# Using Quicken®:

## IBM® Version

# 2nd Edition

Stephen Nelson

**QUE®**
CORPORATION
LEADING COMPUTER KNOWLEDGE

# Using Quicken®:

## IBM® Version

## 2nd Edition

Library of Congress Catalog No.: 90-62948

ISBN 0-88022-644-7

93 92 91 90                                                   4 3 2 1

Interpretation of the printing code: the rightmost double-digit number is the year of the book's printing; the rightmost single-digit number, the number of the book's printing. For example, a printing code of 90-1 shows that the first printing of the book occurred in 1990.

This book is based on Quicken Versions 4.0 and 3.0.

# Stephen Nelson

Stephen Nelson, a certified public accountant, provides financial consulting and computer-based financial modeling services to a variety of firms and investors—principally in the areas of real estate and manufacturing.

Nelson's experience includes a stint as the treasurer and controller of Caddex Corporation, a venture-capital-funded start-up software development company and a pioneer in the electronic publishing field, and, prior to that, as a senior consultant with Arthur Andersen & Co. There, he provided financial and systems consulting services to clients in a variety of industries.

Nelson has written more than 50 articles on personal finance for national publications, including *Lotus Magazine*, *PC Computing*, and *INC Magazine*. He is the author of Que's *Using DacEasy*, 2nd Edition; *Using Harvard Project Manager*; *Using TimeLine*; and *Using Prodigy*; and he is a coauthor of Que's *Using 1-2-3 Release 3*.

Nelson holds a Bachelor of Science degree in accounting from Central Washington University and a Master of Business Administration degree with a finance emphasis from the University of Washington.

**Publishing Director**

Lloyd J. Short

**Acquisitions Editor**

Karen A. Bluestein

**Project Manager**

Paul Boger

**Product Director**

Shelley O'Hara

**Production Editor**

Gregory Robertson

**Editors**

Kelly D. Dobbs
Beth Hoger
Lori A. Lyons
Heidi Weas Muller
Daniel Schnake

**Technical Editor**

Alan L. Gray, CPA

**Editorial Assistant**

Patricia J. Brooks

**Indexer**

Sherry Massey

**Book Design and Production**

Dan Armstrong
Claudia Bell
Brad Chinn
Dan Clemons
Sally Copenhaver
William Hurley
Charles Hutchinson
Bob LaRoche
Jennifer Matthews
Matthew Morrill
Dennis Sheehan
Louise Shinault
Bruce Steed

*Composed in Garamond and Excellent No. 47*
by Que Corporation.

# CONTENTS AT A GLANCE

Introduction . . . . . . . . . . . . . . . . . . . . . . . . . . . . . . . . . . . . . . . . . 1

## Part I      Getting Started with Quicken

Chapter 1    Preparing To Use Quicken . . . . . . . . . . . . . . . . . . . . 11
Chapter 2    Getting Around in Quicken . . . . . . . . . . . . . . . . . . 35
Chapter 3    Describing Your Accounts . . . . . . . . . . . . . . . . . . 47

## Part II     Learning the Basics

Chapter 4    Using the Register . . . . . . . . . . . . . . . . . . . . . . . . . . 63
Chapter 5    Making the Register Easier To Use . . . . . . . . . . . . 83
Chapter 6    Writing and Printing Checks . . . . . . . . . . . . . . . . .115
Chapter 7    Making Check Writing Easier . . . . . . . . . . . . . . . . .133
Chapter 8    Reconciling Your Bank Account . . . . . . . . . . . . . . .161
Chapter 9    Taking Care of Quicken Files . . . . . . . . . . . . . . . . .181

## Part III    Supercharging Quicken

Chapter 10   Organizing Your Finances Better . . . . . . . . . . . . . . .203
Chapter 11   Fine-Tuning Quicken . . . . . . . . . . . . . . . . . . . . . . . . .227
Chapter 12   Tracking Your Net Worth, Other Assets, and
              Liabilities . . . . . . . . . . . . . . . . . . . . . . . . . . . . . . .239
Chapter 13   Monitoring Your Investments . . . . . . . . . . . . . . . . . .259
Chapter 14   Tapping the Power of Quicken's Reports . . . . . . . .301
Chapter 15   Paying Bills Electronically . . . . . . . . . . . . . . . . . . . .353

## Part IV     Putting Quicken To Work

Chapter 16   Budgeting with Quicken . . . . . . . . . . . . . . . . . . . . . .373
Chapter 17   Using Quicken for Home Accounting . . . . . . . . . . .387
Chapter 18   Using Quicken in Your Business . . . . . . . . . . . . . . .399
Chapter 19   Preparing for Income Taxes with Quicken . . . . . . .429

## Part V Protecting Yourself from Forgery, Embezzlement, and Other Disasters

Chapter 20  Protecting Against Forgery and Embezzlement....453
Chapter 21  Protecting Against System Disasters ............467

Appendix A  Tips for Specific Business Situations ............477
Appendix B  Using This Book with Version 3.0..............483
Appendix C  Planning for Your Retirement .................485

Index ..................................................499

# TABLE OF CONTENTS ▼

**Introduction** . . . . . . . . . . . . . . . . . . . . . . . . . . . . . . . . .  1

What Is Quicken? . . . . . . . . . . . . . . . . . . . . . . . . . . . . . . . . .  2

When To Use Quicken . . . . . . . . . . . . . . . . . . . . . . . . . . . .  2

What This Book Contains . . . . . . . . . . . . . . . . . . . . . . . . .  4

## I   Getting Started with Quicken

### 1   Preparing To Use Quicken . . . . . . . . . . . . . . . .  11

Ordering Check Forms . . . . . . . . . . . . . . . . . . . . . . . . . .  11

Picking a Conversion Date . . . . . . . . . . . . . . . . . . . . . .  14

Installing the Software . . . . . . . . . . . . . . . . . . . . . . . . . .  16

    Installing Quicken on a Hard Disk System . . . . . . . . . . . . .  16

    Installing Quicken on a Dual Floppy Disk System . . . . . . . . .  22

    Describing Your Checking Account . . . . . . . . . . . . . . . . . .  22

    Describing Your Printer . . . . . . . . . . . . . . . . . . . . . . . . . .  27

Chapter Summary . . . . . . . . . . . . . . . . . . . . . . . . . . . . . . .  33

### 2   Getting Around in Quicken . . . . . . . . . . . . . . . .  35

Using Help . . . . . . . . . . . . . . . . . . . . . . . . . . . . . . . . . . . .  35

Using and Selecting Menu Options . . . . . . . . . . . . . . . .  37

Collecting Data On-Screen . . . . . . . . . . . . . . . . . . . . . . .  40

    Moving between Fields . . . . . . . . . . . . . . . . . . . . . . . . . . .  40

    Entering and Editing Data On-Screen . . . . . . . . . . . . . . . .  40

    Saving Your Work . . . . . . . . . . . . . . . . . . . . . . . . . . . . . .  42

Using the Calculator . . . . . . . . . . . . . . . . . . . . . . . . . . . .  42

Learning To Use Quicken . . . . . . . . . . . . . . . . . . . . . . . .  45

Chapter Summary . . . . . . . . . . . . . . . . . . . . . . . . . . . . . . .  45

### 3   Describing Your Accounts . . . . . . . . . . . . . . . . .  47

Working with Accounts . . . . . . . . . . . . . . . . . . . . . . . . . .  47

    Adding Another Account . . . . . . . . . . . . . . . . . . . . . . . . .  47

    Editing Existing Accounts . . . . . . . . . . . . . . . . . . . . . . . .  51

    Deleting Existing Accounts . . . . . . . . . . . . . . . . . . . . . . .  51

    Selecting an Account . . . . . . . . . . . . . . . . . . . . . . . . . . . .  52

Working with Account Groups . . . . . . . . . . . . . . . . . . . .  53

    Adding New Account Groups . . . . . . . . . . . . . . . . . . . . . .  53

    Editing Account Group Names . . . . . . . . . . . . . . . . . . . . .  57

    Deleting Account Groups . . . . . . . . . . . . . . . . . . . . . . . . .  58

    Selecting an Account Group . . . . . . . . . . . . . . . . . . . . . . .  59

Chapter Summary . . . . . . . . . . . . . . . . . . . . . . . . . . . . . . .  59

# II  Learning the Basics

## 4  Using the Register ..................... 63

Getting To Know the Register Screen ..................... 64
Recording a Check in the Register ..................... 65
Recording a Deposit in the Register ..................... 70
Recording Other Withdrawals ..................... 72
Recording Transfers between Accounts ..................... 73
Reviewing and Editing Register Transactions ..................... 74
Using Postdated Transactions ..................... 75
Printing a Register ..................... 75
Chapter Summary ..................... 81

## 5  Making the Register Easier To Use ............... 83

Using the Edit Menu Tools ..................... 83
   Recording, Deleting, and Voiding Transactions ........... 84
   Splitting Transactions ..................... 86
   Locating Transactions ..................... 89
      Using the Find Option ..................... 90
      Using Key Word Matches ..................... 92
      Combining Exact and Key Word Matches ............. 94
      Repeating a Find Request ..................... 95
   Using the Go to Date Option ..................... 95
   Using the Go to Transfer Option ..................... 96
Using the Quick Entry Menu Tools ..................... 98
   Memorizing Transactions ..................... 99
   Recalling a Transaction ..................... 101
   Deleting Memorized Transactions ..................... 102
   Listing Memorized Transactions ..................... 103
   Using the Categorize/Transfer Option ..................... 104
   Setting Up a Transaction Group ..................... 105
   Executing a Transaction Group ..................... 108
   Changing and Deleting Transaction Groups ............... 110
Using the Activities Menu ..................... 111
Chapter Summary ..................... 113

## 6  Writing and Printing Checks ..................... 115

Getting To Know the Write Checks Screen ................. 116
Writing a Check ..................... 117
Reviewing and Editing Checks ..................... 122
Postdating Checks ..................... 122
Printing Checks ..................... 124

Reprinting a Check . . . . . . . . . . . . . . . . . . . . . . . . . . . . . . . . . . . 131
Chapter Summary. . . . . . . . . . . . . . . . . . . . . . . . . . . . . . . . . . . . . 132

**7    Making Check Writing Easier**. . . . . . . . . . . . . . . . . 133

Using the Edit Menu Tools. . . . . . . . . . . . . . . . . . . . . . . . . . . . . 133
   Recording and Deleting Checks . . . . . . . . . . . . . . . . . . . . . 134
   Using Split Transactions . . . . . . . . . . . . . . . . . . . . . . . . . . . . 134
   Voiding Checks . . . . . . . . . . . . . . . . . . . . . . . . . . . . . . . . . . . 138
   Using the Find Options . . . . . . . . . . . . . . . . . . . . . . . . . . . . 139
      Finding Exact Matches. . . . . . . . . . . . . . . . . . . . . . . . . . 139
      Finding Key Word Matches . . . . . . . . . . . . . . . . . . . . . 142
      Combining Exact Matches and Key Word Matches . . . . . . 142
      Repeating a Search. . . . . . . . . . . . . . . . . . . . . . . . . . . . 143
   Using Go To Date Option . . . . . . . . . . . . . . . . . . . . . . . . . . 143
   Using the Go To Transfer Option . . . . . . . . . . . . . . . . . . . . 144
Using the Quick Entry Menu Tools . . . . . . . . . . . . . . . . . . . . . 145
   Memorizing Transactions. . . . . . . . . . . . . . . . . . . . . . . . . . . 145
   Recalling a Transaction . . . . . . . . . . . . . . . . . . . . . . . . . . . 147
   Deleting Memorized Transactions . . . . . . . . . . . . . . . . . . . . 149
   Listing Memorized Transactions . . . . . . . . . . . . . . . . . . . . . 150
   Using the Categorize/Transfer Option . . . . . . . . . . . . . . . . . 151
   Setting Up a Transaction Group . . . . . . . . . . . . . . . . . . . . . 152
   Executing a Transaction Group . . . . . . . . . . . . . . . . . . . . . 155
   Changing and Deleting Transaction Groups. . . . . . . . . . . . . 156
Using the Activities Menu. . . . . . . . . . . . . . . . . . . . . . . . . . . . . 157
Chapter Summary. . . . . . . . . . . . . . . . . . . . . . . . . . . . . . . . . . . . 160

**8    Reconciling Your Bank Account**. . . . . . . . . . . . . . . . 161

Reviewing the Reconciliation Process . . . . . . . . . . . . . . . . . . . 161
   Reviewing the Bank Statement . . . . . . . . . . . . . . . . . . . . . . 162
   Checking Cleared Transactions. . . . . . . . . . . . . . . . . . . . . . 162
   Verifying that Balances Correspond. . . . . . . . . . . . . . . . . . . 163
Reconciling Your Account with Quicken . . . . . . . . . . . . . . . . . 163
   Printing Reconciliation Reports . . . . . . . . . . . . . . . . . . . . . 167
   Reviewing the Reconciliation Report. . . . . . . . . . . . . . . . . . 169
   Creating Balance Adjustment Transactions. . . . . . . . . . . . . . 173
Catching Common Errors. . . . . . . . . . . . . . . . . . . . . . . . . . . . . 176
   Transposing Numbers. . . . . . . . . . . . . . . . . . . . . . . . . . . . . 177
   Forgetting To Record Transactions . . . . . . . . . . . . . . . . . . . 178
   Entering Payments as Deposits or Deposits as Payments. . . . 178
   Offsetting Errors . . . . . . . . . . . . . . . . . . . . . . . . . . . . . . . . 178
Chapter Summary. . . . . . . . . . . . . . . . . . . . . . . . . . . . . . . . . . . . 179

**9    Taking Care of Quicken Files** . . . . . . . . . . . . . . . . . . . . **181**

Reviewing the Quicken Files . . . . . . . . . . . . . . . . . . . . . . . . . 181
Backing Up and Restoring Files . . . . . . . . . . . . . . . . . . . . . . . . 182
   Backing Up Your Files . . . . . . . . . . . . . . . . . . . . . . . . . . . . 183
   Restoring Backed-Up Files . . . . . . . . . . . . . . . . . . . . . . . . 186
Shrinking Files . . . . . . . . . . . . . . . . . . . . . . . . . . . . . . . . . . 190
   When To Shrink Files . . . . . . . . . . . . . . . . . . . . . . . . . . . . 190
   How To Shrink Files . . . . . . . . . . . . . . . . . . . . . . . . . . . . . 191
Locating Files . . . . . . . . . . . . . . . . . . . . . . . . . . . . . . . . . . . 194
Exporting and Importing Files . . . . . . . . . . . . . . . . . . . . . . . . 195
   Exporting Files . . . . . . . . . . . . . . . . . . . . . . . . . . . . . . . . 196
   Importing Files . . . . . . . . . . . . . . . . . . . . . . . . . . . . . . . . 198
Chapter Summary . . . . . . . . . . . . . . . . . . . . . . . . . . . . . . . . 200

**III    Supercharging Quicken**

**10    Organizing Your Finances Better** . . . . . . . . . . . . . . . **203**

Working with Categories . . . . . . . . . . . . . . . . . . . . . . . . . . . 203
   Building a List of Categories . . . . . . . . . . . . . . . . . . . . . . . 205
   Using Subcategories . . . . . . . . . . . . . . . . . . . . . . . . . . . . . 210
   Setting Up Categories . . . . . . . . . . . . . . . . . . . . . . . . . . . 212
   Adding Categories . . . . . . . . . . . . . . . . . . . . . . . . . . . . . . 213
   Deleting Categories . . . . . . . . . . . . . . . . . . . . . . . . . . . . . 216
   Editing Categories . . . . . . . . . . . . . . . . . . . . . . . . . . . . . . 217
   Printing a Category and Transfer List . . . . . . . . . . . . . . . . . 218
Working with Classes . . . . . . . . . . . . . . . . . . . . . . . . . . . . . 219
   Defining a Class . . . . . . . . . . . . . . . . . . . . . . . . . . . . . . . 220
   Editing and Deleting Classes . . . . . . . . . . . . . . . . . . . . . . . 222
   Using Subclasses . . . . . . . . . . . . . . . . . . . . . . . . . . . . . . 224
   Recording Classes and Subclasses . . . . . . . . . . . . . . . . . . . 224
Chapter Summary . . . . . . . . . . . . . . . . . . . . . . . . . . . . . . . . 225

**11    Fine-Tuning Quicken** . . . . . . . . . . . . . . . . . . . . . . . . . **227**

Using the Change Setting Menu . . . . . . . . . . . . . . . . . . . . . . 227
   Changing Screen Colors . . . . . . . . . . . . . . . . . . . . . . . . . . 228
   Changing Screen Update Speed . . . . . . . . . . . . . . . . . . . . . 229
   Fine-Tuning with Other Settings . . . . . . . . . . . . . . . . . . . . 230
Starting Quicken with Parameters . . . . . . . . . . . . . . . . . . . . . 234
   Selecting an Account . . . . . . . . . . . . . . . . . . . . . . . . . . . . 235
   Selecting a Main Menu Option . . . . . . . . . . . . . . . . . . . . . . 235
   Using Less Memory . . . . . . . . . . . . . . . . . . . . . . . . . . . . . 236

Using Versions 4.0 and 3.0 Key Definitions . . . . . . . . . . . . . . 237
Chapter Summary. . . . . . . . . . . . . . . . . . . . . . . . . . . . . . . . . . 238

**12   Tracking Your Net Worth, Other Assets, and
      Liabilities**. . . . . . . . . . . . . . . . . . . . . . . . . . . . . . . . 239

Setting Up Accounts for Other Assets and Liabilities. . . . . . . . . 240
Keeping Financial Records . . . . . . . . . . . . . . . . . . . . . . . . . . . 243
Reviewing Tips for Working with Other Assets
   and Liabilities . . . . . . . . . . . . . . . . . . . . . . . . . . . . . . . . . . 247
   Dealing with Cash Accounts . . . . . . . . . . . . . . . . . . . . . . . 247
   Updating Account Balances . . . . . . . . . . . . . . . . . . . . . . . . 248
   Dealing with Credit Card Accounts . . . . . . . . . . . . . . . . . . 251
   Paying Credit Card Bills. . . . . . . . . . . . . . . . . . . . . . . . . . . 252
Measuring Your Net Worth . . . . . . . . . . . . . . . . . . . . . . . . . . 256
Chapter Summary. . . . . . . . . . . . . . . . . . . . . . . . . . . . . . . . . . 257

**13   Monitoring Your Investments** . . . . . . . . . . . . . . . . . . 259

Preparing To Monitor Investments . . . . . . . . . . . . . . . . . . . . . 259
Working with Mutual Funds. . . . . . . . . . . . . . . . . . . . . . . . . . 264
Working with Other Investments . . . . . . . . . . . . . . . . . . . . . . 272
Working with the Investment Register. . . . . . . . . . . . . . . . . . . 280
   Working with the Securities Lists. . . . . . . . . . . . . . . . . . . . 280
   Updating Your Investment Records for Market Values . . . . . . 286
   Reconciling Your Investment Accounts. . . . . . . . . . . . . . . . . 292
   Tips On Investments and Investment Record-Keeping . . . . . . 298
Chapter Summary. . . . . . . . . . . . . . . . . . . . . . . . . . . . . . . . . . 299

**14   Tapping the Power of Quicken's Reports** . . . . . . . 301

Reviewing Printing Basics. . . . . . . . . . . . . . . . . . . . . . . . . . . . 304
Tracking Personal Finances with Personal Reports . . . . . . . . . . 307
   Cash Flow. . . . . . . . . . . . . . . . . . . . . . . . . . . . . . . . . . . . . 308
   Monthly Budget Report . . . . . . . . . . . . . . . . . . . . . . . . . . . 309
   Itemized Category Report . . . . . . . . . . . . . . . . . . . . . . . . . 312
   Tax Summary. . . . . . . . . . . . . . . . . . . . . . . . . . . . . . . . . . . 314
   Net Worth Reports . . . . . . . . . . . . . . . . . . . . . . . . . . . . . . 315
Tracking Your Business Finances with Business Reports . . . . . . 317
   Profit and Loss Statement. . . . . . . . . . . . . . . . . . . . . . . . . . 317
   Cash Flow Report . . . . . . . . . . . . . . . . . . . . . . . . . . . . . . . 319
   A/P by Vendor Report . . . . . . . . . . . . . . . . . . . . . . . . . . . . 320
   A/R by Customer Report . . . . . . . . . . . . . . . . . . . . . . . . . . 321
   Job/Project Report. . . . . . . . . . . . . . . . . . . . . . . . . . . . . . . 324
   Payroll Report . . . . . . . . . . . . . . . . . . . . . . . . . . . . . . . . . . 324
   Balance Sheet. . . . . . . . . . . . . . . . . . . . . . . . . . . . . . . . . . . 326

Tracking Your Investments with Quicken's Investment
    Reports. . . . . . . . . . . . . . . . . . . . . . . . . . . . . . . . . . . . . . . . . . . 328
    Portfolio Value Reports . . . . . . . . . . . . . . . . . . . . . . . . . . . 329
    Investment Performance Reports . . . . . . . . . . . . . . . . . . . . 330
    Capital Gains (Schedule D) Reports . . . . . . . . . . . . . . . . . . 331
    Investment Income Reports . . . . . . . . . . . . . . . . . . . . . . . . 332
    Investment Transactions Reports . . . . . . . . . . . . . . . . . . . . 334
Customizing and Filtering Reports . . . . . . . . . . . . . . . . . . . . . . 334
    Customizing a Report. . . . . . . . . . . . . . . . . . . . . . . . . . . . . . 335
        Entering a Report Title . . . . . . . . . . . . . . . . . . . . . . . . . 336
        Restricting Transactions . . . . . . . . . . . . . . . . . . . . . . . . 337
        Sorting Transactions. . . . . . . . . . . . . . . . . . . . . . . . . . . . 337
        Segregating Transactions . . . . . . . . . . . . . . . . . . . . . . . . 337
        Selecting Accounts . . . . . . . . . . . . . . . . . . . . . . . . . . . . . 338
    Filtering a Report . . . . . . . . . . . . . . . . . . . . . . . . . . . . . . . . 338
        Matching Payees . . . . . . . . . . . . . . . . . . . . . . . . . . . . . . . 339
        Matching Memos . . . . . . . . . . . . . . . . . . . . . . . . . . . . . . . 339
        Matching Categories. . . . . . . . . . . . . . . . . . . . . . . . . . . . 339
        Matching Classes. . . . . . . . . . . . . . . . . . . . . . . . . . . . . . . 340
        Selecting Categories. . . . . . . . . . . . . . . . . . . . . . . . . . . . 340
        Selecting Classes. . . . . . . . . . . . . . . . . . . . . . . . . . . . . . . 341
        Including Only Tax-Related Categories . . . . . . . . . . . . . . 341
        Matching Transaction Amounts . . . . . . . . . . . . . . . . . . . 341
        Specifying Certain Types of Transactions. . . . . . . . . . . . 342
        Specifying Cleared/Uncleared Transactions . . . . . . . . . . . 342
    Setting Report Options. . . . . . . . . . . . . . . . . . . . . . . . . . . . 342
Memorizing Reports. . . . . . . . . . . . . . . . . . . . . . . . . . . . . . . . . 344
Creating a Transaction Report. . . . . . . . . . . . . . . . . . . . . . . . . 346
Creating a Summary Report. . . . . . . . . . . . . . . . . . . . . . . . . . 348
Creating a Budget Report. . . . . . . . . . . . . . . . . . . . . . . . . . . . 348
Creating an Account Balances Report . . . . . . . . . . . . . . . . . . . 350
    Using the Report Title Field . . . . . . . . . . . . . . . . . . . . . . . . 350
    Using the Report Balances on Dates from and through
        Fields. . . . . . . . . . . . . . . . . . . . . . . . . . . . . . . . . . . . . . . 351
    Using the Report at Intervals of Field . . . . . . . . . . . . . . . . . 351
    Using the Use Current/All/Selected Accounts Field. . . . . . . . 351
Chapter Summary. . . . . . . . . . . . . . . . . . . . . . . . . . . . . . . . . . . 352

**15   Paying Bills Electronically**. . . . . . . . . . . . . . . . . . . . 353

Setting Up Your System for Electronic Payment . . . . . . . . . . . . 353
    Completing the CheckFree Paper Work . . . . . . . . . . . . . . . . 354
    Telling Quicken You Will Use Electronic Bill Paying. . . . . . . 354
    Identifying CheckFree Bank Accounts . . . . . . . . . . . . . . . . . 359

Identifying the People You Will Pay. . . . . . . . . . . . . . . . . . . . . . . 362
Paying Bills with CheckFree. . . . . . . . . . . . . . . . . . . . . . . . . . . . . 364
Using the Special CheckFree Functions . . . . . . . . . . . . . . . . . . . 367
    Issuing a Stop Payment Request. . . . . . . . . . . . . . . . . . . . . . . 369
    Making an Electronic Payment Inquiry . . . . . . . . . . . . . . . . . 369
    Sending Electronic Mail . . . . . . . . . . . . . . . . . . . . . . . . . . . . . 369
Chapter Summary. . . . . . . . . . . . . . . . . . . . . . . . . . . . . . . . . . . . . 370

## IV Putting Quicken To Work

## 16 Budgeting with Quicken . . . . . . . . . . . . . . . . . . . . . . 373

Defining Budgeting . . . . . . . . . . . . . . . . . . . . . . . . . . . . . . . . . . 373
    Setting Your Goals . . . . . . . . . . . . . . . . . . . . . . . . . . . . . . . . . 374
    Designing a Game Plan. . . . . . . . . . . . . . . . . . . . . . . . . . . . . . 375
    Monitoring Your Progress . . . . . . . . . . . . . . . . . . . . . . . . . . . 380
Using Quicken for Budgeting. . . . . . . . . . . . . . . . . . . . . . . . . . . 380
    Using Categories . . . . . . . . . . . . . . . . . . . . . . . . . . . . . . . . . . 380
    Creating Budgeting Reports. . . . . . . . . . . . . . . . . . . . . . . . . . 381
Reviewing Tips for Successful Budgeting. . . . . . . . . . . . . . . . . . 382
    Paying Yourself First. . . . . . . . . . . . . . . . . . . . . . . . . . . . . . . . 382
    Recognizing After-Tax Shares of Bonuses and Raises . . . . . . . 384
    Allowing for Unplanned and Emergency Expenses. . . . . . . . . 384
    Using Zero-Based Budgeting . . . . . . . . . . . . . . . . . . . . . . . . . 385
Chapter Summary. . . . . . . . . . . . . . . . . . . . . . . . . . . . . . . . . . . . 385

## 17 Using Quicken for Home Accounting . . . . . . . . . . . 387

Where Quicken Fits In . . . . . . . . . . . . . . . . . . . . . . . . . . . . . . . . 387
    Tracking Income Tax Deductions . . . . . . . . . . . . . . . . . . . . . . 387
    Automating Record Keeping. . . . . . . . . . . . . . . . . . . . . . . . . . 388
    Monitoring a Budget. . . . . . . . . . . . . . . . . . . . . . . . . . . . . . . . 389
        Focusing on Discretionary Items. . . . . . . . . . . . . . . . . . . . 389
        Aggregating Spending Categories. . . . . . . . . . . . . . . . . . . 390
        Thinking about the Spending Method. . . . . . . . . . . . . . . . 392
How To Use Quicken . . . . . . . . . . . . . . . . . . . . . . . . . . . . . . . . . 392
    Using Quicken for Bank Accounts . . . . . . . . . . . . . . . . . . . . . 392
    Using Quicken for Credit Cards . . . . . . . . . . . . . . . . . . . . . . . 393
    Using Quicken for Cash . . . . . . . . . . . . . . . . . . . . . . . . . . . . . 393
    Tracking the Adjusted Basis of Your Home . . . . . . . . . . . . . . 394
    Tracking the Non-Deductible Portions of an IRA . . . . . . . . . . 395
When To Perform Quicken Tasks. . . . . . . . . . . . . . . . . . . . . . . . 396
Chapter Summary. . . . . . . . . . . . . . . . . . . . . . . . . . . . . . . . . . . . 397

**18   Using Quicken in Your Business** ................. 399

Understanding the Basics ................................. 400
   Knowing What Quicken Accounts Track ................. 400
   Defining a Transaction ............................ 401
   Knowing What Categories Calculate .................... 402
Invoicing Customers ..................................... 403
Tracking Customer Payments and Receivables .............. 406
   Recording Customer Payments ......................... 407
   Tracking Customer Receivables ........................ 408
Accounting for Fixed Assets ............................... 411
   Understanding Depreciation .......................... 412
   Recording Fixed Assets and Depreciation ............... 413
Preparing Payroll ........................................ 414
   Getting Ready for Payroll ............................ 414
   Paying Employees ................................... 415
   Paying Payroll Taxes ................................ 418
   Completing Quarterly and Annual Tax Reports ........... 418
   Completing the W-2 and W-3 ......................... 419
   Completing Other Forms and Reports .................. 420
Preparing Inventory Accounting ........................... 420
   Understanding Periodic Inventory Systems .............. 421
   Implementing a Periodic Inventory System .............. 421
   Reviewing the Problems of a Periodic System ........... 423
Job Costing ............................................. 423
Tracking Loans and Notes ................................ 426
Chapter Summary ....................................... 428

**19   Preparing for Income Taxes with Quicken** ...... 429

Using Categories ........................................ 429
Importing Quicken Data into TurboTax ..................... 450
Chapter Summary ....................................... 450

**V   Protecting Yourself from Forgery,
Embezzlement, and Other Disasters**

**20   Protecting Against Forgery
and Embezzlement** ............................ 453

Defining Forgery and Embezzlement ....................... 453
   Preventing Forgery ................................. 454
   Preventing Embezzlement ............................ 457

Keeping Complete Financial Records . . . . . . . . . . . . . . . . . . . 457
   Segregating Duties . . . . . . . . . . . . . . . . . . . . . . . . . . . 458
   Checking Employee Backgrounds . . . . . . . . . . . . . . . . . 458
   Requiring Vacations . . . . . . . . . . . . . . . . . . . . . . . . . . 458
Using Internal Controls. . . . . . . . . . . . . . . . . . . . . . . . . . . 458
   Creating Paper Trails . . . . . . . . . . . . . . . . . . . . . . . . . 459
   Retaining Documents . . . . . . . . . . . . . . . . . . . . . . . . . 460
   Using Passwords . . . . . . . . . . . . . . . . . . . . . . . . . . . . 461
Chapter Summary. . . . . . . . . . . . . . . . . . . . . . . . . . . . . . . 466

**21  Protecting Against System Disasters** . . . . . . . . . . . . . 467
Defining a Few Basic Terms. . . . . . . . . . . . . . . . . . . . . . . . 467
   Files . . . . . . . . . . . . . . . . . . . . . . . . . . . . . . . . . . . . . 468
   Software . . . . . . . . . . . . . . . . . . . . . . . . . . . . . . . . . . 468
   Hardware . . . . . . . . . . . . . . . . . . . . . . . . . . . . . . . . . 469
Preventing Hardware Disasters . . . . . . . . . . . . . . . . . . . . . 469
   Dealing with Dirty Power . . . . . . . . . . . . . . . . . . . . . . 469
   Handling Hard Disk Failures . . . . . . . . . . . . . . . . . . . . 470
   Handling Floppy Disk Problems . . . . . . . . . . . . . . . . . . 470
Reviewing and Preventing Software Disasters. . . . . . . . . . . . 471
   Recovering Deleted Files. . . . . . . . . . . . . . . . . . . . . . . 471
   Protecting Against Viruses . . . . . . . . . . . . . . . . . . . . . . 473
      Defining Viruses . . . . . . . . . . . . . . . . . . . . . . . . . . 473
      Determining Where Viruses Originate . . . . . . . . . . . . 473
      Detecting Viruses . . . . . . . . . . . . . . . . . . . . . . . . . 474
   Working with Beta Software . . . . . . . . . . . . . . . . . . . . 475
Chapter Summary. . . . . . . . . . . . . . . . . . . . . . . . . . . . . . . 476

**A  Tips for Specific Business Situations** . . . . . . . . . . . . 477
Tips for Lawyers, Consultants, and Other Professionals . . . . . . 477
Tips for Restaurants. . . . . . . . . . . . . . . . . . . . . . . . . . . . . . 478
Tips for Retailers . . . . . . . . . . . . . . . . . . . . . . . . . . . . . . . 478
Tips for Churches, Synagogues, and Nonprofit Organizations . . 479
   Tracking Pledges . . . . . . . . . . . . . . . . . . . . . . . . . . . . 480
   Tracking Fund Designations . . . . . . . . . . . . . . . . . . . . . 480
Outgrowing Quicken. . . . . . . . . . . . . . . . . . . . . . . . . . . . . 480
   Becoming More Sophisticated. . . . . . . . . . . . . . . . . . . . 480
   Becoming Too Large for Quicken . . . . . . . . . . . . . . . . . 481
Appendix Summary . . . . . . . . . . . . . . . . . . . . . . . . . . . . . 482

**B  Using This Book with Version 3.0** . . . . . . . . . . . . . . . 483
Version 4.0's Two Major New Features . . . . . . . . . . . . . . . . . 483
Reviewing Other Miscellaneous Changes. . . . . . . . . . . . . . . 484

**C**     **Planning for Your Retirement** . . . . . . . . . . . . . . . . . . . . **485**

      Preparing a Living Expenses Budget . . . . . . . . . . . . . . . . . . . . . 486

      Estimating Tentative Retirement Income . . . . . . . . . . . . . . . . . . 487

      Estimating Needed Retirement Savings . . . . . . . . . . . . . . . . . . . 494

      Some More Tips on Retirement Planning . . . . . . . . . . . . . . . . . . 497

    **Index** . . . . . . . . . . . . . . . . . . . . . . . . . . . . . . . . . . . . . . . . . . . . . . . **499**

# ACKNOWLEDGMENTS ▼

I would like to thank Mari Latterell, product manager at Intuit, for her helpful comments and suggestions, and Joe Sermersheim, of Intuit's technical support staff, for answering my questions about Quicken.

# CONVENTIONS USED IN THIS BOOK

*U*sing Quicken, 2nd Edition, uses several conventions of which you should be aware. They are listed here for your convenience.

Information that you are to type (usually found in examples with numbered steps) is indicated by italic type. For example, "At the prompt, type *cd \quicken4*.

Messages and prompts that appear on-screen are represented here in a special typeface (You are about to delete a memorized transaction).

Tips for certified public accountants are in shaded boxes with *CPA Tip* in the margin.

Menu options are in bold (**Record Transaction**).

Screen names are in initial capital letters (Register screen).

Field names and options in dialog boxes are in a special typeface (1. Delete transaction).

# TRADEMARK ACKNOWLEDGMENTS

Que Corporation has made every effort to supply trademark information about company names, products, and services mentioned in this book. Trademarks indicated below were derived from various sources. Que Corporation cannot attest to the accuracy of this information.

Ashton-Tate and dBASE are registered trademarks of Ashton-Tate Corporation.

DacEasy is a registered trademark of DacEasy, Inc., an Insilco company.

Hewlett-Packard is a registered trademark and LaserJet is a trademark of Hewlett-Packard Co.

IBM is a registered trademark of International Business Machines Corporation.

Lotus, 1-2-3, and Symphony are registered trademarks of Lotus Development Corporation.

Microsoft and MS-DOS are registered trademarks of Microsoft Corporation.

Quicken is a registered trademark and Billminder is a trademark of Intuit.

WordPerfect is a registered trademark of WordPerfect Corporation.

# Introduction

In college, one of my better accounting professors spent most of his lecture one fall day describing how John D. Rockefeller Sr. made his fortune. According to the professor, Rockefeller made his fortune by being a good accountant. The professor's point wasn't that Rockefeller's entry into the oil business didn't amount to perfect timing. He didn't minimize Standard Oil's strategy of vertical integration (it owned the oil fields, the refineries, and even the gas stations). He also didn't discount the effectiveness of Rockefeller's aggressive business tactics. All these, the professor admitted, were important—perhaps even essential. What was more important, the professor said, was that Rockefeller knew better than any of his competitors how much it cost to get the oil, refine the oil, and sell the oil. As a result, he always knew whether he was making money or losing money. And he used this information as a foundation for making his business decisions. In the end, of course, Rockefeller became a billionaire.

Your financial goals—business or personal—are probably more modest than Rockefeller's were. Your reasons for wanting to use Quicken, however, probably resemble Rockefeller's reasons for desiring good, relevant accounting: You want to make better personal or business decisions. That's what this book is really about: making better financial decisions by using financial information—financial information that Quicken can help you collect, store, and use.

If you are considering the installation of a personal or small-business accounting package like Quicken, if you have decided to install Quicken and want a little extra help, or if you already have begun using Quicken and want a reference source that goes beyond the information provided in the user's manual, *Using Quicken: IBM Version*, 2nd Edition, will help. In this text is a wealth of information about Quicken Version 4.0 and about managing your personal or small-business finances.

1

After you read this Introduction, you will know what Quicken Version 4.0 is and whether the program suits your needs. This Introduction also identifies the contents of each chapter.

# What Is Quicken?

Quicken is a computer-based bookkeeping system you can use to manage your personal or business finances. Used in the simplest way, Quicken maintains your check register for you—deducting payments and adding deposits to your checking account balance. Quicken eliminates the possibility of you overdrawing your account because of an arithmetic error.

The real value of Quicken, however, stems from several other features the program provides. First, Quicken enables you to use your computer and printer to generate checks—a real time-saver if you find yourself writing many checks at home every month. Second, Quicken enables you to use the information stored in your check register to report on your income and outgo, track tax deductions, and compare your actual income and expenses to what you originally budgeted. Third, Quicken can be used to perform bookkeeping for most personal and business assets and liabilities, including personal investments, business receivables, personal credit lines and mortgages, and business payables. With these extra features, individuals can track and manage their finances closely, and many small businesses can use Quicken as a full-fledged accounting package. (Quicken enables you to generate personal and business income statements, balance sheets, and cash-flow statements.)

# When To Use Quicken

Answering the question "When should I use Quicken?" depends on whether you are using the program for personal or small-business purposes. If you are considering Quicken for personal use, four factors indicate that Quicken represents a good investment of your time and money:

❑ When check writing and checking-account record keeping take more time than you want to spend. Quicken does most of the work related to keeping your check book: recording transactions, writing checks, reconciling account balances, and maintaining the check register. Because Quicken does the work for you, the program saves you a tremendous amount of time.

❏ When you need to track your tax deductions carefully. Quicken tracks the amounts you spend on tax-deductible items. At the end of the year, totaling your charitable contribution deductions is as simple as printing a report.

❏ When you want to budget income and expense amounts and compare what you earn and spend with what you budgeted. Budgets, contrary to their reputation, are not equivalent to financial handcuffs that prevent you from enjoying life. Budgets are tools that enable you to identify your financial priorities. They help you monitor your progress in organizing your financial life so that you meet your financial objectives. Quicken makes budgeting easy.

❏ When you want to monitor and track personal assets, such as investments, and personal liabilities, such as your mortgages and credit card debt.

If you are considering Quicken for business, three factors indicate that Quicken represents a good investment of your time and money and a reasonable accounting alternative:

❏ You do not need or want to use a small-business accounting package that requires double-entry bookkeeping. Packages such as DacEasy, Peachtree, and others require that you use double-entry bookkeeping. Although this procedure is a powerful and valuable tool, if you are not familiar with double-entry bookkeeping, you probably can spend your time better in ways other than learning accounting methods. Quicken provides a single-entry, easy-to-use accounting system.

❏ You do not need a fancy billing and accounts receivable system. Quicken enables you to perform record keeping for accounts receivable. If you have fewer than two dozen transactions a month, Quicken provides a satisfactory solution. If your transaction volume exceeds this amount, however, you may want to consider a full-fledged accounts receivable package that prepares invoices, calculates finance charges, and easily handles high volumes of customer invoices and payments.

❏ You do not need an automated inventory record keeping system. Although Quicken enables you to set up other assets, such as inventory, the program does not enable you to track the number of units of these other assets—only the dollars. With inventory, however, you not only need to know the dollar value of inventory, you need to know the number of units of inventory. For example, suppose that you sell snow skis. You need to know the number of pairs of skis you have as well as the dollar value of your ski inventory.

# What This Book Contains

*Using Quicken: IBM Version*, 2nd Edition, is divided into 5 parts and 20 chapters. (If you read the book from cover to cover, you may notice a little repetition in some places—inevitable when the book also needs to serve as a reference.)

Part I, "Getting Started with Quicken," includes three chapters that, as the title implies, help you get started.

Chapter 1, "Preparing To Use Quicken," guides you through the steps you need to take before you start using Quicken, including ordering any pre-printed forms you will need, deciding which Quicken options to use, learning to use the system, picking a starting date, and installing the software. Chapter 1 describes each of these steps in detail.

Chapter 2, "Getting Around in Quicken," gives you a quick introduction to the mechanics of actually working with the program. You learn how to start the program, select menu options, tap Quicken's on-line help feature, and use the built-in calculator. If you already have started using Quicken, you may want to skim this material.

Chapter 3, "Describing Your Accounts," walks you through the steps to set up your second and subsequent bank accounts. The chapter also describes a few basic concepts you need to know from the start if you will be using Quicken for more than just a single bank account. If you plan to use Quicken for personal and business purposes, take a few minutes to read through this chapter.

Part II, "Learning the Basics," gives you all the information you need to use Quicken's basic functions.

Chapter 4, "Using the Register," explains the steps for using Quicken's fundamental feature: its register. The chapter doesn't assume that you know anything about Quicken. Rather, you read a complete explanation of what the register is, what information it contains, and how you use it. If you're a new user of Quicken or think you can use a little help with the basics, start with this chapter after you have completed Part I.

Chapter 5, "Making the Register Easier To Use," describes some of the special menu options, which, although not essential, can make the Quicken register easier to use. When you're comfortable with the information covered in Chapter 4, spend some time in Chapter 5. Your time investment should pay rich dividends.

Chapter 6, "Writing and Printing Checks," describes one of Quicken's core features—the capability to print checks. The chapter includes instructions for completing the Write Checks screen, where you provide the information Quicken needs to print a check, and gives instructions for recording, reviewing, editing, and printing checks. Not everyone wants or needs to use Quicken to print checks, but if you do, Chapter 6 is the place to start after you understand the Quicken register.

Chapter 7, "Making Check Writing Easier," describes how to use the special menu options available on the Write Checks screen to speed up the check-writing process. The chapter includes information on the Edit Find, Quick Entry, and Activities function key options. Although this information in Chapter 7 is not essential to writing checks, it will make writing and printing checks even faster.

Chapter 8, "Reconciling Your Bank Account," discusses one of the important steps you can take to protect your cash and the accuracy and reliability of your financial records. This chapter first reviews the reconciliation process in general terms and then describes the steps for reconciling your accounts in Quicken, correcting and catching errors, and printing and using the reconciliation reports that Quicken creates.

Chapter 9, "Taking Care of Quicken Files," describes how to take care of the files that Quicken uses to store your financial records. Chapter 9 describes how to back up and restore your Quicken files, how to make copies of the files, and how to purge from the files old information you no longer need.

Part III, "Supercharging Quicken," moves beyond the simple applications covered in Part II, and helps you get more from Quicken.

Chapter 10, "Organizing Your Finances Better," discusses one of Quicken's optional and most powerful features—the capability to categorize and classify your spending. The categories make it easy to determine tax deductions, the amounts spent for various items, and the types of money that go into your bank accounts. The classes also enable you to look at specific groups of categories, such as personal expenses or business expenses. Chapter 10 defines Quicken's categories and classes, describes why and when you should use them, shows the predefined categories provided within Quicken, and explains how to use these categories. The chapter also outlines the steps for adding, deleting, and modifying your own categories and classes.

Chapter 11, "Fine-Tuning Quicken," describes the two ways you can customize, or fine-tune, Quicken's operation. One way is to use the **Other Settings** option under the Main menu option **Change Settings**. The other way is to start Quicken with parameters. This chapter describes both approaches.

Chapter 12, "Tracking Your Net Worth, Other Assets, and Liabilities," describes some of the special features that Quicken Version 4.0 provides for personal use. You can track cash and other assets, such as real estate, as well as liabilities, such as credit cards and a mortgage.

Chapter 13, "Monitoring Your Investments," describes the new investment register feature that Quicken Version 4.0 provides for investors. If you want to monitor your investments better, read through Chapter 13 to see the new tools and options that Quicken 4.0 provides specifically for managing investments.

Chapter 14, "Tapping the Power of Quicken's Reports," shows you how to sort, extract, and summarize the information contained in the Quicken registers by using the Reports menu options. Quicken's reports enable you to gain better control over and insight into your income, expenses, and cash flow.

Chapter 15, "Paying Bills Electronically," describes how you can use Quicken to pay your bills electronically by using the CheckFree service. Electronic payment isn't for everybody, but if you're a Quicken user, you should at least know what's involved and whether it makes sense for you. Chapter 15 gives you this information.

Part IV, "Putting Quicken to Work," moves away from the mechanics of using Quicken's features and talks about how to incorporate Quicken as a financial-management tool.

Chapter 16, "Budgeting with Quicken," discusses one of Quicken's most significant benefits—budgeting and monitoring your success in achieving a budget. This chapter reviews the steps for budgeting, describes how Quicken helps with budgeting, and provides some tips on how to budget more successfully. If you are not comfortable with the budgeting process, Chapter 16 should give you enough information to get started. If you find budgeting an unpleasant exercise, the chapter also provides some tips on making budgeting a more positive experience.

Chapter 17, "Using Quicken for Home Accounting," discusses how Quicken should be used by individuals for personal financial record keeping. Using any software, and particularly an accounting program, is more than mechanics. This chapter answers questions about where Quicken fits in for home users, how Quicken changes the way you keep your personal financial records, and when Quicken options should be used.

Chapter 18, "Using Quicken in Your Business," covers some of the special techniques and procedures for using Quicken in business accounting. This chapter begins by discussing the overall approach to using Quicken in a business. Next, the following seven basic accounting tasks are detailed: invoicing customers, tracking receivables, tracking inventory, accounting for fixed assets, preparing payroll, job costing, and tracking loans and notes.

Chapter 19, "Preparing for Income Taxes with Quicken," is a short chapter, but an important one. This chapter tells you how to make sure that the financial records you create with Quicken provide the information you will need to prepare your federal and state income tax returns. The chapter also briefly discusses the general mechanics of passing data between Quicken and an income tax preparation package such as Turbotax.

Part V, "Protecting Yourself from Forgery, Embezzlement, and Other Disasters," covers material that usually isn't addressed in computer tutorials—which is too bad, because it's critical information that you should have.

Chapter 20, "Protecting Against Forgery and Embezzlement," describes the steps you can take to protect your Quicken system and the money it counts. The first part of the chapter outlines procedures for protecting yourself from check forgery and embezzlement. The second part of the chapter outlines the ways you can minimize intentional and unintentional human errors with Quicken.

Chapter 21, "Protecting Against System Disasters," also covers some unpleasant topics. The chapter talks about hardware malfunctions, disk failures, computer viruses, and various other software problems. Given the importance of what you're trying to do with Quicken—manage your money better—it seems only reasonable to take a few pages to describe some of the technical problems you may encounter and what you can do to address them.

*Using Quicken: IBM Version*, 2nd Edition, also provides three appendixes.

Appendix A, "Tips for Specific Business Situations," provides a laundry list of accounting tips for different kinds of business people, including lawyers, consultants, other professionals, restaurant managers and owners, retailers and wholesalers, and even nonprofit organizations. If you're planning to use Quicken for a business, consider skimming through Appendix A.

Appendix B, "Using This Book with Version 3.0," outlines the differences between Version 3.0 of Quicken and the current version, Version 4.0.

With this appendix, you should be able to use this book for either version of Quicken.

Appendix C, "Planning for Your Retirement," although not directly related to the operation of Quicken, offers helpful information for everyone. Too often, people fail to plan for retirement until it is too late. Read this appendix to learn how to make the most of your life in retirement.

# I

# Getting Started with Quicken

## Includes

Preparing To Use Quicken

Getting Around in Quicken

Describing Your Accounts

# 1

# Preparing To Use Quicken

**P**reparing to use Quicken is not difficult. But if you are new to computers or to the language and mechanics of installing software on a computer, receiving a little hand-holding and emotional support is nice. This chapter walks you through the steps for preparing to use Quicken. Don't worry if you don't know enough about computers, Quicken, or computer-based accounting systems. Simply follow the instructions and steps described in this chapter. In a few pages, you know which supplies you need to begin using Quicken and when you should begin using Quicken. After reading this chapter, you will have installed Quicken.

## Ordering Check Forms

You don't need to print your checks with Quicken to benefit from using the product, but Quicken's check-writing feature is a time-saver. The time savings, however, do not come cheaply. You spend between $30 and $50 for 250 computer check forms. In most cases, then, you spend more for check forms over the course of a year than you originally spent for Quicken. Obviously, you want to make sure that you make the right decision about ordering check forms. Two situations that merit the expense of the check forms: if you write many, many checks at home or business—say, more than two dozen checks each month; or when you plan to use Quicken for a business and want the professional appearance of computer-printed checks.

*CPA Tip*

> You still will use manual checks—checks you write by hand —even if you choose to use Quicken check forms. Home users, for example, will need manual checks for trips to the store. And business owners will need manual checks for unexpected deliveries that require immediate cash payments.

If you decide to use Quicken to print checks, you must order check forms for every bank account for which you want to print checks using your computer. The cheapest and easiest source of check forms is Intuit, the manufacturer of Quicken.

Complete and mail the order form included in the Quicken package; Intuit prints check forms with your name and address at the top of the form and the bank and account information at the bottom of the form. Do not worry about the bank accepting your new checks.

*CPA Tip*

> When deciding where to start numbering your computer check forms, consider two things: First, you will want to start the computer-printed check form numbers far enough away from your manual check numbers so that they do not overlap or duplicate and cause confusion in your record keeping and reconciliations; second, you may want to start numbering your computer-printed check forms with a number that shows you at a glance whether you wrote a check using Quicken or manually.

When you select check forms, you make a series of choices related to color, style, or lettering, and decide whether the check form is multipart or has voucher stubs. Table 1.1. summarizes your options.

**Table 1.1**
**Summary of Quicken Check Form Options**

| *Name* | *Colors* | *Form Size (inches)* | *Number of Parts* | *Comments* |
|--------|----------|----------------------|-------------------|------------|
| Prestige Antique | Tan | 3.5 × 8.5 | 1 | Antique refers to parchment background; printed three to a sheet. |

| Name | Colors | Form Size (inches) | Number of Parts | Comments |
|------|--------|--------------------|-----------------|----------|
| Prestige Standard | Gray | 3.5 × 8.5 | 1 or 2 | You can choose blue, green, or maroon accent strip; printed three to a sheet. |
| Prestige Payroll/ Voucher | Gray | 7.0 × 8.5 | 1 or 2 | You can choose blue, green, or maroon accent strip; larger form size due to voucher stub. |
| Standard | Blue or Green | 3.5 × 8.5 | 1, 2, or 3 | Printed three to a sheet. |
| Voucher/ Payroll | Blue or Gray | 7.0 × 8.5 | 1, 2, or 3 | Larger form size due to voucher stub. |
| Laser | Blue or Green | 3.5 × 8.5 | 1 | 8.5 × 10.5 sheets— each with 3 check forms— fit into printer paper tray. |
| Laser Voucher/ Payroll | Blue or Green | 3.5 × 8.5 | 1 or 2 | 8.5 × 11 sheets— each with 1 check form—fit into printer paper tray. |
| Wallet-size Computer | Blue or Green | 2-5/6 × 6 | 1 or 2 | Has a 2½-inch check stub so that overall form width is 8.5 inches. |

You are on your own when you select the color, size, and the style of lettering you want. This discussion, however, provides a couple of hints about the number of parts your check form should have and whether or not your check form should have a voucher stub or remittance advice.

The number of parts in a check form refers to the number of printed copies. A one-part form means that only the actual check form that you sign is printed. A two-part form means that a copy of the check is printed at the same time as the original. With a three-part form, you get two copies in addition to the original.

Multipart forms probably are not necessary for most home uses. In a business, however, the second and third parts can be attached to paid invoices as a fast and convenient way of keeping track of which checks paid which invoices. An extra copy of the check form may be valuable to keep in your check register until the canceled check comes back from the bank. You then have all your checks in one place. The third copy also can be placed in a numerical sequence file to help you identify the payee more quickly than if you had only the check number.

One precaution to consider if you use multipart forms is that the forms may wear out your impact printer's head (the points that hit the printer ribbon and cause characters to be printed). Check your printer's multipart form rating by referring to your printer manual. Verify that your printer is rated for at least the number of parts you want to print.

The voucher stub, also called the remittance advice, is the blank piece of paper about the same size as the check form and is attached to the check form. Voucher stubs provide extra space for you to describe or document the reason for the check. You also can use this area to show any calculations involved in arriving at the total check amount. You may, for example, use the voucher stub space to describe how an employee's payroll amount was calculated or to define the invoices for which that check was issued. As with multipart forms, voucher stubs probably make more sense for business use rather than home use.

If you are not sure which check forms to choose, try Quicken's starter kit. The starter kit costs about $35 as of this writing, includes 250 checks, and gives you a chance to experiment with preprinted check forms.

# Picking a Conversion Date

Picking the conversion date is another critical decision you must make before you can enjoy the many advantages of an automated accounting system. The conversion date is the day on which you plan to stop using your old manual system and begin using your new Quicken system. The less you expect from Quicken, the less important the conversion date is.

If you intend to use Quicken to organize your income tax deductions, calculate business profits, or to plan budgets, consider the issue of a clean accounting cutoff point for the date you begin record keeping with Quicken. From the conversion date forward, Quicken provides your accounting information. Before the conversion date, your old accounting system must provide your accounting information. Pick a natural cutoff date that makes switching from one system to another easy. The best time to begin using any accounting package is usually at the beginning of the year. All the income and expense transactions for the new year are recorded in the same place. Picking a good cutoff date may seem trivial, but having your tax deductions for one year recorded and summarized in one place is handy.

If you cannot start using Quicken at the beginning of the year, the next best time is at the beginning of the month. If you start at the beginning of a month, you must combine your old accounting or record-keeping information with Quicken's information to get totals for the year. When calculating tax deductions, for example, you need to add the amounts Quicken shows to whatever your old system shows. Your old system may not be anything fancy—perhaps a shoe box full of receipts.

You should watch for a few things when choosing an accounting cutoff date. You may put the same income or expense transaction in both systems and, therefore, count the transaction twice when you add the two systems together to get the annual totals. You may neglect to record a transaction because you think that you recorded the transaction in the other system. In either case, your records are wrong. To begin using Quicken at the beginning of the month, spend some time summarizing your accounting information from the old system. Make sure that you do not include the same transaction (income received or an expense paid) twice. This repetition can occur if you pay the expense once using the old system and then again using Quicken.

For the same reasons, the worst time to begin using Quicken is in the middle of a month. With no natural cutoff point, you are likely to count some transactions on both systems and forget to record others in either system.

If you don't use Quicken to summarize income and expense transactions or monitor how well you are sticking to a budget, and all you really want is a tool to maintain your checkbook and produce checks, the conversion date isn't as important.

# Installing the Software

To use Quicken, your computer must meet the following minimum hardware requirements:

❏ IBM personal computer or compatible

❏ 320K of memory for Version 4 (Intuit recommends 384K for DOS 3.0 and later, but Quicken will run on 320K); 256K of memory for Version 3 (Use CHKDSK, the DOS command, to determine the amount of memory available on your computer.)

❏ Two floppy disk drives or one floppy disk drive and a hard disk

❏ MS-DOS or PC DOS Version 2.0 or higher (Use VER, the DOS command, to determine the DOS version installed on your computer.)

❏ Any printer (except one that uses thermal paper)

❏ An 80-column color or monochrome monitor

The steps for installing the Quicken system vary depending on whether your computer uses only floppy disks or has a floppy and a hard disk drive. Refer to the appropriate section that follows to install Quicken on your system.

## Installing Quicken on a Hard Disk System

If you haven't been using Version 3 of Quicken, you should know a few things about the Quicken hard disk installation program, INSTALL, before you use the program. INSTALL creates a directory named QUICKEN4 on your hard disk, in which the program files are stored. Your data files also are stored in the QUICKEN4 directory unless you change the system settings (described in Chapter 11). (In case you are not familiar with the terms, program files refer to the files that contain the actual Quicken software instructions and data files refer to the files that contain your financial information.)

INSTALL also creates a batch file named Q.BAT so that all you have to do is type *q* at the C› prompt to run QUICKEN. If you already have a Q.BAT file (if you have been using Quicken Version 2, for instance), INSTALL renames the old file Q2.BAT.

INSTALL also verifies that the CONFIG.SYS file's BUFFERS statement equals or exceeds 10 and that the FILES statement equals or exceeds 10. INSTALL resets these statements because Quicken runs with several files open and performs many reads from the hard disk. For more information on the CONFIG.SYS file and the BUFFERS and FILES statements, see your DOS manual. If you do not have a CONFIG.SYS file, INSTALL creates one with the appropriate BUFFERS and FILES statements. If the CONFIG.SYS file you currently have does not have these statements, INSTALL adds them. If the statements exist, but are set to less than 10, INSTALL increases the statement settings to 10. INSTALL does not cause any problems by changing your computer's CONFIG.SYS file.

To install Quicken on a hard disk system, do the following:

1. Turn on your computer and monitor. Make sure that the correct system date and time are set. (Type *date* or *time* at the C› prompt.) DATE is the DOS command for setting the system date. TIME is the DOS command for setting the system time. Refer to your DOS user's manual if you need help using the DATE or TIME commands.

2. Place the Quicken help disk in drive A. (If you have a 3½-inch disk, the help and program portions of Quicken are on the disk.) Type *a:install* and press Enter.

The introductory Install screen, shown in figure 1.1, appears.

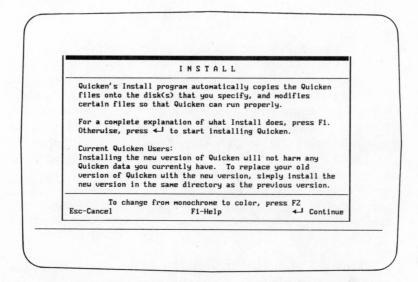

*Fig. 1.1. The introductory Install screen.*

3. Press Enter, and Quicken displays the screen you use to specify on which disk you want to install Quicken, as shown in figure 1.2. (Press F2 to change the display on your monitor from monochrome to color or from color to monochrome.)

   *Note:* If you have two floppy drives, the screen shown in figure 1.2 includes both floppy drives.

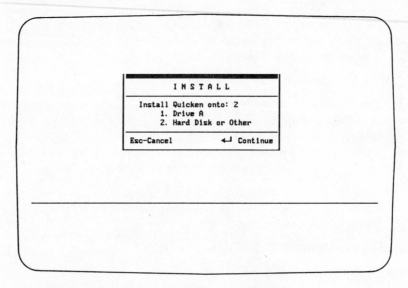

*Fig. 1.2. The specify disk on which to install screen.*

4. Select the appropriate number to designate a hard disk installation and press Enter to continue. Quicken displays the specify directory location screen shown in figure 1.3. The default directory that Quicken creates and installs itself into is \QUICKEN4. (If you previously used Version 3 of Quicken and stored the program and data files in QUICKEN3, the default directory is QUICKEN3. Installing Quicken Version 4 in the QUICKEN3 directory will not damage the Quicken Version 3 data files.) If you want to use some other directory, you specify it here by typing the default directory. When the correct directory is displayed, press Enter. (Version 2 of Quicken stores files in the directory C:\QUICKEN2. Do not specify the directory as C:\QUICKEN2 because you will overwrite these records.)

5. Quicken asks whether or not you want the Billminder option installed, as shown in figure 1.4. Press Enter to answer yes or Esc to answer no.

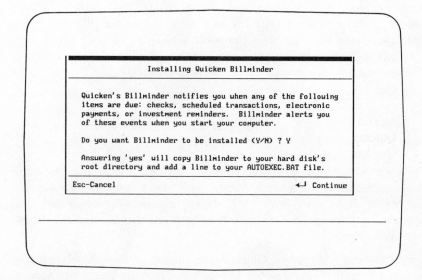

```
        INSTALL

Type the drive and/or directory you want Quicken installed in.
If the directory does not exist, it will be created.

Specify drive/directory: C:\QUICKEN3

Esc-Cancel                                    ↵ Continue
```

**Fig. 1.3.** *The Specify Directory screen.*

The Billminder reminds you of bills you should pay. When you turn on your computer or when you enter Quicken, you are reminded that bills must be paid. This handy feature can save you the price of Quicken and this book many times over by eliminating or minimizing late-payment fees.

```
        Installing Quicken Billminder

Quicken's Billminder notifies you when any of the following
items are due: checks, scheduled transactions, electronic
payments, or investment reminders.  Billminder alerts you
of these events when you start your computer.

Do you want Billminder to be installed (Y/N) ? Y

Answering 'yes' will copy Billminder to your hard disk's
root directory and add a line to your AUTOEXEC.BAT file.

Esc-Cancel                                    ↵ Continue
```

**Fig. 1.4.** *The Installing Quicken Billminder screen.*

Quicken completes the first part of the installation and prompts you to insert the program disk in drive A, as shown in figure 1.5. Billminder alerts you that you have entered checks that need to be printed. (See Chapters 6 and 11 for more about the Billminder option.)

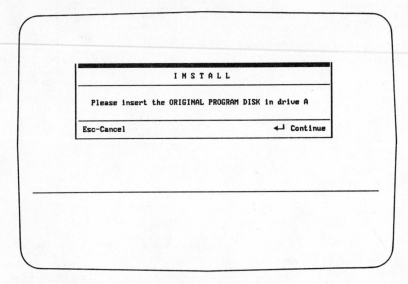

*Fig. 1.5.* *The insert program disk prompt.*

If you decide to use the Billminder option, the INSTALL program adds a line to the end of your AUTOEXEC.BAT file that runs the Billminder program every time you start your computer. (INSTALL does not destroy the old AUTOEXEC.BAT file; the program renames the file AUTOEXEC.B00 in case you want to retrieve or re-use the original file.)

After you insert the program disk and press Enter, Quicken continues with the installation. Quicken tells you when the installation is complete by displaying the screen shown in figure 1.6. To return to the C› prompt, press Enter.

To begin using Quicken, type *q* at the C› prompt. Before displaying the Main menu, Quicken might ask whether you have a color monitor. Type *1* for yes or *2* for no. (Figure 1.7, which also is used when installing Quicken on a floppy disk system, shows the screen Quicken uses to ask you this question.)

*Note:* On some computers, Quicken also might simply indicate that it is setting the monitor speed to fast, but alert you that the speed may need to be reset to slow.

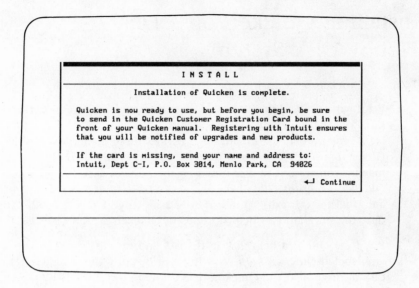

**Fig. 1.6.** *The Installation of Quicken Is Complete screen.*

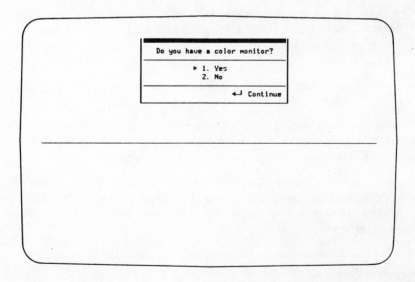

**Fig. 1.7.** *Quicken asks whether your monitor is color.*

# Installing Quicken on a Dual Floppy Disk System

To install Quicken on a dual floppy disk system, do the following:

1. Place your DOS disk in drive A and turn on your computer and monitor. Make sure that your system has the correct date and time set. (Type *date* at the A› prompt.) Format three blank floppy disks. (Refer to your DOS manual for information on the FORMAT command if you are not sure of how to format disks.) Label the first disk *Quicken program copy*; label the second disk *Quicken help copy*, and label the third disk *Quicken data disk*. (If you have a 3 1/2-inch disk, the program and help portions of Quicken are on one disk.)

2. Place the Quicken help disk in drive A and the disk you formatted and labeled *Quicken help copy* in drive B. Copy the Quicken help disk in drive A to the Quicken help copy disk in drive B by typing *copy a:*.* b:* at the A› prompt and pressing Enter. Repeat these steps to make a copy of the Quicken program disk.

3. After the copies are complete, remove the Quicken program disk from drive A and put the program and help disks in a safe place. Move the Quicken help copy disk to drive A and the Quicken data disk to drive B.

4. To start Quicken from the help copy disk, type *q* and press Enter. (In the future, you also start Quicken this way.)

If Quicken cannot determine what kind of monitor you use, you see the screen shown in figure 1.7. To respond to the monitor question, type *1* to indicate a color monitor or *2* to indicate a monochrome monitor.

If you did not set the date, Quicken asks for the correct date. To enter the correct date, type today's date in MM/DD/YY format (for example, 11/26/90). After you respond to these queries, press Enter. Quicken's Main menu appears, as shown in figure 1.8.

# Describing Your Checking Account

You need to describe the bank account for which you will be recording check and deposit transactions. To describe an account, you enter the account's current balance; the account name; and a longer, textual description of the bank account. The longer, textual description might

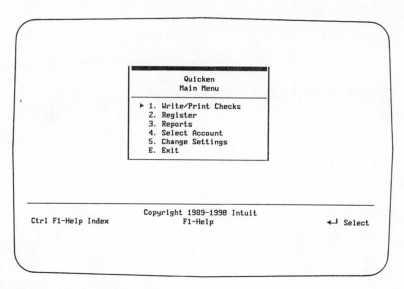

```
                    Quicken
                   Main Menu

        ▶ 1. Write/Print Checks
          2. Register
          3. Reports
          4. Select Account
          5. Change Settings
          E. Exit
```

```
                    Copyright 1989-1990 Intuit
Ctrl F1-Help Index           F1-Help              ↵ Select
```

*Fig. 1.8.* *The Quicken Main menu.*

include, for example, the bank name and bank account number. (If you want to create personal or business balance sheets or use multiple bank accounts, you also need to set up additional accounts for other checking accounts, assets, or liabilities. Chapter 12 describes how to set up other accounts.)

*CPA Tip*

In describing your bank account, you may want to abbreviate the bank name and then use the last four digits to distinguish between various accounts at the same bank. For example, Standard Bank of Washington, account 9173526471, would become StdWash 6471. Standard Bank of Oregon, account 7386427389, would become StdOre 7389. Standard Bank of Washington, account 9173533721, would become StdWash 3721. This procedure enables you to separate the different accounts for the same banks.

To set up accounts for the first time, follow these steps:

1. From Quicken's Main menu, select the **Register** option by typing *2* or by using the down-arrow key to highlight the option and then pressing Enter. The First Time Setup screen appears (see fig. 1.9).

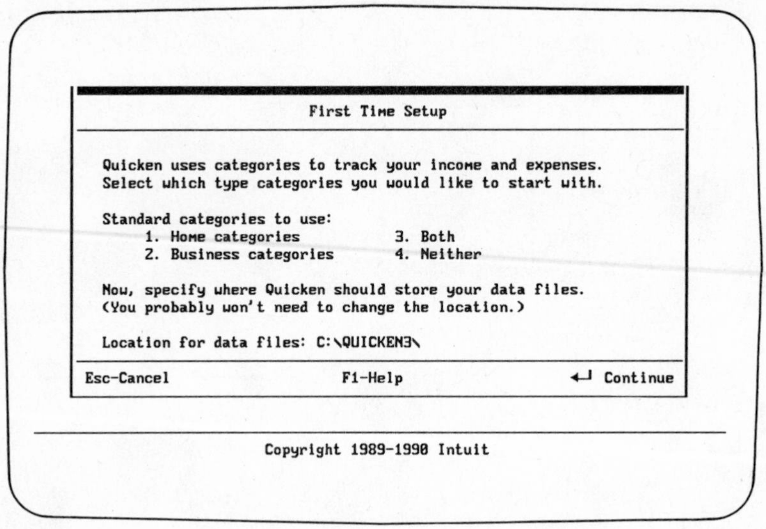

```
                          First Time Setup

   Quicken uses categories to track your income and expenses.
   Select which type categories you would like to start with.

   Standard categories to use:
        1. Home categories        3. Both
        2. Business categories     4. Neither

   Now, specify where Quicken should store your data files.
   (You probably won't need to change the location.)

   Location for data files: C:\QUICKEN3\

   Esc-Cancel                F1-Help                 ←┘ Continue
```

Copyright 1989-1990 Intuit

*Fig. 1.9. The First Time Setup screen.*

At this point, you need to decide whether you want to use the standard categories predefined by Quicken or your own categories. If you want to use Quicken's categories, you can direct Quicken to use one or both of the predefined category lists.

2. Type *1* if you want to use Quicken's home categories. Type *2* if you want to use Quicken's business categories. If you want to use both, type *3*. If you want to use neither, type *4*.

   A category describes and summarizes common business and personal income and expenses, such as salary, insurance, utilities, and so on. (Chapter 7 describes Quicken's categories in more detail.)

   You also can specify the data directory Quicken should use to store your records. For hard disk users, the default directory is QUICKEN3 or QUICKEN4. For floppy disk users, the default directory is B:\.

3. If you want to use a different directory, enter that directory name on the First Time Setup screen. You might want separate directories to separate significant accounting periods; for example, QUICKEN90 for the 1990 files, QUICKEN91 for the 1991 files. Or, perhaps you have an existing business and are starting a new one; name one directory QUICKOLD and the second QUICKNEW.

4. (Optional) Quicken Version 2.0 users must convert the Quicken 2.0 files before continuing, because Quicken 4.0 uses a different file format. Refer to your program's documentation for instructions on converting files.

*Note:* Version 3.0 users do not need to convert their files for use with Version 4.0.

5. After you complete the First Time Setup screen, press Enter, and the Set Up New Account screen appears (see fig. 1.10). This screen provides several fields that you need to fill in with information, including account name, account type, the starting account balance, the starting date, and account description.

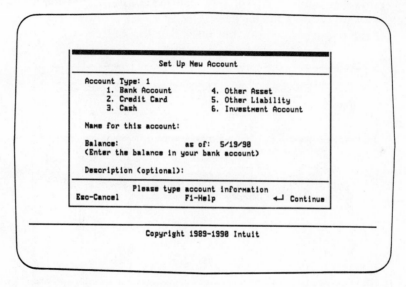

*Fig. 1.10. The Set Up New Account screen.*

6. In the Account Type field, indicate whether the account is an asset or a liability and what kind of asset or liability. If you are setting up a bank account, the account type should be 1. Press Enter to move to the Name field.

7. Enter a description of the account using the Name field. The Name field can be up to 15 characters long and can use any characters except [ ] / and : . You also can include spaces. Press Enter to move to the Balance field.

8. Enter the starting account balance. For a bank account, this amount should be the current account balance according to your records. You must enter a balance, even if it is 0.

9. Enter the date. The as of date should be the date on which the balance you entered is correct.

10. (Optional) Fill in the Description field to provide an additional 21 characters of account description.

11. When you finish entering information for the Set Up New Account screen, press Enter.

    Quicken completes the installation and displays the Register screen shown in figure 1.11. The only information showing is the balance forward transaction Quicken recorded to set your opening balance. (The register is described in more detail in Chapter 4.)

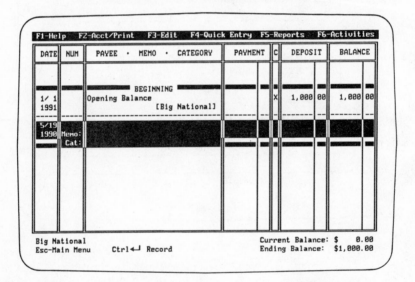

**Fig. 1.11.** *The empty register screen.*

12. To exit the Register screen, press Esc. Quicken returns you to the Main menu. To exit from Quicken, type *e* for exit.

Congratulations! You have installed Quicken.

# Describing Your Printer

The final part of installing Quicken is identifying the printer or printers you will use to print the Quicken register and perhaps the Quicken check forms and reports. To describe your printer, follow these steps:

1. Start Quicken, if the program isn't already running, by typing *q*. Select the **Change Settings** option from Quicken's Main menu by typing *5* when the Main menu is displayed. Quicken displays the Change Settings menu (see fig. 1.12).

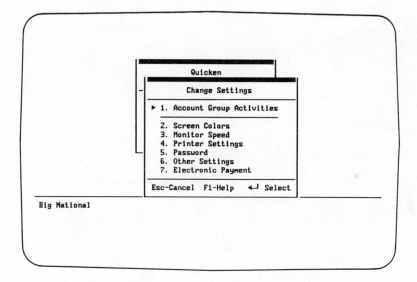

*Fig. 1.12. The Change Settings menu.*

2. Select the **Printer Settings** option from the Change Settings menu by typing *4*. Quicken displays the Printer Settings submenu (see fig. 1.13).

   The Printer Settings submenu provides three options:

   ```
   1. Check Printer Settings
   2. Report Printer Settings
   3. Alternate Printer Settings
   ```

3. Select the **Check Printer Settings** option by typing *1*. Quicken displays the Printer List screen (see fig. 1.14).

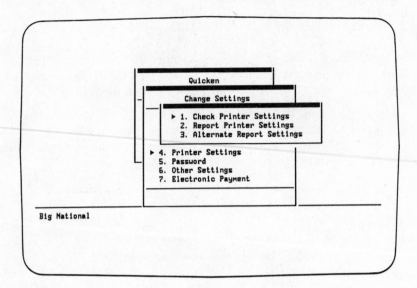

**Fig. 1.13.** *The Printer Settings submenu.*

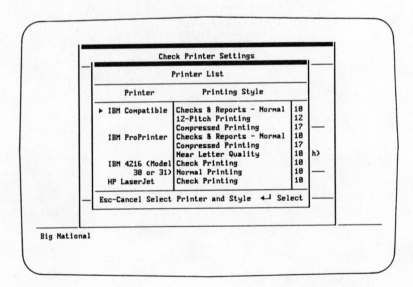

**Fig. 1.14.** *The Printer List screen.*

4. Use the Printer List screen to identify your printer. To choose a printer from the list, highlight your choice by using the up- and down-arrow keys. If you cannot find your printer, select another

printer that your printer emulates. You should be able to find which printers your printer emulates by checking the printer user's manual. If you cannot find your printer on the list and also cannot find a printer your printer emulates, select the undefined printer option. After you select the printer, press Enter. Quicken displays the Check Printer Settings screen (see fig. 1.15).

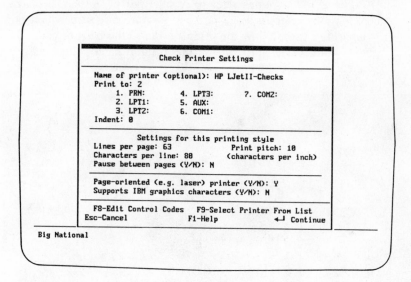

***Fig. 1.15.*** *The Check Printer Settings screen.*

If you select a printer from the printer list, Quicken correctly fills out the Printer Settings screen. Use the Printer Settings screen to describe your printer.

5. Save the printer settings by pressing Enter when the cursor is positioned on the Supports IBM Graphics Characters field. Or, press Ctrl-Enter or F10 when the cursor is positioned on the Printer settings option on the Change Settings menu. Quicken redisplays the Change Settings menu. Press Esc to return to the Main menu. From the Main menu, press E to exit.

To define a report printer and an alternate report printer, repeat steps 3 through 5. When you repeat step 3, however, type *2* if you are defining a report printer and type *3* if you are defining an alternate report printer.

If you selected the undefined printer steps, you must follow these additional steps (before saving the printer setting):

1. (Optional) Type the name of the printer. Figure 1.15, for example, shows HP LJetII-Checks, which is an abbreviation for the Hewlett-Packard LaserJet Series II.

2. (Optional) Press Enter or Tab to move the cursor to the Print to field. The Print to field tells Quicken which communications port should be used to send checks and reports to the printer. The PRN, LPT1, LPT2, LPT3 options refer to parallel ports. The AUX, COM1, and COM2 options refer to serial ports. If you are not sure which port your printer uses, follow the printer cable to the back of your computer. The socket into which the printer cable plugs may be labeled.

*CPA TIP*

If you have a choice about how your printer and computer should communicate, choose a parallel port. Parallel connections mean that the printer and computer can talk to each other at the same time—in parallel, which usually results in faster communication.

When you choose a serial port, the computer can send information to the printer only when the printer is not sending information back to the computer. The printer can send information to the computer only when the computer is not sending information back to the printer. With a serial port, your computer and printer take turns communicating with each other.

3. (Optional) Press Enter or Tab to move the cursor to the Indent field. Use the Indent field to tell Quicken how many characters to move in from the left margin of the form or paper to begin printing. Each time Quicken begins printing a line, the program moves that many characters to the right. Enter a number from 0 to 80, but be careful that you do not enter a number so large that Quicken does not have room to print. For laser printers, you can use an indent setting equal to 0. For impact printers, start with an indent setting equal to 0, but you may need to increase this setting if Quicken starts printing too far on the left side of your paper. If Quicken prints off the page on the right side of the paper, reduce your indent setting.

4. (Optional) Press Enter or Tab to move to the Lines Per Page field. Use the Lines Per Page setting to tell Quicken how many lines you want printed on a page. Quicken assumes that 6 lines equal an inch.

If you are using 11-inch paper, therefore, set this value to 66. If you are using 14-inch paper, set this value to 84.

To tell whether the lines per page setting is correct, compare where Quicken starts printing on successive pages. If the printing doesn't start at the same distance from the top of the page, you need to adjust the lines per page setting. The setting is too high if Quicken starts printing lower on the second page than on the first. Your setting is too low if Quicken starts printing higher on the second page than on the first.

5. (Optional) Press Enter or Tab to move to the Print Pitch field. Use the print pitch setting to tell Quicken how many characters your printer prints in an inch. Typical pitch, or characters per inch, settings are 10, 12, and 15. Check your printer manual to determine your printer's pitch. You also can use a ruler to measure the number of characters, including blank spaces, printed in one inch on a sample of the printer's output.

6. (Optional) Press Enter or Tab to move to the Characters Per Line field. Use the Characters Per Line field setting to tell Quicken how many characters fit on a line. This setting usually equals 80 if your pitch setting is 10. The characters per line usually equal 96 if your pitch setting is 12.

7. (Optional) Press Enter or Tab to move the cursor to the Pause Between Pages field. Use this field to tell Quicken whether to stop after printing a full page so that you can insert a new piece of paper or adjust the printer. Press Y for yes or N for no.

8. (Optional) Press Enter or Tab to move to the Page-oriented Printer field. Printers that use individual sheets of paper are, from Quicken's perspective, page-oriented. Use the Page-oriented Printer field to tell Quicken whether your printer uses individual sheets of paper. Press Y for yes or N for no.

9. (Optional) Press Enter or Tab to move to the Supports IBM Graphics Characters field. Use this field to tell Quicken whether your printer supports the extended IBM character set. If available on your printer, Quicken uses IBM graphics characters in the extended character set in headings on your reports. Press Y for yes or N for no.

10. (Optional) Press F8 to access the Printer Control Codes screen (see fig. 1.16). You use the Printer Control Codes screen to enter the special sequences of letters, numbers, and other keyboard characters that cause your printer to perform in a specific manner or print in a certain style (such as condensed print). To determine which

printer control codes are appropriate for your printer, look them up in your printer manual. Type the control code that Quicken should initially send your printer in the Before Printing field. Press Enter or Tab to move the cursor to the After Printing field and type the control code that Quicken should send your printer when finished printing. Press Enter or Tab to move the cursor to the Start of Page field and type the control code that Quicken should send your printer as it starts a new page. If you are using a laser printer to print check forms, press Enter or Tab to move the cursor to the Landscape Mode field and type the control code that Quicken should send to a laser printer to print in landscape mode. Figure 1.16 shows the printer control codes that Quicken provides for a Hewlett-Packard LaserJet Series II. The precise control codes that you use, however, depend on your printer. To return to the Printer Settings screen, press Enter when the cursor is positioned on the Landscape Mode field.

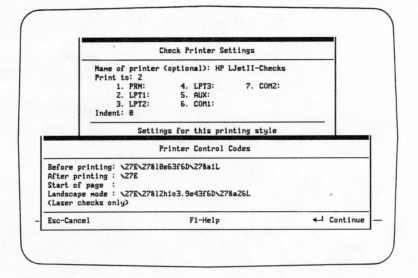

**Fig. 1.16.** *The Printer Control Codes screen.*

11. Save the printer settings by pressing Enter when the cursor is positioned on the Supports IBM Graphics Characters field. Or, press Ctrl-Enter or F10 when the cursor is positioned on any other screen in the system. Quicken redisplays the Change Settings menu. Press Esc to return to the Main menu. From the Main menu, type *e* to exit.

# Chapter Summary

This chapter described the steps you take to prepare to use Quicken: ordering check forms, picking the conversion date, and installing the software. Now that you have Quicken installed, you are ready to begin using the system. Before you start entering actual checks and deposits, writing checks, or reconciling accounts, take a few minutes to peruse the contents of the next chapter. Chapter 2 covers the basics of using the Quicken program and should make getting the most from Quicken that much easier.

# 2

# Getting Around
# in Quicken

Quicken is not difficult to use, especially when you begin by learning the helpful operations described in this chapter. You will learn about accessing Quicken's help screens, selecting menu options, using the Quicken screens to collect financial information for storage, and using Quicken's calculator.

## Using Help

Think of Quicken's Help feature as a user's manual stored in your computer's memory. You can access this manual from anywhere in Quicken by pressing F1. Quicken's Help feature is context-sensitive; that is, it provides the manual and opens it to the correct page. If you select **Help** from Quicken's Main menu, for example, you receive information about the Main menu options (see fig. 2.1).

Often, the information provided by the Help key (F1) requires more than one screen. Use the PgDn and PgUp keys to see the next or preceding pages of information. After you read the help information, press Esc to return to the program. Quicken returns to where you were when you pressed the Help key.

If you press F1 twice, you access the Select Help Topic screen, which lists 59 topics for which you can get help (see fig. 2.2). To select a topic, move the selection triangle so that it marks the desired topic and press

Enter. To leave the Select Help Topic screen without choosing a topic, press Esc.

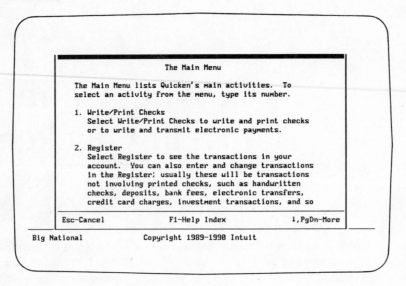

```
                    The Main Menu

    The Main Menu lists Quicken's main activities.  To
    select an activity from the menu, type its number.

    1. Write/Print Checks
       Select Write/Print Checks to write and print checks
       or to write and transmit electronic payments.

    2. Register
       Select Register to see the transactions in your
       account.  You can also enter and change transactions
       in the Register; usually these will be transactions
       not involving printed checks, such as handwritten
       checks, deposits, bank fees, electronic transfers,
       credit card charges, investment transactions, and so

    Esc-Cancel           F1-Help Index          ↓,PgDn-More

    Big National         Copyright 1989-1990 Intuit
```

**Fig. 2.1.** *Help for Quicken's Main menu.*

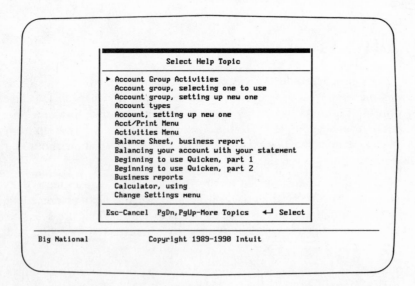

```
                  Select Help Topic

    ▸ Account Group Activities
      Account group, selecting one to use
      Account group, setting up new one
      Account types
      Account, setting up new one
      Acct/Print Menu
      Activities Menu
      Balance Sheet, business report
      Balancing your account with your statement
      Beginning to use Quicken, part 1
      Beginning to use Quicken, part 2
      Business reports
      Calculator, using
      Change Settings menu

    Esc-Cancel  PgDn,PgUp-More Topics   ↵ Select

    Big National         Copyright 1989-1990 Intuit
```

**Fig. 2.2.** *The Select Help Topic screen.*

# Using and Selecting Menu Options

Quicken provides the following four ways to select menu options:

- ❏ Typing the number of the option
- ❏ Highlighting the option and pressing Enter
- ❏ Using the shortcut keys
- ❏ Using the function keys

The first way to select an option from a menu is to type the number of that option. If you want to select the **Write/Print Checks** option from the Main menu, for example, you can type *1*. Quicken will display the Write Checks screen (see fig. 2.3). To exit the screen and return to the Main menu, press Esc.

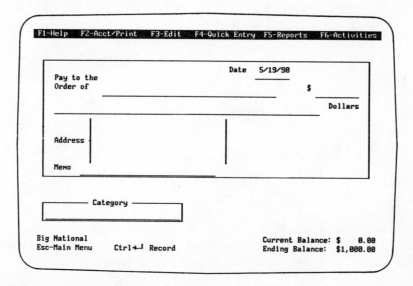

**Fig. 2.3.** *The Write Checks screen.*

The second way to select menu options is to use the cursor-movement keys to highlight the appropriate selection. If you press the up- and down-arrow keys, the small triangle to the left of the menu option numbers moves up and down. When the small triangle is next to the option you want to select, press Enter.

The third way to select menu options is to use one of the shortcut key combinations. Not every menu option has a shortcut key, but most of the options you use regularly do. To execute a shortcut, hold down the Ctrl key and press the appropriate letter key. For example, one way to delete a check or deposit in the register is to select the **Delete transaction** option from the Edit menu, and confirm that you want to delete a transaction by pressing Enter. You also can press the Ctrl and D keys to accomplish the same thing. Quicken shows you the shortcut keys (for example, Ctrl-D) to the right of the options (see fig. 2.4). Chapter 5 describes the **Delete Transaction** option in detail.

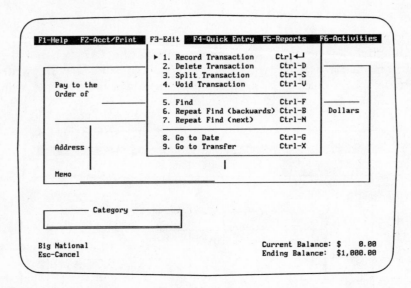

*Fig. 2.4. Quicken menus show shortcut combinations.*

Shortcut keys are described more in the chapters discussing the associated menu options. For now, remember that shortcut keys are another way to execute menu options and that they save time.

From Quicken screens, such as the Write Checks screen (described in Chapter 6) and the Register screen (described in Chapter 4), you use the fourth method for selecting menu options: press one of the function keys. Function-key options fall into one of two groups: function keys that access an option you also may access from the Main menu, and keys that provide options related to entering information on-screen.

As an example of the first group of function-key options, pressing F5 from the Write Checks screen accesses the Reports menu. You also can move to the Reports menu by selecting the Reports option from Quicken's Main menu.

The first group of function-key options may seem confusing initially, but this group of shortcuts enables you to jump around the Quicken menu structure. You can move from one aspect of Quicken to another without leaving what you are working on currently or backtracking through the menus to find the option you want. (A menu map at the back of the book diagrams the Quicken menu structure.)

You also access the second group of function-key options (for entering information on-screen) from one of the Quicken screens. From a screen, you can access two groups of options by using only a function key: the Edit and the Quick Entry options under the Write/Print Checks and Register selections on the Main menu. F3 accesses the Edit menu options shown in figure 2.4, and F4 accesses the Quick Entry menu options shown in figure 2.5. These options provide tools you can use to make the screen related to the options easier to use. (Chapters 5 and 7 describe the applicable menus and their options.)

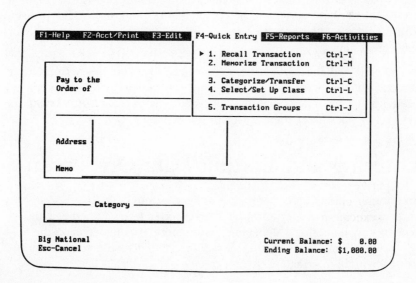

*Fig. 2.5.* *The Quick Entry menu.*

# Collecting Data On-Screen

Collecting data on-screen involves moving between fields, entering and editing fields, and saving your work. Quicken provides you with a variety of ways to accomplish these tasks, explained in the following sections. To follow this information on your computer, move to the Write Checks screen by selecting the **Write/Print Checks** option from Quicken's Main menu.

## Moving between Fields

Quicken provides a variety of ways to move between fields. You can move from field to field by pressing Enter. You can move to the next field by pressing Tab and to the preceding field by pressing Shift-Tab. You can move between fields by using the arrow keys. Pressing Ctrl-← moves the cursor to the beginning of the preceding field, and pressing Ctrl-→ moves the cursor to the beginning of the next field. Finally, you also can use the Home and End keys to move to the first and last fields on the screen. If the cursor is at the start of the field, pressing Home moves the cursor to the first field on the screen; if the cursor is at the end of the field, pressing End moves the cursor to the last field. Table 2.1 summarizes the cursor-movement keys.

If you followed the earlier discussion and moved to the Write Checks screen and you want to practice using the cursor-movement keys, try each of the keys or key combinations listed in table 2.1. (*Note:* Trying the keys really does make them easier to understand.)

## Entering and Editing Data On-Screen

Entering or editing a field of data is as easy as moving between fields. To enter data into a field, type the appropriate characters. Whether Quicken accepts only numeric or alphabetic and numeric data depends on the field you are entering. Refer to the chapter pertaining to the screen you are using for more information.

Generally, type dollar amounts as numeric data by using the number keys on your keyboard. Do not enter the dollar symbol or any commas because Quicken adds these symbols for you. If an amount represents a negative number, however, precede the number with a minus sign, as in $-1.47$. Quicken assumes that the number is an even dollar amount unless you use

**Table 2.1**
**Cursor-Movement Keys for Moving between Fields**

| Key | New Cursor Placement |
| --- | --- |
| Enter | The next field |
| Tab | The next field |
| Shift-Tab | The preceding field |
| Arrow Keys | The next or preceding field, according to the arrow |
| Ctrl-← | The beginning of the preceding field |
| Ctrl-→ | The beginning of the next field |
| Home | The first field on the screen (from start of a field) |
| End | The last field on the screen (from end of a field) |

a decimal when entering the number. For example, entering 1245 displays as $1,245.00, and entering 12.45 displays as $12.45.

If you make an error while entering an amount, use the arrow keys to position the cursor on the numbers you want to change. You also can use Home and End to move the cursor within a field. Press Home to move the cursor to the start of a field, and press End to move the cursor to the end of a field. To delete numbers, use the Backspace or Del key. The Backspace key removes the number preceding the cursor location; the Del key removes the number at the cursor location. To delete the entire field, press Ctrl-Backspace.

Most of the remaining data stored in the system (data other than dollar amounts) can be alphabetic, numeric, or both. Where alphabetic characters are allowed, you can use upper- or lowercase characters. Try typing the name of someone to whom you frequently write checks, such as the bank. You can use spaces, capital letters, numbers, and whatever else you want or need.

You can edit or change an entry in a text field by retyping the field's contents or by using the arrow keys to position the cursor on the characters you want to change. To delete characters, use the Backspace or Del key. To add characters to existing text, press the Ins key and type the needed characters. To add characters to the end of the text, position the cursor at the end of the text, using the right-arrow key, and type the remaining characters. Again, if you just want to clear the field so that you can start over, press Ctrl-Backspace.

For date fields, Quicken provides a special editing capability. By pressing the + key, you can add one day to the date; by pressing the − key, you can subtract one day. Try this feature by entering 1/1/91 in the Date field. Pressing + changes the date to 1/2/91, and pressing − changes the date to 12/31/90. If the date is only the month and year—as in a few places in the Quicken system—you can move the date ahead one month by pressing the + key and back one month by pressing the − key.

## Saving Your Work

When you finish entering data on-screen and want to save the data, you have three ways to save your work:

❑ Press F10

❑ Press Enter from the last field on-screen

❑ Press Ctrl-Enter

If you are recording a check, Quicken displays a blank Write Checks screen so that you can enter another check. If you are recording a transaction in the register, Quicken displays the next empty row in the register so that you can record another transaction.

## Using the Calculator

One of Quicken's tools (beginning with Version 3) is the on-line calculator that you can use by pressing the shortcut key combination Ctrl-O. Figure 2.6 shows the Calculator screen.

Quicken verifies that Num Lock (number lock—a key on the keypad) is on so that you can use the numeric keypad to enter numbers. If the Num Lock key is off, Quicken temporarily toggles the key on while you are using the calculator.

Use the on-line calculator as you do a regular calculator. For example, to add three invoices for $12.87, $232.01, and $49.07, and subtract a $50 credit memo, you press the following keys:

12.87 + 232.01 + 49.07 − 50

Press Enter or the equal sign. Quicken performs the math and displays the results as shown in figure 2.7. The calculator tape shows both the numbers and the math operators. To clear the on-line calculator, press C. If you do not clear the calculator tape, Quicken saves the numbers and the math operators and they will reappear the next time you access the calculator.

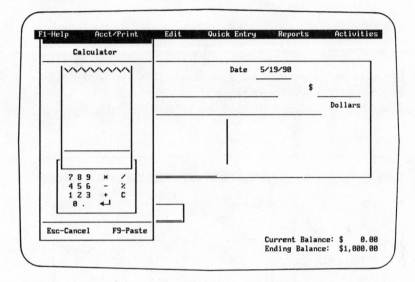

**Fig. 2.6.** *The calculator screen before you begin entering numbers.*

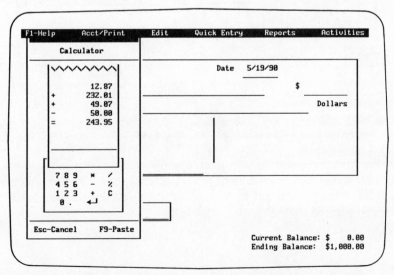

**Fig. 2.7.** *The Calculator tape shows both the numbers and the math operators.*

To multiply numbers, use the asterisk. For example, to multiply $232.01 by .25, press the following keys:

232.01*.25

Press Enter or the equal sign.

To divide numbers, use the slash. For example, to divide $527.32 by 2, you press the following keys:

527.32/2

Press Enter or the equal sign.

If you want to add or subtract a percentage, the on-line calculator also provides a percent key. For example, to add 25% to 200, press 200 + 25% and then Enter. Quicken calculates and displays the result shown in figure 2.8.

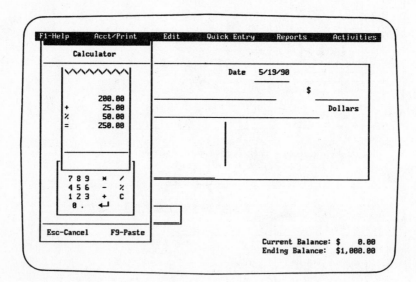

***Fig. 2.8.*** *Using the percent key.*

Press Esc to exit the on-line calculator. If you are calculating an amount to enter as a value in a screen field, you also can press F9, and Quicken enters the calculation result into the field where the cursor was located when you pressed Ctrl-O.

# Learning To Use Quicken

Using Quicken is usually easy, but you may sometimes be perplexed and find yourself scratching your head. To minimize the hassles and heartaches of learning a new program, consider several additional resources.

For a sturdy foundation, read the Quicken user's manual and this book—or at least the chapters that apply to those parts of the program you will use.

Talk to other Quicken users who might be working through problems similar to yours and finding helpful solutions. Formal and informal users' groups are excellent support systems. The store that sold you Quicken, the store or computer consultant who helps you with your hardware and software, or the CPA who prepares your annual financial statements or tax return may be able to direct you to Quicken users' groups.

Spend some time experimenting with the software. Try different transactions, explore the menus and screens, and pore over the reports. Experimenting increases your confidence in the system, gives you experience in working with live business or family data, and most importantly, confirms which options accomplish which tasks.

# Chapter Summary

This chapter described the basics of getting around in Quicken: using help, selecting menu options, collecting data on screens, and using the calculator. The chapter also provided some tips for learning Quicken. If you need to define more than one bank account, you need to read Chapter 3. If you don't need to define more than one bank account, you are ready to learn the basics of using Quicken—such as writing and printing checks, using Quicken's register, reconciling your bank account, and taking care of Quicken's files—which are covered beginning with Chapter 4.

# 3

# Describing Your
# Accounts

I f you followed the steps outlined in Chapter 1, you already have
defined one bank account as part of installing Quicken, but you may
want to define other bank accounts. For instance, you may have more
than one checking account, a savings account or two, and even certificates of deposit for which you will keep records with Quicken. If you
want to use Quicken to track more than one account, you need to
describe these accounts to Quicken. You then can use Quicken to record
changes in the accounts and track transfers between accounts.

## Working with Accounts

The next few paragraphs cover the basics of working with the Quicken
accounts. These basics include how to add another account, how to edit
and delete accounts, and how to tell Quicken which account you want.
You also receive some tips on creating accounts—information that should
make working with multiple accounts easier.

## Adding Another Account

You need to describe, or identify, accounts for each bank account you
want to track with Quicken. You defined only one account as part of
installing the software, but you can have as many as 255 accounts in a
group, and you can have multiple groups. (*Note:* Account groups are discussed in more detail later in the chapter.)

To set up another bank account, choose the **Select Account** option from Quicken's Main menu (see fig. 3.1). Quicken then displays the Select Account to Use screen shown in figure 3.2. The Select Account to Use screen already will show the bank account defined as part of installing the Quicken program.

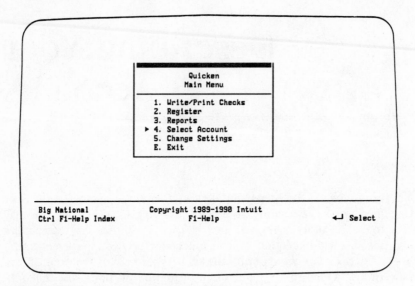

*Fig. 3.1. Selecting from Quicken's Main menu.*

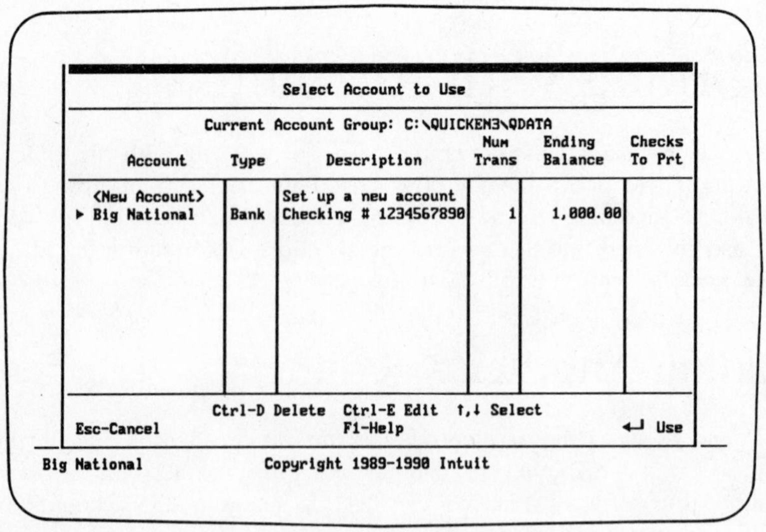

*Fig. 3.2. The Select Account to Use screen.*

To add another account, follow these steps:

1. With the arrow keys, select the New Account entry on the Select Account to Use screen.

2. Press Enter. The Set Up New Account screen appears as shown in figure 3.3.

3. With the cursor on the Account Type field, press 1 to choose Bank Account. (Chapter 12 describes setting up credit card, cash, other asset, and other liability accounts. Chapter 13 describes setting up investment accounts.)

4. Move the cursor to the Name field. Type a name or short description of the bank account in the Name field. Use characters, letters, spaces, and any symbols except brackets ([ ]), a slash (/), or a colon.

---

*CPA Tip*

Remember that you have only 15 spaces for the account name. Use an abbreviation of the bank's name (Big National could become Big Natl). This leaves room for the last four digits of the account number. You then can distinguish accounts easily, as shown by the following example:

BigNatl-1234 for a checking account
BigNatl-3272 for a savings account
BigNatl-7113 for CDs

---

5. Move the cursor to the Balance field. Type the bank account balance as of the conversion date. Do not use commas or dollar signs when you enter the balance.

6. Move the cursor to the as of date field. Type the date of the balance amount using the MM/DD/YY format. Remember that you can use the + and − keys to move the date ahead and back one day.

7. (Optional) Move the cursor to the Description field. Type a further description of the account, such as the account number.

8. Press Enter to save your changes and return to the Select Account to Use screen. To add more accounts, repeat steps 1 through 8.

When you first set up accounts for Quicken, creating accounts can get out of hand. You might, for example, define Quicken accounts for every checking account you have regardless of whether the account is active. You also might define Quicken accounts for each of your savings accounts, credit unions, money market accounts, and perhaps even

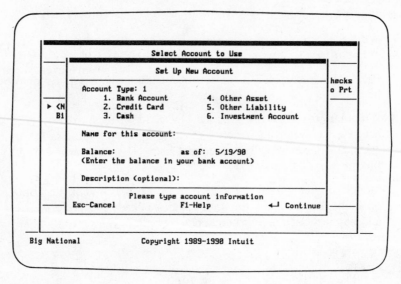

**Fig. 3.3.** *The Set Up New Account screen.*

accounts for certificates of deposit. Rather than indiscriminately define accounts for every bank account you have, consider a few ideas and rules for determining which of your bank accounts also should be Quicken accounts:

❏ If you want to write checks on the account with Quicken, you must define a Quicken account.

❏ If you want to use Quicken's reconciliation feature to explain differences between your records and the bank's, credit union's, or brokerage house's statement, you must define a Quicken account.

❏ If you have transactions in an account that you want to include in Quicken's tax deduction summaries or profit and loss statements, you must define a Quicken account. For example, you might have charitable contributions or mortgage interest transactions.

Other factors can indicate that you probably do not need to define a bank, credit union, or brokerage house account as a Quicken account:

❏ If you do not have any deposits into or withdrawals from the account other than interest income or bank service fees, your monthly statement will suffice for your financial records.

❏ If you have only a handful of transactions a month—fewer than a dozen—and none represents an account transfer from or to an account for which you will use Quicken, you probably do not need to track the account in Quicken. This choice, however, is a matter of personal preference.

❏ If you otherwise would not keep track of an account, you probably should not bother to put the account into Quicken—even if you have the best of intentions about becoming more diligent in your record keeping.

# Editing Existing Accounts

You also can use the Select Account to Use screen to edit the names and descriptions of existing accounts. You might do this, for example, if you originally described the account incorrectly. Or, you may want to edit an account name and description if you have transferred the account in total to a new account number or even a new bank. Maybe you moved from Denver to San Francisco and are still using the same bank, but a different branch. Quicken does not, however, enable you to change the account type, balance, or "as of" date after you add the account. If these dates are wrong, you need to delete and then re-create the account. To edit an account, follow these steps:

1. With the arrow keys, mark the account you want to edit on the Select Account to Use screen.

2. Press Enter. The Set Up New Account screen appears, filled out with the current information for the account.

3. (Optional) Edit the bank account name in the Name field.

4. (Optional) Move the cursor to the Description field. Edit the bank account description in the Description field.

5. Press Enter to save your changes and return to the Select Account to Use screen.

To edit additional accounts, repeat steps 1 through 5.

# Deleting Existing Accounts

You also can use the Select Account to Use screen to delete accounts you no longer use. Perhaps you closed an account or maybe you have decided an account isn't worth tracking with Quicken. To delete an account, follow these steps:

1. With the arrow keys, mark the account you want to delete on the Select Account to Use screen.

2. Press Ctrl-D. The Deleting Account message box appears (see fig. 3.4), providing the name of the account to be deleted and alerting you to the permanence of the deletion.

3. Type *yes* to delete the selected account. If you do not want to delete the account, press Esc.

*Note:* When you delete an account, you delete both the account description and any transactions you have recorded in the account. Be sure you really want to delete the account before taking the steps to do so.

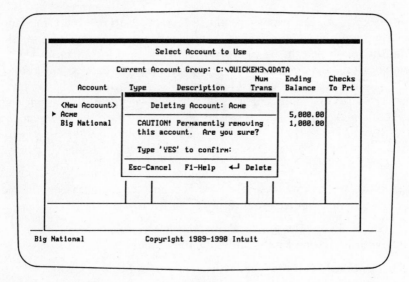

*Fig. 3.4.* The Deleting Account *message box.*

## Selecting an Account

As soon as you start working with multiple accounts, you will need to tell Quicken which account you want to use. Suppose that you decide to use Quicken to track a savings and a checking account. Whenever you enter a savings account deposit, make sure that you record the deposit for the savings account and not the checking account. Similarly, if you withdraw money from the checking account, you need to make sure the withdrawal is correctly recorded there, and not in the savings account. To record accounts correctly, you again use the Select Account to Use screen. Use the arrow keys to mark the account you want and then press Enter.

> Entering all transactions for an account at one time is more effi-
> cient. Consider collecting several transactions for an account and
> then recording them at one time.

*CPA Tip*

# Working with Account Groups

As soon as you begin defining multiple accounts, you also run head on
into the issue of account groups. Quicken stores accounts you define in
account groups, and it enables you to have more than one account group.
The obvious question, then, when you begin defining new accounts is to
which account group an account should be added. You usually will find
these decisions fairly easy to make.

The general rule is that you store related accounts together in their own
account group. Accounts are related when they pertain to the same business or the same household. If you use Quicken for home accounting and
for a commercial printing business, you use two account groups—one for
home and one for business. If you use Quicken for three businesses—a
consulting practice, a small publishing business, and restaurant—you use
three account groups—one for each of the three businesses.

## Adding New Account Groups

By default, Quicken defines one account group, named QDATA, when you
install the Quicken program. Until you define a second account group, any
accounts you define are added to QDATA. To define a new account group,
follow these steps:

1. Select **Change Settings** from the Quicken Main menu to display
   the Change Settings menu (see fig. 3.5).

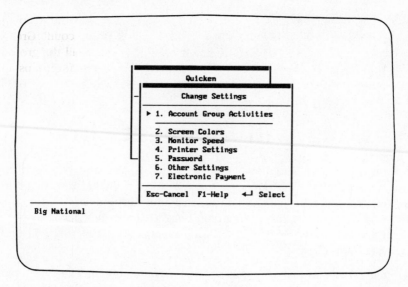

*Fig. 3.5. The Change Settings menu.*

2. Select the **Account Group Activities** option from the Change Settings menu to display the Account Group menu (see fig. 3.6).

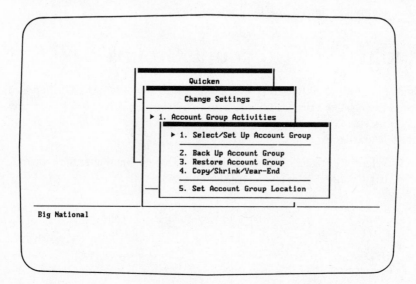

*Fig. 3.6. The Account Group menu.*

3. Select the **Select/Set Up Account Group** option from the Account Group menu. Quicken displays the Select/Set Up Account Group screen (see fig. 3.7). The Select/Set Up screen shows all the groups in the directory C:\QUICKEN3. To see the account groups in another directory, press F9. Quicken displays the Set Account Group Location screen for specifying another directory (see fig. 3.8).

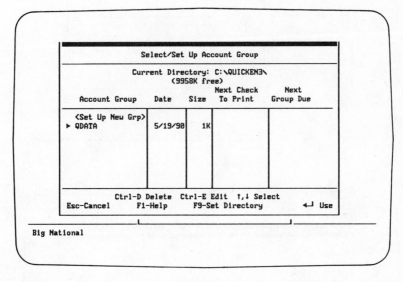

*Fig. 3.7.* *The Select/Set Up Account Group screen.*

4. Use the arrow keys to mark the Set Up New Grp item on the Select/ Set Up Account Group screen. Press Enter to display the Set Up Account Group screen (see fig. 3.9).

5. Enter the name you want to use for the account group. Whatever you enter must be a valid DOS file name, which means it can use any combination of up to eight characters and letters, but no blanks. For example, "PRINTING", "LEGAL", "HOME", and "TAVERN2" are all valid DOS file names and, therefore, acceptable as account group names. The blank space in "PRINT 1" makes this name invalid, though, and "RESTAURANT" fails because it uses more than eight characters. (Consult your DOS user's manual for additional rules for using symbols in these names.)

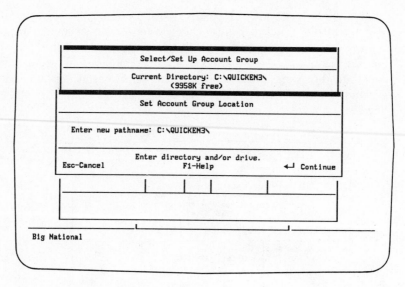

**Fig. 3.8.** *The Set Account Group Location screen.*

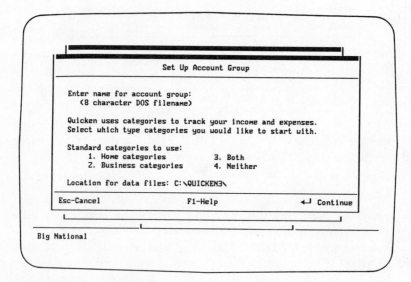

**Fig. 3.9.** *The Set Up Account Group screen.*

6. Move the cursor to the Standard categories to use field and press 1
   if you want to use Quicken's predefined home accounting categories, 2 for Quicken's predefined business categories, 3 for both sets
   of categories, and 4 for neither set of categories. (Chapter 10
   describes Quicken's predefined categories.)

*Note:* There is nothing tricky here. The predefined categories you should select correspond to your use of Quicken. If you are using Quicken for home accounting, for example, press 1. If you are using Quicken for business accounting, press 2, and so on.

7. (Optional) By default, Quicken puts the account group data file it creates for storing your financial records in the directory C:\QUICKEN3\ if you are using Version 3, or in QUICKEN4 if you are using Version 4. You can, however, change the directory. To do so, move the cursor to the Location for data files field. Type a valid path name you want to use. Refer to your DOS user's manual for more information on path names.

*Note:* You really shouldn't need to change the default directory name, except out of personal preference. Quicken enables you to change it, however, if you want.

# Editing Account Group Names

You also can use the Select/Set Up Account Group screen to edit the names of existing account groups. You may want to edit an account group name, for example, if you named the group incorrectly. If you name account groups based on whatever business it is you do accounting for with Quicken, changing the name of the business also may mean you want to change the name of the account group. For example, suppose the account group for the business "Acme Manufacturing" is ACME_MFG. If the business name changes to "Acme, Incorporated," you can change the account group name to ACME_INC. To edit an account group's name, follow these steps:

1. (Optional) To edit an account group in some directory other than C:\QUICKEN3\ or C:\QUICKEN4\, press F9. Quicken displays the Set Account Group Location screen (see fig. 3.8) for specifying another location for Quicken's account groups. Press Enter.

2. Select the account group you want to edit from the Select/Set Up Account screen by using the arrow keys.

3. Press Ctrl-E. The Rename an Account Group screen appears (see fig. 3.10).

4. Edit the account group name in the Name field. Be sure to enter a valid DOS file name.

5. Press Enter to save your changes and return to the Select/Set Up Account Group screen. To edit additional account groups, repeat steps 1 through 5.

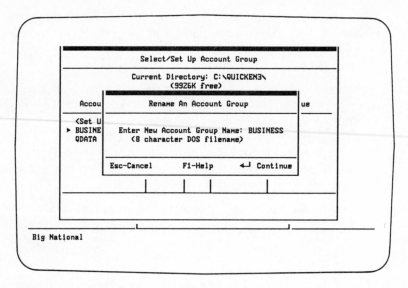

**Fig. 3.10.** *The Rename an Account Group screen.*

## Deleting Account Groups

You also can use the Select/Set Up Account Group screen to delete accounts. Generally, you should never delete an account group, because when you do, you are essentially deleting all the accounts in the group. If you no longer are tracking any of the accounts in the account group, you can delete the group. This may be the case if you set up a special account for learning to use Quicken and you no longer use the account. You also no longer need the account group used for a business if you sell the business. To delete an account, follow these steps:

1. (Optional) If you want to delete an account group in some directory other than C:\QUICKEN3\ (or \QUICKEN4), press F9. Quicken displays the Set Account Group Location screen (see figure 3.8), which you can use to specify some other directory as the location in which to look for Quicken account groups. Press Enter.

2. Select the account group you want to delete from the Select/Set Up Account screen by using the arrow keys.

3. Press Ctrl-D. Quicken displays the Deleting Account Group message box (see figure 3.11). The message box gives the name of the account group that Quicken is about to delete, and asks you to confirm the deletion.

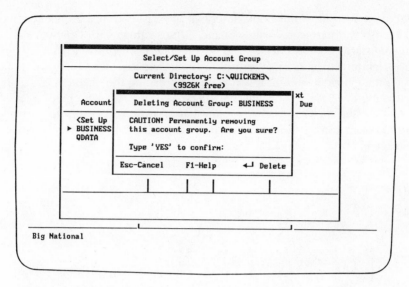

Fig. 3.11. The Deleting Account Group message box.

4. Type *yes* to delete the account group. If you do not want to delete the account group, press Esc.

5. Press Enter to complete the deletion and return to the Select/Set Up Account Group screen. To delete additional account groups, repeat steps 1 through 5.

## Selecting an Account Group

When you work with more than one account group, you need to tell Quicken with which account group you want to work. To do this, use the Select/Set Up Account Group screen. Use the arrow keys to mark the account group you want and then press Enter.

# Chapter Summary

This chapter described how you add, edit, and delete bank account descriptions. You also learned about account groups. With the information in the first three chapters, you should be ready to use Quicken. In essence, these first three chapters covered the details of getting started with Quicken—the things you need to do before you actually start working with the program.

The next section of the book describes the basics of using Quicken and covers such things as recording financial transactions with Quicken, printing registers, writing checks, and so on. These chapters don't cover as much about business and personal accounting topics as they do about using the Quicken system. When you finish reading the chapters in Part II, "Learning the Basics," you will be well-acquainted with the mechanics of actually using the Quicken program. That knowledge is essential to turning Quicken into a tool you can use for business or personal financial management.

# II

# Learning the Basics

## Includes

Using the Register

Making the Register Easier To Use

Writing and Printing Checks

Making Check Writing Easier

Reconciling Your Bank Account

Taking Care of Quicken Files

# 4

# Using the Register

Your checkbook, or check register, is your most fundamental financial tool. You probably agree that your check register largely summarizes your financial life. Money flows into the account in the form of wages for a household or sales collections for a business. Money flows out of the account to pay expenses.

Moving your check register to Quicken provides two major benefits. First, Quicken does the arithmetic of deducting withdrawals and adding deposits—a trivial contribution until you remember the last time an error in your arithmetic caused you to bounce a check. Second, Quicken records each of your checking account transactions in the check register so that you can use Quicken's Reports feature to summarize and extract information from the register—information that helps you plan and control your finances more effectively.

Quicken's register is the program's major component. Every other program feature—writing checks, reconciling accounts, and printing reports—depends on the register. Every user works with Quicken's register by directly entering transactions in the register and by indirectly using the information stored in the register. In fact, any of the financial transactions you record can be entered directly into the Quicken register. (*Note:* If you want to use Quicken to write checks, the Write/Print Checks screen and option probably provide a more convenient format for collecting the information Quicken prints on the face of the check.)

This chapter describes the basics of using Quicken's register, including the following:

❏ Getting to know the Register screen

❏ Recording transactions in the register

❑ Reviewing and editing register transactions

❑ Printing the register

Chapter 5, "Making the Register Easier," describes three additional sets of menu options—Edit, Quick Entry, and Activities—to make using the check register even easier. Chapter 12, "Accounting for Other Assets and Debts," describes how you can use the register to keep track of assets besides cash and even to track liabilities like credit cards and bank loans. Chapter 13, "Monitoring Your Investments," describes a special set of tools that the newest version of Quicken provides for managing your investments.

# Getting To Know the Register Screen

You select the **Register** option on Quicken's Main menu to access the Register screen. You use the Register screen, shown in figure 4.1, to record most of the checking account transactions—manual checks, deposits, interest, bank fees, and so on—that affect your checking account.

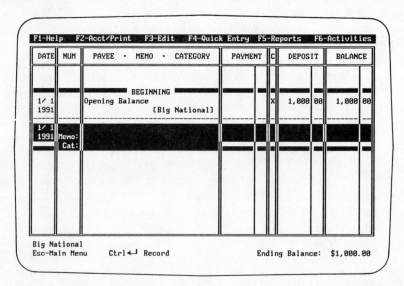

**Fig. 4.1.** *The Register screen.*

The only transaction you do not record with the **Register** option is a check you record and print with the **Write/Print Checks** option (see Chapters 5 and 6). After collecting the information, Quicken records the transaction in the register and updates the account balance. The steps you take to record a transaction on the Register screen are described in the next section.

The Register screen can be broken down into three parts: the menu bar at the top of the screen, the actual check register, and the information bar at the bottom of the screen.

The menu bar shows the function keys you can use on the Register screen to access menus of options:

F1    Accesses help

F2    Accesses the Acct/Print menu

F3    Accesses the Edit menu (see Chapter 5)

F4    Accesses the Quick Entry menu (see Chapter 5)

F5    Accesses the same menu accessed by the **Reports** option on Quicken's Main menu (see Chapter 14)

F6    Accesses the Activities menus (see Chapter 5)

The second part of the Register screen is the actual check register you use to record account transactions. Take a minute to review the register—it probably resembles the register you now use to record checks manually. (The fields are described later in the chapter.)

The third part of the Register screen is the information bar at the bottom. This bar shows the bank account name (checking), information on what the Esc and Enter keys do, and the balance in the account.

Before you start recording transactions in a register, you can use this information to make sure that you have selected the correct account and to gauge the effect of the transactions you want to record.

# Recording a Check in the Register

Recording a check in the Quicken register closely parallels recording a check by hand in a paper checkbook register. The Register screen, however, makes the whole process easier. (*Note:* You can record any check in the register, including checks you want to print. Typically, however, you record checks you have written previously by hand directly into the register. You record checks you want to print using the Write/Print Checks screen and option, which are described in Chapter 6.)

To record a check, take the following steps:

1. Select **Register** from Quicken's Main menu if the register is not displayed already. Quicken displays the Register screen (see fig. 4.1). *Note:* If you are working with more than one account, you may need to select the account first (see Chapter 3).

2. Enter the check date in the Date field. Enter the check date in the month/day/year format.

   The first time you use Quicken, the program fills the Date field with the system date. After you record your first transaction using the Register screen, Quicken fills the Date field with the last date you used. To edit the date, you have two choices. First, you can move to the month, day, or year you want to change and type over what already is showing on-screen. Second, you can use the + and − keys to change the date one day at a time. Each time you press the + key, Quicken moves the date ahead one day. Each time you press the − key, Quicken moves the date back one day.

*CPA Tip*

Businesses and individuals often receive discounts for paying bills early. Consider early payment in setting the check date. Not taking early payment discounts is an extremely expensive way to borrow money from the vendor. Suppose that a vendor normally requires payment within 30 days but allows a 2 percent discount for payments received within 10 days. If you pay within 30 rather than 10 days, you essentially pay the vendor a 2 percent interest charge for paying 20 days later. Because one year contains roughly 18 20-day periods, the 2 percent for 20 days equals approximately 36 percent annually.

Although you may need to "borrow" this money, you probably can find a much cheaper lender. As a rule of thumb, if a vendor gives you a 1 percent discount for paying 20 days early, you are borrowing the vendor's money at about an 18 percent annual interest rate if you do not pay early. A 3 percent discount works out to a whopping 54 percent a year.

3. Press Enter or Tab and Quicken moves the cursor to the Num field. Enter the number of the check in the Num field. *Note:* Checks you recorded on the Write/Print Checks screen but have not printed show asterisks as their numbers.

   If you want to enter a check you later want to print, you can enter the check number as asterisks. The Write/Print Checks screen and option, however, provide a more convenient method of writing and printing checks. Refer to Chapter 6 for detailed information on Quicken's Write/Print Checks feature.

4. Press Enter or Tab to move the cursor to the Payee field. Enter the name of the person or business the check pays. You have space for up to 31 characters.

5. Press Enter or Tab to move the cursor to the Payment field. Enter the check amount, using up to 10 numbers for the amount. You can enter a check as large as $9,999,999.99. The decimal point counts as one of the ten characters but the commas do not.

6. Press Enter or Tab to reach the cleared (C) field, which shows whether a transaction has been recorded by the bank. Use this field as part of reconciling, or explaining the difference between your check register account balance and the balance the bank shows on your monthly statement. To mark a transaction as cleared, enter an asterisk, the only character Quicken accepts here, in the C field. During reconciliation, Quicken changes the asterisk to an X (see Chapter 8).

7. (Optional) Press Enter or Tab twice to move the cursor through the Deposit field and to the Memo field. Use the Memo field to describe the reasons for a transaction. You can use up to 31 characters to describe a transaction. If you are making several payments a month to the bank, the Memo field enables you to specify the house payment, the school loan, the hot tub, the boat, and so on.

8. (Optional) Press Enter or Tab to move the cursor to the Category field. You use the Category field to describe the category into which a transaction falls, such as utilities expense, interest expense, or entertainment. Use Ctrl-C to access the existing categories provided by Quicken or those you have added previously (see fig. 4.2). Now, use the arrow keys to mark the category into which the check falls and press Enter.

   You also can use the Category field to describe the class into which a transaction falls. (Categories and classes are described in Chapter 10.) Figure 4.3 shows a check to the Seattle Power Company. The category is Utilities.

*CPA Tip*

Quicken 4.0 provides a new feature called "Auto-completion," which you can use when you know a few of the category names. If you type enough of a category name to uniquely identify that name and then press Enter, Quicken types the rest of the category name for you. Suppose that you have a category named "Utilities" and it is the only category name that starts with the letter "u." If you type *u* in the Category field and press Enter, Quicken types the remaining letters of the word—*tilities*. The only trick to the auto-completion feature is that you need to type enough of the category name to uniquely identify it. You also can use the auto-completion feature to enter the account number for a field.

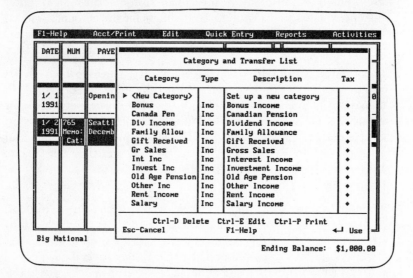

*Fig. 4.2. Press Ctrl-C to see a list of predefined categories.*

9. Record the transaction by pressing Enter when the cursor is on the last field, Category, or record the transaction while the cursor is on any screen field by pressing Ctrl-Enter or F10. Quicken asks you to confirm that you want to record the transaction. If you select Record transaction, the transaction is recorded (see fig. 4.4).

Whenever you record a transaction, a flashing message in the lower left-hand corner of the screen says RECORDING. (If your computer is very fast, you can hardly read the message.) When Quicken finishes recording the

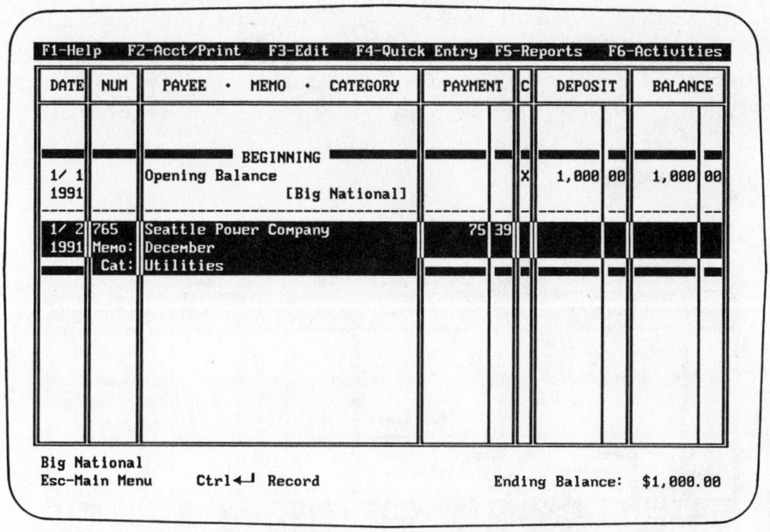

*Fig. 4.3.* A sample check entered in the register.

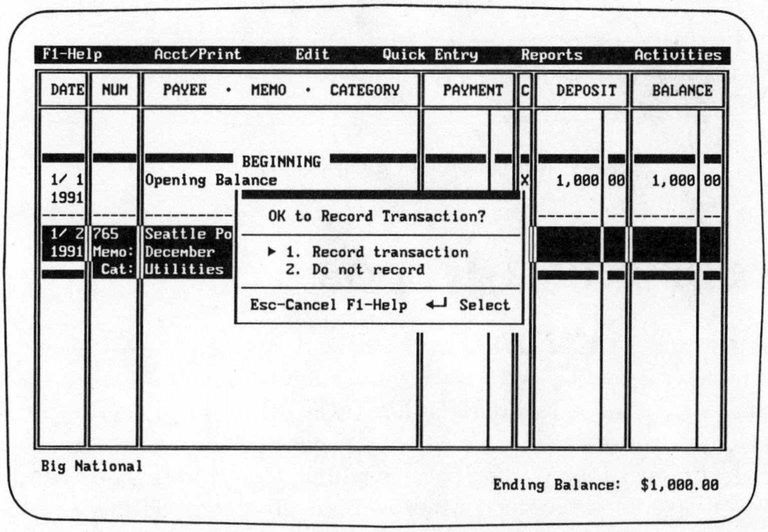

*Fig. 4.4.* The message box that asks whether you want to record the check.

transaction, your computer beeps and an empty row is added to the bottom of the register, with the cursor positioned at the empty Date field. Because Quicken arranges checking account transactions by date, it rearranges transactions if you enter them in an order other than the order of their dates.

Quicken also calculates the new Balance field when you record a transaction (see fig. 4.5). If the balance is too large for a positive or negative number to display, Quicken displays asterisks in the Balance field. Quicken uses negative numbers to indicate you have overdrawn your account. If you have a color monitor, Quicken displays negative amounts in a different color.

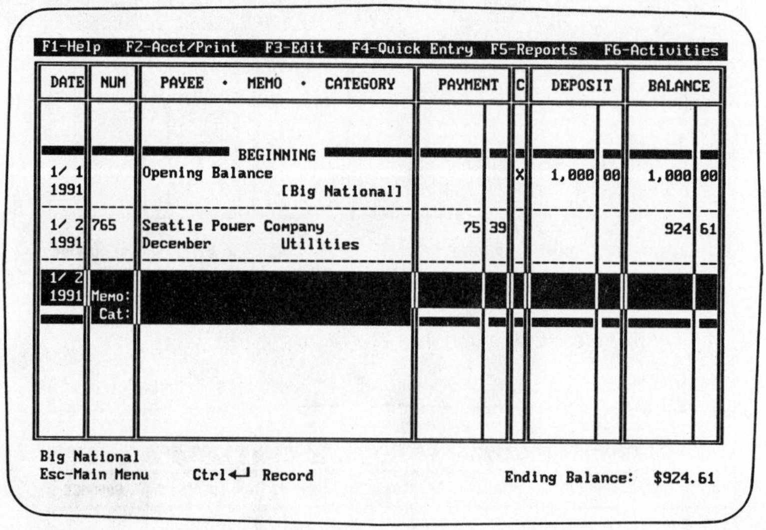

*Fig. 4.5. The register showing the new balance after a check is recorded.*

# Recording a Deposit in the Register

As you might expect, recording a deposit in the Quicken register is like recording a deposit in your checkbook's paper register.(*Note:* You should not have to record the starting balance with a deposit transaction because it should have been recorded when you initially described the account.)

To record a deposit or starting balance, follow these steps:

1. Select **Register** from Quicken's Main menu if the register is not displayed already. Quicken displays the Register screen. *Note:* If you are working with more than one account, you may need to select the account first (see Chapter 3).

2. Enter the deposit date in the Date field in month/day/year format. Remember that you can use the + and − keys to change the date one day at a time.

3. (Optional) Press Enter or Tab to move cursor to the Num field. Enter the receipt number of the deposit in the Num field.

4. Press Enter or Tab to move the cursor to the Payee field. Enter a description of the deposit transaction. You have space for up to 31 characters. For example, a business recording a deposit from a customer might describe the deposit by using the customer name, such as "Acme Manufacturing." A home user recording a payroll deposit might describe the deposit as "payroll check." Interest might be described as "October interest income."

5. Press Enter or Tab three times to move the cursor through the Payment and C fields to the Deposit field. As with the Payment field, Quicken enables you to enter only numbers, with amounts under $9,999,999.99.

6. (Optional) Press Enter or Tab to move the cursor to the Memo field. Use the Memo field to describe the reasons for a transaction. You can use up to 31 characters to describe a transaction. For example, a business may note the invoice a customer deposit paid. A home user may indicate the payroll period covered by a payroll check.

7. (Optional) Press Enter or Tab to move the cursor to the Category field for describing the deposit's category, such as gross sales, wages, or interest income. Use Ctrl-C to access the existing categories provided by Quicken or those you have previously added. Use the arrow keys to mark the category into which the check falls, and then press Enter.

   You also can use the Category field to describe the income category into which a transaction falls. (Categories and classes are described further in Chapter 10.) Figure 4.6 shows a deposit for recording interest income.

8. Record the transaction by pressing Enter when the cursor is on the last field, Category, or record the transaction while the cursor is in any field by pressing Ctrl-Enter or F10. Quicken displays a prompt, asking you to confirm that you want to record the transaction. If you select Record transaction, the transaction is recorded.

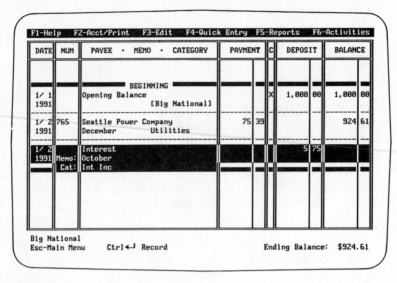

**Fig. 4.6.** *A sample deposit recorded in the register.*

# Recording Other Withdrawals

The steps for recording other withdrawals—such as automated teller machine transactions, wire transfers, and automatic payments—parallel the steps for recording a check. You enter the date, number, payee, the payment amount, and, optionally, a memo description and a category. Record the withdrawal by pressing Enter when the cursor is in the Category field or by pressing Ctrl-Enter or F10 when the cursor is in any other field.

*CPA Tip*

Consider the monthly service fees a bank charges in choosing a bank and in keeping minimum balances. Most banks charge monthly service fees of about $5. Some banks waive the $5 fee if you keep a balance of $200 at all times in your account. The $5 a month translates into $60 a year. Because $60 in fee savings equals $60 in interest, the interest rate the bank pays people who keep their minimum balance at $200 is $60/$200 or 30 percent. The return is even better than that for most people because the interest income gets taxed, but the fee savings do not. Probably no other $200 investment in the world is risk-free and pays 30 percent interest.

# Recording Transfers between Accounts

You can use the Category field to record transfers from one account to another. Suppose, for example, that you are recording a check drawn on your checking account for deposit to your credit union account with the Acme Credit Union. The check is not an expense, so it should not be categorized as utilities, medical, insurance, or something else. It is a transfer of funds from one account to another. You can identify such transfers by entering the account name in brackets, as shown in figure 4.7.

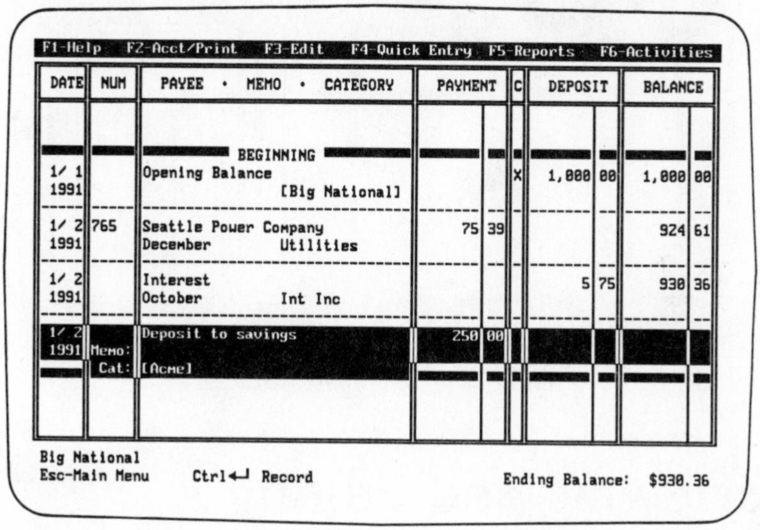

```
 F1-Help   F2-Acct/Print   F3-Edit   F4-Quick Entry  F5-Reports   F6-Activities

 DATE  NUM   PAYEE  ·  MEMO  ·  CATEGORY     PAYMENT  C   DEPOSIT     BALANCE


                   ▀▀▀ BEGINNING ▀▀▀
 1/ 1       Opening Balance                          X  1,000 00   1,000 00
 1991                         [Big National]
 ---------------------------------------------------------------------
 1/ 2 765   Seattle Power Company              75 39                 924 61
 1991       December         Utilities
 ---------------------------------------------------------------------
 1/ 2       Interest                                       5 75      930 36
 1991       October         Int Inc
 ---------------------------------------------------------------------
 1/ 2       Deposit to savings               250 00
 1991 Memo:
      Cat: [Acme]




 Big National
 Esc-Main Menu     Ctrl↵ Record              Ending Balance:  $930.36
```

*Fig. 4.7.* The Category *field completed to record a transfer between accounts.*

Be sure the account has been set up first before you try to transfer to or from the account. Quicken enables you to add categories, but not accounts, during the use of the register. The accounts are located at the end of the category list and you can access them more quickly by pressing the End key to reach the end of the list. When you have located the proper account, press Enter and Quicken inserts the account name in the Description field in the register.

*Note:* When you press Ctrl-C, Quicken not only lists categories, but also accounts. Accordingly, you also can use the Ctrl-C technique to see accounts for transfers.

If you record a transfer, Quicken records the transfer in the registers for both accounts. In the transaction shown in figure 4.7, a payment of $250 is recorded for the checking account and, at the same time, a deposit of $250 is recorded for the credit union savings account. Figure 4.8 shows the register for the credit union savings account with the $250 deposit. You can toggle between the two registers by pressing Ctrl-X.

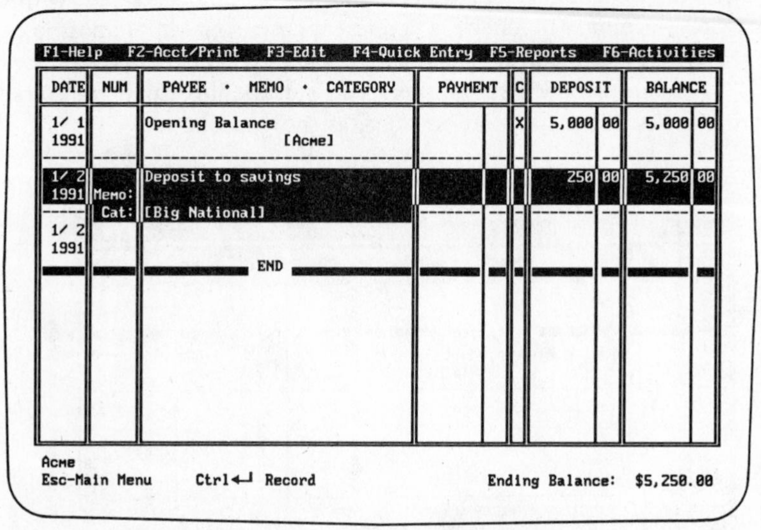

**Fig. 4.8.** *The other part of the transfer transaction.*

# Reviewing and Editing Register Transactions

You can review and edit transactions using the **Register** option from the Main menu at any time. You may want to review a transaction to make sure that you recorded the transaction correctly. You also may want to review a transaction to see whether you received a deposit and to see whether you remembered to pay a particular bill. Use the following keys to move among transactions:

| | |
|---|---|
| Arrow keys | Move from row to row |
| Tab | Move forward among fields within a row |
| Shift-Tab | Move backward among fields within a row |

| PgUp | Move up a page |
| PgDn | Move down a page |
| Home | Move to the first transaction in the register |
| End | Move to the last transaction in the register |

To edit a transaction, move to the transaction you want to change, edit the fields that you want to change, and re-record the transaction by pressing Ctrl-Enter or F10 or by pressing Enter while the cursor is on the Category field.

# Using Postdated Transactions

Postdated transactions are checks and deposits dated in the future. Traditionally, people use postdated checks as a way to delay a payment. The payee cannot or should not cash the check before the future date. With Quicken, you can use postdated transactions to delay checks being cashed. Perhaps more importantly, you can forecast your cash flows and balances by entering those checks and deposits that you know are in the future.

The steps for entering postdated transactions mirror those for entering regular transactions. The only difference, of course, is that the check or deposit date is in the future. When you enter postdated transactions, Quicken calculates two account balances: the current balance, which is the account balance for the current date, and the ending balance, which is the account balance after the last postdated transaction. Quicken determines the current date by looking at the system date.

Figure 4.9 shows the Big National register with a postdated transaction. The ending balance, $180.36, incorporates all the transactions for the account, including postdated transactions.

Quicken also displays the current balance, $680.36, the account balance at the current date.

# Printing a Register

You will want to print a paper register each time you enter a group of check and deposit transactions. A printed copy of the register enables you

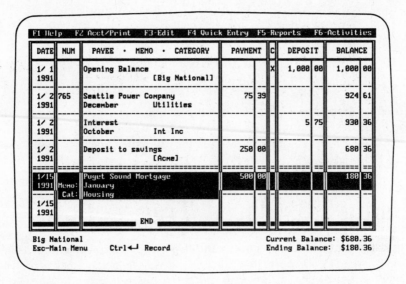

**Fig. 4.9.** *The register showing a postdated transaction, the current balance, and the ending balance.*

to review checking account transactions without turning on your computer. It also can provide a way to recover your financial records if no backup files exist. (Chapter 9 describes the steps for backing up your Quicken data files.)

The Acct/Print menu, which you use to print the register, has six options (see fig. 4.10). This chapter discusses only the second option: **Print Register**. The **Select/Set Up Account** option is the same as the Main menu option **Select Account**, described in Chapter 3. **Change Printer Settings** is the same as the **Printer Settings** option on the Change Settings menu, described in Chapter 1. **Back Up All Accounts**, **Export**, and **Import** are described in Chapter 9.

To print a register, take the following steps:

1. Press F2 to display the Acct/Print menu and then select the **Print Register** option (see fig. 4.10), or press Ctrl-P. Quicken displays the Print Register screen (see fig. 4.11).

2. Verify that your printer is set to use regular paper—and not check forms.

3. Enter the date of the first check or deposit transaction you want printed on the register. If you are printing only the transactions for

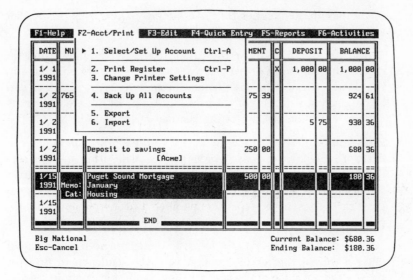

**Fig. 4.10.** *The Acct/Print menu.*

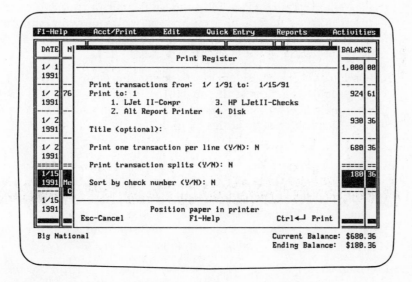

**Fig. 4.11.** *The Print Register screen.*

the day's batch of transactions, enter the Print transactions from date as the current date. If you are printing a copy of the month's transactions, enter the Print transactions from date as the first day of the month. Remember that the + and − keys change the date one day at a time.

4. Press Enter or Tab to move the cursor to the to date field. Enter the date of the last check or deposit transaction. If you are printing only the transactions for the day's batch of transactions, enter the to date as the current date. If you are printing a copy of the month's transactions, enter the to date as the last day of the month.

5. Press Enter or Tab to move the cursor to the Print to field. Use the Print to field to specify which printer will print the register. Quicken lists up to three printers you might have defined as part of the installation process, and it lists a fourth option, Disk. To specify the Print to setting, type the number that corresponds to the printer you want to use.

6. (Optional) Press Tab or Enter to move the cursor to the Title field. Enter a special title or description you want Quicken to print on the top of each page of the register. You might, for example, choose "June Check Register" for June's register.

7. (Optional) Press Enter or Tab to move the cursor to the Print one transaction per line field. Press Y if you want Quicken to print the register in a compact form using only one line per transaction and using abbreviations for many of the fields.

8. (Optional) Press Enter or Tab to move the cursor to the Print transaction splits field. If you split transactions—you used more than one category for the transaction—you can cause Quicken to print each of those categories by pressing Y in this field (see Chapter 5.)

9. (Optional) Press Enter or Tab to move the cursor to the Sort by check number field. Usually, Quicken arranges the check and deposit transactions by date. You can, however, press Y to arrange transactions by the check numbers. If a check deposit does not have a number or has the same number as another transaction, Quicken uses the date as a secondary sorting tool.

10. (Optional) If you select 4 at the Print to field, you can create an ASCII file on disk. Quicken displays the Print To Disk box, which collects the file name you want to use for the ASCII file, the number of lines per page, and the page width. Enter the name you want Quicken to use for the ASCII file in the File field. If you want to use a data directory different from the Quicken data directory,

QUICKEN3, you also can specify a path name. (See your DOS user's manual for information on path names.) Set the number of register lines Quicken prints between page breaks in the Lines per page field. If you are using 11-inch paper, the page length is usually 66 lines. Set the number of characters, including blanks, that Quicken prints on a line in the Width field. If you are using 8½-inch paper, the characters per line figure usually is 80. Figure 4.12 shows a completed Print To Disk box.

11. When the Print Register screen is complete and you are ready to print, press Ctrl-Enter.

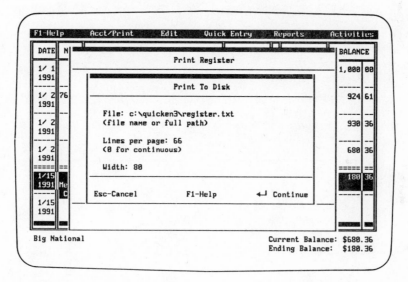

**Fig. 4.12.** *The Print To Disk box.*

Quicken generates a copy of the register like that shown in figure 4.13 or figure 4.14. Figure 4.13 shows the register when the Print one transaction per line field is set to the N default. Figure 4.14 shows the same register when the field is set to Y.

```
                              Check Register

Big National
1/ 2/91                                                                    Page 1

        Date  Num         Transaction          Payment  C  Deposit   Balance
        -----  -----  ---------------------  ----------  -  ---------- ----------

        1/ 1       Opening Balance                      X  1,000.00   1,000.00
        1991 memo:
             cat: [Big National]

        1/ 2 765   Seattle Power Company        75.39               924.61
        1991 memo: December
             cat: Utilities

        1/ 2       Interest                                5.75      930.36
        1991 memo: October
             cat: Int Inc

        1/ 2       Deposit to savings          250.00               680.36
        1991 memo:
             cat: [Acme]

        1/15       Puget Sound Mortgage        500.00               180.36
        1991 memo: January
             cat: Housing
```

*Fig. 4.13.* The register with transactions printed on several lines.

```
                              Check Register

Big National                                                               Page 1
1/ 2/91

 Date   Num       Payee           Memo          Category        Amount  C  Balance
 ------  -----  ----------------  ----------  -------------  ----------  -  ----------
 1/ 1/91      Opening Balance                 [Big National]   1,000.00 X  1,000.00
 1/ 2/91 765  Seattle Power Company December  Utilities         -75.39     924.61
 1/ 2/91      Interest           October      Int Inc            5.75      930.36
 1/ 2/91      Deposit to savings              [Acme]           -250.00     680.36
 1/15/91      Puget Sound Mortgage January    Housing          -500.00     180.36
```

*Fig. 4.14.* The register with one transaction printed on each line.

*CPA Tip*

At the end of each month, print a copy of the register for the transactions you entered in that month. Store the register with the bank statement for the month. That way, if you ever have questions about a previous month—or the bad luck to lose your data files—you can reconstruct transactions from previous months. You can discard the now redundant individual registers that show each of the groups of transactions for the month. You will not need these with a copy of the entire month.

# Chapter Summary

This chapter introduced you to Quicken's register—the central repository of all your checking account information. The basics include knowing the components of the check register screen; using the register to record checks, deposits, and other checking account transactions; reviewing and editing register transactions; and printing the register.

The next chapter describes three additional sets of tools to facilitate your use of the register: the Edit menu, the Quick Entry menu, and the Activities menu.

# 5

# Making the Register
# Easier To Use

Chapter 5 can make your work with registers more efficient by describing sets of options on the Edit (F3), Quick Entry (F4), and Activities (F6) menus. Among other functions, these menus can help you search through your register for specific transactions or save and re-use information you record repeatedly in your check register. The Edit menu provides options that make it easier for you to add, modify, and remove transactions. The Quick Entry menu offers features that speed up the process of recording transactions. The Activities menu options, although not directly related to the register, make working with the Quicken program easier.

## Using the Edit Menu Tools

The Edit menu, shown in figure 5.1, provides you with nine options. As noted earlier, the Edit menu essentially provides features that make it easier for you to record transactions in the register. The actions that many of the menu options produce probably are already well-known to you by now; for that reason, many of the following descriptions are brief.

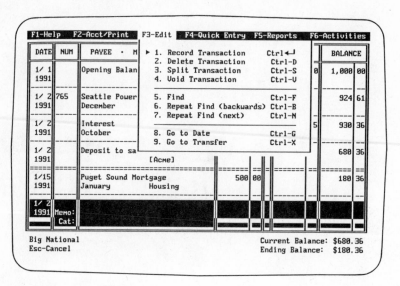

**Fig. 5.1.** *The Edit menu.*

# Recording, Deleting, and Voiding Transactions

The Edit menu lists three basic options: **Record Transaction**, **Delete Transaction**, and **Void Transaction**. None of these three options is difficult to use, so you will not need a step-by-step discussion. Rather, each can be described in a few sentences.

❏ **Record Transaction** (Ctrl-Enter) is the same as pressing Ctrl-Enter or F10. Selecting **Record Transaction** from the Edit menu records the transaction in the register and your disk.

❏ **Delete Transaction** (Ctrl-D) removes the selected transaction from the register and your disk. You also can use **Delete Transaction** to erase the Register screen's fields if you have not yet recorded the transaction. After you select **Delete Transaction**, Quicken asks you to confirm the deletion by displaying the message shown in figure 5.2. To delete the transaction, select the first option. If you change your mind, select the second option or press Esc.

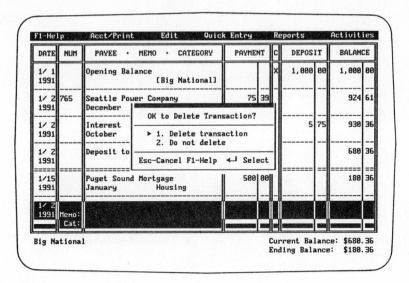

**Fig. 5.2.** *The* OK to Delete Transaction *message.*

❏ **Void Transaction** (Ctrl-V) is the fourth option on the Edit menu. If you select **Void Transaction**, Quicken inserts the word VOID before the payee name, changes the payment or deposit amounts to zero, and sets the cleared flag to X to indicate that the transaction isn't outstanding. Figure 5.3 shows the now voided check to Puget Sound Mortgage. (*Note:* If you void a previously recorded transaction, Quicken doesn't update the balance until you record the voided transaction.)

If you void a transaction that is part of a transfer from one account to another, voiding any part of the transaction also voids the other parts of the transaction—those recorded in the other registers.

**Void Transaction** enables you to keep track of voided transactions in your check register alongside actual transactions. You should keep an audit trail, or record, of voided and stop-payment checks. Use **Void Transaction** to perform this sort of record keeping. Chapter 19 treats audit trails.

*CPA Tip*

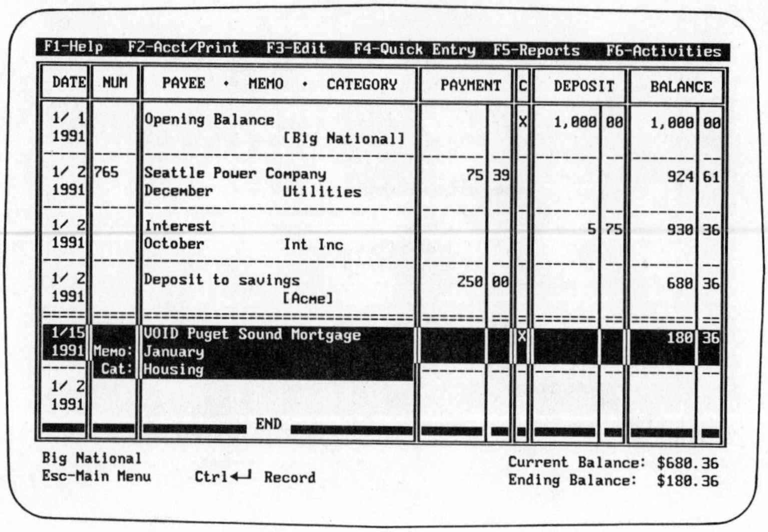

**Fig. 5.3.** *A voided check.*

# Splitting Transactions

The regular register screen provides one field for recording the category into which a check fits. A check written to the power company, for example, might belong in the "Utilities" category and a payroll deposit might be "Wages." But some transactions fit in more than one category. A check written to the bank to pay a mortgage payment, for example, might actually pay principal, interest, insurance, and property taxes. So occasionally, you need to be able to break down a transaction into multiple categories. Selecting **Split Transaction** (Ctrl-S) from the Edit menu provides additional Category fields so that you can use more than one category for a transaction or further describe a transaction. To split a transaction, take the following steps:

1. Press F3 to display the Edit menu and select **Split Transaction**, or press Ctrl-S. Selecting this option accesses the Split Transaction screen, shown in figure 5.4.

2. Enter the category name in the Category field. The Category field on the Split Transaction screen is used like the Category field on the Register screen. You also can use the field to record transfers. Thirty lines are available on the Split Transaction screen for descriptions or for categories.

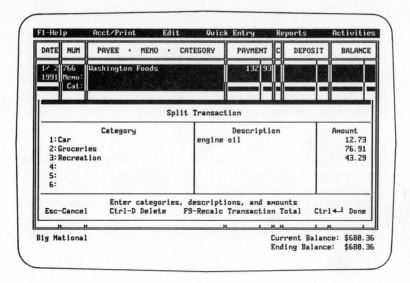

**Fig. 5.4.** *The Split Transaction screen.*

*Note:* Remember that Quicken provides predefined home and business categories. The home category list has descriptions for most general household expenses, and the business category list has general business income and expense categories. Press Ctrl-C to view and select from a list of the predefined categories.

3. (Optional) Press Enter or Tab to move the cursor to the Description field. Type a description of the category or the amount. The Description field provides a 27-character space for further description of a transaction or an explanation of your category choice.

4. **Press Enter or Tab** to move the cursor to the Amount field. You use the Amount field in two ways, depending on whether you select **Split Transaction** before or after you enter the payment or deposit amount on the Register screen.

   If you select **Split Transaction** before you enter a figure in the Amount field, Quicken adds each of the amounts you enter in the Amount fields on the Split Transaction screen together. Quicken then takes the total of these amounts and puts that total in the Payment or the Deposit field on the Register screen. If the total of the split transaction amounts is negative, Quicken places the amount in the Payment field; if the total is positive, Quicken places the amount in the Deposit field.

If you select **Split Transaction** after you enter the payment or deposit amount on the Register screen, Quicken pulls the amount entered onto the Split Transaction screen into the first Amount field. When you enter the register amount as a payment, Quicken pulls the amount onto the Split Transaction screen as a negative number; when you enter the amount as a deposit, Quicken pulls the amount onto the screen as a positive number. If you then enter a number in the first Amount field on the Split Transaction screen, Quicken calculates the difference between the Register screen amount and the amount you have entered, and places this difference in the second Amount field on the Split Transaction screen.

5. Press Enter or Tab to move to the next line of the Split Transaction screen. Repeat steps 2, 3 and 4 for each category and amount combination you want to record. You can record up to 30 category and amount combinations.

   *Note:* If you use all 30 of the Split Transaction Amount fields, the sum of the split transaction amounts may not equal the register amount. In this case, you must adjust manually the Register screen amount or one of the Split Transaction screen amounts. You also can press F9 to total the Amount fields on the Split Transaction screen and to insert that total into the Amount field on the Register screen.

6. Press Ctrl-Enter or F10 to leave the Split Transaction screen and return to the register.

7. After making your changes on the Split Transaction screen, press Ctrl-Enter or F10 to record the transaction. You are prompted to record the transaction. Press 1 to record the transaction; press 2 not to record the transaction. Quicken indicates a transaction is split by displaying the word SPLIT below the transaction number (see fig. 5.5).

   If you split transactions, you may want to see the extra category names, descriptions, and amounts on the printed version of the register. When you select **Print Register** from the Acct/Print menu, the Print Register field includes a Print Split Transactions setting switch. Use this switch to tell Quicken whether you want the additional categories and amounts of a split transaction printed on the register. (See Chapter 4, "Using the Register," for more information on printing the register.)

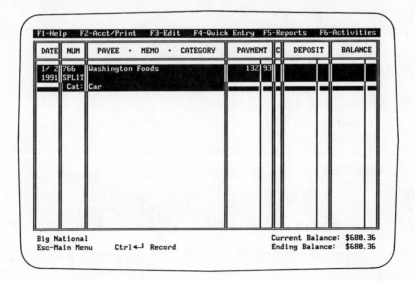

**Fig. 5.5.** *Quicken identifies split transactions with the word* Split *under the* Num *field.*

# Locating Transactions

You may write only a handful of checks and make only one or two deposits in a month. Even with such low volumes, however, you will soon have several dozen transactions in a register. As you write more checks and make additional deposits, searching through your register for specific transactions becomes more and more difficult. You may eventually want to know whether you recorded a deposit or paid a bill, or when you last paid a vendor. Quicken provides three Edit menu options for locating specific transactions: **Find**, **Repeat Find (backwards)**, and **Repeat Find (next)**.

You can search through the register for transactions using any of the fields you store for transactions. For example, you can look for transactions where the payee is "Stouffer's Office Supplies," where the category is "utilities," or where the amount is "$54.91."

# Using the Find Option

To search through the transactions you recorded in the register, follow these steps:

1. Press F3 to display the Edit menu, and then select the **Find** option or press Ctrl-F. Quicken displays the Transaction to Find screen shown in figure 5.6

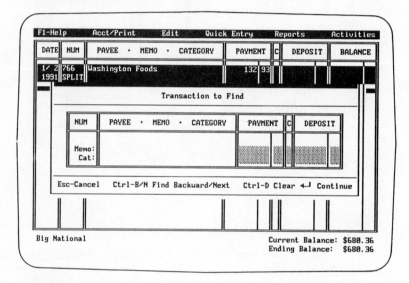

**Fig. 5.6.** *The Transaction to Find screen.*

2. (Optional) To search through the register for a transaction equal to a specific amount, enter the amount in either the Payment or the Deposit field. The amount you look for is called a *search argument*.

   If you enter an amount in the Payment field on the Transaction to Find screen, Quicken searches through the checks in the register for that amount. If you enter an amount in the Deposit field, Quicken searches for that amount among the deposits in the register. If Quicken finds a transaction that matches your search argument, the transaction is highlighted on the Register screen.

3. (Optional) To search through the register for checks or deposits with a specific entry in the Payee field, enter the appropriate entry in the Transaction to Find Payee field.

4. (Optional) To search through the register for checks or deposits with a specific entry in the Memo field, enter what the transaction you want to find shows in its Memo field.

5. (Optional) To search through the register for checks or deposits with a specific entry in the Num field, enter what the transaction you want to find shows in its Num field.

6. (Optional) To search through the register for checks or deposits with a specific entry in the C field, enter what the transaction you want to find shows in its C field ($, X, or *). You might want to perform such a search to find cleared or outstanding transactions.

7. When you finish entering the search argument or arguments, press Ctrl-Enter or F10, or press Enter when the cursor is on the C field.

   Quicken asks which direction you want to search by displaying the screen shown in figure 5.7. Find backwards (Ctrl-B) looks through transactions with dates earlier than the transaction currently selected on the Register screen. Find next (Ctrl-N) looks through transactions with dates later than the date of the transaction currently selected on the Register screen.

8. Select Find backwards or Find next.

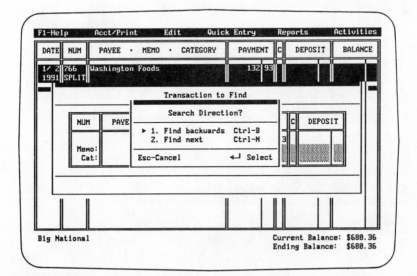

***Fig. 5.7.*** *The Search Direction screen.*

Quicken searches for an exact match to what you type. If you enter an asterisk in the C field, for example, Quicken searches for those transactions that you marked as cleared with an asterisk. If you enter *Walt Lumens* in the Payee field, Quicken searches for transactions with the Payee description field exactly equal to Walt Lumens. Quicken does not recognize case; WALT LUMENS, walt lumens, and wALT lUMENS are all exact matches from Quicken's perspective. If the Payee field is Walter Lumens, W. Lumens, or Mr. Walt Lumens, however, Quicken does not find the transaction.

If Quicken does not find a transaction that matches your search argument, the program displays the message No matching transactions were found, shown in figure 5.8.

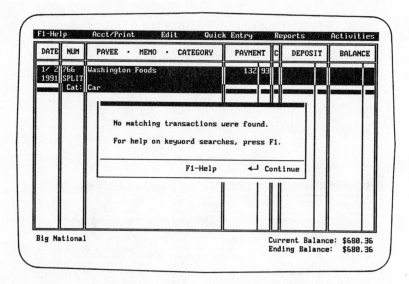

**Fig. 5.8.** *The* No matching transactions were found *message.*

## Using Key Word Matches

Key word matches enable you to search a field that includes or excludes certain letters, characters, or series of characters. Key word matches use three characters: the period (.), question mark (?), and tilde (˜). Periods are wildcard indicators that can represent any character, a group of characters, or even no characters. The question mark represents any character. The tilde identifies a word, character, or characters you want to exclude from your search. Table 5.1 summarizes what various search arguments do and do not find.

**Table 5.1**
**Summary of Search Arguments Using Special Characters***

| Argument | What It Finds | What It Does Not Find |
|---|---|---|
| ..interest | interest<br>car loan interest<br>mortgage interest | car loan<br>interest expense<br>mortgage expense<br>war loan |
| interest.. | interest<br>interest expense | car loan<br>car loan interest<br>mortgage expense<br>mortgage interest<br>war loan |
| ..interest.. | interest<br>car loan interest<br>interest expense<br>mortgage interest | car loan<br>mortgage expense<br>war loan |
| ~.interest | car loan<br>interest expense<br>mortgage expense<br>war loan | interest<br>car loan interest<br>mortgage interest |
| ~ interest.. | car loan<br>car loan interest<br>mortgage expense<br>mortgage interest<br>war loan | interest<br>interest expense |
| ~ ..interest.. | car loan<br>mortgage expense<br>war loan | car loan interest<br>interest<br>interest expense<br>mortgage interest |
| ?ar loan | car loan<br>war loan | car loan interest<br>interest<br>interest expense<br>mortgage expense<br>mortgage interest |

*Table 5.1 continues*

**Table 5.1**—*continued*

| Argument | What It Finds | What It Does Not Find |
|---|---|---|
| ~ ?ar loan | interest | car loan |
| | car loan interest | war loan |
| | interest expense | |
| | mortgage expense | |
| | mortgage interest | |

\* For a sample list of memo descriptions containing the following: car loan, car loan interest, interest, interest expense, mortgage expense, mortgage interest, and war loan.

## Combining Exact and Key Word Matches

You can search with more than one exact match or key word argument. Figure 5.9, for example, shows the Transaction to Find screen set to search for transactions with the phrase "big national bank" in the Payee field and an asterisk in the cleared field.

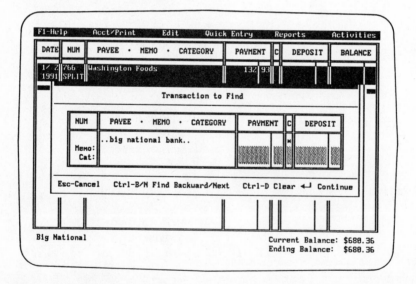

**Fig. 5.9.** *Searching for transactions that include the phrase "big national bank" in the* Payee *field.*

If you use more than one match test, the Find operation locates any transactions that meet all match tests. With the Transaction to Find screen shown in figure 5.9, for example, Find does not locate transactions with the phrase "big national bank" used in the Payee field unless the asterisk character also is used in the C field. Find also does not locate transactions with the asterisk character used in the C field unless the phrase "big national bank" also is used in the Payee field.

## Repeating a Find Request

When Quicken executes a Find operation, it selects the first transaction that meets the search argument or arguments you entered. If you were precise in specifying the exact match or key word match, the first transaction Quicken finds may be the one you want. That transaction also could be similar to the one you want, but not an exact match, so Quicken gives you two additional Find options: **Repeat Find backwards** (Ctrl-B) and **Repeat Find next** (Ctrl-N). **Repeat Find backwards** (Ctrl-B) executes the find operation already specified on the Transaction to Find screen, and it looks through checks and deposits before the selected transaction. Similarly, **Repeat Find next** executes the find operation already specified on the Transaction to Find screen, but it looks through checks and deposits after the selected transaction.

# Using the Go to Date Option

You may have wondered about the absence of a date field on the Transaction to Find screen. You use the **Go to Date** option (Ctrl-G) on the Edit menu to look for a transaction or account balance for a specific date. Specify the date you want to use as the basis for your search on the Go to Date screen, shown in figure 5.10.

Quicken initially displays the current system date as the Go to Date. You can change the date by typing the date you want over the default date. You also can use the + and − keys to move the date forward or backward one day at a time.

After you set the date you want, Quicken finds and displays the first transaction with the date you entered. If no transaction has the date you entered, the transaction with the date closest to the date you entered is displayed.

Because Quicken arranges transactions in the register by date, you do not need to specify a search direction for the **Go to Date** option. By comparing the date on the currently selected transaction to the Go to Date,

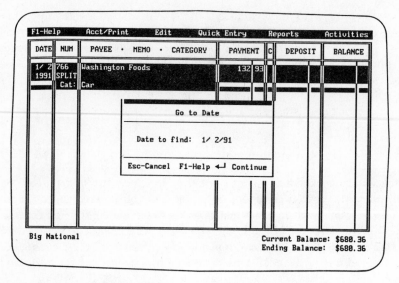

*Fig. 5.10. The Go to Date screen.*

Quicken determines which direction it needs to search. If the Go to Date is earlier than the date on the selected transaction, Quicken looks through the previous transactions; if the Go to Date is later than the date on the selected transaction, Quicken searches succeeding transactions.

## Using the Go to Transfer Option

If the currently selected transaction is a transfer, you can use the **Go to Transfer** option on the Edit menu to display the register with the corresponding transaction. For example, figure 5.11 shows that the deposit to savings check is selected. By looking at the Category field, which displays [Acme], you can see that this is a transfer transaction. The name of the account to which the transfer is taking place is shown in the Category field with brackets around the name.

If you select **Go to Transfer** (Ctrl-X) from the Edit menu, Quicken displays the account register with the corresponding transaction selected. Figure 5.12 shows the corresponding transaction in the savings register. In the first account, Big National, the transaction is a payment because it reduces that account balance. In the second account, Acme, the transaction is listed as a deposit.

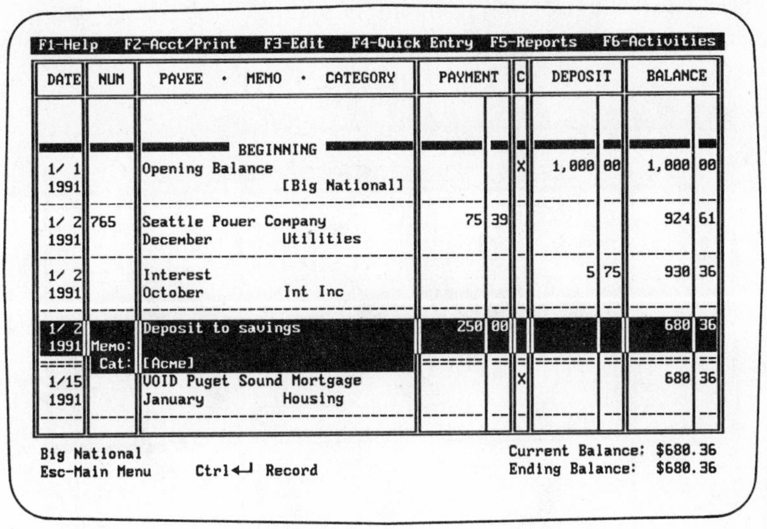

```
F1-Help   F2-Acct/Print   F3-Edit   F4-Quick Entry   F5-Reports   F6-Activities
┌──────┬─────┬──────────────────────────────┬─────────┬──┬───────────┬──────────┐
│ DATE │ NUM │  PAYEE · MEMO · CATEGORY     │ PAYMENT │C │  DEPOSIT  │ BALANCE  │
├──────┼─────┼──────────────────────────────┼─────────┼──┼───────────┼──────────┤
│      │     │      ══ BEGINNING ══          │         │  │           │          │
│ 1/ 1 │     │ Opening Balance              │         │X │ 1,000 00  │ 1,000 00 │
│ 1991 │     │              [Big National]  │         │  │           │          │
│ 1/ 2 │ 765 │ Seattle Power Company        │   75 39 │  │           │   924 61 │
│ 1991 │     │ December        Utilities    │         │  │           │          │
│ 1/ 2 │     │ Interest                     │         │  │      5 75 │   930 36 │
│ 1991 │     │ October         Int Inc      │         │  │           │          │
│ 1/ 2 │     │ Deposit to savings           │  250 00 │  │           │   680 36 │
│ 1991 │Memo:│                              │         │  │           │          │
│      │Cat: │ [Acme]                       │         │  │           │          │
│ 1/15 │     │ VOID Puget Sound Mortgage    │         │X │           │   680 36 │
│ 1991 │     │ January         Housing      │         │  │           │          │
└──────┴─────┴──────────────────────────────┴─────────┴──┴───────────┴──────────┘
 Big National                                     Current Balance:  $680.36
 Esc-Main Menu    Ctrl↵  Record                   Ending Balance:   $680.36
```

*Fig. 5.11.* *The deposit to savings check is part of a transfer.*

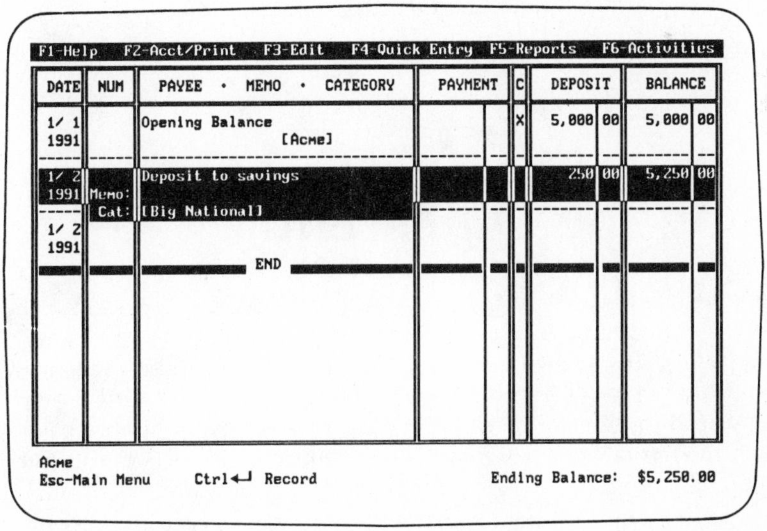

```
F1-Help   F2-Acct/Print   F3-Edit   F4-Quick Entry   F5-Reports   F6-Activities
┌──────┬─────┬──────────────────────────────┬─────────┬──┬───────────┬──────────┐
│ DATE │ NUM │  PAYEE · MEMO · CATEGORY     │ PAYMENT │C │  DEPOSIT  │ BALANCE  │
├──────┼─────┼──────────────────────────────┼─────────┼──┼───────────┼──────────┤
│ 1/ 1 │     │ Opening Balance              │         │X │ 5,000 00  │ 5,000 00 │
│ 1991 │     │              [Acme]          │         │  │           │          │
│ 1/ 2 │     │ Deposit to savings           │         │  │   250 00  │ 5,250 00 │
│ 1991 │Memo:│                              │         │  │           │          │
│      │Cat: │ [Big National]               │         │  │           │          │
│ 1/ 2 │     │                              │         │  │           │          │
│ 1991 │     │          ══ END ══           │         │  │           │          │
│      │     │                              │         │  │           │          │
└──────┴─────┴──────────────────────────────┴─────────┴──┴───────────┴──────────┘
 Acme
 Esc-Main Menu    Ctrl↵  Record                   Ending Balance:   $5,250.00
```

*Fig. 5.12.* *The corresponding transfer transaction.*

If you use the **Go to Transfer** option on a split transaction, Quicken asks you to identify the category you want to go to (see fig. 5.13). With a split transaction, you can make transfers to more than one account. If you try to change a split transaction from one of the other registers, Quicken tells you that the transaction was created through a transfer, and you must return to the original transaction to make changes.

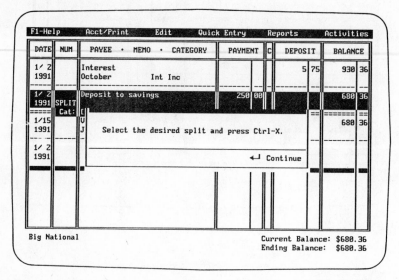

**Fig. 5.13.** *Quicken prompts you to indicate which account you want to go to.*

# Using the Quick Entry Menu Tools

Quicken already may be fast enough for you. After all, it does not take that much time to type in the half dozen fields you enter to record a check or a deposit. But you can streamline your record keeping further with several of the options on the Quick Entry menu (see fig. 5.14). You can use the **Recall Transaction** and **Memorize Transaction** options to store and then re-use recurring transactions. With the **Transaction Groups** option, you can store and then re-use whole sets of transactions. (Normal **Categorize/Transfer** and **Select/Set Up Class** options are covered in Chapter 10.)

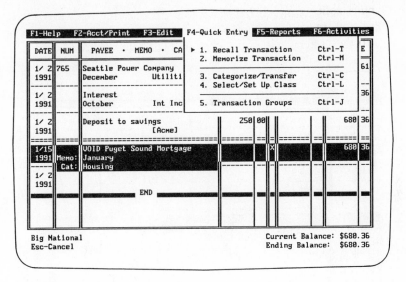

**Fig. 5.14.** *The Quick Entry menu.*

# Memorizing Transactions

Many of the checks you write and the deposits you make are often similar or identical to previous checks and deposits. A household, for example, may register the mortgage check, the car loan check, the utility bill check, and the payroll deposit each month. A business may write checks for the monthly rent, payroll, and expenses like supplies or insurance.

Because so many register transactions are largely the same every month, Quicken gives you the capability to store transaction information in a memorized transactions list. Rather than entering the information over and over, you can re-use transaction information. To memorize a transaction, follow these steps:

1. Select the register transaction you want to memorize, such as the one shown in figure 5.15.

2. Press F4 to display the Quick Entry menu, and then select the **Memorize Transaction** option, or press Ctrl-M. Quicken highlights the selected transaction and alerts you that the marked information is about to be memorized (see fig. 5.16). The marked information includes the payee, payment or deposit amounts, cleared memo, and category; the Date and Cleared fields are not marked.

3. To finish the memorize operation, press Enter. Quicken saves a copy of the transaction in the memorized transaction list. The copy is named after what is in the Payee field.

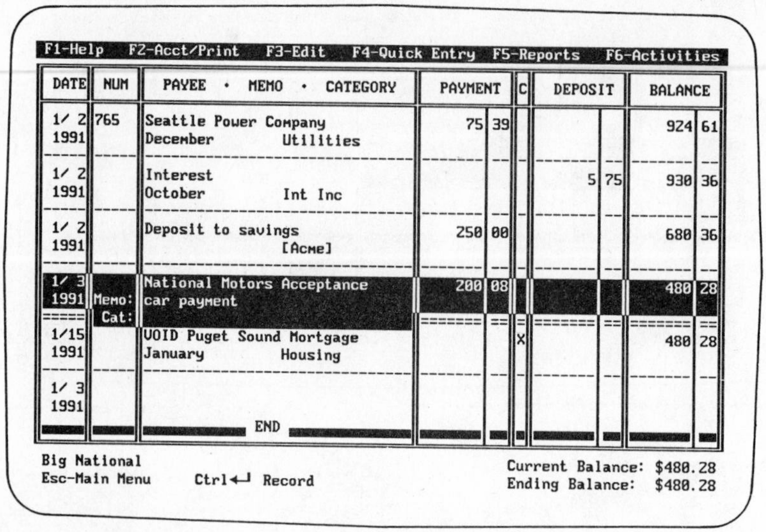

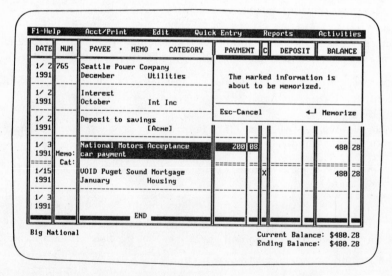

*Fig. 5.15.* *You might decide to memorize a monthly loan payment.*

*Fig. 5.16.* *The memorization message.*

# Recalling a Transaction

The **Recall Transaction** option works in conjunction with the **Memorize Transaction** option just described. Selecting **Recall Transaction** (Ctrl-T) enables you to fill a row in the register with memorized transactions. Suppose that Quicken memorizes the payment shown in figure 5.15. When you need to record the payment the following month, select **Recall Transaction** from the Quick Entry menu. The Memorized Transactions List is displayed, as shown in figure 5.17. Only the loan payment is shown, because this transaction is the only one that has been memorized.

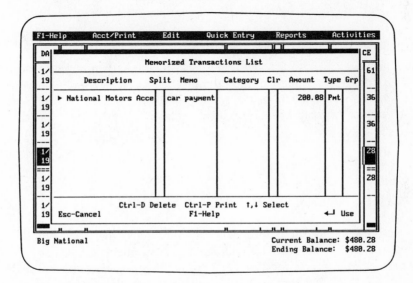

***Fig. 5.17.*** *The Memorized Transactions List screen.*

Figure 5.17 shows the information saved as part of the Memorize Transaction operation. Eight fields are shown on-screen, all of which may have been filled to record a register transaction.

The payee name is in the Description column; the memo is in the Memo column; the category name is in the Category column, and the check amount is in the Amount column. If you split a check transaction, an S appears in the Split column. Quicken also places the abbreviation *Pmt* in the Type field to identify the transaction as a payment, *Dep* in the Type field to identify the transaction as a deposit, or *Check* in the Type field to identify the transaction as a check. The Clr column shows whether you have marked the transaction as cleared (see Chapter 8). The Grp column identifies whether the memorized transaction is part of a group of transactions (described a little later in the chapter).

To use, or recall, a memorized transaction, take the following steps:

1. Press F4 to display the Quick Entry menu and then select the **Recall Transaction** option, or press Ctrl-T. Quicken displays the Memorized Transaction List (see fig. 5.17).

2. Move the selection triangle to the left of the Description field to the transaction you want to use.

3. Press Enter, and Quicken fills the next empty row in the register with the information from the memorized transaction.

4. Edit the information from the memorized transaction so that it correctly reflects the transaction you want to record. For a check, you probably will want to enter a check number. For both checks and deposits, you often will want to edit the Amount and Memo fields. The current date is automatically entered in the register. (**Note:** You cannot postdate a memorized transaction.)

5. To record the check, press Ctrl-Enter. Quicken records the transaction in the register.

## Deleting Memorized Transactions

You also use the **Recall Transaction** option to delete memorized transactions from the Memorized Transactions List. You might want to delete a memorized transaction, for example, with the final payment on a house or car loan. To delete a memorized transaction, follow these steps:

1. Press F4 to display the Quick Entry menu, and then select the **Recall Transaction** option, or press Ctrl-T. Quicken displays the Memorized Transactions List.

2. Highlight the transaction you want to delete.

3. When the transaction you want to delete is marked, press Ctrl-D. Quicken alerts you that it is about to delete a memorized transaction, as shown in figure 5.18. To delete the transaction, press Enter; otherwise, press Esc.

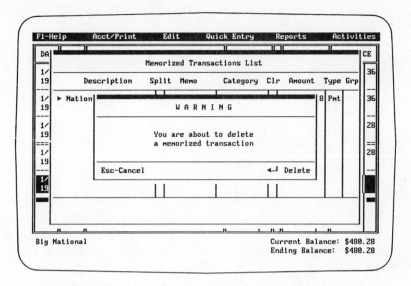

**Fig. 5.18.** *The* you are about to delete a memorized transaction *message.*

# Listing Memorized Transactions

Quicken also enables you to print a list of the transactions you have memorized. Most of the time, you will not need this feature. As long as
Quicken is running, the memorized transactions list is at your finger-
tips anyway if you press Ctrl-T. One example of when you might want a
printed list is for an annual review of transactions. If you decide that you
want a printed copy of the list, follow these steps:

1. Press F4 to display the Quick Entry menu and then select the
   **Recall Transaction** option, or press Ctrl-T. Quicken displays the
   Memorized Transactions List.

2. Press Ctrl-P. Quicken displays the Print Memorized Transactions
   List screen, which you use to specify settings for printing the list.
   (This screen is like the Print Register screen.)

3. Indicate printer settings and Quicken then prints the list (see
   fig. 5.19.)

```
                                          Memorized Transactions List                    Page 1
      QDATA
      1/ 3/91

              Payee/Memo/Category        Clr     Type        Amount
      ----------------------------        ---    -------    ------------

      National Motors Acceptance                 Payment      -200.08
        car payment

      Seattle Power Company                       Payment       -75.39
        December
        Utilities
```

**Fig. 5.19.** *A printed Memorized Transactions List.*

*CPA Tip*

Consider each of the transactions you now regularly record as candidates for the Memorized Transactions List: rent, house payment, utility payment, school loans, payroll deposits, bank service fees, and so on. The easiest time to memorize transactions is when you initially record a transaction, so every time you enter a transaction, ask yourself whether the transaction is one you will enter repeatedly. You also can memorize split transactions.

# Using the Categorize/Transfer Option

With the **Categorize/Transfer** option (Ctrl-C), you can create or retrieve a category. Creating a new category is described in Chapter 10, but Quicken provides predefined home and business categories that you can retrieve.

To find and use a predefined category, take the following steps:

1. Press F4 to display the Quicken Entry menu, and then select the **Categorize/Transfer** option, or press Ctrl-C. Quicken displays the Category and Transfer List screen with predefined categories and any accounts you may have created (see fig. 5.20).

2. Select the category or account you want to use and press Enter. Quicken retrieves the category or account name from the list and puts it in the Category field.

You also can use the PgUp, PgDn, Home, and End keys to move quickly through long lists of categories. Pressing PgUp displays the preceding page of categories in the list; pressing PgDn displays the next page of categories in the list; pressing Home displays the first page of categories, and pressing End displays the last page of categories.

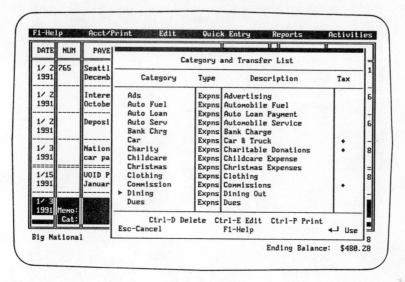

**Fig. 5.20.** *The Category and Transfer List screen.*

# Setting Up a Transaction Group

Frequently, you might encounter a set of consistent monthly transactions. A household might have the monthly bills: a mortgage, the utility bill, and the car payment. A business might have employee payroll checks. Instead of memorizing and recalling individual transactions, you can set up a group of memorized transactions. Transaction groups enable you to recall several memorized transactions at the same time.

To create a transaction group, follow these steps:

1. Following the steps described earlier in this chapter, memorize each of the transactions you want to include in a transaction group.

2. Press F4 to display the Quick Entry menu, and then select the **Transaction Groups** option, or press Ctrl-J. Quicken displays the Select Transaction Group to Execute screen, as shown in figure 5.21.

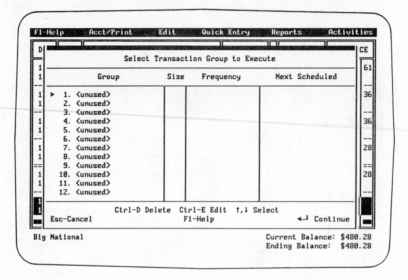

**Fig. 5.21.** *The Select Transaction Group to Execute screen.*

3. Use the up- and down-arrow keys to mark the first unused transaction group and then press Enter. Quicken displays the Describe Group screen (see fig. 5.22). (**Note:** If you are defining your first transaction, you will mark group 1 and press Enter. If a transaction group already exists, choose an empty group.)

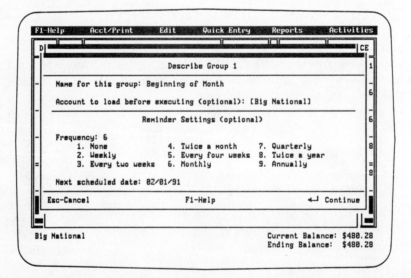

**Fig. 5.22.** *The Describe Group screen.*

4. Give a name or description to the group. You can use a maximum of 20 characters to describe the group.

5. Press Enter or Tab to move the cursor to the Account to load before executing field. Enter the account name for which the transactions should be recorded. This action causes the appropriate account to be selected before you recall the transactions in a group. If you only work with one account, you do not need to fill in this field.

6. Press Enter or Tab to move the cursor to the Frequency field. Set the frequency using one of the nine settings shown in figure 5.22: None, Weekly, Every two weeks, Twice a month, Every four weeks, Monthly, Quarterly, Twice a year, or Annually. Select the frequency you want by typing the number that corresponds to the desired frequency.

7. If you set the frequency to something other than None, you also must set the next scheduled date. Press Enter or Tab to move the cursor to the Next scheduled date field. Enter the date in the MM/DD/YY format. You can use the standard Quicken + and − keys to change this date to the one desired.

8. Press Enter, and Quicken displays the Assign Transactions to Group screen (see fig. 5.23). The Assign Transactions to Group screen lists all the possible memorized transactions.

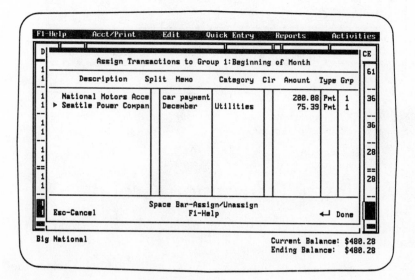

**Fig. 5.23.** *The Assign Transactions to Group screen.*

9. Use the arrow keys to mark memorized transactions that should be part of the transaction group. When a transaction that should be included is marked, press the space bar to assign the transaction to the group. The last column on the Assign Transactions to Group screen, Grp, displays the group number. To unassign a transaction, press space bar again. Figure 5.23 shows two memorized transactions selected for transaction group 1: the monthly car payment and the utilities payment.

10. After the transactions that should be assigned to a group are all marked, press Enter to save your work.

Quicken redisplays the Select Transaction Group to Execute screen. The newly defined transaction group appears (see fig. 5.24.).

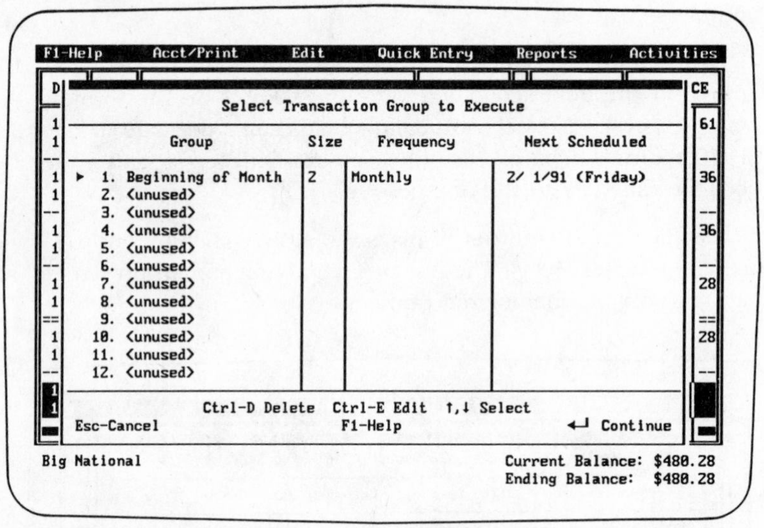

```
┌───────────────────────────────────────────────────────────────────────┐
│ F1-Help      Acct/Print     Edit     Quick Entry    Reports   Activities│
├───────────────────────────────────────────────────────────────────────┤
│ D│▐▔▔▔▔▔▔▔▔▔▔▔▔▔▔▔▔▔▔▔▔▔▔▔▔▔▔▔▔▔▔▔▔▔▔▔▔▔▔▔▔▔▔▔▔▔▔▔▔▔│       │CE│
│ 1│             Select Transaction Group to Execute             │       │61│
│ 1│                                                             │       │  │
│ 1│     Group            Size    Frequency        Next Scheduled │       │--│
│ 1│   ▸ 1. Beginning of Month  2   Monthly      2/ 1/91 (Friday) │       │36│
│ 1│     2. <unused>                                             │       │  │
│ --│     3. <unused>                                             │       │--│
│ 1│     4. <unused>                                             │       │36│
│ 1│     5. <unused>                                             │       │  │
│ --│     6. <unused>                                             │       │  │
│ 1│     7. <unused>                                             │       │28│
│ 1│     8. <unused>                                             │       │  │
│ --│     9. <unused>                                             │       │  │
│ ==│    10. <unused>                                             │       │==│
│ 1│    11. <unused>                                             │       │28│
│ 1│    12. <unused>                                             │       │  │
│ --│                                                             │       │--│
│ 1│         Ctrl-D Delete   Ctrl-E Edit   ↑,↓ Select            │       │  │
│  │   Esc-Cancel            F1-Help              ↵ Continue     │       │  │
├───────────────────────────────────────────────────────────────────────┤
│  Big National                             Current Balance:  $480.28    │
│                                           Ending Balance:   $480.28    │
└───────────────────────────────────────────────────────────────────────┘
```

**Fig. 5.24.** *A newly defined transaction group appearing on the Select Transaction Group to Execute screen.*

# Executing a Transaction Group

To create a set of register transactions using a transaction group, follow these steps:

1. Press F4 to display the Quick Entry menu, and then select the **Transaction Groups** option, or press Ctrl-J. Quicken displays the Select Transaction Group to Execute screen (see fig. 5.21).

2. Move the selection triangle to the left of the Description field for the transaction group you want to use.

3. Press Enter, and Quicken prompts you for the Transaction Group Date, as shown in figure 5.25.

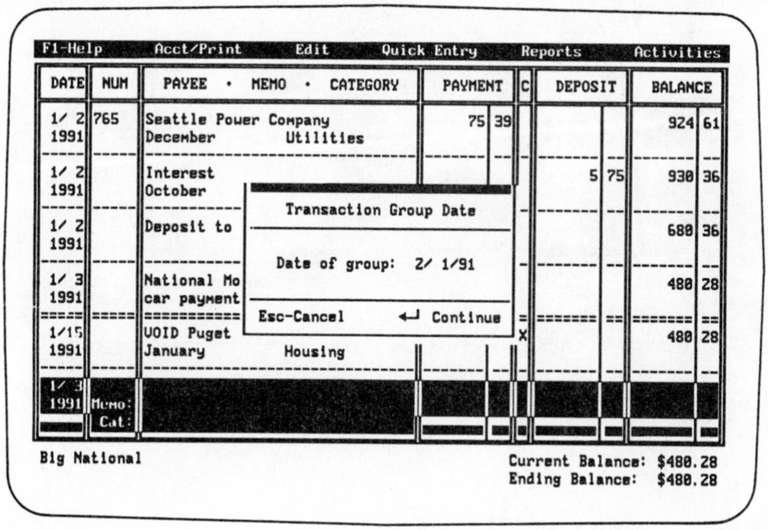

**Fig. 5.25.** *The Transaction Group Date screen.*

4. Enter the date you want checks and deposits in the transaction group to show when they are recorded in the register. Remember that you can use the + and − keys to change the date one day at a time.

5. Press Enter when the Transaction Group Date field is correct. Quicken records the memorized transactions in the register, saves the transactions, and displays the message shown in figure 5.26.

6. As necessary, edit the information for each of the memorized transactions added as part of the transaction group, and then record the transaction.

The execute transaction group operation also moves the next scheduled date for the transaction group forward, using whatever interval you specified.

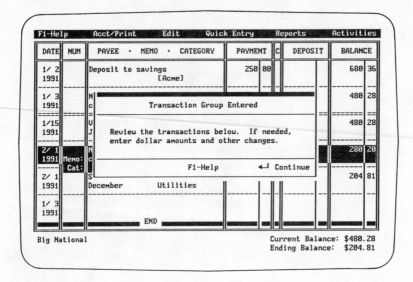

**Fig. 5.26.** *The* Transaction Group Entered *message.*

# Changing and Deleting Transaction Groups

If you want to change or modify a transaction group, you again use the **Transaction Groups** option on the Quick Entry menu and select the previously set-up transaction group. Access the Describe Group and Assign Transactions screens, as shown in figures 5.22 and 5.23. Make the required changes on the appropriate screen and press Enter to continue to the next screen.

Because transaction groups segregate your checks into groups you pay together at one time, changes in payment due dates mean that you need to change the transaction group. For example, if you refinance your mortgage, the due date might change from the fifth to the fifteenth. If you have separate transaction groups for checks you write at the beginning of the month and those you write during the middle of the month, you may need to change your transaction groups.

If you want to delete a transaction group, you also select the **Transaction Groups** option from the Quick Entry menu. Use the arrow keys to mark the group you want to delete and press Ctrl-D. Quicken displays a message alerting you that it is about to delete the marked transaction group. To remove the transaction group, press Enter.

# Using the Activities Menu

The register Activities menu has five options, as shown in figure 5.27. The **Write Checks** option (Ctrl-W) accesses the Write Checks screen, as does the **Write/Print Checks** option on Quicken's Main menu. You use the **Write Checks** option so that Quicken prints checks for you. The **Write/ Print Checks** option is described in Chapters 6 and 7. The **Reconcile** option accesses the Reconciliation screen and options (see Chapter 8).

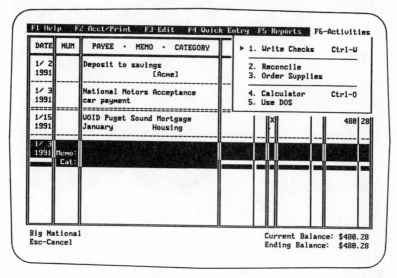

**Fig. 5.27.** *The Activities menu.*

The **Order Supplies** option displays the Print Supply Order Form screen, shown in figure 5.28, which you print and then use as a three-page order form for purchasing supplies. These forms can be used to order check forms and envelopes from Intuit (the manufacturer of Quicken). Although the actual order form is not shown here, the form is similar to the order form that Intuit provides in the Quicken package.

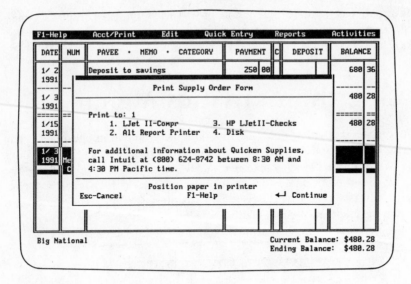

**Fig. 5.28.** *The Print Supply Order Form screen.*

The fourth Activities menu option, **Calculator** (Ctrl-O), accesses the on-line, 10-key calculator. Figure 5.29 shows the calculator, described in Chapter 2.

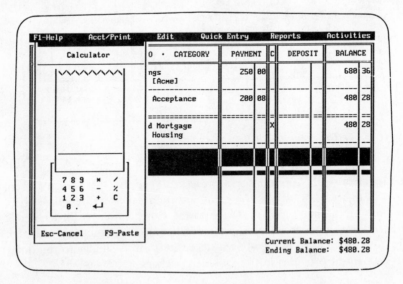

**Fig. 5.29.** *The calculator available from the Activities menu.*

The **Use DOS** option brings up DOS and displays the DOS prompt, as follows:

```
To return to Quicken, type EXIT.
Microsoft® MS-DOS® Version 3.30
©Copyright Microsoft Corp 1981-1987
C:\QUICKEN3›
```

This feature is handy when you want to execute DOS commands before leaving Quicken. For example, you may want to format a disk to make a backup copy of a bank account.

# Chapter Summary

This chapter described the three register menus not covered in the preceding chapter. The Edit menu provides tools you can use to make easier recording, editing, and deleting of individual transactions. The Quick Entry menu provides tools for memorizing and re-using transactions you record repeatedly. The Activities menu provides a grab bag of options.

# 6

# Writing and Printing
# Checks

With Quicken's check-printing feature, you can write checks and pay bills faster and more efficiently than you ever thought possible. You can pay bills faster because Quicken provides a collection of short-cuts and time-saving techniques that automate and speed up check writing and bill paying. You can pay bills more efficiently because Quicken helps you keep track of the bills coming due and provides categories with which you can classify the ways you are spending your money.

As noted in Chapter 4, you don't actually ever have to use the **Write/ Print Checks** option that Quicken includes on the Main menu. You need to use this feature only if you want to print checks with Quicken. If you do want to print checks, the Write/Print Checks screen has some advantages. First, the screen enables you to include the address of the person to whom you will be writing the check—something the register does not allow you to do. Second, you use a screen that resembles the actual check form, which often makes entering the data easier. Also, using the Write/ Print Checks screen and option doesn't mean additional work because Quicken records the information you collect directly into the Quicken register.

This chapter describes the basics of using the **Write/Print Checks** option on the Main menu. Included in this chapter are discussions of the following topics:

❏ Getting to know the Write Checks screen

❏ Writing a check

**115**

❏ Reviewing and editing checks

❏ Printing and reprinting checks

# Getting To Know the Write Checks Screen

You use the Write Checks screen, shown in figure 6.1, to collect the information you use to print check forms. After collecting the information, Quicken records the check in the check register. You then can print the check. To access the Write Checks screen, select the **Write/Print Checks** option from Quicken's Main menu.

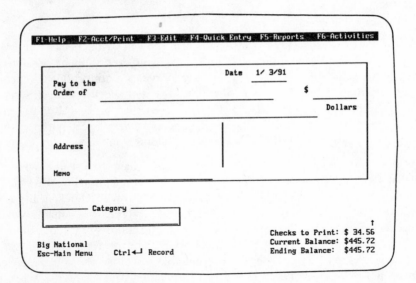

**Fig. 6.1.** *The Write Checks screen.*

The Write Checks screen can be broken down into three parts: the menu bar at the top of the screen, the check form, and the information bar at the bottom of the screen.

The menu bar shows the function keys you use from the Write Checks screen to access menus. These keys should look familiar if you have worked with the Register screen:

| F2 | Accesses the Acct/Print Checks menu |
| F3 | Accesses the Edit menu (see Chapter 7) |
| F4 | Accesses the Quick Entry menu (see Chapter 7) |
| F5 | Accesses the Reports menu (see Chapter 14) |
| F6 | Accesses the Activities menu (see Chapter 7) |

The second part of the screen is the actual check form you complete to have your checks printed. The steps for completing the form are described in the following section, "Writing a Check."

The third part of the Write Checks screen is the information bar at the bottom of the screen. This bar shows several pieces of information, including the account you currently are using, descriptions of what the Esc and Enter keys do, the Checks to Print total, and the ending balance in the account. Figure 6.1 shows the bank account as "Big National," the Checks to Print total as $34.56, and the current ending balances as $445.72. (**Note:** The Checks to Print total is the total of all the checks you are writing in this session.)

# Writing a Check

The mechanics of writing a check with Quicken closely resemble those for manually writing a check. The only real difference is that Quicken's Write Checks screen makes the process easier. With Quicken, writing a check means you simply complete the Write Checks screen. You fill in as many as seven fields: Date, Payee, Amount, Address, Message, Memo, and Category. After you write the check, you're ready to record and print it.

To write a check, you take the following steps:

1. Select the **Write/Print Checks** option from Quicken's Main menu, or, if you're already on the Register screen, press F6 to display the Activities menu and select the **Write Checks** option. Quicken displays the Write Checks screen shown in figure 6.1.

2. Enter the date of the check in the Date field. Write the date in the month/day/year format (i.e., *12/11/90*). The first time you use Quicken, the program fills the Date field with the system date (the current date according to your computer's internal memory). After you write your first check using the Write Checks screen, Quicken fills the Date field with the last date used. To edit the date, you have two choices. First, you can move the cursor to the part of the date—month, day, or year—you want to change and type over what is already on-screen. Second, you can use the + and − keys to

change the date one day at a time. Each time you press the + key, Quicken moves the date ahead one day. Each time you press the − key, Quicken moves the date back one day.

**CPA Tip**

As mentioned in Chapter 4, businesses and individuals often receive discounts for paying bills early, so consider early payment in setting the check date. In effect, not taking early payment discounts is an extremely expensive way to borrow money from the vendor. Suppose that a vendor normally requires payment within 30 days but gives a two percent discount for payments received within 10 days. If you pay within 30 rather than 10 days, you pay the vendor a two percent interest charge for paying 20 days later. Because one year contains roughly 18 20-day periods, the two percent for 20 days equals approximately 36 percent annually.

Although you may need to borrow this money, you probably can find a much cheaper lender. As a rule of thumb, if a vendor gives you a one percent discount for paying 20 days early, you are borrowing money from him at about an 18 percent annual interest rate if you do not pay early. A three percent discount works out to a whopping 54 percent per year.

3. Press Enter or Tab to move the cursor to the Pay to the Order of field. This field is where you enter the name of the person or business, called the *payee*, that the check pays. Type in the field the name you want to appear on the check.

   Because you have space for up to 40 characters, you should not have any problem fitting in the payee's name. In fact, you should have room to enter "and" and "or" payees. (An "and" payee, for example, is *Vader Ryderwood and Russell Dardenelle*. Both Vader and Russell must endorse such a check to cash it. An "or" payee is entered as *Vader Ryderwood or Russell Dardenelle* and requires Vader *or* Russell to endorse the check to cash it.)

4. Press Enter or Tab to move the cursor to the Amount field. The Amount field shows the amount of the check. You can use up to 10 characters to input the amount. Quicken enables you to enter only numbers, commas, and periods in the Amount field. Quicken enters commas if you do not and if room is available for them. The largest value you can enter in the Amount field is 9999999.99. Because this number is difficult to read without commas (the number is $9,999,999.99), you probably will want to use commas. If you use

some of the 10 characters for commas, the largest value you can enter is 999,999.99. When you complete the Amount field and press Enter, Quicken writes out the amount on the next line of the check —just as you do when writing a check manually. To save space, Quicken may abbreviate hundred as Hndrd, thousand as Thsnd, and million as Mill.

5. (Optional) Press Enter or Tab to move the cursor to the next field, the first line of the Address block. The optional Address field provides five 30-character lines. If you use envelopes with windows and enter the payee's address in this field, the address shows in the envelope window. You save time that otherwise is spent addressing envelopes.

    Assuming that you are using the Address field, you need to type the payee's name on the first line. Quicken provides a shortcut for you. If you type ' (apostrophe) or " (double quotation mark), Quicken copies the name from the Pay to the Order of field. (Because the Pay to the Order of field has space for 40 characters and the address lines have only 30 characters, this shortcut may cut off up to the last 10 characters of the payee's name.)

6. (Optional) If you set the extra message line switch to yes, press Enter or Tab to move the cursor to the Msg field. The extra message switch is on the Change Settings menu under the **Other Settings** option and is described in Chapter 11. This field gives you another 24 characters for additional information you want printed on the check, such as an account number for a credit card or a loan number for a mortgage. Because this information does not show through an envelope window, do not use the line for address information.

7. (Optional) Press Enter or Tab to move the cursor to the second line of the address block. Enter the street address or post office box.

8. (Optional) Press Enter or Tab to move the cursor to the third line of the address block. Enter the city, state, and ZIP code.

9. (Optional) Press Enter or Tab to move the cursor to the other address lines—there are six altogether—and enter any additional address information.

10. (Optional) Press Enter or Tab to move the cursor to the Memo field. You can use this field as you use the extra message line to further describe the reasons for a check, such as "May rent," or you can use the line to tell the payee your account number or loan number.

11. (Optional) Press Enter or Tab to move the cursor to the Category field. You use the Category field to describe the category into which a check falls, such as utilities expense, interest expense, or entertainment. You also can use the Category field to describe the class into which a check falls. (Categories and classes are described in Chapter 10, "Organizing Your Finances Better.") Quicken provides a listing of the most typical categories for home or business use to enable you to quickly categorize your most frequent transactions. You access the predefined list by pressing Ctrl-C. To use the Category field to describe a category, enter the name you used to define the category.

*CPA Tip*

Quicken 4.0 provides a new feature called "Auto-completion," which you can use after you have learned a few of the category names. If you type enough letters of a category name to uniquely identify the category and then press Enter, Quicken types the rest of the category name for you. Suppose, for example, that you have a category named "Entertainment," and that it is the only category name that starts with the three letters "ent." If you type *ent* and press Enter, Quicken types the remaining letters of the word for you—*ertainment*. You also can use the auto-completion feature in other situations, most of which apply to the investment monitoring features and are described in Chapter 13. You also can use the auto-completion feature to enter an account name in the Category field when transferring money to another account.

12. To record the check, press Enter when the cursor is on the Category field. Alternatively, you can press F10 or Ctrl-Enter when the cursor is on any of the fields. Figure 6.2 shows a completed Write Checks screen.

13. After you press Ctrl-Enter or F10, Quicken displays the prompt shown in figure 6.3 and asks you to confirm that you want to record the check. If you select Record transaction, the check is recorded.

Whichever method you choose to record a check, you briefly see a flashing message in the lower left-hand corner of the screen that says RECORDING. (If you use a very fast computer, you may not be able to read the message because it appears and disappears so quickly.) After Quicken finishes recording the check, your computer beeps, and the recorded check scrolls off the screen. A new, blank check form that was hidden by the preceding check is left on-screen—ready to be filled.

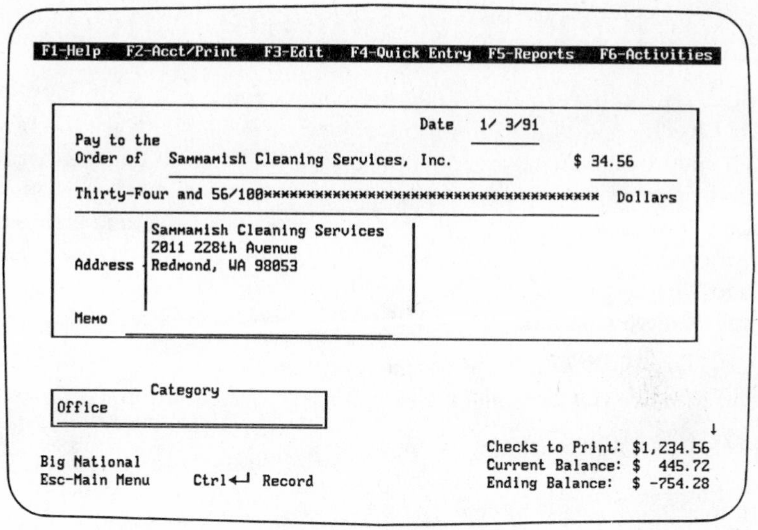

**Fig. 6.2.** *A completed Write Checks screen.*

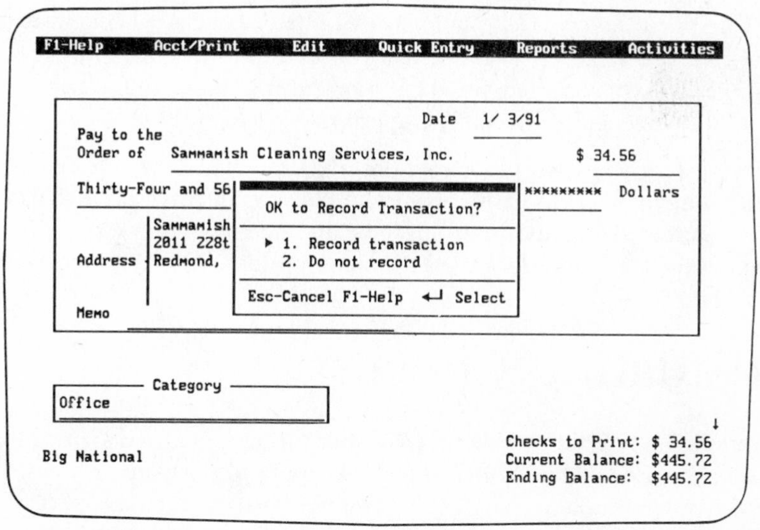

**Fig. 6.3.** *The* OK to Record Transaction *message.*

# Reviewing and Editing Checks

You can return to, review, and edit the checks you create with the **Write/ Print Checks** option until you print them. For example, you can correct errors and change check amounts for new bills. Suppose that you write a check to pay several bills from the same person or business—perhaps the bank with whom you have your mortgage, your car loan, and a personal line of credit. If you receive another bill from the bank, you may need to change the check amount. After printing, you need to use the Main menu's **Register** option, which is described in Chapters 4 and 5.

You can use the PgUp, PgDn, Home, and End keys on the Write Checks screen to move through the checks you have created but not yet printed:

| | |
|---|---|
| PgUp | Displays the preceding check |
| PgDn | Displays the next check |
| Home | Displays the first check |
| End | Displays the last check |

Quicken arranges by date the checks you have created with the Write Checks screen but have not printed. Those checks with the earliest dates are listed first, followed chronologically by later checks. Checks with the same date are arranged in the order you entered them. To edit a check you already have recorded, press PgUp or PgDn to move to the check you want to change and then edit the appropriate fields.

If you decide you don't want to print a check, you simply delete it. To delete the check, press Ctrl-D while the check is displayed. You also can select **Delete Transaction** from the Edit menu on the Write Checks screen. Chapter 7 describes the Edit menu options.

# Postdating Checks

Chapter 4, "Using the Register," talks about using postdated transactions. All the same reasons described there also apply to postdated checks. But when writing checks with Quicken, postdating takes on an added feature. Quicken can review postdated checks for those that you should print. To do this, Quicken uses a built-in program called the Billminder. Billminder looks for postdated checks it thinks you should print. The process works slightly differently depending on whether you're using Quicken on a hard disk system or on a floppy disk system. On a hard disk system, you are reminded of postdated checks and of transactions groups every time you turn on your computer. Quicken uses a pop-up message box (see fig. 6.4).

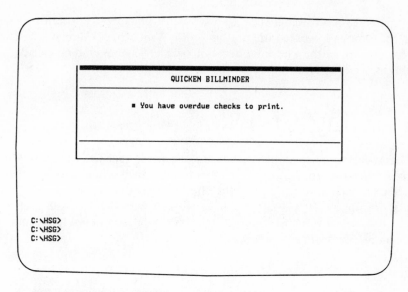

*Fig. 6.4. The pop-up Billminder message box.*

On a floppy disk system, you are reminded of postdated checks and of transaction groups every time you start Quicken. On a floppy disk system, Quicken displays a message at the bottom of the Main menu like that shown in figure 6.5.

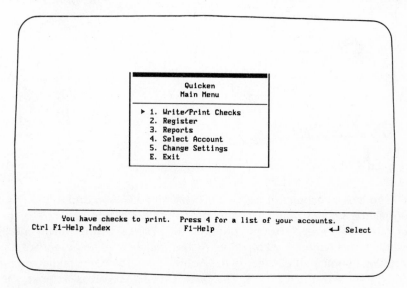

*Fig. 6.5. The Billminder feature also displays a reminder message at the bottom of the Main menu.*

If you enter postdated checks, Quicken adds the current account balance to the information bar at the bottom of the Write Checks screen. The current balance is the checking account balance—not including postdated checks (refer again to figure 6.3).

# Printing Checks

The Acct/Print menu, which you use to print the register, has six options (see fig. 6.6). This chapter describes only the second option—**Print Checks**—which you use to print checks created with the **Write/Print Checks** option. (If you already have worked with the Quicken register, you will notice that the Write Checks Acct/Print menu closely resembles the register's Acct/Print menu.)

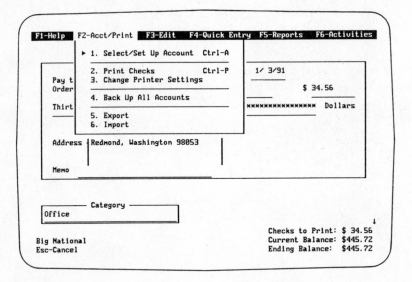

*Fig. 6.6. The Acct/Print menu.*

Refer to other chapters of *Using Quicken: IBM Version*, 2nd Edition, for information on the other five options. **Change Printer Settings** is the same as the **Printer Settings** option on the Change Settings menu and is described in Chapter 1, "Preparing To Use Quicken." The **Select/Set Up Account** option is the same as the **Select Account** Main menu option and is described in Chapter 3. The **Back Up All Accounts**, **Export**, and **Import** options are described in Chapter 9, "Taking Care of Quicken Files."

To print checks, follow these steps:

1. Load the check forms into your printer in the same way that you load regular paper.

   If you are using an impact printer, insert the continuous form checks into the printer as you would insert continuous form paper. If you are using a laser printer, place the check form sheets in the printer paper tray, as you would regular sheets of paper. (You use continuous form checks for impact printers and check form sheets for laser printers.)

2. Press F2 to display the Acct/Print menu and then select the **Print Checks** option.

   Quicken displays the Print Checks screen, shown in figure 6.7. The Print Checks screen displays two messages that give you information about the checks ready to be printed and provides three fields for you to use to control the printing of your checks. The two messages tell you how many checks you have to print, and, if relevant, how many checks are postdated. Figure 6.7 shows that you have two checks to print and that one check is postdated.

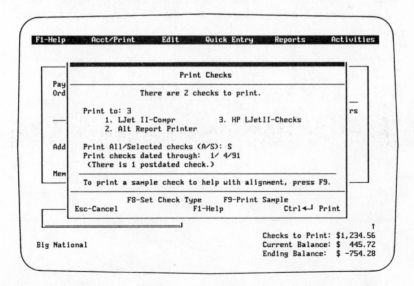

*Fig. 6.7. The Print Checks screen.*

3. With the cursor positioned on the Print to field, select the printer you want to use by pressing 1, 2, or 3. If you described your printer when installing Quicken, you should see your printer name here. If

you don't see it, refer to the Chapter 1 section called "Describing Your Printer."

4. Press Enter or Tab to move the cursor to the Print All/Selected checks field. To print all the checks entered on the Write Checks screen, leave this field set to A for All. To print only some of the checks, press S.

5. Press Enter or Tab to move the cursor to the Print checks dated through field. The Print postdated checks through field accepts a date through which you want Quicken to print postdated checks.

   Suppose that today is 5/10/91 and that the checks waiting to be printed are dated 5/10/91, 5/11/91, and 5/12/91. (The number of postdated checks appears below the Print postdated checks through field.) If you set the date of this field to 5/11/91, Quicken prints the checks dated 5/10/91 and 5/11/91. It does not, however, print the check dated 5/12/91.

6. (Optional) Use F9 to print a sample check. Pressing F9 prints one check form with the fields filled. Sample checks are essential for vertically and horizontally aligning checks if you are using an impact printer. (If you use a laser printer, you do not need to use this feature.) Figure 6.8 shows the sample check printed by Quicken.

*Fig. 6.8.* *A sample check.*

The Date field is filled as XX/XX/XX. The Pay to the Order of field is filled with Payee. The Amount fields are filled with XX,XXX.XX and Zero and 00/100***. The Memo field is filled with the phrase This is a void check.

Quicken also prints a pointer line, as shown in figure 6.8. The pointer line enables you to tell Quicken how the check form is aligned vertically. Quicken uses this information to align the check forms vertically.

For impact printers, if you elect to use the sample check feature, Quicken displays the Type Position Number screen, which you can use to align the check form vertically. To use this alignment capability, enter the number from the check form's pin-feed strips that the pointer line points to. (Pin-feed strips are the strips of holes on the sides of the check forms. Your printer uses these holes to move the check forms through the printer.) Only even numbers show on the pin-feed strips. The odd numbers are identified by hash marks. (The pin-feed strips aren't shown in figure 6.8, but take a look at the actual check form in your computer.)

To align the check horizontally, manually adjust the check form in the printer to the right or left. You may decide, for example, that the fields shown in figure 6.8 are a little too far, perhaps an eighth of an inch, to the left. In that case, you manually move the check forms over to the left an eighth of an inch. Quicken prints the next check with its check form spaces filled an eighth of an inch to the right compared to the preceding check form.

7. Press F8 to access the Set Check Type screen that you use to tell Quicken what kind of check form you are using. Figure 6.9 shows the Type of Checks screen used to specify the type of check form:

| | |
|---|---|
| 1 | Designates regular checks |
| 2 | Designates wallet checks |
| 3 | Designates voucher checks |
| 4 | Designates laser checks |
| 5 | Designates laser voucher checks |
| 6 | Designates laser wallet checks |

If you are using multipart laser check forms, you need to specify the number of additional copies that should be printed.

If you are using regular checks, such as those shown in figure 6.8, press 1. (Chapter 1, "Preparing To Use Quicken," describes in more detail Quicken's various check form options.)

8. To leave the Type of Checks screen, press Enter when the cursor is on the last field, or press Ctrl-Enter or F10. Quicken displays the Print Checks screen again.

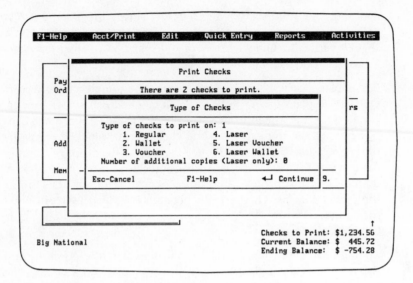

**Fig. 6.9.** *The Type of Checks Screen.*

(Optional) If you answered the Print All/Selected checks field with an S, Quicken then displays the Select Checks to Print screen (see fig. 6.10), from which you can select the checks you want to print. To select a check you want printed, use the arrow keys to

```
 F1-Help      Acct/Print      Edit      Quick Entry      Reports      Activities

                          Select Checks to Print

        Date        Payee              Memo            Amount

    ▶  1/ 3/91  Sammamish Cleaning Se                     34.56    Print
       1/ 9/91  Big National Bank    mortgage payment  1,200.00









                   Space Bar-Select/Deselect      F9-Select All
       Esc-Cancel                    F1-Help                    ↵  Continue
                                                                             ↑
                                               Checks to Print: $1,234.56
       Big National                            Current Balance: $   445.72
                                               Ending Balance:  $  -754.28
```

**Fig. 6.10.** *The Select Checks to Print screen.*

move the selection triangle. When the selection triangle is next to the check you want to print, press the space bar to select the check. To deselect a check previously marked for printing, move the selection triangle to that check and press the space bar again.

If you selected the checks to print, press Enter, F10, or Ctrl-Enter to leave the Select Checks to Print screen. Quicken then asks for the next check number.

9. Quicken uses the Type Check Number screen to ask you for the number of the next check to print (see fig. 6.11). Quicken displays the number of the next check. If the number Quicken displays is the same as the number that appears in the upper left corner of the next check form, press Enter to print the check. If the number Quicken displays is not correct, type the correct check number. You also can use the + and − keys to change the number.

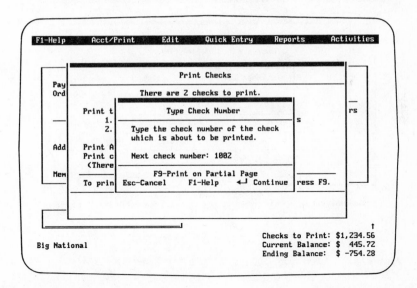

**Fig. 6.11.** *The Type Check Number screen.*

10. Press Enter to print the checks. Figure 6.12 shows a sample check to Big National Bank printed with the vertical and horizontal alignment correct. After Quicken finishes printing the checks, the program asks you if the checks printed correctly. Figure 6.13 shows the screen that Quicken uses to ask the question. If each of your checks printed correctly, press Enter.

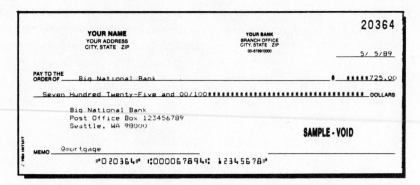

**Fig. 6.12.** *A sample check made payable to Big National Bank.*

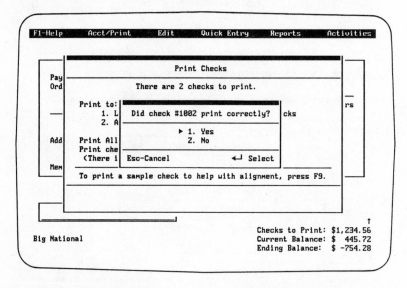

**Fig. 6.13.** *Quicken asks whether the checks printed correctly.*

If one or more of your checks printed incorrectly—perhaps the alignment was not right or the check forms jammed in the printer halfway through printing—answer No. Quicken asks for the number of the first check that printed incorrectly. Quicken then returns to the Print Checks screen, and you repeat each of the Print Checks steps to reprint the checks that printed incorrectly. Quicken allows only the check numbers printed to be entered.

*CPA Tip*

Write "VOID" in large letters across the face of checks that Quicken incorrectly prints. This precaution prevents you and anyone else from later signing and cashing the checks.

# Reprinting a Check

If you decide later, even after leaving the Print Checks screen, that you want to reprint a check, you can do so. Suppose that the original check somehow gets lost or destroyed. You still have to pay the person, so you need to reprint the check. Rather than re-enter all the same information a second time, you can reprint the original information. (*Note:* If you lose a check, consider placing a stop-payment order with your bank.)

When you describe checks you want to print using the Write Checks screen, Quicken actually records the checks in the register. Because Quicken hasn't assigned check numbers, however, the check number field shows asterisks. These asterisks indicate that the check is one that you have set up to print using the Write Checks screen (see fig. 6.14.) When Quicken prints the checks, it replaces the asterisks with the actual check number.

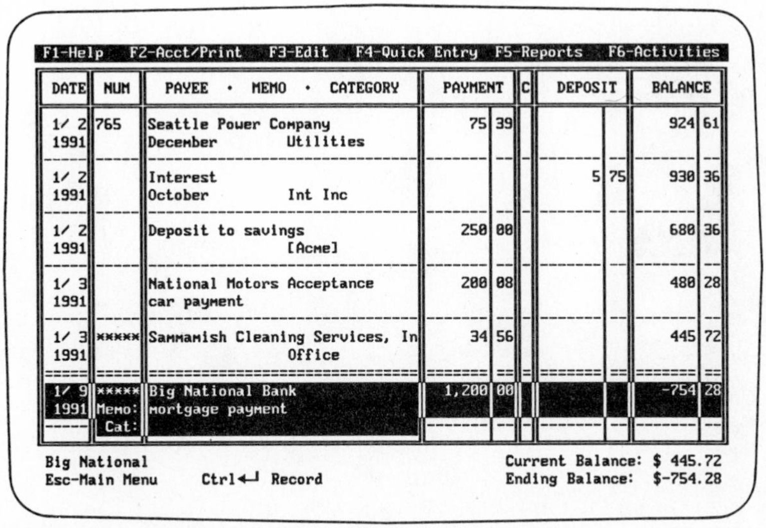

| DATE | NUM | PAYEE · MEMO · CATEGORY | PAYMENT | C | DEPOSIT | BALANCE |
|------|-----|-------------------------|---------|---|---------|---------|
| 1/ 2 1991 | 765 | Seattle Power Company<br>December        Utilities | 75 39 | | | 924 61 |
| 1/ 2 1991 | | Interest<br>October          Int Inc | | | 5 75 | 930 36 |
| 1/ 2 1991 | | Deposit to savings<br>            [Acme] | 250 00 | | | 680 36 |
| 1/ 3 1991 | | National Motors Acceptance<br>car payment | 200 08 | | | 480 28 |
| 1/ 3 1991 | xxxxx | Sammamish Cleaning Services, In<br>            Office | 34 56 | | | 445 72 |
| 1/ 9 1991 | xxxxx Memo:<br>Cat: | Big National Bank<br>mortgage payment | 1,200 00 | | | -754 28 |

Big National                                    Current Balance: $ 445.72
Esc-Main Menu        Ctrl↵ Record              Ending Balance:  $-754.28

F1-Help   F2-Acct/Print   F3-Edit   F4-Quick Entry   F5-Reports   F6-Activities

*Fig. 6.14.* Quicken stores checks to be printed in the register and identifies them by setting the check numbers to asterisks.

This bit of information itself isn't all that exciting, but it does enable you to trick Quicken into reprinting a check. All you need do is change a check's number to asterisks. Quicken then assumes that the check is one you want to print and that you created it on the Write Checks screen. To print the check after you have changed the number to asterisks, you follow the steps described earlier for printing a check.

# Chapter Summary

This chapter described the basics of using another of Quicken's major time-saving features—the Write/Print Checks tool. These basics include the components of the Write Checks screen; how to use the write checks screen to record and postdate checks; and how to review, edit, and print checks. The next chapter describes the three sets of tools you can use to make using the Write Checks option even easier to use.

# 7

# Making Check Writing Easier

T he basic features of the **Write/Print Checks** option described in the preceding chapter make writing and printing checks with Quicken fast and easy. You can write checks faster and more easily if you use three additional Write Checks menu options:

    Edit
    Quick Entry
    Activities

This chapter describes how you can use each of these options. If you have worked with the Register screen's Edit, Quick Entry, and Activities menus, you will recognize that the corresponding Write Checks menus work similarly. In fact, the only real difference between working with these options in the Register screen or working with them on the Write/Print Checks screen is that the screens are different. For this reason, if you already are familiar with these menus, you might want to skim this chapter. (The one Write Checks menu option not yet discussed, **Reports**, accesses the same menu as the **Reports** option on the Main menu and is described in Chapter 13.)

## Using the Edit Menu Tools

The Edit menu, shown in figure 7.1, provides you with nine options. Each Edit menu option is described in the following sections. Essentially, all nine options enable you to modify the unprinted checks.

**133**

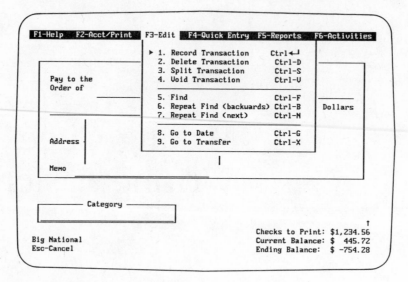

*Fig. 7.1. The Edit menu provides you with nine options.*

# Recording and Deleting Checks

The **Record Transaction** option records (saves) checks in the register and on your hard or floppy disk. You also can record checks by pressing Ctrl-Enter or F10.

The **Delete Transaction** option removes the check displayed on the Write Checks screen from the register and from your hard or floppy disk. You also can use the **Delete Transaction** option to erase information in the Write Checks screen's fields if you have not yet recorded the check. When you select **Delete Transaction** (or press Ctrl-D), Quicken asks you to confirm that you want to delete the transaction (see fig. 7.2).

To delete the check, select the first option, **Delete transaction**. If you change your mind, select **Do not delete** or press Esc.

# Using Split Transactions

The Write Checks screen provides a field for recording the category into which a check fits. For example, a check written to the power company might be described as belonging in the Utilities category. A check written to pay for office supplies might belong in the Supplies category. Many transactions, however, do not fit into one category. When you need to

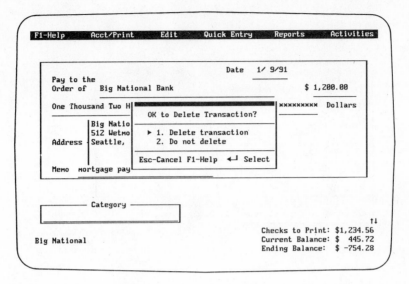

*Fig. 7.2. The* OK to Delete Transaction *prompt.*

break a check down into more than one category, use the **Split Transaction** option from the Edit menu. The **Split Transaction** option provides additional category fields and more space to describe and document a check.

To split a transaction, follow this procedure:

1. Press F3 to display the Edit menu and select **Split Transaction** (or press Ctrl-S). The Split Transaction screen appears (see fig. 7.3).

2. Enter the category name in the Category field. You can use the Category field on the Split Transaction screen in the same way as the Category field on the Write Checks screen. You also can use the Category field to record transfers. Thirty lines are available on the Split Transaction screen for descriptions or categories.

   *Note:* Quicken provides predefined home and business categories. The home category list provides descriptions for most general household expenses, and the business category list includes general business income and expense categories. To access these categories, press Ctrl-C from either the Write/Print Checks or the Register screen.

3. (Optional) To move the cursor to the Description field, press Enter or Tab. Type a description of the category or the amount. The Description field provides a 27-character space you can use to

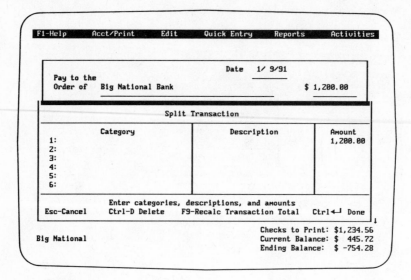

*Fig. 7.3. The Split Transaction screen.*

describe a transaction, to explain why you selected a category, or to explain how you calculated the check amount.

4. Press Enter or Tab to move the cursor to the Amount field. You can use the Amount field in two ways, depending on whether you select **Split Transaction** before or after you enter the amount on the Write Checks screen.

If you select **Split Transaction** before you enter anything in the Amount field on the Write Checks screen, Quicken adds together each of the amounts you enter in the Amount field on the Split Transaction screen. Quicken then puts that total in the Amount field on the Write Checks screen.

If you select **Split Transaction** after you have entered an amount on the Write Checks screen, Quicken shows the amount in the first Amount field on the Split Transaction screen. If you then enter a number in the first Amount field on the Split Transaction screen, Quicken calculates the difference between the Write Checks screen amount and the new amount you have entered and places this difference in the second Amount field on the Split Transaction screen.

5. Press Enter or Tab to move to the next line of the Split Transaction screen. Repeat steps 2, 3, and 4 for each category and amount combination that you want to record. You can record up to 30 category

and amount combinations. Figure 7.4 shows a completed Split Transaction screen.

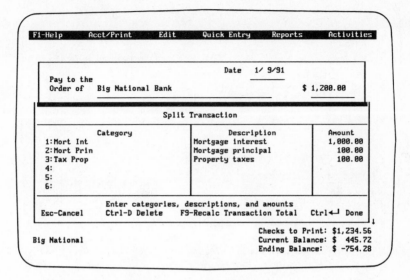

```
 F1-Help      Acct/Print     Edit      Quick Entry     Reports      Activities

                                    Date    1/ 9/91
      Pay to the
      Order of   Big National Bank                          $ 1,200.00

                              Split Transaction

              Category                  Description            Amount
      1:Mort Int               Mortgage interest             1,000.00
      2:Mort Prin              Mortgage principal              100.00
      3:Tax Prop               Property taxes                  100.00
      4:
      5:
      6:

                  Enter categories, descriptions, and amounts
      Esc-Cancel    Ctrl-D Delete    F9-Recalc Transaction Total   Ctrl↵ Done

                                    Checks to Print: $1,234.56
      Big National                  Current Balance: $  445.72
                                    Ending Balance:  $ -754.28
```

***Fig. 7.4.*** *A completed Split Transaction screen.*

*Note:* If you use all 30 of the split transaction Amount fields, Quicken has nowhere to make the Write Checks screen amount equal to the total Split Transaction amount. You must adjust manually the Write Checks screen amount or one of the Split Transaction screen amounts. You also can press F9 to total the Amount fields on the Split Transaction screen and to insert that total into the Amount field on the Write Checks screen.

6. Press Ctrl-Enter or F10 to leave the Split Transaction screen and return to the Write Checks screen.

7. After making your changes on the Split Transaction screen, you are prompted to record the transaction. Press 1 to record the transaction; press 2 not to record the transaction. Quicken indicates a split transaction by displaying the word SPLIT below the Category field (see fig. 7.5).

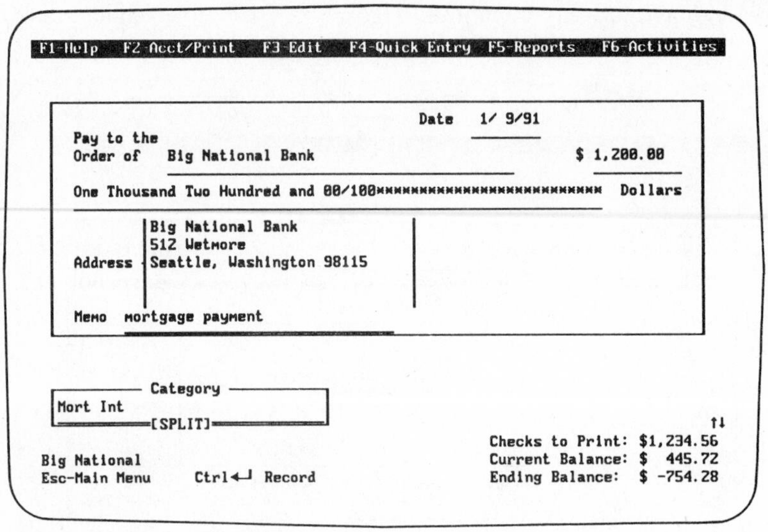

```
F1-Help  F2-Acct/Print  F3-Edit  F4-Quick Entry  F5-Reports  F6-Activities

                                    Date   1/ 9/91
        Pay to the
        Order of   Big National Bank                      $ 1,200.00

        One Thousand Two Hundred and 00/100****************************  Dollars

                   Big National Bank
                   512 Wetmore
        Address ─ Seattle, Washington 98115

        Memo   mortgage payment


              ── Category ──
        Mort Int
        ─────────[SPLIT]─────────                                   ↑↓
                                        Checks to Print: $1,234.56
        Big National                    Current Balance: $  445.72
        Esc-Main Menu     Ctrl↵ Record  Ending Balance:  $ -754.28
```

**Fig. 7.5.** *Quicken identifies a split transaction with the word* SPLIT *below the* Category *field on the Write Checks screen.*

*CPA Tip*

If you use check forms with vouchers and enter individual invoices and invoice amounts on the Split Transaction screen, Quicken prints this information on the voucher. Vendors then can record your payments correctly, and you no longer have to spend time trying to explain which invoice a check pays. Remember that there is room on the voucher only for the first 15 lines of the Split Transaction screen. If you happen to use all 30 lines of the Split Transaction screen, only half of your split transaction detail appears.

# Voiding Checks

Just as you can void transactions in the register, you also can void unprinted checks. You may void a check that, after entering, you decide not to pay but still want to keep records for. Voiding a check means you keep a record of the fact that you wrote a check, but didn't actually send the check. To void unprinted checks, follow this procedure:

1. Select the **Void Transaction** option from the Edit menu (or press Ctrl-V) while the check you want to void is displayed. Quicken displays the register with the recently voided transaction highlighted.

2. To complete the voiding process, press Ctrl-Enter.

3. Press Ctrl-W to return to the Write Checks screen.

# Using the Find Options

The Edit menu provides three Find options: **Find**, **Repeat Find (backwards)** and **Repeat Find (next)**. These Find options enable you to search rapidly through checks you have created (but have not printed) with the Write Checks screen.

## Finding Exact Matches

One way to search through unprinted checks is to use an exact match. An exact match means you look for a check that has a payee, the amount, the category, or some other piece of check information exactly equal to what you want. The amount you are looking for is called a *search argument*.

To search through checks you have created but have not printed, follow these steps:

1. Press F3 to display the Edit menu and select the **Find** option (or press Ctrl-F). Quicken displays the Transaction to Find screen shown in figure 7.6.

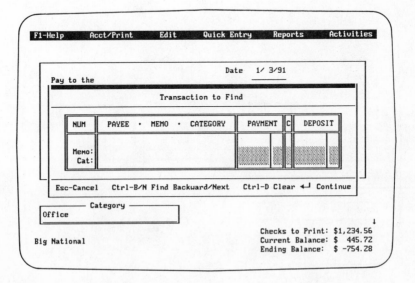

**Fig. 7.6.** *The Transaction to Find screen.*

2. Perform one or more of the following searches:

   (Optional) To search for checks equal to a specific amount, enter the amount in the Payment field. Quicken searches through the unprinted checks for the amount you entered. The amount you are looking for is called the search argument.

   (Optional) To search through the register for checks with a specific entry in the Payee field, enter the payee entry of the check you are seeking in the Payee field.

   (Optional) To search for unprinted checks with a specific Memo field entry, enter the memo entry of the check you are seeking in the Memo field.

   **Note:** Do not enter an amount in the Num, C, or Deposit fields. Although the Num, C, and Deposit fields appear on the Transaction to Find screen, they do not appear on the Write Checks screen. Therefore, you cannot use the Num, C, or Deposit fields to find checks created with the Write Checks screen.

3. After you enter your search arguments, press Ctrl-Enter or F10. Alternatively, press Enter when the cursor is on the C field.

   Quicken asks in which direction you want to search by displaying the screen shown in figure 7.7. You have two options: **Find backwards** and **Find next**. **Find backwards** (Ctrl-B) searches through

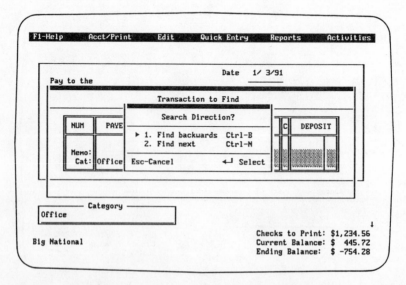

**Fig.** 7.7. *Quicken asks whether you want to search through checks dated before or after the currently selected transaction.*

transactions dated earlier than the transaction currently selected on the Register screen. **Find next** (Ctrl-N) searches through transactions dated later than the transaction currently selected on the Register screen.

4. Select **Find backwards** or **Find next**.

Quicken searches for the exact words that you type. For example, if you enter 75 in the Payment field, Quicken searches for checks equal to $75.00. If you enter *mortgage* in the Memo field, Quicken looks for checks with *mortgage* in that field. Because the case of the letters does not matter, *Mortgage*, *MORTGAGE*, and *mortgage* are all exact matches from Quicken's perspective. If the Memo field reads *May mortgage*, however, Quicken does not find the check.

If Quicken finds a check that matches your search argument, Quicken displays the check on the Write Checks screen. If Quicken does not find a check that matches your search argument, the program displays the message No matching transactions were found (see fig. 7.8).

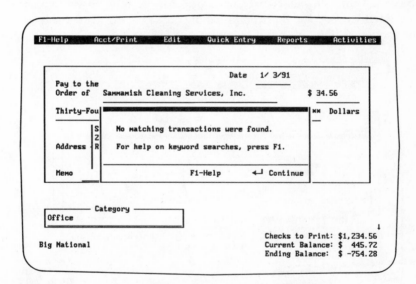

**Fig. 7.8.** *The* No matching transactions were found *message.*

# Finding Key Word Matches

Key-word matches enable you to search based on a field including or excluding certain letters, characters, or series of characters. Key-word matches use three special characters: periods, question marks, and tildes (~). Periods act as wild card indicators that can represent any character, group of characters, or even no character. The question mark can represent any one character. The tilde character identifies a word, character, or group of characters that you want to exclude from your search.

# Combining Exact Matches and Key Word Matches

You can search by using more than one exact match or key-word search argument. Figure 7.9, for example, shows the Transaction to Find screen filled to search for checks using *big national* in the Payee field and *mortgage* in the Memo field. The same tricks and techniques that work for searching through your register work for searching through your unprinted checks. For more information on key-word matches, refer to the section "Using Key Word Matches" in Chapter 5.

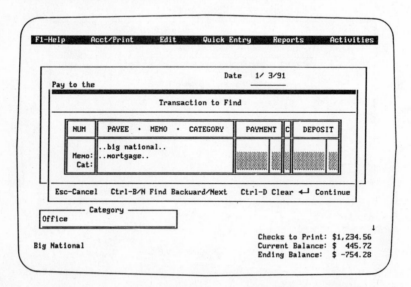

**Fig. 7.9.** *Using key-word matches on the Transaction to Find screen.*

If you use more than one match test, Quicken locates only those checks that meet all the tests. Given the Transaction to Find screen shown in figure 7.9, Quicken does not locate checks with the phrase *big national* in the Payee field unless the word *mortgage* is in the Memo field and vice versa.

## Repeating a Search

When executing a Find operation, Quicken selects the first check that matches the search arguments you entered. If you were precise in specifying the exact match or key-word match, the first check Quicken finds may be the one you want. Because other times the first check Quicken finds will not be the one you want, however, Quicken gives you two additional Find options: **Repeat Find (backwards)** and **Repeat Find (next)**. **Repeat Find (backwards)** executes the find operation already specified on the Transaction to Find screen—**Repeat Find (backwards)** searches through checks dated before the currently displayed check. Similarly, **Repeat Find (next)** executes the find operation already specified on the Transaction to Find screen. **Repeat Find (next)** searches through checks dated after the displayed check.

# Using the Go To Date Option

To search for a specific day's transactions, use the **Go to Date** option or press Ctrl-G. Specify the date you want to use as the basis for your search on the Go to Date screen, shown in figure 7.10.

Initially, Quicken displays the current system date on the Go to Date screen. To specify a date for your search, type the date you want over the default date. You also can use the + and − keys to move the date forward or backward one day at a time.

After you specify a date and press Enter, Quicken finds and displays the first check with the date you entered. If no check with the date you entered is found, Quicken displays the check with the date closest to the date you entered.

Because Quicken arranges checks by the check date, you do not need to specify a search direction when using the **Go to Date** option. By comparing the date on the currently displayed check to the date you enter, Quicken determines which direction to search. If the date you want to search for is before the date on the current check, Quicken looks through the previous checks. If the date you want to search for is after the date on

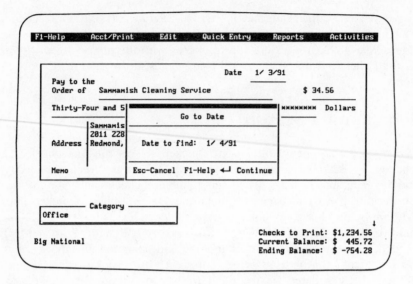

*Fig. 7.10. Quicken can search through checks using a date.*

the current check, Quicken looks through checks dated after the current check.

# Using the Go To Transfer Option

You can select the **Go to Transfer** option (Ctrl-X) if you want to go to the transfer transaction related to the currently displayed check. If you entered the transfer account in the Category field, recorded the check, and then executed the **Go to Transfer** option, Quicken displays the Account register showing the corresponding transaction. Pressing Ctrl-X again returns you to the original check register.

In almost every case, the reason you will be entering an account here is because you're transferring money from your checking account to some other bank account by writing a check. To review account transfers, see Chapters 4 and 5.

# Using the Quick Entry Menu Tools

To speed up the check-writing process, Quicken's Quick Entry menu provides several options (see fig. 7.11).

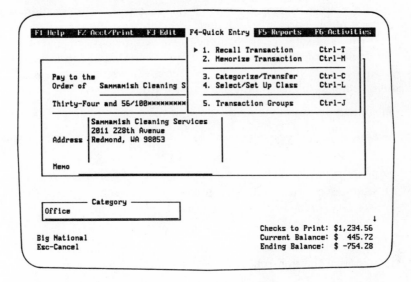

**Fig. 7.11.** *The Quick Entry menu provides tools for speeding up check writing.*

The following paragraphs describe how you can use the **Recall Transaction** and **Memorize Transaction** options to store and reuse recurring transactions, how you can use the **Categorize/Transfer** option, and how you can use the **Transaction Groups** option to store and reuse whole sets of transactions. The **Select/Set Up Class** option is discussed in Chapter 10.

# Memorizing Transactions

Many of the checks you write probably are similar from week to week and month to month. For your household, you may write a mortgage check, a car loan check, a utility bill check, and so on. For your business, you may write weekly payroll checks to employees and monthly checks to major vendors. Because checks often are similar, Quicken enables you to store check information in a special list called the Memorized Transactions List. Instead of re-entering the same information, you can reuse transaction information. The **Memorize Transaction** option is particularly valuable if you address checks, because you do not have to re-enter the payee's address every time you write a check.

If you have read Chapter 5, you already know about using memorized transactions in the register. **Memorize Transaction** works similarly on the Write Checks screen. Accordingly, if you feel well-versed in the mechanics of memorized transactions, skip or skim the next few paragraphs. The only substantive difference between memorized transactions for the register and memorized transactions for unprinted checks is that if you memorize an unprinted check, Quicken memorizes the address information. (Address information doesn't appear in the register.)

To memorize a transaction, follow these steps:

1. Display the check you want to memorize on the Write Checks screen (see fig. 7.12).

2. Press F4 to display the Quick Entry menu, and then select the **Memorize Transaction** option. Alternatively, press Ctrl-M. Quicken alerts you that the marked information is about to be memorized (see fig. 7.13).

3. To complete the memorization process, press Enter. Quicken saves a copy of the transaction in the Memorized Transactions List.

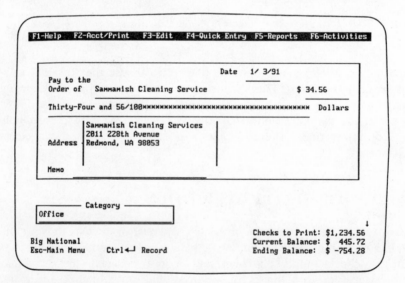

*Fig. 7.12. You might decide to memorize a monthly house cleaning or janitorial check.*

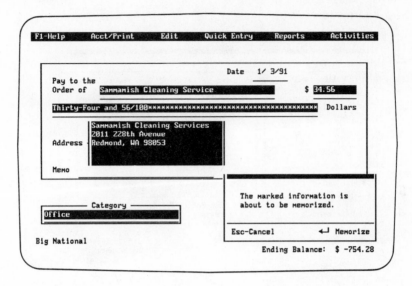

**Fig. 7.13.** *Quicken tells you that the marked information is about to be memorized.*

## Recalling a Transaction

Selecting **Recall Transaction** (Ctrl-T) enables you to complete the Write Checks screen using information from memorized transactions. Suppose that you use the **Memorize Transaction** option to memorize the monthly cleaning payment shown in figure 7.12. When you need to pay Sammamish Cleaning Services again, select **Recall Transaction** from the Quick Entry menu or press Ctrl-T. Either approach displays the Memorized Transactions List shown in figure 7.14. The Memorized Transactions List screen shows all memorized transactions. You only want to recall, however, those transactions that show Chk in their Type column. Chk indicates that the transaction was memorized from the Write Checks screen. Chk transactions will include information that appears only on the Write Checks screen, such as the address data and the extra message line.

Figure 7.14 shows some of the information saved as part of the **Memorize Transaction** operation. The address information and message are also saved, but the address and message do not show on the Memorized Transactions List.

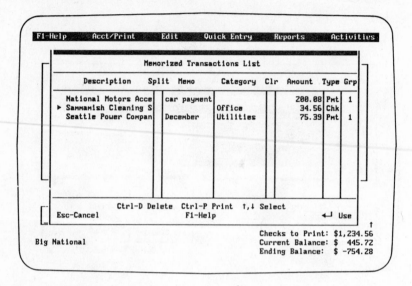

**Fig. 7.14.** *The Memorized Transactions List.*

The payee name is in the `Description` field, the memo is in the `Memo` field, the category name is in the `Category` field, and the check amount is in the `Amount` field. If you split a check transaction, an S appears in the `Split` field. Quicken also places the abbreviation Chk in the `Type` field to identify the transaction as a check. The `Grp` field indicates whether the memorized transaction is part of a group of transactions. Transaction groups are described later in the chapter.

To use (or recall) a memorized transaction, take the following steps:

1. If you have not done so already, press F4 to display the Quick Entry menu and select the **Recall Transaction** option. Alternatively, press Ctrl-T. Quicken displays the Memorized Transactions List (see fig. 7.14).

2. Use the up- and down-arrow keys to move the selection triangle to the left of the `Description` field of the check you want to write.

3. Press Enter. Quicken uses the memorized transaction to fill the Write Checks screen.

4. Edit the information from the memorized transaction so that the information correctly reflects the check you want to write.

5. To record the check, press Ctrl-Enter. Quicken records the check transaction in the register.

# Deleting Memorized Transactions

At some point, the original reasons you had for memorizing a transaction might no longer apply. Eventually, for example, you may pay off the mortgage or a car loan, children may outgrow the need for day care, or you may choose to stop spending money on some item such as club dues or cable television.

You can use the **Recall Transaction** option to delete memorized transactions from the Memorized Transactions List.

To delete a transaction from the list, follow these steps:

1. Press F4 to display the Quick Entry menu and select the **Recall Transaction** option (or press Ctrl-T). Quicken displays the Memorized Transactions List (see fig. 7.14).

2. Use the up- and down-arrow keys to highlight the transaction you want to delete.

3. After you highlight the transaction you want to delete, press Ctrl-D. Quicken alerts you that you are about to delete a memorized transaction (see fig. 7.15).

4. To delete the memorized transaction, press Enter. If you do not want to delete the memorized transaction, press Esc.

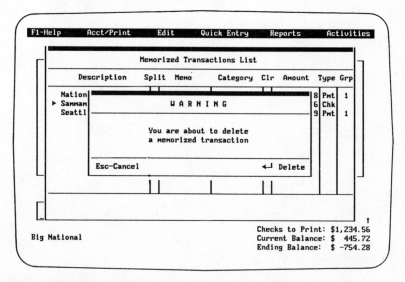

**Fig. 7.15.** *The* You are about to delete a memorized transaction *message.*

# Listing Memorized Transactions

Quicken enables you to print lists of memorized transactions. Assuming you entered payee addresses, a printed list of memorized transactions can act as a directory of the people and businesses to whom you write checks.

To print a list of memorized transactions, follow these steps:

1. Press F4 to display the Quick Entry menu and then select the **Recall Transaction** option (or press Ctrl-T). Quicken displays the Memorized Transactions List screen (see fig. 7.14).

2. Press Ctrl-P. Quicken displays the Print Memorized Transactions List screen, which is similar to the Printed Checks screen described in the preceding chapter. Specify the printer setting you want to use to print the report.

3. Indicate the printer you want to use. Press Enter, and Quicken prints the list (see fig. 7.16).

```
                            Memorized Transactions List
QDATA                                                                    Page 1
1/ 4/91

        Payee/Memo/Category          Clr    Type        Amount
----------------------------------    ---   -------   -------------

Big National Bank                            Check       -1,200.00
  mortgage payment

           ADDRESS
Big National Bank
512 Wetmore
Seattle, Washington 98115


                          SPLITS
Mort Int                  Mortgage interest       -1,000.00
Mort Prin                 Mortgage principal        -100.00
Tax Prop                  Property taxes            -100.00

Sammamish Cleaning Service           Check          -34.56

Office

           ADDRESS
Sammamish Cleaning Services
2011 228th Avenue
Redmond, WA 98053
```

*Fig. 7.16. The printed Memorized Transactions List.*

> Consider as candidates for the Memorized Transactions List each of the checks you regularly write using Quicken: rent, house payment, utility payment, school loans, and so on. Using the **Memorized Transaction** option saves you time you otherwise would spend typing, finding addresses, and describing checks.

*CPA Tip*

# Using the Categorize/Transfer Option

With the **Categorize/Transfer** option (Ctrl-C), you can create or retrieve a category. Remember that Quicken provides predefined home and business categories. (Creating new categories is discussed in Chapter 10.)

To find and use a predefined category, follow this process:

1. Press F4 to display the Quick Entry menu and select the **Categorize/Transfer** option (or press Ctrl-C). Quicken displays the Category and Transfer List screen, which lists each of the predefined categories and any account you have created (see fig. 7.17). The accounts are listed at the end of the Category and Transfer List.

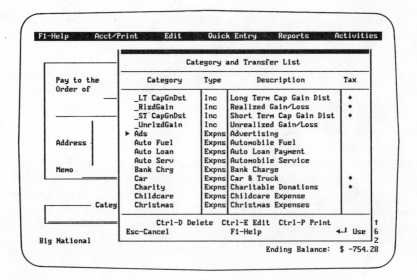

*Fig. 7.17. The Category and Transfer List screen.*

2. Use the up- and down-arrow keys to select the category or account you want to use and then press Enter. Quicken retrieves the category or account name from the list and puts the name in the Category field.

You also can use the PgUp, PgDn, Home, and End keys to move quickly through long lists of categories. Pressing PgUp displays the preceding page of categories in the list, pressing PgDn displays the next page of categories in the list, pressing Home displays the first page of categories, and pressing End displays the last page of categories.

# Setting Up a Transaction Group

The capability to recall a single memorized check saves time, but Quicken provides you with another option: you can recall sets of memorized transactions called *transaction groups*. Transaction groups enable you to recall several memorized checks at the same time. Rather than repeatedly using **Recall Transaction** to retrieve checks from the Memorized Transactions List, you can recall an entire group of checks in one step.

The first step to using a transaction group is creating a transaction group. To create a transaction group, follow these steps:

1. Follow the steps described earlier (in the "Memorizing Transactions" section) to memorize the transactions you want to include in a transaction group.

2. Press F4 to display the Quick Entry menu and select the **Transaction Groups** option (or press Ctrl-J). Quicken displays the Select Transaction Group to Execute screen, as shown in figure 7.18.

3. Use the up- and down-arrow keys to mark the first unused transaction group, and then press Enter. Quicken displays the Describe Group screen (see fig. 7.19). If you are defining your first transaction group, mark Group 1 and press Enter. If you previously have defined a transaction group, use Group 2. (Group 1 was used for figures in Chapter 5, so Group 2 will be used here.) Quicken provides twelve empty transaction groups.

4. Enter a name or description for the transaction group. You can use a maximum of 20 characters to describe the group.

5. Press Enter or Tab to move the cursor to the Account to load before executing field. Enter the account on which the checks should be written. (This causes the appropriate account to be selected before you recall the check transactions in a group. You

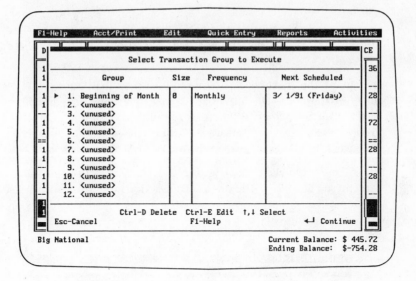

**Fig. 7.18.** *The Select Transaction Group to Execute screen.*

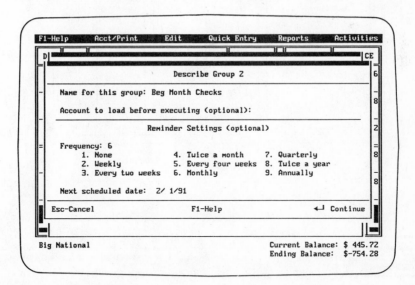

**Fig. 7.19.** *The Describe Group screen.*

don't need this field, obviously, if you're working with only one account.)

6. Press Enter or Tab to move the cursor to the Frequency field. Set the frequency using one of the nine settings shown in figure 7.19:

None, Weekly, Every two weeks, Twice a month, Every four weeks, Monthly, Quarterly, Twice a year, or Annually. Select the frequency you want by typing the number that corresponds with the desired frequency.

7. If you set the frequency to something other than None, you also must set the next scheduled date. (*Note:* The next scheduled date is the date for which Billminder reminds you of the transaction group.) Press Enter or Tab to move the cursor to the Next scheduled date field. Enter the date in the MM/DD/YY format.

8. Press Enter. Quicken displays the Assign Transactions to Group screen (see fig. 7.20). The Assign Transactions to Group screen lists all memorized transactions.

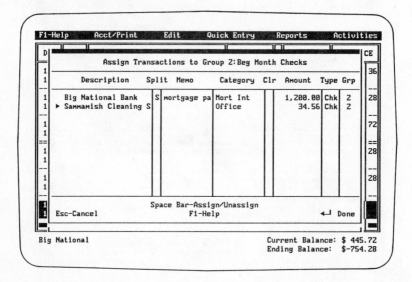

*Fig. 7.20. The Assign Transactions to Group screen.*

9. Use the arrow keys to mark memorized transactions that will be part of the transaction group. When a transaction is marked, press the space bar to assign the transaction to the group. When a transaction has been assigned to a group, the Grp field on the Assign Transactions screen displays the group number. To "unassign" a transaction, press the space bar again while the transaction is highlighted. Figure 7.20 shows memorized transactions selected for Group 2.

10. When you have marked all the memorized transactions that will be part of the transaction group, press Enter to save your work. Quicken displays the Select Transaction Group to Execute screen with the newly defined transaction group listed (see fig. 7.21).

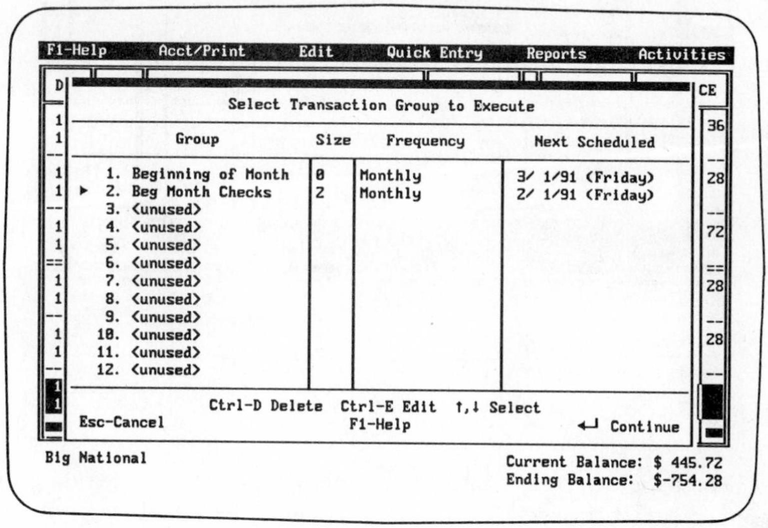

```
F1-Help      Acct/Print      Edit      Quick Entry      Reports      Activities
 D                                                                           CE
 1                       Select Transaction Group to Execute
 1                                                                           36
 1           Group            Size    Frequency           Next Scheduled
 1        1. Beginning of Month  0    Monthly         3/ 1/91 (Friday)       28
 1    ▶   2. Beg Month Checks    2    Monthly         2/ 1/91 (Friday)
         3. <unused>
 1       4. <unused>                                                         72
 1       5. <unused>
==       6. <unused>                                                         ==
 1       7. <unused>                                                         28
 1       8. <unused>
         9. <unused>
 1      10. <unused>                                                         28
 1      11. <unused>
        12. <unused>
            Ctrl-D Delete   Ctrl-E Edit   ↑,↓ Select
    Esc-Cancel                 F1-Help              ↵ Continue

 Big National                                Current Balance: $ 445.72
                                             Ending Balance:  $-754.28
```

*Fig. 7.21. The newly defined transaction group appears on the Select Transaction Group to Execute screen.*

# Executing a Transaction Group

After you create a transaction group of memorized check transactions, you can use the transaction group to recall simultaneously the entire set of memorized checks.

To write a series of checks using a transaction group, follow these steps:

1. Press F4 to display the Quick Entry menu and select the **Transaction Groups** option. Quicken displays the Select Transaction Group to Execute screen (see fig. 7.18).

2. Use the up- and down-arrow keys to move the selection triangle to the left of the Description field of the transaction group you want to use.

3. Press Enter. Quicken prompts you for the Transaction Group Date, as shown in figure 7.22. (Quicken switches to the register when displaying the Transaction Group Date screen.)

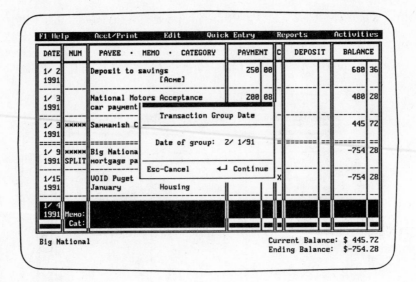

**Fig. 7.22.** *The Transaction Group Date screen.*

4. Enter the date you want shown on checks in the transaction group. Remember that you can use the + and − keys to change the date one day at a time.

5. Press Enter when the Transaction Group Date screen has the correct date. Quicken writes each of the checks and displays the Transaction Group Entered screen shown in figure 7.23. Quicken also moves forward the next scheduled date for the transaction group, using the frequency you specified. (***Note:*** The next scheduled date is the date for which Billminder reminds you of the transaction group.)

6. Edit the information on each of the checks as necessary. To use the Write Checks screen to edit, press Ctrl-W.

# Changing and Deleting Transaction Groups

Because transaction groups segregate your checks into groups you pay together at one time, changes in payment due dates mean you need to change the transaction group. For example, if you refinance your mortgage, the due date might change from the fifth to the fifteenth. If you have

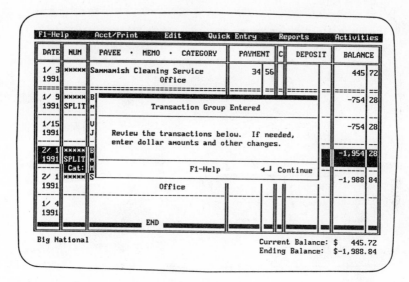

**Fig. 7.23.** *The Transaction Group Entered screen.*

separate transaction groups for checks you write at the beginning of the month and those you write during the middle of the month, you may need to change your transaction groups.

If you want to modify a transaction group, use the **Transaction Groups** option on the Quick Entry menu and select a transaction group. Access the Describe Group and Assign Transactions to Group screens shown in figures 7.19 and 7.20. Make the required changes on the appropriate screen and press Enter to continue to the next screen.

If you want to delete a transaction group, select the **Transaction Groups** option from the Quick Entry menu. Use the arrow keys to mark the group you want to delete and then press Ctrl-D. Quicken displays a message alerting you that the marked transaction group is about to be deleted. To delete the transaction group, press Enter. Press Esc if you do not want to delete the transaction group.

# Using the Activities Menu

The Write/Checks Activities menu provides access to other Quicken tools you may need when writing checks. The Write Checks Activities menu has five options, as shown in figure 7.24.

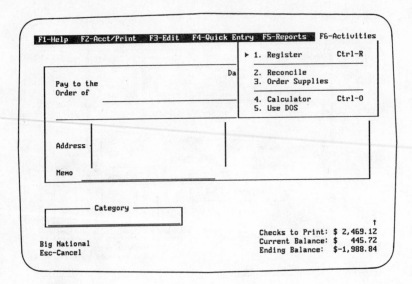

**Fig. 7.24.** *The Write Checks Activities menu.*

Choosing **Register** accesses the Register screen and menu options, just as the **Register** option on Quicken's Main menu does. The register is described in Chapters 4 and 5.

Selecting **Reconcile** accesses the Reconciliation screen and options, just as the **Reconcile** option on Quicken's Main menu does. Reconciling is described in Chapter 8.

Selecting **Order Supplies** accesses the Print Supply Order Form screen, shown in figure 7.25. You print this three-page order form to purchase supplies, such as check forms and envelopes, from Intuit, the manufacturer of Quicken. The supply order form is similar to the order form that Intuit provides in the Quicken package.

Choosing **Calculator** accesses the on-line, 10-key calculator that Quicken provides (see fig. 7.26). Chapter 2 describes the on-line calculator in detail.

Selecting **Use DOS** calls up DOS and displays the DOS prompt:

```
To return to Quicken, type EXIT.
Microsoft® MS-DOS® Version 3.30
(C) Copyright Microsoft Corp 1981-1987
C:\QUICKEN3>
```

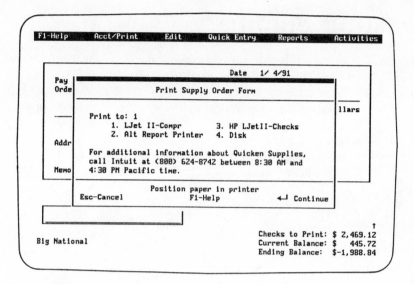

**Fig. 7.25.** *The Print Supply Order Form screen.*

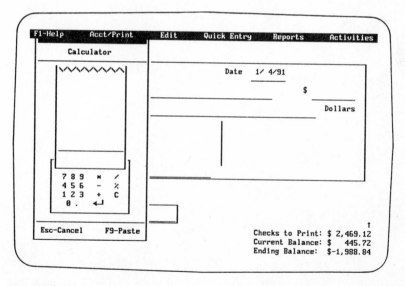

**Fig. 7.26.** *The on-line calculator.*

The **Use DOS** feature is handy when you want to execute DOS commands before leaving Quicken. For example, you may want to format a disk to make a backup copy of an account. To return to Quicken from DOS, type *exit* at the C> prompt.

# Chapter Summary

This chapter described the details of using the three sets of Write Checks menu options not covered in the preceding chapter: the Edit, Quick Entry, and Activities menus. The options on these three menus make using the Write Checks screen even easier and faster. The Edit menu options make recording, editing, and deleting checks easier; the Quick Entry menu options speed the process of using Quicken to print checks; and the Activities menu options access other Quicken and system features you may need while writing and printing checks.

# 8

# Reconciling Your
# Bank Account

Regularly reconciling your bank account is one of the most important steps you can take to protect your cash and the accuracy and reliability of your financial records. But most people probably don't do it—except out of a sense of guilt or frustration. The work is tedious, and usually aggravating as you search, often futilely, for the transaction that will explain the difference between the bank's records and your personal records. Fortunately, Quicken provides a fast and easy method of reconciliation. This chapter describes the steps for reconciling your accounts in Quicken, printing and using reconciliation reports and correcting and catching reconciliation errors.

## Reviewing the Reconciliation Process

Reconciling your bank account is not difficult. You probably already understand the mechanics of the reconciliation process. For those readers who are a bit rusty with the process, however, the next few paragraphs briefly describe how reconciliation works.

To reconcile a bank account, you perform three basic steps:

1. Review the bank statement for new transactions and errors. You want to verify that you have recorded each transaction correctly.

2. Determine which transactions have not been recorded by the bank, or cleared, and total these transactions.

3. Verify that the difference between the check register balance and the bank balance equals the total of the cleared transactions. If it doesn't, you need to repeat steps 1 and 2.

*Note:* If you still find the process confusing, examine your monthly bank statement. The back of your current bank statement probably explains the whole process step-by-step.

## Reviewing the Bank Statement

The first step in reconciling your account is to review the bank statement. You first should find any new transactions that the bank recorded and that you now need to record. These transactions might include bank service fees, overdraft charges, and interest income. You need to record these transactions in your register before proceeding further with the reconciliation.

For each transaction, confirm that the checking account transaction recorded in your register and on your bank statement are the same amount. If you find a transaction not recorded in both places for the same amount, review the discrepancy and identify which transaction is incorrect.

*CPA Tip*

Carefully review each canceled check for authenticity. If a check forger successfully draws a check on your account, you can discover the forgery by reviewing canceled checks. As Chapter 19 explains, you need to find such forgeries if you hope to recover the money.

## Checking Cleared Transactions

The second step in checking account reconciliation is to calculate the total dollar value of those transactions that have not cleared the bank. By adding up any checks that have not cleared (usually called *outstanding checks*) and also any deposits (usually called *deposits in transit*), you calculate an amount that represents the logical difference between the bank's records and your records.

Usually, the actual mechanics of this step go something like this: you look through your bank statement to identify checks and deposits that have cleared and then mark cleared transactions in the register. After you have marked all the cleared transactions in the register, it's a simple matter to add up all the transactions that have not cleared.

## Verifying that Balances Correspond

The final step is a quick one: you verify that the difference between the check register balance and the bank statement balance is the total of the transactions that haven't cleared. If you have correctly performed steps 1 and 2 in the reconciliation process, the two amounts should differ by the total of the transactions that haven't cleared. If the two amounts don't differ by precisely this amount, you must repeat steps 1 and 2 until you locate and correct the error.

# Reconciling Your Account with Quicken

Quicken makes reconciling your bank account easier by automating the steps and doing the arithmetic. To reconcile your account, follow these steps:

1. Select **Reconcile** from the Activities menu on the Write Checks or Register screen. Quicken then displays the screen shown in figure 8.1.

2. In the Bank Statement Opening Balance field, type the bank statement balance shown at the start of the period your statement covers, if the balance is different from the one shown. This number will appear on your bank statement.

3. Press Enter or Tab to move the cursor to the Bank Statement Ending Balance field and type the bank statement balance shown at the end of the period your bank statement covers. This number will appear on your bank statement.

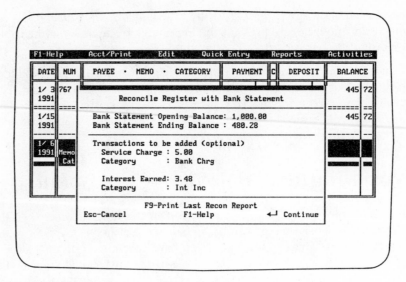

*Fig. 8.1. The Reconcile Register with Bank Statement screen.*

4. Press Enter or Tab to move the cursor to the Service Charge field. If you have not recorded monthly service fees, record them now by entering the appropriate amount in the Service Charge field.

5. (Optional) Press Enter or Tab to move the cursor to the Service Charge Category field. If you entered an amount in the Service Charge field and want to assign the charge to a category, enter the appropriate category name in the Service Charge Category field. (Remember that you can access the Category and Transfer List screen by pressing Ctrl-C.)

6. Press Enter or Tab to move the cursor to the Interest Earned field. If you have not recorded monthly interest income on the account, record it now by entering the appropriate amount in the Interest Earned field.

7. (Optional) Press Enter or Tab to move the cursor to the Interest Earned Category field. If you entered an amount in the Interest Earned field and want to assign the income to a category, enter the appropriate category name here.

8. Press Enter to access the Transaction List screen, which shows each checking account transaction (see fig. 8.2).

```
 F1-Help      Acct/Print      Edit      Quick Entry      Reports      Activities

 NUM  │C│   AMOUNT   │  DATE  │      PAYEE       │       MEMO
                5.75   1/ 2/91  Interest           October
      │*│      3.48   1/ 6/91  Interest Earned
            -250.00   1/ 2/91  Deposit to savings
      │*│     -5.00   1/ 6/91  Service Charge
 765        -75.39    1/ 2/91  Seattle Power Company  December
 766       -200.08    1/ 3/91  National Motors Accept  car payment
 767        -34.56    1/ 3/91  Sammamish Cleaning Ser

 ■ To Mark Cleared Items, press Space Bar  ■ To Add or Change Items, press F9

                       RECONCILIATION SUMMARY
           Items You Have Marked Cleared (*)
          ------------------------------------  Cleared (X,*) Balance      998.48
             1    Checks, Debits        -5.00   Bank Statement Balance     480.28
             1    Deposits, Credits      3.48   Difference                 518.20

 F1-Help            F8-Mark Range        F9-View as Register       Ctrl F10-Done
```

*Fig. 8.2. Checking account transactions shown in a list.*

9. Mark checks and deposits that have cleared, or been recorded by, the bank. To mark an item as cleared, use the up- and down-arrow keys to move the selection triangle to the left of the transaction you want to mark. When the triangle is in place, press the space bar. Quicken enters an asterisk in the cleared column.

   If you want to mark a range of transactions as cleared, press F8. Quicken displays the Mark Range of Check Numbers as Cleared screen (see fig. 8.3). You use this screen to specify that all the transactions with check numbers within the indicated range should be marked as cleared. As you mark transactions, the Transactions List screen includes the number and dollar amount of the check and deposit transactions you marked as cleared, the cleared transaction total, the ending balance, and the difference between the two. You are finished with the reconciliation when the difference equals zero.

10. (Optional) To correct transactions that were entered incorrectly in your register, press F9 to redisplay the same information in an abbreviated form of the standard register. Edit the transactions in the register in the usual manner. To change the displayed screen back to the abbreviated transaction list, press F9 again. (Chapter 5 describes how to use the Quicken register.)

    Figure 8.4 shows sample transactions as they appear in the register.

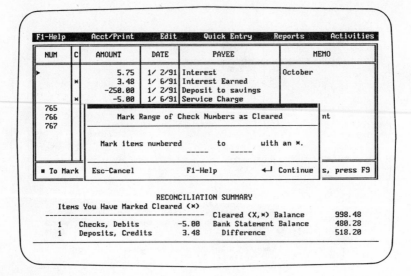

**Fig. 8.3.** *The Mark Range of Check Numbers as Cleared screen.*

```
F1-Help  F2-Acct/Print  F3-Edit  F4-Quick Entry  F5-Reports  F6-Activities
┌────┬────┬─────────────────────────┬─────────┬─┬─────────┬─────────┐
│DATE│NUM │PAYEE · MEMO · CATEGORY   │ PAYMENT │C│ DEPOSIT │ BALANCE │
├────┼────┼─────────────────────────┼─────────┼─┼─────────┼─────────┤
│1/ 2│    │Interest                 │         │ │    5 75 │  930 36 │
│1991│Memo:│October                 │         │ │         │         │
│    │Cat:│Int Inc                  │         │ │         │         │
│1/ 2│    │Deposit to savings       │  250 00 │ │         │  680 36 │
│1991│    │          [Acme]         │         │ │         │         │
│1/ 3│766 │National Motors Acceptance│ 200 08 │ │         │  480 28 │
│1991│    │car payment              │         │ │         │         │
│1/ 3│767 │Sammamish Cleaning Service│  34 56 │ │         │  445 72 │
│1991│    │          Office         │         │ │         │         │
└────┴────┴─────────────────────────┴─────────┴─┴─────────┴─────────┘
                    RECONCILIATION SUMMARY
        Items You Have Marked Cleared (*)
        ---------------------------------   Cleared (X,*) Balance   998.48
            1    Checks, Debits     -5.00    Bank Statement Balance  480.28
            1    Deposits, Credits   3.48    Difference              518.20

Esc-Main Menu     F8-Mark Range      F9-View as List     Ctrl F10-Done
```

**Fig. 8.4.** *Checking account transactions shown in the register.*

11. When the difference between the cleared balance and the bank statement balance is zero, press Ctrl-End to indicate that you are finished with the reconciliation. When you press Ctrl-End, Quicken

changes each asterisk in the C field to an X, and asks whether you want to print a reconciliation report (see fig. 8.5).

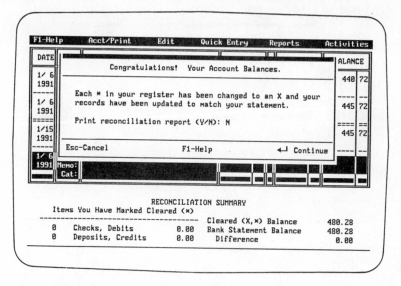

**Fig. 8.5.** *Quicken congratulates you when your account balances.*

**Note:** If you understand double-entry bookkeeping, you probably recognize that Quicken uses the labels Debit and Credit incorrectly from your perspective. Do not be confused by this usage. The screen uses the terms from the bank's perspective to further help people who do not understand double-entry bookkeeping.

# Printing Reconciliation Reports

Many people like to keep printed records of their reconciliations. Printed copies of the reconciliation report show how you reconciled your records with the bank, indicate which checks and deposits are still outstanding, and show which transactions cleared the bank in a given month—information that can be very helpful if you subsequently discover the bank has made an error or you have made a reconciliation error.

To print a reconciliation report, follow these steps:

1. Press Y (from the screen shown in figure 8.5) if you want to print a reconciliation report. Quicken displays the Print Reconciliation Report screen, shown in figure 8.6.

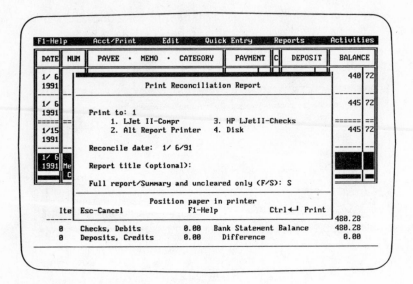

*Fig. 8.6. The Print Reconciliation Report screen.*

2. Complete the Print to field by pressing 1 for printer 1, 2 for printer 2, 3 for printer 3, or 4 for disk.

   If you used printer names on the Printer Settings screen, you see those printer names on the Print Reconciliation Report screen. Figure 8.6 shows, for example, that your first printer is LJetII-Compr.

   If you choose to print to disk an ASCII file, select Disk on the Print Reconciliation Report screen. Quicken then requests three additional pieces of information: the file name, the number of lines per page, and the width (see fig. 8.7). In the File field, enter the name you want Quicken to use for the created ASCII file. If you want to use a data directory different from QUICKEN3, enter the drive and directory you have chosen, such as C:\QUICKEN3\PRNT_TXT. Next, enter the number of lines per page, usually 66. Finally, enter the width of the page (80), unless you are using a condensed mode, which might be 132.

3. Press Enter or Tab to move the cursor to the Reconcile date field, and then enter the date you performed the reconciliation.

4. Press Enter or Tab to move the cursor to the Report title field, and then enter a report title for the reconciliation report. You may want to use the month and year so as to distinguish one report from another.

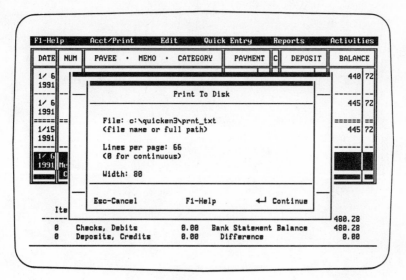

*Fig. 8.7. The Print To Disk screen.*

5. Press Enter or Tab to move the cursor to the Full report/Summary and uncleared only field. This field enables you to choose how much detail shows on your reconciliation report. The default is Summary, because Full includes all the detail on every transaction you mark as cleared. Answer the Full report/Summary and uncleared only field by pressing F for Full or S for Summary.

6. Verify that your printer is turned on and loaded with paper. Press Ctrl-Enter to print the reconciliation report. Quicken warns you if the printer is not ready.

## Reviewing the Reconciliation Report

The printed reconciliation report includes three distinct components: the Reconciliation Summary, the Cleared Transaction Detail, and the Uncleared Transaction Detail. (If you select Summary, only the first and third parts of the reconciliation report print.)

The Reconciliation Summary report, shown in figure 8.8, essentially re-states the Reconciliation Summary shown at the bottom of the abbreviated check register screen. The Reconciliation Summary has two sections:

Bank Statement—Cleared Transactions
Your Records—Uncleared Transactions

```
                                         January Reconcilation
      Big National                                                              Page 1
      1/ 6/91
                                         RECONCILIATION SUMMARY



             BANK STATEMENT -- CLEARED TRANSACTIONS:

                     Previous Balance:                                 1,000.00
                                                                      ---------------
                         Checks and Payments:         4 Items          -530.47
                         Deposits and Other Credits:  2 Items            10.75
                                                                      ---------------
                     Ending Balance of Bank Statement:                   480.28


             YOUR RECORDS -- UNCLEARED TRANSACTIONS:


                     Cleared Balance:                                    480.28
                                                                      ---------------
                         Checks and Payments:         1 Item            -34.56
                         Deposits and Other Credits:  0 Items            0.00
                                                                      ---------------
                     Register Balance as of  1/ 6/91:                    445.72
                                                                      ---------------
                         Checks and Payments:         0 Items            0.00
                         Deposits and Other Credits:  0 Items            0.00
                                                                      ---------------
                     Register Ending Balance:                            445.72
```

**Fig. 8.8.** *The Reconciliation Summary report.*

The first section calculates the ending balance according to the bank statement by subtracting the cleared checks and adding the cleared deposits from the beginning bank balance. The second section calculates the ending register balance by subtracting the outstanding checks and adding the deposits in transit from the ending bank balance.

The Reconciliation Summary report isn't a report you read—rather the report documents how you reconciled the account. For this reason, you don't actually need to spend time reviewing this report—unless, for some reason, you need to go back later and explain to the bank what its balance should have been or go back and see which transactions were outstanding when you reconciled.

The Cleared Transaction Detail report, shown in figure 8.9, shows each of the cleared checks and payment transactions and each of the cleared deposits and other credit transactions you marked with an asterisk as part of the most recent reconciliation. The report does not include transactions you marked as cleared in some prior reconciliation.

```
                              January Reconciliation
Big National                                                              Page 2
1/ 6/91
                              CLEARED TRANSACTION DETAIL


        Date   Num     Payee           Memo          Category    Clr   Amount
        -------- -----  ---------------  ---------------  ---------------  ---  -----------

        Cleared Checks and Payments

        1/ 2/91 765   Seattle Power Co December        Utilities    X      -75.39
        1/ 2/91       Deposit to savin                 [Acme]       X     -250.00
        1/ 3/91 766   National Motors  car payment                 X     -200.08
        1/ 6/91       Service Charge                   Bank Chrg    X       -5.00
                                                                          -----------
        Total Cleared Checks and Payments             4 Items             -530.47


        Cleared Deposits and Other Credits

        1/ 2/91       Interest         October         Int Inc      X        5.75
        1/ 6/91       Interest Earned                  Int Inc      X        5.00
                                                                          -----------
        Total Cleared Deposits and Other Credits      2 Items               10.75

                                                                          ===========
        Total Cleared Transactions                    6 Items             -519.72
```

*Fig. 8.9. The Cleared Transaction Detail report.*

The Cleared Transaction Detail report includes most of the information related to a transaction, including the transaction date, the check or transaction number, the payee name or transaction description, any memo description, and the amount. Checks and payments are displayed as negative amounts because they decrease the account balance. Deposits are displayed as positive amounts because they increase the account balance. Because of space constraints, some of the Payee, Memo, and Category field entries are truncated on the right. The total amount and number of cleared transactions on the Cleared Transaction Detail report support the data shown in the first section of the Reconciliation Summary.

The Uncleared Transaction Detail report, shown in figures 8.10 and 8.11, is identical to the Cleared Transaction Detail report except that the still uncleared transactions for your checking account are summarized. The report is broken down into transactions dated prior to the reconciliation date and transactions dated subsequent to the reconciliation date.

Like the Cleared Transaction Detail report, the Uncleared Transaction Detail report includes most of the information related to a transaction, including the transaction date, the check or transaction number, the payee name or transaction description, any memo description, and the amount. Checks and payments are shown as negative amounts because they decrease the account balance. Deposits are shown as positive amounts because they increase the account balance. The total amount and total number of cleared transactions on the Uncleared Transaction Detail report support the data shown in the second section of the Reconciliation Summary.

```
                                      January Reconciliation
Big National                                                                      Page 3
1/ 6/91

                         UNCLEARED TRANSACTION DETAIL UP TO  1/ 6/91


           Date    Num       Payee           Memo          Category    Clr   Amount
           ------- -----  --------------- --------------- --------------- --- -----------

           Uncleared Checks and Payments

             1/ 3/91 767   Sammamish Cleani                Office               -34.56
                                                                            -----------
           Total Uncleared Checks and Payments             1 Item             -34.56


           Uncleared Deposits and Other Credits

                                                                            -----------
           Total Uncleared Deposits and Other Credits      0 Items             0.00

                                                                           ============
           Total Uncleared Transactions                    1 Item             -34.56
```

**Fig. 8.10.** *Uncleared transactions dated prior to the reconciliation date.*

```
                                      January Reconciliation
Big National                                                                      Page 4
1/ 6/91

                         UNCLEARED TRANSACTION DETAIL AFTER  1/ 6/91


           Date    Num       Payee           Memo          Category    Clr   Amount
           ------- -----  --------------- --------------- --------------- --- -----------

           Uncleared Checks and Payments

                                                                            -----------
           Total Uncleared Checks and Payments             0 Items             0.00


           Uncleared Deposits and Other Credits

                                                                            -----------
           Total Uncleared Deposits and Other Credits      0 Items             0.00

                                                                           ============
           Total Uncleared Transactions                    0 Items             0.00
```

**Fig. 8.11.** *Uncleared transactions dated subsequent to the reconciliation date.*

# Creating Balance Adjustment Transactions

If you cannot reconcile your account, that is, if the difference amount shown on the Reconciliation Summary equals something other than zero, as a last resort you may want to make a balance adjustment. A balance adjustment means that Quicken creates a transaction that forces the difference amount to equal zero. You can make a balance adjustment by pressing Esc on the Register screen before you have reduced the difference between the cleared balance and the bank statement balance to zero. Quicken then displays the Reconciliation is Not Complete screen, shown in figure 8.12.

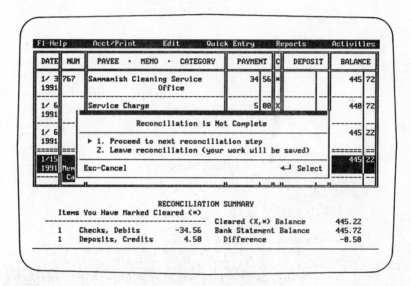

*Fig. 8.12. The Reconciliation Is Not Complete screen.*

The Reconciliation is Not Complete screen identifies two alternatives: Proceed to next reconciliation step, and Leave reconciliation (your work will be saved). If you select the second alternative, Quicken returns to the Main menu.

If you select the first alternative, Quicken displays the screen shown in figure 8.13. This screen informs you of the magnitude of the problem and possible causes. If you still want to create an adjustment transaction, follow these steps:

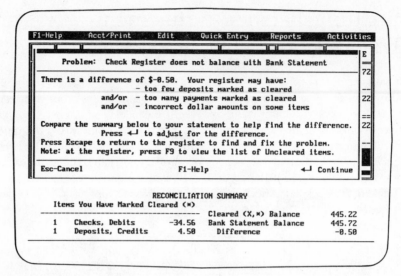

*Fig. 8.13. The Check Register Does Not Balance with Bank Statement screen.*

1. Press Enter to continue. Quicken alerts you that the difference still exists by displaying the Check Register Does Not Balance with Bank Statement screen (see fig. 8.13).

2. Press Enter to continue. Quicken displays the Adding Balance Adjustment Entry screen shown in figure 8.14, which alerts you that the adjustment is about to be made and suggests that you reconsider your decision.

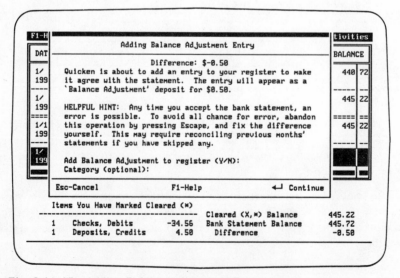

*Fig. 8.14. The Adding Balance Adjustment Entry screen.*

3. To make the adjustment, press Y for Yes. If you do not want to make the adjustment, press N for No. If you want to leave this screen and return to the Abbreviated Register screen, press Esc.

4. (Optional) To categorize your adjustment transaction (press Ctrl-C to see a Category and Transfer List screen), enter a category name in the optional `Category` field.

Quicken next tells you that the register has been adjusted to agree with the bank statement balance and displays a screen you can use to print the reconciliation report, as shown in figure 8.15. To print a reconciliation report, press Y for Yes. Quicken displays the Print Reconciliation Report screen, which you use as described earlier in this chapter to print the reconciliation report. Figure 8.16 shows a sample adjustment transaction.

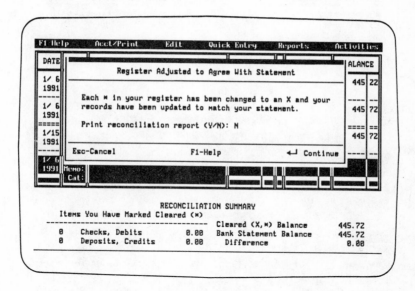

**Fig. 8.15.** *The Register Adjusted to Agree with Statement screen.*

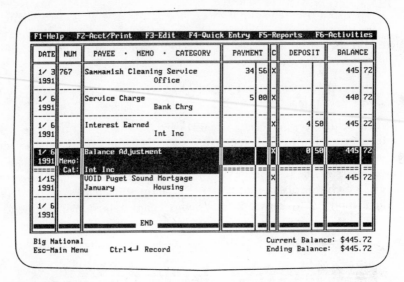

*Fig. 8.16. A sample adjustment transaction created by Quicken.*

**CPA Tip**

Although Quicken provides the adjustment feature, you probably should not use the feature because it camouflages errors in your register. As a result, you never really can be sure where the error occurs. Your difference amount equals something other than zero because you are missing some transaction in your register or because you incorrectly marked a transaction as cleared, or maybe you have transposed some numbers (i.e., writing $87.00 as $78.00). The difference also may occur because someone has forged checks or embezzled from your account. If you cannot reconcile your account, make sure that the previous month's reconciliation resulted in a difference equal to zero. If the previous month's reconciliation shows a difference other than zero, you must reconcile that month, and perhaps the months prior to that one, before you can get the current month's difference to be displayed as zero.

# Catching Common Errors

You easily can make several errors when recording transactions in your checking account; these errors may make reconciling your account difficult or even impossible. Because it sometimes is helpful not just to look for errors, but to look for certain kinds of errors, the next few paragraphs identify some common errors and explain tricks for catching those errors.

# Transposing Numbers

Transposing numbers is a frequent error in recording any financial transaction. People accidentally transpose two of the numbers in an amount. If the difference is divisible by 9, a transposition error is likely. For example, you may write a check for $32.67 and record the check as $23.67 or $32.76. This error appears to be obvious, but is surprisingly easy to make and sometimes difficult to catch. When you review each transaction, you see all the correct numbers; however, they are arranged in a slightly different order.

When searching for transposed numbers you can focus on the decimal places of the transaction where the transposition error might have occurred. Table 8.1 summarizes by amounts where the transposition error might have occurred.

**Table 8.1**
**Possible Locations of Transposition Errors**

| Error Amount | Decimal Places of Transposition |
| --- | --- |
| $.09 to $.72 | In cents. For example, $.12 vs. $.21 or $1.19 vs. $1.91. |
| $.90 to $7.20 | Between the dollar decimal position immediately to left of decimal place and the cents decimal position to right of decimal place. For example, $32.56 versus $35.26 or $2004.56 versus $2005.46. |
| $9.00 to $72.00 | Between the two positions immediately to the left of decimal place. For example, $1423 versus $1432 or $281 versus $218. |
| $90 to $720 | Between second and third positions immediately to the left of decimal place. For example, $1297 versus $1927 or $1124 versus $1214. |

# Forgetting To Record Transactions

The most common mistake many people make is forgetting to record transactions. In a personal checking account, these omissions often include decreases in the account—for example, automated teller machine withdrawals—and increases in the account, such as interest income. In a business checking account, manual checks seem to be a common culprit; you tear out a blank check for a purchasing trip and forget to record the check later.

If the amounts differ as a result of one transaction, identifying the missing transaction can be as easy as finding a transaction on the bank statement that equals the difference. You also should check the sequence of checks to see whether any are missing.

# Entering Payments as Deposits or Deposits as Payments

Another error is to enter a payment transaction as a deposit transaction or a deposit transaction as a payment transaction. Until you find this error, it can be particularly frustrating. If you look at your register, you see that every transaction is recorded, and every number is correct.

An easy way to find such an error is to divide your error by half and see whether the result equals some transaction amount. If it does, you may have recorded that transaction incorrectly. For example, suppose that you currently have a difference of $1,234.56 between the register and the bank statement balances. If you divide $1,234.56 by 2, you get an amount of $617.28. If you see a $617.28 transaction in your register, verify that you recorded that transaction in the correct column. If you recorded the $617.28 as a deposit when you should have recorded it as a payment, or if you recorded it as a payment when it should have been a deposit, the difference will equal twice the transaction amount, or $1,234.56.

# Offsetting Errors

You may have more than one error in your account, and these errors may partially offset each other. Suppose that you forgot to record an automated teller machine withdrawal of $40, for example, and made a transposition error in which you recorded a deposit as $216 instead of the correct amount of $261. The difference equals $5, which is the combined effect of both transactions and can be calculated as

$$-40 + (261 - 216) = \$5$$

Despite the fact that the difference seems small, you actually have two large errors in the account.

With offsetting errors, remember that finding one of the errors sometimes makes it seem as if you are getting further away from your goal of a zero difference. Do not get discouraged if one minute you are $5 away from completing the reconciliation, and the next minute, you are $50 away from completing the reconciliation. Clearly, you are making progress if you are finding errors—even if the difference is getting bigger.

# Chapter Summary

This chapter described how to reconcile your account with Quicken. You learned about the Reconciliation screen, menu options, and reports that you can use to simplify the process of reconciling your bank accounts. The **Reconcile** option helps you turn what once was an unpleasant financial chore into a quick and easy task.

# 9

# Taking Care of
# Quicken Files

Quicken stores in files the financial information you enter into the register. This chapter, the last in the "Learning the Basics" section, covers how to take care of Quicken files. The chapter will review which files Quicken creates, how to back up and restore files, how to shrink files to get rid of out-dated information, and how to export and import file data.

## Reviewing the Quicken Files

To operate Quicken, you do not need to know the function of each of the program's files. Sometimes, however, this knowledge is helpful. For example, if a file is damaged or corrupted, knowing whether the file is important to your use of Quicken is valuable. If you use one of the popular hard disk management programs, knowing "which files are which" is helpful if you want to compress or encrypt certain files. (You might want to compress files so that they occupy less space on your hard disk. To ensure the confidentiality of your financial records, you might want to encrypt your files so that they are impossible for others to read.)

When you install Quicken, the following series of program files is copied to your hard disk or to your program floppy disk:

Q-EXE, Q.OVL          The actual Quicken program files

| Q.HLP | On-line help file accessed with F1 |
|---|---|
| BILLMIND.EXE | Program to look for checks, groups due |
| QCHECKS.DOC | Blank supply order form |
| CONVERT.COM | Quicken 2 data file conversion program |
| PRINTERS.DAT | Printer driver file |
| HCAT.QMT | Predefined home category list |
| BCAT.QMT | Predefined business category list |
| TCAT.QMT | Combined home and business category list |

Quicken also creates the following files:

| Q.CFG | Configuration and set-up information |
|---|---|
| Q.BAT | A batch file that starts Quicken |
| Q3.DIR | List of account descriptions and check due dates |

For each account group you set up, Quicken creates four additional files by combining the account group name with four different file extensions. Assuming that you use an account group named QDATA, Quicken creates the following files:

| QDATA.QDT | Data file for account group |
|---|---|
| QDATA.QNX | Data file index for account group (used to sort transactions) |
| QDATA.QMT | Memorized transaction list for account group (stores memorized transactions) |
| QDATA.QDI | Dictionary file for account group (stores words that you can enter with the Auto-completion feature) |

# Backing Up and Restoring Files

*Backing up* means making a second copy of your Quicken data files (including Q3.DIR, QDATA.QDT, QDATA.QNX, QDATA.QMT, and QDATA.QDI). The reason you should back up your files is clear: If your original Quicken data files are damaged, you can use your backup copies to restore your files or their original condition. You can back up and restore using DOS file commands or one of the popular hard disk management programs. But for the sake of convenience, you probably will find using the Quicken back up and restore options easier. This section discusses those back up and restore options.

## Backing Up Your Files

You need to make two important decisions about backing up your files. First, you must decide how often you need to back up. Although opinions on the subject vary, you generally should back up your data files after completing any session in which you enter or change accounting data. For example, when you finish entering your first set of account transactions, you should back up your files.

Most people back up their account records daily, weekly, or monthly. After you have worked with Quicken and become familiar with account group restoration procedures, you can estimate more accurately how often you need to back up your account groups. For example, if you discover that backing up your files requires as much effort as re-creating six months of record keeping, you may decide to back up your Quicken data files only every six months.

Second, you need to decide how many old backup copies you should keep. Usually, two or three copies are adequate. (This rule of thumb is called the grandfather, father, and son scheme.) Suppose that you back up your account groups every day. On Thursday, someone accidentally deletes the group. If you keep two old backup copies in addition to the most recent backup copy, you have backups from Wednesday, Tuesday, and Monday. If the Wednesday copy is damaged (an unlikely but possible situation), you still have the Tuesday and Monday copies. The more recent a backup copy, the easier data is to recover, but using an old backup copy is easier than re-entering all the data from the original documents.

Store your account group backup copies in a safe place. Do not keep all backup copies in the same location. If you experience a fire or if someone burglarizes your business or house, you may lose all your copies— no matter how many backups you keep. Store at least one copy at an off-site location. If you use Quicken at home, you can keep a backup copy in your desk at work; if you use Quicken for business, keep a backup copy at home.

To back up your Quicken files, follow these steps:

1. Select the **Change Settings** option from Quicken's Main menu. (Quicken displays the Change Settings menu shown in figure 9.1.)

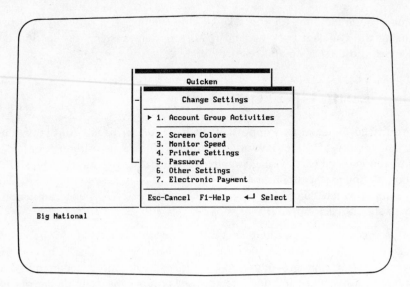

*Fig. 9.1. The Change Settings menu.*

2. Select the **Account Group Activities** option from the Change Settings menu. (Quicken displays the Account Group Activities menu shown in figure 9.2.)

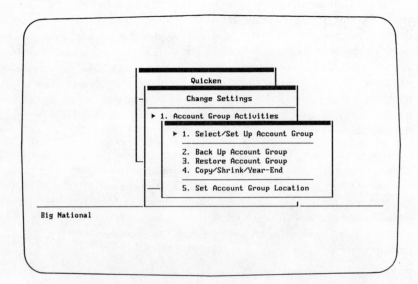

*Fig. 9.2. The Account Group Activities menu.*

3. Select **Back Up Account Group** from the Account Group Activities menu. Quicken prompts you to insert the backup floppy disk in the appropriate disk drive (see fig. 9.3). After you insert the backup disk and press Enter, Quicken displays the Select Account Group to Back Up screen shown in figure 9.4. This screen is similar to the Select/Set Up Account Group screen—only the title is different.

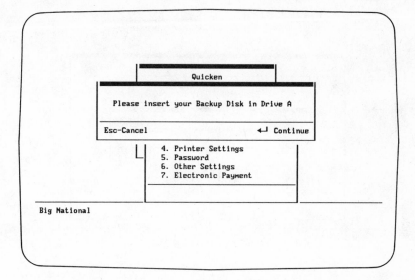

**Fig. 9.3.** *The* Please insert your Backup Disk in Drive A *message.*

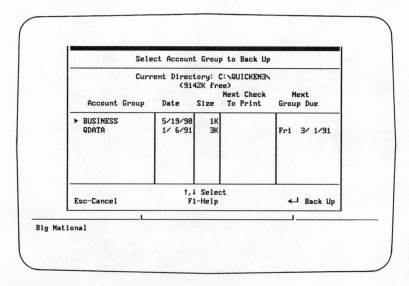

**Fig. 9.4.** *The Select Account Group to Back Up screen.*

4. Use the up- and down-arrow keys to move the selection triangle to the left of the account group you want to back up and press Enter.

The message Backing Up then appears as Quicken copies the selected account group to the backup disk. When Quicken finishes backing up, the message Account Group backed up successfully appears, as shown in figure 9.5.

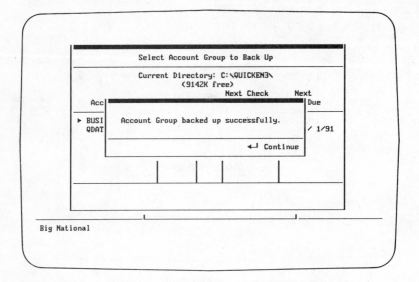

**Fig. 9.5.** *The* Account Group backed up successfully *message.*

*Note:* If the account group you are trying to back up does not fit on the disk, an error message alerts you that the disk is full, and you should press Esc to cancel. Quicken then displays the warning message Account not backed up. If the disk is full, press Esc, insert a different backup disk, and repeat steps 1-4.

5. Remove the backup disk from the disk drive and store the disk in a safe place.

# Restoring Backed-Up Files

Eventually, someone or something accidentally will delete or destroy an account group. Your computer may malfunction; someone may spill the contents of the pencil sharpener or a cup of coffee on the floppy disk containing the Quicken data files. But if you have backed up your files recently, and if you have been diligent about printing copies of your register, you should not have any serious problems. You will be able to restore your Quicken files using your backup copies.

To retrieve the data you copied with the **Back Up Account Group** option, follow this procedure:

1. Select the **Change Settings** option from Quicken's Main menu. Quicken displays the Change Settings menu shown in figure 9.1.

2. Select the **Account Group Activities** option from the Change Settings menu. Quicken displays the Account Group Activities menu shown in figure 9.2.

3. Select the **Restore Account Group** option. Quicken prompts you to insert the backup disk in drive A (see fig. 9.3). After you insert the backup disk and press Enter, Quicken displays the Select Account Group to Restore screen (see fig. 9.6).

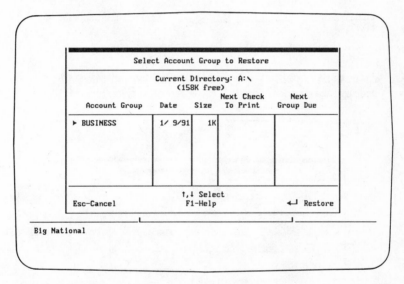

**Fig. 9.6.** *The Select Account Group to Restore screen.*

4. Use the up- and down-arrow keys to move the selection triangle to the left of the account group you want to restore and then press Enter.

   *Note:* Quicken alerts you that the restoration operation will overwrite the existing account group (see fig. 9.7). To continue with the restoration, press Enter.

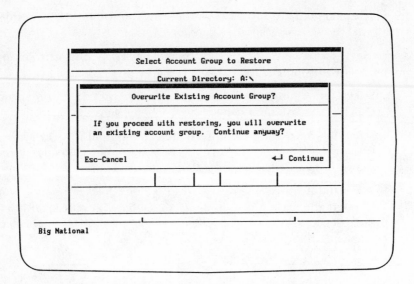

*Fig. 9.7. The* Overwrite Existing Account Group *message.*

When the restoration is complete, Quicken displays the Account Group restored successfully message shown in figure 9.8.

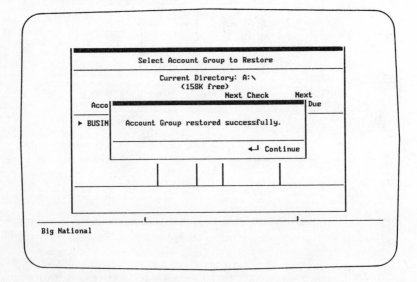

*Fig. 9.8. The* Account Group restored successfully *message.*

You cannot restore the currently selected account group. If you try to restore the currently selected group, the message shown in figure 9.9 alerts you to this error. If you originally set up only one group, you need to set up a second, dummy account group that you can select as the current group before you use the restore option.

*Note:* Remember that in Quicken you can work with several accounts. Chapter 3 lists the steps for setting up accounts. Refer to Chapter 3 if you have questions about this procedure.

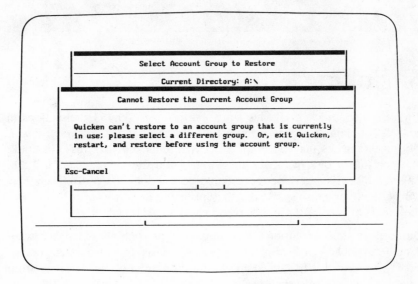

*Fig. 9.9.* The Cannot Restore the Current Account Group *message.*

5. Using the most recent copy of the register, re-enter every transaction that you entered between the time you backed up and the time you lost the data. You need to re-enter transactions for each account.

6. Back up your files in case another accident causes you to lose your Quicken files again.

*CPA Tip*

If some disaster befalls data files that you did not back up, you must re-enter each register transaction. Your up-to-date printed copies of each register will show what should be re-entered. If you don't have up-to-date copies of each of the registers, you will need to re-enter each of the transactions using the original source documents—checks, deposits receipts, and so on. Obviously, you don't ever want to find yourself re-entering data from original documents, so regularly back up your files and store the backup disks in safe place.

# Shrinking Files

Theoretically, Quicken enables you to store up to 65,353 transactions in an account group's registers. Practically, the limitations are much lower. Floppy disk users may be limited by their Quicken data disks: a 360K, 5¼-inch floppy disk has space for about 3,000 transactions, and a 720K, 3½-inch disk has space for about 6,000 transactions. Hard disk users may not be limited by disk space, but they probably do not want to work with thousands or tens of thousands of transactions in registers.

Quicken provides a solution for dealing with the problem of ever-growing data files: Quicken enables you to purge old transactions that occur before a date that you specify. Quicken calls the purging of old transactions from a new copy of the file *shrinking*.

# When To Shrink Files

The basic rule is that you should shrink files when you no longer need the detailed information in a transaction. Usually, you no longer need transaction details when two conditions are met:

❏ The transactions have cleared the bank so that you will not need to mark them as cleared as part of reconciling the account.

❏ The transactions have appeared on the Quicken reports you use to track income, expenses, and deductions.

For most users, the most convenient time to shrink the files—the time when both the basic conditions are met—is after you complete your annual income tax return and any year-end reporting. By that time, all transactions from the prior year should have cleared the bank, and you will have printed all necessary Quicken reports.

# How To Shrink Files

To shrink files, use the **Copy/Shrink Year-End** option on the Account Group Activities menu (see fig. 9.2). Because you can shrink only the currently selected account, you need to use the **Select/Set Up Account Group** option to select an account to shrink. (If you do not select an account before using the **Copy/Shrink Year-End** option, Quicken warns you that it is about to shrink your files.)

When you are ready to shrink files, follow these steps:

1. Select the **Change Setting** option from Quicken's Main menu. Quicken displays the Change Settings menu (see fig. 9.1).

2. Select the **Account Group Activities** option from the Change Settings menu. Quicken displays the Account Group Activities menu (see fig. 9.2).

3. Select the **Copy/Shrink Year-End** option from the Account Group Activities menu. Quicken displays the Copy Account Group screen shown in figure 9.10.

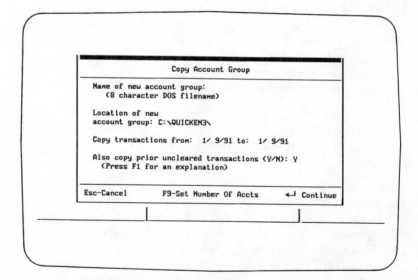

*Fig. 9.10. The Copy Account Group screen.*

4. Enter a new name for the account group. Mechanically, you create shrunken versions of files by copying a portion of the original file. Because you actually are creating a new file, you need to provide a

new account group name. What you enter as the account group name must be a valid DOS file name. (If you are unsure of DOS file-naming conventions, see your DOS user's manual.)

*CPA Tip*

> If you create a separate set of Quicken data files for each year, consider including the year number in the account group name. For example, the data files from 1989 might be named QDATA89, the data files from 1990 named QDATA90, the data files from 1991 QDATA91, and so on. Including the year number in account group names enables you to determine easily which year's records are contained in a particular data file.

5. (Optional) Press Enter or Tab to move the cursor to the Location of a new account group field. If you do not want to use the default directory—C:\QUICKEN3 for hard disk users and drive B for floppy disk users—you can specify a different directory in which the copied account group will be stored. Remember that the drive and directory you specify must be a valid path name.

6. Press Enter or Tab to move the cursor to the Copy transactions from field. Enter the date from which you want transactions included in your register. If you are creating one copy of the register for each year of transactions, the From date should be January 1 of the current year. (Remember that the + and − keys provide a quick way to change the date one day at a time.)

7. Press Enter or Tab to move the cursor to the Copy transactions to field. Enter the date through which you want transactions included in your register. If you are creating one copy of the register for each year of transactions, the To date should be December 31 of the current year.

8. Press Enter or Tab to move the cursor to the Also copy prior uncleared transactions field. Press Y for Yes if you will reconcile your bank account and N for No if you will not reconcile your bank account. (Prior uncleared transactions most often are checks and deposits that occurred before the Copy transaction from date but have not yet been recorded by the bank. You need these prior uncleared transactions to reconcile your bank account.)

9. (Optional) By default, Quicken sets a limit on the number of accounts in any single group. Quicken's default limit is 64. You can increase this limit, however, to as much as 255 groups. To increase

the limit, press F9. Quicken displays the Set Maximum Accounts in Group box (see fig. 9.11). Type the number of groups you want as the maximum and press Enter.

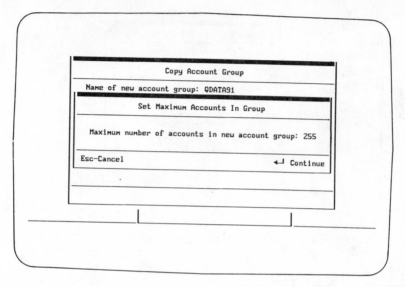

**Fig. 9.11.** *The Set Maximum Accounts in Group screen.*

10. When you have filled the fields with the appropriate information, press Enter. Quicken makes a copy of the account group in the specified location with the specified name. This new copy is the shrunken file. You will use the shrunken file in the future as the account group into which you record transactions.

    Quicken next displays the message box shown in figure 9.12. Quicken tells you that the account group was copied successfully and asks whether you want to reload the original group or load the new group.

11. Press 2 to load the new group, and Quicken returns the Main menu to the screen.

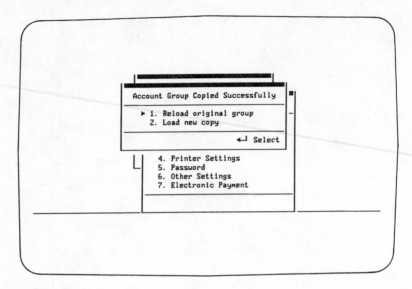

**Fig. 9.12.** *The Account Group Copied Successfully screen.*

# Locating Files

If you accept the program defaults, Quicken stores data files in C:\QUICKEN3 for hard disk users and drive B for floppy disk users. You have the option, however, of having Quicken locate the files somewhere besides the default location. You do this when you specify where the files for an account group should be located when you set up or shrink an account group.

If you locate Quicken files in other places, you need to tell Quicken where those files are. To inform Quicken of the location of your files, use the **Set Account Group Location** option on the Account Group Activities menu.

To use the **Set Account Group Location** option, follow these steps:

1. Select the **Change Settings** option from Quicken's Main menu. Quicken displays the Change Settings menu.

2. Select the **Account Group Activities** option from the Change Settings menu. Quicken displays the Account Group Activities menu.

3. Select the **Set Account Group Location** option on the Account Group Activities menu. Quicken displays the Set Account Group Location screen shown in figure 9.13.

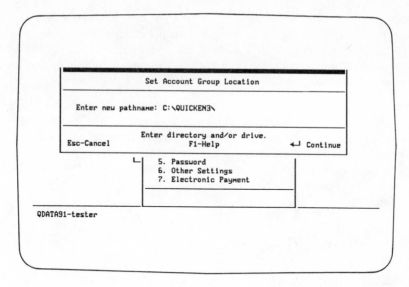

**Fig. 9.13.** *The Set Account Group Location screen.*

4. Enter the drive and directory where the Quicken data files are located.

   The drive and directory you enter must be a valid DOS path name. The drive letter must be valid and followed by a colon. Directories and subdirectories must have been created previously. (The hard disk installation program creates the directory QUICKEN3.) If you use a directory and subdirectory together, they must constitute a valid path name. The subdirectory specified must be in the directory specified. (For more information on directories, subdirectories, and path names, see your DOS user's manual.)

5. Press Enter to save your changes.

# Exporting and Importing Files

*Exporting* is the process by which a software program makes a copy of a file in a format that another program can read. For example, you might want to export the information stored in the Quicken register so that you can retrieve and use the information in a database program, such as dBASE, or in a spreadsheet program, such as 1-2-3.

*Importing* is the process by which information created by one software program is retrieved by a second software program. For example, you might want to import into Quicken the information created by an accounting program, such as DacEasy, so that you can use Quicken's reports to summarize the information.

Exporting and importing really represent two sides of the same coin: exporting creates a file using the information stored in the Quicken register, and importing retrieves information from another file into the Quicken register. Although most Quicken users never will need to export or import files, Quicken provides the tools to do both. **Export** and **Import** options appear on the Write Checks and Register versions of the Acct/Print menus.

## Exporting Files

The **Export** option enables you to create an ASCII text file from register transactions. You then can use the ASCII file in another software program. Word processing, spreadsheet, and database applications, for example, commonly enable you to import ASCII text files from Quicken.

To execute an export operation, take the following steps:

1. While on the Write Checks or the Register screen, press F2 to display the Acct/Print menu (see fig. 9.14).

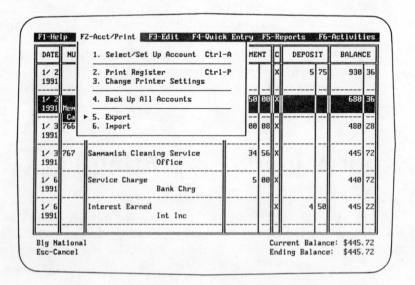

*Fig. 9.14. The Acct/Print menu.*

2. Select **Export** from the Acct/Print menu. Quicken displays the Export Transactions to QIF File screen shown in figure 9.15.

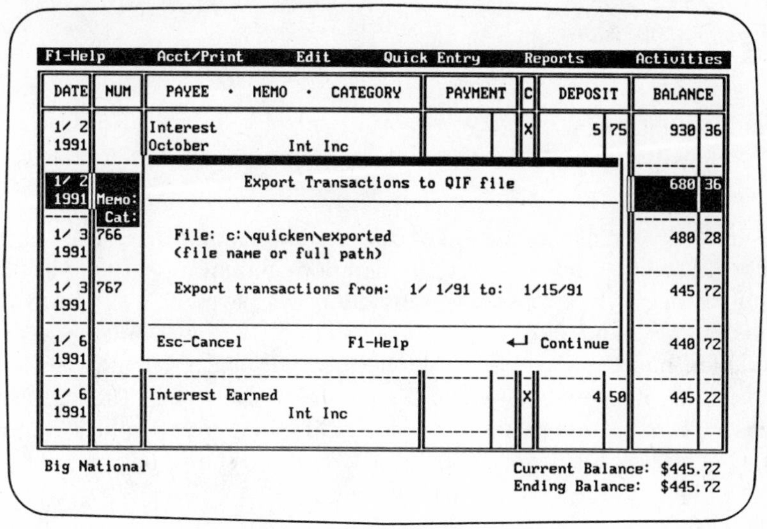

```
F1-Help      Acct/Print      Edit      Quick Entry      Reports      Activities

DATE  NUM    PAYEE  ·  MEMO  ·  CATEGORY    PAYMENT  C   DEPOSIT    BALANCE

1/ 2        Interest                                 X        5 75    930 36
1991        October              Int Inc

1/ 2|Memo:              Export Transactions to QIF file                680 36
1991| Cat:
1/ 3 766      File: c:\quicken\exported                               480 28
1991          <file name or full path>

1/ 3 767      Export transactions from:  1/ 1/91 to:  1/15/91        445 72
1991

1/ 6          Esc-Cancel          F1-Help          ⏎ Continue        440 72
1991

1/ 6        Interest Earned                         X        4 50    445 22
1991                             Int Inc

Big National                                  Current Balance: $445.72
                                              Ending Balance:  $445.72
```

***Fig. 9.15.*** *The Export Transactions to QIF File screen.*

3. In the `File` field, enter the DOS file name that you want Quicken to use for the new ASCII file. You also can include a path name. For example, figure 9.15 shows the Export Transactions screen used to create an ASCII file named EXPORTED on drive C of your hard drive in the QUICKEN directory.

4. (Optional) To limit exported transactions to those within a certain range of dates, fill in the `Export transactions from` and `to` date fields. You can use the + and − keys to change the date one day at a time.

5. To start the export operation, press Enter when the cursor is on the `Export transaction to` date field. Alternatively, press Ctrl-Enter or F10 when the cursor is on one of the other screen fields.

Quicken creates an ASCII file containing the exported transactions. At the beginning of the file, Quicken prints a line to identify the type of account from which transactions were exported. This information begins with an exclamation point and the word `type` and is followed by the actual type name. For example, transactions exported from a bank account would show `Bank` as the first line.

The following is the actual ASCII information that Quicken uses to record each transaction in the register.

```
D7/24/89
T − 1,000.00
         CX
         N*****
PBig National Bank
L[Savings]
^
```

The first line begins with D and shows the transaction date. The second line begins with T and shows the transaction amount as − 1000.00. (The amount is negative because the transaction is a payment.) The third line begins with a C and shows the cleared status. The fourth line shows the transaction number set to asterisks because the check has not yet been printed. The fifth line begins with P and shows the payee. The sixth line begins with L and shows the Category field entry. If you split a transaction, Quicken creates several L lines. The last line shows only a caret (^), which designates the end of a transaction.

The **Export** option does not produce the same ASCII file as the **Print to Disk** option described in Chapters 4 and 6. **Export** creates an ASCII file with each transaction field on a separate line. You might use this option if you were trying to import the Quicken data into another software program—such as an accounting program—that will use the information. The Print Register's **Print to Disk** setting creates an ASCII text file that looks like a printed check register. You might use this option if you want to create a list of certain Quicken transactions that can be retrieved by a word-processing program, edited with that program, and then printed or used in a document.

## Importing Files

The **Import** option retrieves files stored in the Quicken export format. This is the exact same format that Quicken uses when it exports data (see preceding section). The steps for importing parallel those for exporting data.

To import files, take the following steps:

1. While on the Write Checks or Register screen, press F2 to display the Acct/Print menu (see fig. 9.14).

2. Select **Import** from the Acct/Print menu. Quicken displays the Import from QIF File or CheckFree screen shown in figure 9.16.

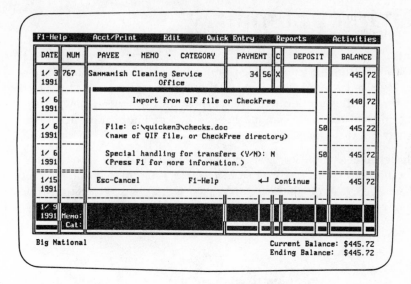

**Fig. 9.16.** *The Import from QIF File or CheckFree screen.*

3. Enter the DOS file name of the file you want Quicken to import. You also can include a path name. For example, figure 9.16 shows the Export Transactions screen ready to import CHECKS.DOC on drive C of your hard drive in the QUICKEN3 directory.

4. (Optional) Press Enter or Tab to move the cursor to the Special handling for transfers field. If you want to import transactions with account transfers included in the Category field, press N for No and the press Enter.

5. To import the file, press Enter when the cursor is on the Special handling for transfers field. Alternatively, press Ctrl-Enter or F10 when the cursor is on one of the other screen fields. Quicken imports the file and records the transaction in the register.

6. You may be prompted to add categories if the imported file does not contain categories.

7. Quicken will tell you that the import was successful upon completion.

# Chapter Summary

This chapter described the steps and the logic for taking care of Quicken data files. The chapter identified the Quicken files and explained how to back up and restore files, how to shrink files, and how to tell Quicken where the files are located. The chapter also described how to export information from Quicken and how to import information from another program into a Quicken register.

This chapter completes "Learning the Basics." You now are ready for the next three sections of *Using Quicken: IBM Version*, 2nd Edition: "Supercharging Quicken," "Putting Quicken To Work," and "Protecting Yourself from Forgery, Embezzlement, and Other Disasters."

# III

# Supercharging Quicken

## Includes

Organizing Your Finances Better

Fine-Tuning Quicken

Tracking Your Net Worth, Other Assets, and
Liabilities

Monitoring Your Investments

Tapping the Power of Quicken's Reports

Paying Bills Electronically

# 10

# Organizing Your
# Finances Better

M any of the earlier chapters of this book mention Quicken's categories. Categories enable you to summarize the information in your check register, track tax deductions, and monitor the money flowing into and out of your checking account. Earlier discussions of Quicken's categories, however, have been rather superficial. In fact, this book so far has touched only on the power of categories.

This chapter goes into depth on the subject of categories and how you can use them to organize your finances better. This chapter describes categories, tells why and when you should use them, and shows the predefined categories Quicken provides for business and personal use. This chapter also describes the steps for adding, deleting, and editing your own categories. Finally, the chapter covers a related tool, Quicken's classes.

## Working with Categories

To review briefly, categories enable you to group the payments that flow out of your account and the deposits that flow into your account. The deposits into your account may stem from two sources: earned wages from a full-time job and profits from a part-time business. Your payments can stem from four expenditures: rent, food, transportation, and your part-time business expenses. By grouping each payment from and each deposit into your account, Quicken easily adds up the totals for each type of payment and deposit. You then can see exactly how much each category contributes to your cash flow. You may find, for example, that your cash flows into and out of your account look like those summarized in table 10.1.

**Table 10.1**
**Personal Cash Flows**

| Deposits | |
|---|---|
| Wages from job | $15,400 |
| Business profits | 4,300 |
| Total Deposits | 19,700 |
| | |
| *Withdrawals* | |
| Housing | 6,000 |
| Food | 3,000 |
| Transportation | 3,000 |
| Business Expenses | 500 |
| Total Withdrawals | 12,500 |
| | |
| Cash Flows | 7,200 |

Is the information shown in table 10.1 valuable? Usually it is. Categorizing your income and outgo is the first step in beginning to manage your personal or business finances. For example, categories enable you to do the following:

❏ Track and tally income tax deductions for individual retirement accounts, mortgage interest deductions, or charitable contributions

❏ Break down checking account deposits and payments into groups of similar transactions so that you can summarize your personal income and outgo

❏ Budget income and outgo and compare budgeted amounts with actual amounts

If you want to use Quicken for a business, the predefined categories enable you to prepare most of the reports you need for managing your business finances. These reports include the following:

❏ A report that resembles and performs most of the arithmetic required to complete your federal income tax form, Schedule C. (The Schedule C form reports the profits or losses from a business or profession.)

❏ Income and cash-flow statements on a monthly and annual basis that enable you to understand your cash flows and measure your business profits or losses

❏ Employee payroll checks and reports

If any of the reports listed look like benefits you want to enjoy as part of using Quicken, you want to use Quicken's categories. How involved or complicated your use of the categories becomes depends on your goals.

# Building a List of Categories

Your information needs determine the various categories you want to use to group similar payments or deposits. Three basic rules apply when building a list of categories.

First, if you want to use categories for tallying and tracking income tax deductions, you need a category for each deduction. If you use the individual retirement account deduction, the mortgage interest deduction, and the state and local taxes deduction, you need categories for each of these deductions. The following list shows the itemized deductions you may want to track to more easily prepare your personal income tax return. The list is based on the federal income tax form, Schedule A.

*Sample personal tax deduction categories*

Medical and dental*
Medical and dental—other*
State and local income taxes
Real estate taxes
Other taxes, including personal property taxes
Deductible home mortgage interest paid to financial institutions
Deductible home mortgage interest paid to individuals
Deductible points
Deductible investment interest
Deductible personal interest (being phased out)
Contributions by cash or check
Contributions other than by cash or check
Casualty or theft losses**
Moving expenses**
Unreimbursed employee expenses
Union dues, tax preparation fees, investment publications, and fees

Individual retirement account
Other miscellaneous expenses

* The first medical expense category includes prescription medicines and drugs, insulin, doctors, dentists, nurses, hospitals, and medical insurance premiums. The second includes items like hearing aids, dentures, eyeglasses, transportation, and lodging.

** This itemized deduction must be supported by an additional tax form. Therefore, you also want to consider setting up the individual amounts that need to be reported on that form as categories.

The following list shows the income and deduction categories you may want to use to prepare your business income tax return. (The list is based on the federal income tax form, Schedule C.)

*Income categories*

Gross receipts or sales
Sales returns and allowances
Cost of goods sold*
Rental/interest
Other income

*Deduction categories*

Advertising
Bad debts from sales or services
Bank service charges
Car and truck expenses
Commissions
Depletion
Depreciation**
Dues and publications
Employee benefit programs
Freight
Insurance
Interest—mortgage
Interest—other
Laundry and cleaning
Legal and professional services
Office expense
Pension and profit-sharing plans
Rent on business property
Repairs
Supplies
Taxes (payroll and business)
Travel
Meals and entertainment

Utilities and telephone

Wages

Wages—job credit

Other deductions

\* The cost of goods sold needs to be calculated or verified using part III of Schedule C.

\*\* This deduction amount must be supported by an additional tax form; consider setting up the individual amounts reported on that form as categories.

Second, if you want to use categories to summarize your cash inflows and outflows, you need a category for each income or expense account you want to use in your summaries. For example, if you want to account for your work expenses and your spouse's work expenses, you need categories for both.

Third, if you want to use categories to budget (so that you later can compare what you budgeted and what you actually spent), you need a category for each comparison you want to make. If you want to budget entertainment expenses and clothing expenses, you need categories for both.

By applying these three rules, you should be able to build a list of the categories you want to use. As an aid in creating your own list, figure 10.1 shows the category list that Quicken provides for personal accounts. Figure 10.2 shows the category list Quicken provides for business accounts.

Consider these lists as starting points. The predefined personal, or home, category list provides a long list of income and spending categories that may be useful for personal accounting. Depending on your particular situation, some categories may be provided that you don't need, and other categories may be missing that you do need. Similarly, the predefined business list provides income and spending categories that may be useful in business accounting. If you apply the rules described earlier for devising your own categories, you should have no problem using the predefined lists as starting points from which you construct a category list that works well for you.

After you complete your list, review the categories for any redundancies produced by two of the rules calling for the same category. For example, for personal use of Quicken, you can add a category to budget for monthly individual retirement account (IRA) payments. You also can add a category to tally IRA payments because they represent potential tax deductions. Because both categories are the same, you can cross one off your list.

```
                                Category and Transfer List
HOME                                                                      Page 1
1/ 9/91


                                    Tax
        Category        Description   Rel  Type  Budget Amount
        --------        -----------   ---  ----  -------------
        Bonus           Bonus Income      *  Inc
        Canada Pen      Canadian Pension  *  Inc
        Div Income      Dividend Income   *  Inc
        Family Allow    Family Allowance  *  Inc
        Gift Received   Gift Received     *  Inc
        Int Inc         Interest Income   *  Inc
        Invest Inc      Investment Income *  Inc
        Old Age Pension Old Age Pension   *  Inc
        Other Inc       Other Income      *  Inc
        Salary          Salary Income     *  Inc
        Auto Fuel       Automobile Fuel      Expns
        Auto Loan       Auto Loan Payment    Expns
        Auto Serv       Automobile Service   Expns
        Bank Chrg       Bank Charge          Expns
        Charity         Charitable Donations *  Expns
        Childcare       Childcare Expense    Expns
        Christmas       Christmas Expenses   Expns
        Clothing        Clothing             Expns
        Dining          Dining Out           Expns
        Dues            Dues                 Expns
        Education       Education            Expns
        Entertain       Entertainment        Expns
        Gifts           Gift Expenses        Expns
        Groceries       Groceries            Expns
        Home Rpair      Home Repair & Maint. Expns
        Household       Household Misc. Exp  Expns
        Housing         Housing              Expns
        Insurance       Insurance            Expns
        Int Exp         Interest Expense  *  Expns
        Invest Exp      Investment Expense *  Expns
        Medical         Medical & Dental  *  Expns
        Misc            Miscellaneous        Expns
        Mort Int        Mortgage Interest Exp *  Expns
        Mort Prin       Mortgage Principal   Expns
        Other Exp       Other Expenses    *  Expns
        Recreation      Recreation Expense   Expns
        RRSP            Reg Retirement Sav Plan Expns
        Subscriptions   Subscriptions        Expns
        Supplies        Supplies          *  Expns
        Tax Fed         Federal Tax       *  Expns
        Tax FICA        Social Security Tax *  Expns
        Tax Other       Misc. Taxes       *  Expns
        Tax Prop        Property Tax      *  Expns
        Tax State       State Tax         *  Expns
        Telephone       Telephone Expense    Expns
        UIC             Unemploy. Ins. Commission *  Expns
        Utilities       Water, Gas, Electric Expns
        bank                                 Bank
```

**Fig. 10.1.** *The category list that Quicken provides for personal or household use.*

```
                                    Category and Transfer List
BUSINESS                                                                        Page 1
1/ 9/91


                                      Tax
        Category         Description    Rel  Type   Budget Amount
   ---------------   ------------------  ---  -----  -------------
     Gr Sales        Gross Sales          *   Inc
     Other Inc       Other Income         *   Inc
     Rent Income     Rent Income          *   Inc
     Ads             Advertising              Expns
     Car             Car & Truck          *   Expns
     Commission      Commissions          *   Expns
     Freight         Freight              *   Expns
     Int Paid        Interest Paid        *   Expns
     L&P Fees        Legal & Prof. Fees   *   Expns
     Late Fees       Late Payment Fees    *   Expns
     Office          Office Expenses      *   Expns
     Rent Paid       Rent Paid            *   Expns
     Repairs         Repairs              *   Expns
     Returns         Returns & Allowances *   Expns
     Taxes           Taxes                *   Expns
     Travel          Travel Expenses      *   Expns
     Wages           Wages & Job Credits  *   Expns
     bank                                     Bank
```

*Fig. 10.2. The category list that Quicken provides for business use.*

Sometimes, however, overlapping or redundant categories are not as easy to spot. A tax deduction you need to calculate may be only a portion of a budgeting category, or a budgeting amount you need to calculate may be only a portion of a tax-deduction category. You need to use categories that are smaller than the tax-deduction amount or the budgeting amount so that you can add up the individual categories that make up a tax deduction, accounting amount, or budgeted amount.

Categories act as building blocks you use to calculate the amounts you really want to know. For example, you can use the following categories to calculate the tax-deduction amounts and the budgeted amounts shown in table 10.2:

Mortgage interest
Mortgage principal
Mortgage late-payment fees
Credit card late-payment fees
Property taxes

**Table 10.2**
**Personal Budget and Tax Amounts**

| Amounts | Categories Used |
|---|---|
| Late fees (a budgeted amount) | Mortgage late-payment fees |
| | Credit card late-payment fees |
| Housing (a budgeted amount) | Mortgage principal |
| | Mortgage interest |
| | Property taxes |
| Mortgage interest (deduction) | Mortgage interest |
| | Mortgage late-payment fees |
| Property taxes (deduction) | Property taxes |

# Using Subcategories

If you want to use categories as building blocks to calculate other budgeted or tax-deduction amounts, you need to know about subcategories. Suppose that, taking the first row of the data from table 10.2, you create two building block categories to track late-payment fees on your mortgage and credit cards—LMortgage and LCredit. (The L stands for late.) If you also set up a category for late fees, LateFees, you can assign mortgage late-payment fees to the category-subcategory combination LateFees and LMortgage. You also can assign credit card late-payment fees to the category-subcategory combination LateFees and LCredit.

To record the subcategories, enter the primary income or expense category first, a colon, and then the subcategory. If you calculate further categorized LateFees by the two types of late fees you may pay, LMortgage and LCredit, you record late fees on your mortgage by entering *LateFees:LMortgage*. And you record late fees on your credit card by entering *LateFees:LCredit*. Figure 10.3 shows the Category field on the Register screen filled with both a category and a subcategory.

On your reports, the totals for LMortgage and LCredit as well as LateFees will show. Figure 10.4 shows an example of a report that illustrates the effect of subcategories.

```
 F1-Help   F2-Acct/Print   F3-Edit   F4-Quick Entry  F5-Reports   F6-Activities

┌─────┬────┬──────────────────────────────┬─────────┬─┬─────────┬─────────┐
│DATE │NUM │ PAYEE · MEMO · CATEGORY       │ PAYMENT │C│ DEPOSIT │ BALANCE │
├─────┼────┼──────────────────────────────┼─────────┼─┼─────────┼─────────┤
│1/ 3 │767 │Sammamish Cleaning Service    │  34 56  │X│         │  445 72 │
│1991 │    │              Office          │         │ │         │         │
│1/ 6 │    │Service Charge                │   5 00  │X│         │  440 72 │
│1991 │    │              Bank Chrg       │         │ │         │         │
│1/ 6 │    │Interest Earned               │         │X│    4 50 │  445 22 │
│1991 │    │              Int Inc         │         │ │         │         │
│1/ 6 │    │Balance Adjustment            │         │X│    0 50 │  445 72 │
│1991 │    │              Int Inc         │         │ │         │         │
│1/15 │    │VOID Puget Sound Mortgage     │         │X│         │  445 72 │
│1991 │    │January       Housing         │         │ │         │         │
│1/ 9 │    │Big National Bank             │ 128 70  │ │         │         │
│1991 │Memo│January Visa                  │         │ │         │         │
│     │Cat:│Latefees:LMortgage            │         │ │         │         │
└─────┴────┴──────────────────────────────┴─────────┴─┴─────────┴─────────┘

 Big National                        Current Balance:  $445.72
 Esc-Main Menu    Ctrl⏎  Record      Ending Balance:   $445.72
```

*Fig. 10.3. Separate categories and subcategories with a colon.*

```
                        Showing Subcategories on a Report
                           1/ 1/91 Through 1/31/91
 Bank,Cash,CC Accounts                                            Page 1
 1/ 9/91
                                          1/ 1/91-
                      Category Description  1/31/91
                      ------------------- ----------

                      INFLOWS
                        Interest Income        10.75
                                             --------
                      TOTAL INFLOWS            10.75

                      OUTFLOWS
                        Automobile Service     34.91
                        Bank Charge             5.00
                        Entertainment          28.94
                        Home Repair & Maint.   24.53
                        Housing                 0.00
                        Late fees:
                          Late payment fees-credit   11.59
                          Late payment fees-mortg.   28.73
                                             --------
                        Total Late fees        40.32
                        Office Expenses        34.56
                        Water, Gas, Electric   75.39
                        Outflows - Other      200.08
                                             --------
                      TOTAL OUTFLOWS          443.73

                                             --------
                      OVERALL TOTAL          -432.98
                                             ========
```

*Fig. 10.4. Using subcategories gives you the ability to show more detail.*

Within Quicken, you cannot produce reports comparing the actual amounts spent for a subcategory with a budgeted amount because Quicken enables you to enter a budgeted amount for only the category, not the subcategory. If you set up the category, LateFees, and the two subcategories, LMortgage and LCredit, the budgeted amount Quicken shows on the budget reports is for LateFees.

# Setting Up Categories

When you create account groups, you can use the predefined home or business categories on the Set Up Account Group screen as the foundation of your own category list (see fig. 10.5).

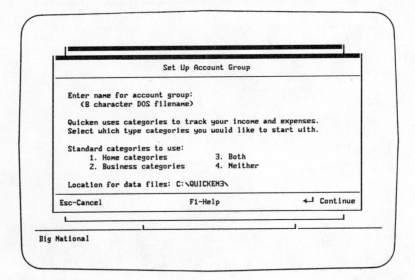

```
                          Set Up Account Group


       Enter name for account group:
         (8 character DOS filename)

       Quicken uses categories to track your income and expenses.
       Select which type categories you would like to start with.

       Standard categories to use:
            1. Home categories          3. Both
            2. Business categories       4. Neither

       Location for data files: C:\QUICKEN3\

   Esc-Cancel                   F1-Help              ↵ Continue


   Big National
```

*Fig. 10.5. Setting up categories.*

If you specify that the home categories should be used, you already have set up the categories shown in figure 10.1. If you specify that the business categories should be used, you already have set up the categories shown in figure 10.2. Even if you elect to use one of the sample category lists, however, you may need to modify the category list.

CPA Tip

Review last year's tax return to help you identify tax-deductible expenses. On your Form 1040 (Federal Individual Tax Return), Schedule A lists deductible itemized expenses, including medical bills, personal interest, contributions, moving expenses, investments, and so on. Call your CPA if you have specific questions when trying to identify a potential tax-deductible expense.

## Adding Categories

You can add categories in two ways. Both are described here, and you can pick whichever you find more convenient. To add categories using the Quick Entry menu option, **Categorize/Transfer**, follow these steps:

1. Press F4 to access the Quick Entry menu from the Write/Print Checks or Register screens (which you access from the Main menu).

2. Select **Categorize/Transfer** or use the shortcut key combination Ctrl-C. After you select **Categorize/Transfer**, the Category and Transfer List screen appears, as shown in figure 10.6.

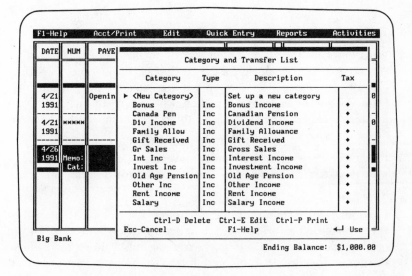

**Fig. 10.6.** *The Category and Transfer List screen.*

3. Select the first item on the list, New Category. You can use the home key to move to the first item on the list. Quicken then displays the Set Up Category screen, shown in figure 10.7.

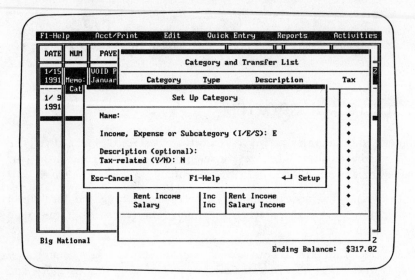

***Fig. 10.7.*** *The Set Up Category screen.*

4. Type the category name you want to use in the Name field.

5. Press Enter or Tab to move the cursor to the Income, Expense, or Subcategory field. Type an *i* if the category is for income, an *e* if the category is for expenses, and an *s* if the category is a subcategory. (You do not need to tell Quicken whether a subcategory is an income or expense figure because the program knows this by looking at the subcategory's category.)

6. (Optional) Press Enter or Tab to move the cursor to the Description field. You can use up to 25 characters to describe the category.

7. (Optional) Press Enter or Tab to move the cursor to the Tax-related field. The Tax-related field determines whether or not the tax reports include the category. You use this field to mark those categories for which you need totals to prepare your personal income tax returns.

8. To save the category, press Enter when the cursor is on the Tax-related field. Alternatively, press Ctrl-Enter or F10 when the cursor is on any of the screen fields.

You can short-cut the entire process of adding a category. To use the shortcut, follow these steps:

1. Move the cursor to the Category field on the Write/Print Checks screen, the Register screen, or the Split Transactions screen (which can be accessed by pressing Ctrl-S from the Write/Print Checks or Register screens).

2. Type the new category name you want to add. If the category doesn't already exist, Quicken displays the Category Not Found message box (see fig. 10.8).

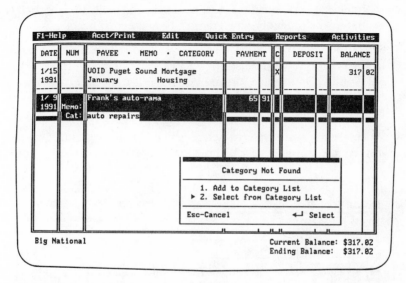

**Fig. 10.8.** *The Category Not Found box.*

3. To add a category, choose Add to Category List. Quicken displays the Set Up New Category box, which you complete as discussed in steps 4 through 8 of the first procedure described to add categories.

**Note:** If you choose the Select from Category List option, Quicken displays the Category List screen and marks the category that comes closest to whatever you entered.

You generally should have plenty of room for as many categories as you need. The precise maximum number, however, depends on your available memory, the length of your category names and descriptions, and the other information stored in memory. You should have room for about 150 categories with 320K of memory and more than 1,000 categories with 512K of memory.

# Deleting Categories

You also might want to delete categories—either because you don't use a particular category or because you added the category incorrectly. Deleting categories is even easier than adding categories. To delete categories, follow these steps:

1. Press F4 to access the Quick Entry menu from the Write/Print Checks or Register screens.

2. Select **Categorize/Transfer** from the Quick Entry menu, or use the shortcut key combination Ctrl-C. After you select **Categorize/ Transfer**, the Category and Transfer List screen appears.

3. Select the item on the list that you want to delete. Use the arrow keys to move down the list of categories one item at a time, or use PgUp and PgDn to move up and down the list one screen at a time. Pressing Home moves you to the beginning of the list and pressing End moves you to the end of the list.

4. When the item you want to delete is marked, press Ctrl-D. Quicken displays the warning screen shown in figure 10.9.

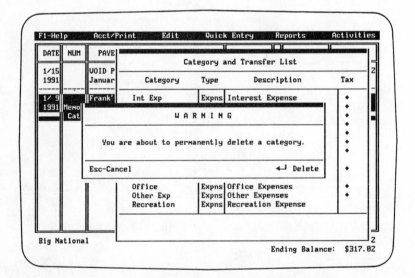

**Fig. 10.9.** *Quicken warns you that it's about to permanently delete a category.*

5. To remove the category from the category list, press Enter. If you don't want to remove the category, press Esc.

After you delete a category, you cannot use the category unless you add the category again. If you already have used the deleted category to describe transactions, you need to return to the register and change the invalid category to current, valid categories. (Chapter 4 and 5 describe how to use the register.)

# Editing Categories

You also can edit a category. Suppose that you run a business and use Quicken to account for, among other things, the wages you pay. Further, suppose that the Wages category has always been used for employees working in Washington state. If you create a new category called OR_WAGES to account for the wages you pay to employees working in Oregon, you might want to change the name of your Wages category to WA_WAGES to reflect the change in the significance of the account.

The steps for editing a category roughly parallel those for adding one. To edit a category, follow these steps:

1. Press F4 to access the Quick Entry menu from the Write/Print Checks or Register screens.

2. Select **Categorize/Transfer** from the Quick Entry menu, or use the shortcut key combination Ctrl-C. After you select **Categorize/Transfer**, the Category and Transfer List screen appears, as shown in figure 10.6.

3. Select the item on the list that you want to edit. Use the arrow keys to move down the list of categories one item at a time. Use PgUp and PgDn to move up and down the list one screen at a time. Pressing Home moves the cursor to the first item on the list; pressing End moves the cursor to the last item on the list.

4. When the item you want to edit is marked, press Ctrl-E. Quicken displays the Edit Category screen shown in figure 10.10.

5. (Optional) Retype or edit the category name you want to use in the Name field.

6. (Optional) Press Enter or Tab to move the cursor to the Income, Expense, or Subcategory field. If necessary, change the Income, Expense, or Subcategory field by typing an *i* for income, an *e* for expenses, or an *s* for subcategory.

7. (Optional) Press Enter or Tab to move the cursor to the Description field. If necessary, retype or edit the existing description.

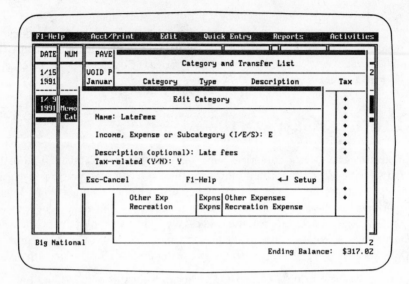

**Fig. 10.10.** *The Edit Category screen.*

8. (Optional) Press Enter or Tab to move the cursor to the Tax-related field. If necessary, change the Tax-related field.

9. To save the changes to the category, press Enter when the cursor is on the Tax-related field, or press Ctrl-Enter or F10 when the cursor is on any of the screen fields.

## Printing a Category and Transfer List

When you select **Categorize/Transfer** from the Quick Entry menu, Quicken displays a list of categories and accounts. Occasionally, you may want a printed copy of this list. You may want to review the list with your tax advisor at her office to verify you are tracking any tax deduction categories, or you may want to keep a paper copy of the list as an aid to entering transactions. To print a copy of the category and transfer list, follow these steps:

1. Press F4 to access the Quick Entry menu from the Write/Print Checks or Register screens.

2. Select **Categorize/Transfer** or use the shortcut combination, Ctrl-C. After you select **Categorize/Transfer**, the Category and Transfer List screen appears (see fig. 10.6).

3. Press Ctrl-P. Quicken displays the Print Category and Transfer List box. The screen, which resembles the Print Register screen, provides fields that you use to select the printer settings you want to use.

4. Indicate which printer settings you want to use—press 1 for the first setting, 2 for the second setting, and so on. Next, press F10 or Ctrl-Enter. Quicken prints a copy of the Category and Transfer List (see Figs. 10.1 and 10.2).

*Note:* For help in completing the Print Category and Transfer List screen, refer to the discussion in Chapter 4 on printing a register. The Print Register screen, which you use to print a register, works the same way as the Print Category and Transfer List screen.

# Working with Classes

Classes add a second dimension to the income and expense summaries that categories provide. Non-business use of Quicken probably does not require this second dimension. Business owners, however, will find Quicken's classes a powerful way to view their financial data from a second perspective.

For example, in addition to using two categories—Product and Service—to track income, you can use classes to determine which salespeople actually are booking the orders. With three salespeople, use these three classes: Joe, Bill, and Sue. In addition to seeing the sales of company products and company services, you also can see things like the sales that Bill made, the product sales that Joe made, and the service sales that Sue made. In effect, you have two different perspectives on your income —type of income, which shows either as a product or service, and salespeople, which shows as Joe, Bill, or Sue (see table 10.3).

### Table 10.3
### Two Perspectives on Income

| Type of income | Salespeople booking orders | | |
|---|---|---|---|
| | *Joe* | *Bill* | *Sue* |
| Product | Joe's product sales | Bill's product sales | Sue's product sales |
| Service | Joe's service sales | Bill's service sales | Sue's service sales |

Categories and subcategories group revenues and expenses by the type of transaction. For example, income transactions may be categorized as gross sales, other income, and so forth. Expense transactions may be categorized as car and truck expenses, supply expenses, utilities, and so on. But you may want to slice the data in other ways. You also may want to see income or expenses by job or project, by salesman or product line, and by geographic location or functional company areas.

# Defining a Class

The first step in using classes is to define the classes you want to use. Which classes you choose depend on how you need or want to view the financial data you collect with Quicken. Unfortunately, giving specific advice on picking appropriate classes is difficult. Classes usually are very specific to your particular personal or business finances. Here is one rough rule of thumb, however: Look at the sorts of questions you currently ask yourself, but cannot answer by using categories alone. A real estate investor may want to uses classes that correspond to individual properties. A law firm may want to use classes that represent each of the partners. And, of course, other businesses have still different views of the Quicken financial data that they want to use. After you define the classes you want to use, you are ready to add the classes in Quicken. You can add as many classes as you want.

To add classes, follow these steps:

1. Press F4 to access the Quick Entry menu from the Write/Print Checks or Register screens.

2. Choose the **Select/Set Up Class** option from the Quick Entry menu. Quicken displays the Class List screen shown in figure 10.11.

3. Mark the New Class item on the list and press Enter. Quicken displays the Set Up Class screen (see fig. 10.12).

4. Type the name you want to use for the class.

5. (Optional) Press Enter or Tab to move the cursor to the Description field. Type a description for the class.

6. To save the class, press Enter when the cursor is on the Description field, or press Ctrl-Enter or F10 when the cursor is on the Name or Description field.

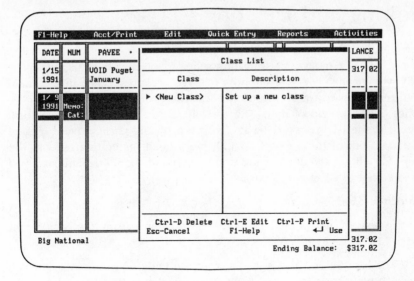

***Fig. 10.11.*** *The Class List screen.*

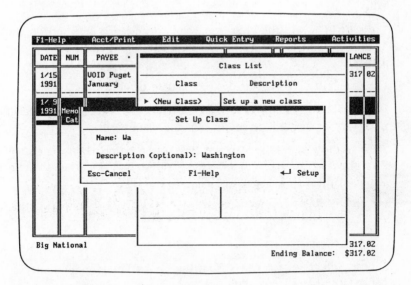

***Fig. 10.12.*** *The Set Up Class screen.*

# Editing and Deleting Classes

If you start defining classes, you also need to know how to edit and delete those classes. Whatever classification scheme you decide to use undoubtedly will change over time. Suppose that you are a real estate investor and you use classes to track your properties. You probably buy and sell properties over a period of time. Alternatively, if you are a bookkeeper for a law firm, the lawyers working at the firm probably change over a period of time. Both of these examples indicate a need for editing classes. The steps for editing and deleting are not difficult and should be familiar if you have edited or deleted categories.

To edit a class, follow these steps:

1. Press F4 to access the Quick Entry menu from the Write/Print Checks or Register screens.

2. Choose **Select/Set Up Class** from the Quick Entry menu. Quicken displays the Class List screen shown in figure 10.11.

3. Use the up- and down-arrow keys to move to the class you want to edit.

4. Press Ctrl-E while the class you want to delete is selected on the Class List. Quicken displays the Edit Class box, as shown in figure 10.13.

5. (Optional) If necessary or desired, retype or edit the class name.

6. (Optional) Press Enter or Tab to move to the Description field. If necessary or desired, retype or edit the class description.

7. To save the your changes to the class, press Enter when the cursor is on the Description field, or press Ctrl-Enter or F10 when the cursor is on the Name or Description field.

To delete a class, follow these steps:

1. Press F4 to access the Quick Entry menu from the Write/Print Checks or Register screens.

2. Choose **Select/Set Up Class** from the Quick Entry menu. Quicken displays the Class List screen shown in figure 10.11.

3. Use the up- and down-arrow keys to move to the class you want to delete.

4. Press Ctrl-D while the class you want to delete is selected on the Class List. Quicken warns you, as shown in figure 10.14, that a class is about to be deleted.

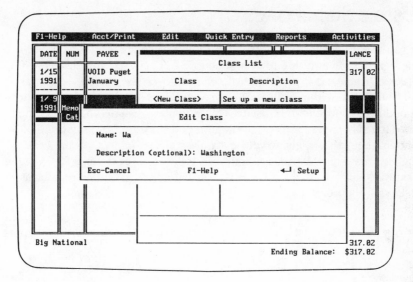

**Fig. 10.13.** *The Edit Class screen.*

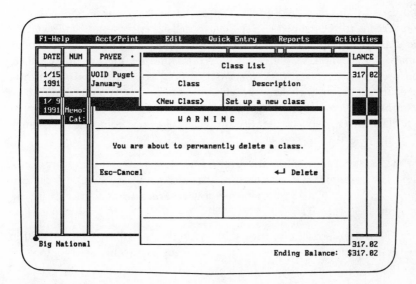

**Fig. 10.14.** *Quicken warns you that a class is about to be deleted.*

5. Press Enter to complete the deletion or press Esc to cancel the deletion.

# Using Subclasses

If you use classes to add another dimension to your reporting and recording, you also may want to use subclasses. Subclasses are classes within classes. If you use a geographical scheme to create classes, your classes may be states. Within each state, you may choose to use subclasses corresponding to portions of the state. For example, Washington, a class, might have the subclasses Eastern Washington and Western Washington. California, another class, might have the subclasses Northern California (excluding the Bay Area), Bay Area, Southern California (excluding Los Angeles County), and Los Angeles County. You enter, edit, and delete subclasses following the same procedures described earlier for classes.

Subclasses can be helpful for sales taxes that are based on a state, county, or city with different tax rates for each jurisdiction, or if you must report sales within each jurisdiction.

# Recording Classes and Subclasses

You use the Category field on the Write Checks, Register, or Split Transaction screens to record classes. To record a class, enter a slash followed by the class name in the Category field after any category or subcategory names. For example, if you want to record the income category, SALES, and the California class, CAL, for a transaction, you enter *sales/cal* in the Category field on the data screen. The same auto-completion feature described earlier in the book also applies to classes. If you type enough of a class for Quicken to identify the class, Quicken completes the entry for you.

If you use subclasses, enter the primary class, a colon, and then the subclass. For example, if the class CAL has the subclass NORTH, you can record sales for Northern California by entering *sales/cal:north* in the Category field (see fig. 10.15).

If you have more then one subclass—classes within classes within classes—you also separate the subclasses from each other with colons.

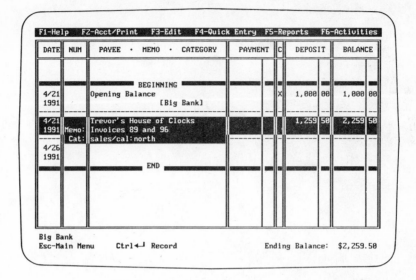

**Fig. 10.15.** *An example of a class and subclass used with a category.*

*CPA Tip*

The Quicken user's manual describes a whole series of ways you can use classes. And, for the most part, the ideas are good. Some accounting problems exist with many of the manual's suggestions. From the start, you should think about the problems so that you don't go to a lot of work and then find out you have wasted your time. The basic problem with classes is that they don't give you a way to budget. You cannot, for example, budget by classes. This may not seem all that important to you right now, but before you begin to use classes, review Chapter 16. Business users probably also will benefit by perusing Chapter 18.

# Chapter Summary

Quicken's categories and classes give you a means to organize your finances better. This chapter described how you can modify Quicken's predefined categories and how you use subcategories. This chapter also defined classes; described when you should use them; and detailed the steps for adding, editing, and deleting classes.

# 11

# Fine-Tuning Quicken

Quicken works fine if you install the program as described in Chapter 1. But you can do a few things to fine-tune Quicken. First, the Change Settings menu provides several options that enable you to control how Quicken works. Second, Version 4.0 of Quicken enables you to start the program with parameters that control how Quicken runs. This chapter covers both topics.

## Using the Change Settings Menu

Three of the options on the Change Settings menu (see fig. 11.1) give you varying degrees of control over how the Quicken program operates. These three options are **Screen Colors**, **Monitor Speed**, and **Other Settings**. (*Note:* Other chapters cover the remaining Change Settings options: Chapter 1 describes the **Printer Settings** option, Chapter 9 describes the **Account Group Activities** option, Chapter 15 describes the **Electronic Payment** option, and Chapter 20 describes the **Password** option.)

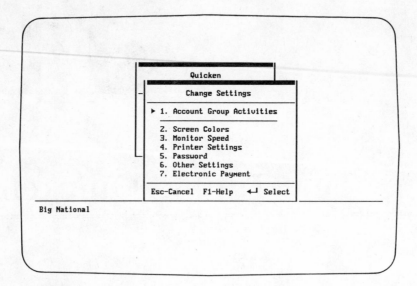

**Fig. 11.1.** *The Change Settings menu provides options that enable you to fine-tune Quicken's operation.*

# Changing Screen Colors

Quicken gives you control over the colors the program uses on menus and screens. If your monitor is monochrome, you can choose between monochrome and shades of gray. If your monitor is color, you can choose a navy and azure combination, white and navy, and red and gray. You cannot hurt anything by experimenting with the various color combinations.

To change the color settings that Quicken uses, follow these steps:

1. Select the **Change Settings** option from Quicken's Main menu.

2. Select the **Screen Colors** option from the Change Settings menu. Quicken displays the Change Color Scheme screen, as shown in figure 11.2.

3. Use the arrow keys to move the cursor to the color combination you want to use and press Enter. Alternatively, press the number of the color scheme: 1 for Monochrome, 2 for Navy/Azure, 3 for White/Navy, and so on.

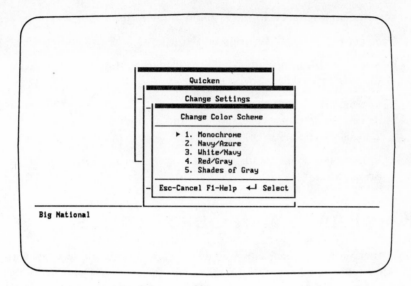

*Fig. 11.2. The Change Color Scheme screen.*

The default color option for a monochrome monitor is **Monochrome**, but you also should try **Shades of Gray** to see which works best for you. If you have a monochrome monitor and the screen display is unclear or portions of the screen don't show, you probably have the monitor type defined as color. The default color scheme for a color monitor is **Navy/ Azure**, but you should try each of the other color schemes to see which works best. If you are color blind, for example, one of the other color schemes may be easier to see.

# Changing Screen Update Speed

The **Monitor Speed** option on the Change Settings menu enables you to choose between slow and fast for the screen update speed. Quicken initially assumes that you want the fast option. If Quicken ascertains that your monitor update speed should be fast, the program does not enable you to change the setting to slow. If Quicken determines that your monitor may not be able to handle the fast speed, it enables you to change the speed to slow.

If your monitor cannot handle the fast speed setting, you may see little flecks and patches—sometimes called snow—on-screen. If you notice snow on your monitor, set the monitor speed to slow.

To set the monitor speed to slow, follow these steps:

1. Select the **Change Settings** option from Quicken's Main menu.

2. Select **Monitor Speed** from the Change Settings menu. Quicken displays the Monitor Speed screen.

3. Use the arrow keys to move the cursor to the speed setting—Slow or Fast—you want to use. Or press the number of the speed setting: 1 for Slow and 2 for Fast.

4. When the triangle cursor marks the speed setting you want to use, press Enter.

## Fine-Tuning with Other Settings

The Other Settings screen, shown in figure 11.3, enables you to work with 13 other settings. You can use these settings to fine-tune Quicken so that the program operates in the fashion you find most helpful. The settings on this screen are described in the following sections. If you want to change any of these settings, first perform these two steps:

1. Select the **Change Settings** option from Quicken's Main menu.

2. Select the **Other Settings** option from the Change Settings menu. Quicken displays the Other Settings screen as shown in figure 11.3.

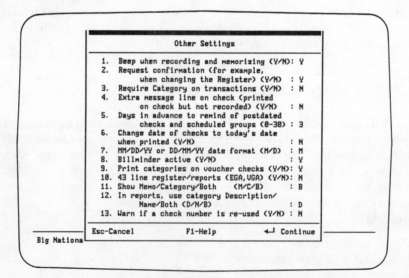

**Fig. 11.3.** *The Other Settings screen.*

3. (Optional) Use the arrow keys or the Tab key to move the cursor to the Beep when recording and memorizing setting. Press N if you want to turn off the beep that Quicken makes when the program records and memorizes transactions; leave the setting at Y if you want to keep the beep. (You may want to consider this option if you enter a lot of transactions. You also use this setting to turn on the beep noise if you previously have turned the beep off.)

4. (Optional) Use the arrow keys or the Tab key to move the cursor to the Request confirmation setting. To turn off the confirmation messages, press N. The Request confirmation setting turns on and off the pop-up confirmation messages that display to give you a second chance before executing many Quicken operations. Because the confirmation messages may save you from accidentally doing something you would rather not do, you probably should leave this switch set to Y.

5. (Optional) Use the arrow keys or the Tab key to move the cursor to the Require category on transactions setting. If you want Quicken to display a reminder message that asks you to confirm transactions you enter without a valid category, press Y. You do not have to use categories if this switch is set to Y, but you have to confirm that you do not want to use a category. If you plan to use categories, you should set this switch to Y for Yes. (Chapter 10 describes the categories feature in detail.)

6. (Optional) Use the arrow keys or the Tab key to move the cursor to the Extra message line on check setting. To see and use the extra message line that appears to the right of the address box on your checks, press Y. To remove the extra message line, press N.

7. (Optional) Use the arrow keys or the Tab key to move the cursor to the Days in advance to remind of postdated checks setting. Type the number of days in advance that Billminder should remind you of postdated checks and scheduled transaction groups. The number of days can be from 0 to 30. (Billminder is described in Chapters 2, 4, and 6.)

8. (Optional) Use the arrow keys or the Tab key to move the cursor to the Change date of checks to today's date when printed setting. If, when Quicken prints checks, you want Quicken to print the current system date as the check date, press Y. When the check date you enter differs from the check printing date, the check's date will be changed.

*CPA Tip*

Quicken reminds hard disk users in a way slightly different from floppy disk users. Because of this difference, the rules for specifying the Days in advance setting also differ. Hard disk users are reminded of postdated checks and scheduled transaction groups every time they turn on the computer. If you are a hard disk user, therefore, you should set the days in advance to one less than the number of days between times you turn on your computer. For example, if you use your computer every other day, the difference in days between use is two. One number less than two is one. Therefore, you should set the days in advance as one. Whenever you turn on your computer, you are reminded of the bills that should be paid that day and the bills that can be paid the next day. But the bills that can be paid the next day need to be paid today because you will not use your computer tomorrow.

Floppy disk users follow a slightly different procedure. Floppy disk users are reminded of postdated checks and scheduled transaction groups on the Quicken Main menu. Quicken reminds floppy disk users, therefore, only when the Quicken program is started. If you are a floppy disk user, set the Days in advance field to one day less than the number of days between times you use Quicken. If you use Quicken on a weekly basis—for example, every Saturday morning—set the Days in advance field to 6. You are reminded every Saturday morning of the bills to be paid for the next six days.

9. (Optional) Use the arrow keys or the Tab key to move the cursor to the Date format setting. If you want dates to appear in month/day/year format—June 1, 1991 appears as 6/1/91, for example—press M for month first. If you want the dates to appear in day/month/year—June 1, 1991 appears as 1/6/91—press D for day first.

10. (Optional) Use the arrow keys or the Tab key to move the cursor to the Billminder active setting. If you then want to use the Billminder feature, set this switch to Yes by pressing Y. The Billminder Active setting enables you to determine whether or not Quicken reminds you of postdated checks and transaction groups.

11. (Optional) Use the arrow keys or the Tab key to move the cursor to the Print categories on voucher checks setting. If you want what you enter in the Category field or the Split Transaction screen fields to appear on the voucher portion of checks, set this setting to yes by pressing Y.

You do not need the Category field information printed on the voucher stub unless someone you pay a check to needs to know which income and expense categories a check affects. If you decide not to use the category fields to record categories, and instead use the fields for information such as the invoices a check pays, you can have this information printed on the check stub. This field does not apply unless your checks have voucher stubs.

12. (Optional) Use the arrow keys or the Tab key to move the cursor to the 43 line register/reports setting. If your computer uses an Enhanced Graphics Adapter (EGA) or video graphics adapter (VGA) monitor and card, you can set the 43 line register/reports field to Y for Yes, which doubles—from six to twelve—the number of lines Quicken displays in the register. If you have an EGA monitor, try the option. Having more register information on-screen is helpful. If the compressed version of the register strains your eyes, set the toggle back to N.

*Note:* All the figures in this book use the standard, uncompressed versions of the register and report screens.

13. (Optional) Use the arrow keys or the Tab key to move the cursor to the Show memo/category/both setting. This setting determines which information appears on the memo line of the check register when the transaction isn't selected. Press M to designate that only the memo should appear; press C to designate that only the category should appear; press B to designate that both the memo and category should appear. Because you do not have enough room to fully display both the Memo and Category fields, if you select B, Quicken abbreviates the two fields.

14. (Optional) Use the arrow keys or the Tab key to move the cursor to the reports use category Description/Name/Both setting. This field determines whether the category name, category description, or both appear on reports. You have three choices: pressing D designates that only the description appears; pressing N designates that only the name appears; pressing B designates that both the name and description appear. D is the default setting and the one you probably want to use.

15. (Optional) Use the arrow keys or the Tab key to move the cursor to the Warn if a check number is re-used setting. If you want Quicken to display a message in a pop-up box when you use a check number you have used previously, set this field to Y for Yes. Figure 11.4 shows the warning message that Quicken uses.

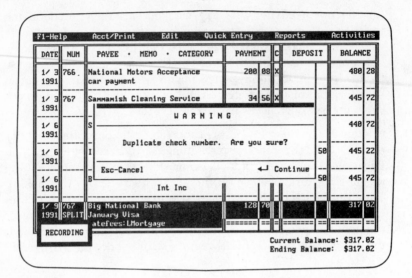

**Fig. 11.4.** *The warning message Quicken uses to alert you that you are entering a previously used check number.*

16. When the Other Settings screen correctly reflects the settings you want to use when you run Quicken, press Enter when the cursor is on the Warn if check number is re-used field. Alternatively, you can press F10 or Ctrl-Enter when the cursor is on one of the other fields. Quicken returns you to the Change Settings menu.

# Starting Quicken with Parameters

The newest version of Quicken enables you to start the program with parameters. (Parameters are codes you type following the *q* you type to start the program.) These parameters enable you to select an account as part of starting Quicken. These parameters also enable you to select one of the Main menu options as part of starting Quicken. Finally, Quicken even has a special parameter that saves memory by loading only certain pieces of the Quicken program so that you have more room in memory for your data. Although the parameters may sound complicated, they really are not difficult. The following sections describe how to use the parameters that Quicken provides.

# Selecting an Account

To start Quicken, type the letter *q* from the DOS prompt. You can specify which account should be selected by following the letter *q* with the name of the account. For example, to start Quicken and simultaneously select the account named "checking," type the following at the DOS prompt:

    Q CHECKING

(**Note:** Leave a space between the letter "q" and the word "checking.")

Quicken selects the account "checking" in the current account group. (If you have questions about selecting an account, refer to Chapter 3.)

If an account isn't in the current group, you also can identify the account group as a second parameter. For example, if you want to select the account "Checking" in the account group "QDATA," type the following at the DOS prompt:

    Q CHECKING QDATA

(**Note:** Leave a space between the letter "q" and the word "checking," and between the words "checking" and "QDATA.")

Selecting an account when you start Quicken isn't difficult and can be quite handy. You do need to remember one trick, however. If the account is two words, you need to enclose the account in quotation marks so that Quicken doesn't think one part of the name is the account group name. For example, in the case of an account named "Big National" in the QDATA account group, you enter the parameter in the applicable one of the two forms shown here:

    Q "BIG NATIONAL"

    Q "BIG NATIONAL" QDATA

# Selecting a Main Menu Option

You also can start Quicken with a parameter that selects one of the Main menu options. Each Main menu option is identified by a number (see fig. 11.5). The numeral 1 indicates the **Write/Print Checks** option, 2 indicates the **Register** option, 3 indicates the **Reports** option, 4 indicates the **Select Account** option, 5 indicates the **Change Settings** option, and E indicates **Exit**.

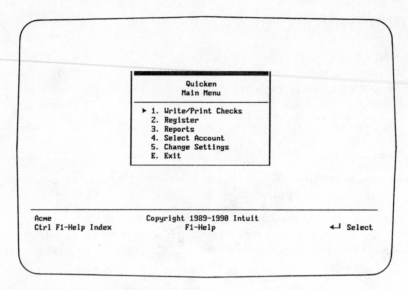

*Fig. 11.5. The Quicken Main menu.*

To select one of the Main menu options, you can follow the letter "q" with the Main menu option number. For example, to start Quicken and select the **Write/Print Checks** option, enter the following at the DOS prompt:

Q 1

(***Note:*** Leave a space between the letter "q" and the number "1.")

You can combine parameters to select an account and Main menu option. For example, to select the account "acme" and choose the second option on the Main menu, type:

Q ACME 2

(***Note:*** Leave a space between the letter "q" and the word "acme," as well as between the word "acme" and the number "2.")

## Using Less Memory

For some Quicken operations, you actually may run out of memory. This should occur only if you are working with an account with many transactions or if you are requesting a very large report. Nevertheless, if you run out of memory, you have a problem that needs to be handled. In the long term, you probably will need to shrink one or more accounts (see Chapter 9).

As a short- or intermediate-term solution, however, you can start Quicken in a way that uses less memory. You use the "/n" parameter. For example, type the following at the DOS prompt:

Q /N

(*Note:* Again, leave a space between the "q" and the character sequence "/n.)

# Using Versions 4.0 and 3.0 Key Definitions

Quicken 4.0 and 3.0 use slightly different key definitions of the Home and End keys. Table 11.1 summarizes the different definitions.

**Table 11.1**
**Key Definitions**

| Key or Key Combination | Version 4.0 | Version 3.0 |
|---|---|---|
| Home | First character in field | First transaction in register |
| End | Last character in field | Last transaction in register |
| Home Home | First field on-screen | Not used |
| End End | Last field on-screen | Not used |
| Ctrl-Home | First transaction in register | Same as Home |
| Ctrl-End | Last transaction in register | Same as End |

Although Version 4.0 key definitions are more consistent with the standard uses of the two keys, you may want to use Version 3.0 key definitions and "/a" parameter. For example, to use the Version 3.0 key definitions for the Home and End keys, type the following at the DOS prompt.

Q /A

(*Note:* Leave a space between the letter "q" and the character sequence "/a.")

After you start Quicken using the "/a" parameter, Quicken continues to use the Version 3.0 key definitions until you tell Quicken to stop. To tell Quicken to stop using the Version 3.0 key definitions and return to the Version 4.0 definitions, use the "/s" parameter. For example, type the following at the DOS prompt:

Q /S

(*Note:* Again, leave a space between the letter "q" and the character sequence "/s.")

# Chapter Summary

You can fine-tune Quicken's operation in two ways: with the Change Settings menu options and with parameters you include when you start Quicken. This chapter described both methods. Understanding how you can fine-tune Quicken and having the steps for doing so laid out might mean you can get Quicken to work just the way you want.

# 12

# Tracking Your Net Worth, Other Assets, and Liabilities

Quicken was designed originally as a checking account record-keeping tool. The newest releases of Quicken, Versions 3.0 and 4.0, however, can do much more than just keep track of your checking account. Using Quicken's familiar check-register format, you can maintain financial records for any asset or liability.

Assets refer to things that you own and that have lasting value. For individuals, assets include items such as a house, cars, furniture, and investments. For businesses, assets include the money customers owe, the inventory held for resale, and any fixtures or equipment used in the business. Liabilities refer to money you owe others. For individuals, liabilities include mortgages, car loans, credit card debts, and income taxes. For businesses, liabilities include amounts owed suppliers, wages payable to employees, and loans from banks and leasing companies.

The benefits of using Quicken to track your assets (other than bank accounts) and to track your liabilities essentially match the benefits associated with tracking bank accounts. By carefully tracking other assets, you know what those assets currently are worth and why they have changed in value. By carefully tracking your liabilities, you maintain firm control over your debts, ensure your ability to continue regular payments, and keep records of why the dollar amounts of your debts have changed. By carefully tracking your assets and liabilities, you can use Quicken to generate reports that calculate your personal or business financial net worth.

(*Note:* The only real drawback, or cost, of tracking your other assets and liabilities is the additional effort required on your part. In many cases, however, the benefits discussed earlier more than merit the cost.)

This chapter describes in general terms how to use Quicken to perform record keeping for other assets and liabilities and then delivers information on why and how you can use Quicken to generate balance sheets. (If you become enthused about the record-keeping possibility of Quicken, you also will want to peruse Chapter 13, Chapter 17, and Chapter 18.)

# Setting Up Accounts for Other Assets and Liabilities

You need to set up a Quicken account for each asset or liability for which you want to keep records with Quicken. You can track any asset or liability you want. No real limit or restriction exists on what you can or cannot do, except that within an account group, you can have only up to 255 accounts. The only thing you need to remember is that the accounts you want to appear together on a balance sheet must be set up in the same account group. Typically, that means all your business accounts need to be in one group and all your personal accounts need to be in another group. After you define the account groups, you take the following steps to set up accounts:

1. Choose the **Select Account** option on Quicken's Main menu. Quicken displays the Select Account to Use screen shown in figure 12.1.

2. To add a new account, select New Account from the list. Quicken then displays the Set Up New Account screen shown in figure 12.2.

3. Enter a description of the account using the Name field. The Name field can be up to fifteen characters long and can use any characters except [, ], /, and :. You can include spaces.

4. Press Enter or Tab to move the cursor to the Account Type field and type the account type.

   Quicken provides four asset account types to choose from: Bank Account, Cash, Other Asset, and Investment Account. If the asset is a bank account, set the account type to 1. If the asset is cash in your wallet or in the petty cash box, set the account type to 3. If the account is an investment, set the account type to 6. (Refer to Chapter 13 for the specifics of defining an investment account.) For any

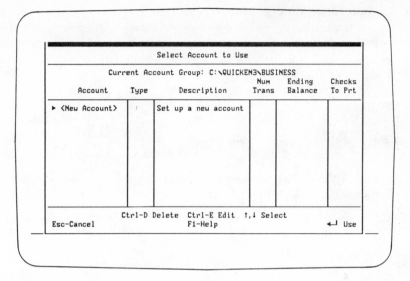

*Fig. 12.1. The Select Account to Use screen.*

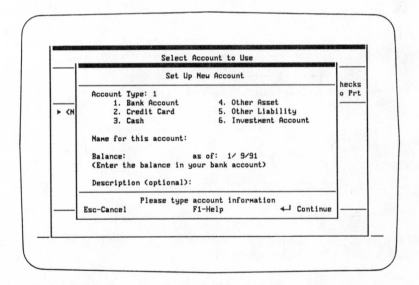

*Fig. 12.2. The Set Up New Account screen.*

other asset—accounts receivable, real estate, and so on—enter the account type as 4. Quicken also provides two liability account types: Credit Card and Other Liability. If the liability is the balance on your VISA or MasterCard account, set the account type to 2; otherwise, set the account type to 5.

5. Press Enter or Tab to move to the starting account Balance field. If you want to set up an opening balance for an asset or liability, enter this amount here. Assets can, for example, be listed at their original cost or their current fair market value. Liabilities can be listed at the current balances.

*CPA Tip*　Be sure to make a note in your records as to the basis of your assets—for example, original cost, fair market value, and so on.

6. Press Enter or Tab to move the cursor to the As of date field. Enter the date on which the balance you entered is correct.

7. If you enter your credit cards, Quicken asks for the credit limit on your cards (see fig. 12.3).

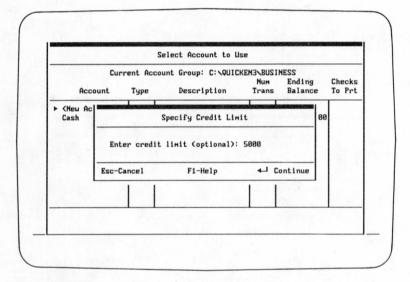

*Fig. 12.3. Quicken prompts you to enter the credit card limit if you define an account type as credit card.*

8. (Optional) Press Enter or Tab to move the cursor to the Description field. Fill in the Description field to provide an additional 21 characters of account description.

9. When you finish entering information for the new asset or liability account, press Enter.

# Keeping Financial Records

After you initially set up an account—whether an asset or a liability—you maintain the account in one of two ways.

First, you can select the account using the **Select Account** option, and then you can use the **Register** option to enter transactions that increase or decrease the account, just as you do for a checking account. (***Note:*** To select an account, choose **Select Account** from Quicken's Main menu. Quicken displays the Select Account to Use screen shown in figure 12.1. Use the arrow keys to mark the account you want and then press Enter.)

Figure 12.4 shows how a register of a major real estate asset—a personal residence—may look. The Other Assets register looks almost identical to the regular Bank Account register and works the same way. Transaction amounts that decrease the asset account balance are recorded in the Decrease field of the register. (On the bank account version of the Register screen, this field is labeled Payment.) Transaction amounts that increase the asset account are recorded in the Increase field of the register. (On the bank account version of the check register, this field is labeled Deposit). The total Real Estate account balance shows at the bottom right corner of the screen. If you have postdated transactions—those with dates in the future—the current balance also shows.

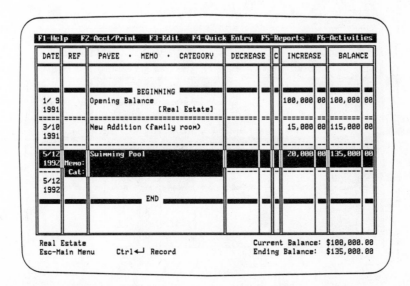

**Fig. 12.4.** *A sample register used to record the value of a personal residence.*

In the example shown in figure 12.4, the opening balance of $100,000 shows what you may have paid originally for your home. The two subsequent transactions shown—one for the addition of a new family room and the other for a new backyard swimming pool—show the events that changed the value of your home. By keeping these records, you may be able to keep better track of the value of your home and the reasons for any change in your home's value.

When working with the Other Assets register, you can access the same menu options as when you are working with the Bank Account register, except that **Update Account Balances** replaces **Reconcile**. (See "Updating Account Balances" later in this chapter.)

Figure 12.5 shows a register that you can use to track what you owe on a loan such as a business credit line or a home mortgage. The Other Liability register also mirrors the check register in appearance and operation. Transaction amounts that increase the amount owed are recorded in the Increase field of the register. (On the bank account version of the register screen, this field is labeled Payment.) Transaction amounts that decrease the amount owed are recorded in the Decrease field of the register. (On the bank account version of the register, this field is labeled Deposit.) The total liability balance shows at the bottom right corner of the screen. If you have postdated transactions, the current balance also shows. You do not use the C field when tracking a liability account.

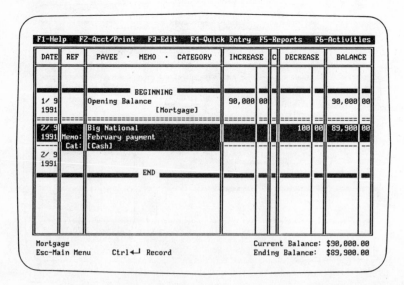

**Fig. 12.5.** *The register used to track the balances on a loan.*

In the example shown in figure 12.5, the opening balance of $90,000 shows what you may have borrowed originally on a mortgage. The subsequent transaction shown—the February mortgage payment—shows the reduction in the outstanding loan balance stemming from the principal portion of the February loan payment.

When working with the Other Liability register, the menu options you can use are the same as when working with the Bank Account register, except that, again, the **Update Account Balances** option replaces the **Reconcile** option.

> If you want to keep track of what you owe on a particular mortgage or loan, you may need an amortization schedule, which the lender should provide. An amortization schedule shows the portion of your payments that goes to paying interest and the portion that goes to reducing the principal you owe. Only the principal reductions are recorded in the register for a loan or mortgage. The interest portion is reported as interest expense.

*CPA Tip*

Entering transactions directly into a register is one way to maintain correct account balances for another asset or liability account. You can, however, choose a second way to maintain correct account balances for other assets and liabilities. Quicken enables you to use an account name in the Category field on the Write/Print Checks and Register screens. Quicken then uses the information from the checking account transaction to record the appropriate transaction in one of the other asset or liability accounts. If you are writing a check to the bank that holds your mortgage and enter the account name *mortgage* in the Category field to show the principal portion of the payment, Quicken records a decrease in the mortgage liability account equal to the principal portion of the payment you are making from your checking account. Figure 12.6 shows a $1,000 check being written to Big National Bank for a mortgage payment. The principal amount of this payment that is applied to the current mortgage balance is $100. When you record the check, a $100 decrease in your Mortgage account also is recorded, as shown in figure 12.7.

> A convenient way to jump between different parts of the same transfer transaction is to use the Edit menu option **Go to Transfer**. You can use the shortcut key combination, Ctrl-X.

*CPA Tip*

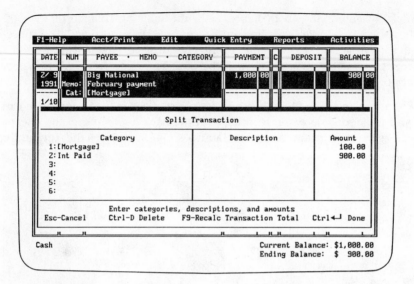

**Fig. 12.6.** *A $1000 check being written to the mortgage company.*

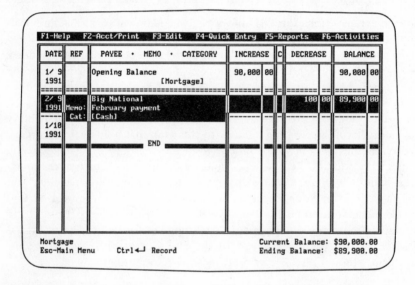

**Fig. 12.7.** *When you record the check, Quicken records a $100 decrease in your mortgage liability.*

# Reviewing Tips for Working with Other Assets and Liabilities

The register basically works the same, regardless of the account type. A few tips and techniques, however, can help you when using Quicken to account for other assets and liabilities. These tips and techniques include dealing with the nuances and subtleties of the cash and credit card account type, using the **Update Account Balances** option for cash accounts and the **Pay Credit Card Bill** option accessed from the Credit Card register.

## Dealing with Cash Accounts

The cash account option works well when you want to keep complete, detailed records of all your miscellaneous cash outlays that are paid out of pocket and not with a check—such as $5.00 for stamps, $12.00 for lunch, $7.50 for parking, and so on. Often, you do not need this level of control or detail. When you do want to keep detailed records, the cash account type provides just the tool to get the job done. Quicken warns you, however, that you cannot use the **Write/Print Checks** option with this type of account.

> For businesses, the cash account type is a convenient way to keep track of petty-cash expenditures and reimbursements. Even very large businesses can benefit by using Quicken for petty-cash accounting.

*CPA Tip*

Figure 12.8 shows the Cash account register screen. Notice that this screen is almost identical to the Bank Account register screen. Money flowing in and out of the account is recorded in the Spend and Receive fields. On the Bank Account register screen, money flowing out of the account is recorded in the Payment field and money flowing into the account is recorded in the Deposit field. On the Other Assets and Other Liability account register screens, money flowing into and out of the account is recorded in the Increase and Decrease fields.

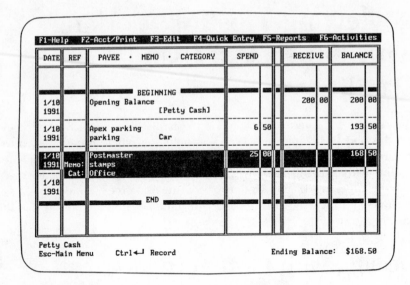

*Fig. 12.8. The cash account type register.*

As with the Other Assets and Other Liability account registers, the C field usually is not used. You can use this column, however, to match receipts against entries to indicate that you have backup records.

# Updating Account Balances

On the Activities menu for cash accounts, other assets, and other liabilities accounts, **Update Account Balances** replaces **Reconcile**. (On the credit card account Activities menu, **Pay Credit Card Bill** replaces **Reconcile**. This option is described later in the chapter.) Figure 12.9 shows the cash account Activities menu.

Selecting **Update Account Balances** provides a screen you use to reconcile, or adjust, an account. Suppose that the register you use to keep track of your petty cash or pocket cash shows $168.50 as the on-hand cash balance, but the actual balance is $161.88. You can use the Update Account Balance screen to record an adjustment, as shown in figure 12.10.

To adjust an account's balance, follow these steps:

1. Select the **Register** option from the Main menu.

2. Press F6 to display the Activities menu.

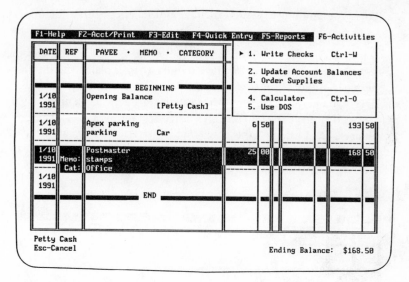

**Fig. 12.9.** *The cash account type Activities menu.*

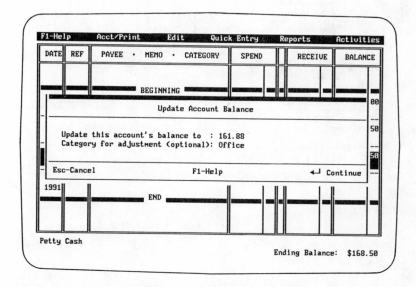

**Fig. 12.10.** *The Update Account Balance screen.*

3. Choose **Update Account Balance** from the Activities menu. Quicken displays the Update Account Balance screen (see fig. 12.10).

4. Enter the amount to which the account balance should be adjusted in the Update this account's balance to field.

5. (Optional) Press Enter or Tab to move the cursor to the Category for adjustment field. Enter the category that explains the difference between the old and new account balances, and then press Enter to have Quicken create the adjustment transaction. Remember that you can press Ctrl-C to see the Category and Transfer List screen. Figure 12.11 shows the adjustment transaction created by the Update Account Balance transaction so that the account balance shows as $161.88.

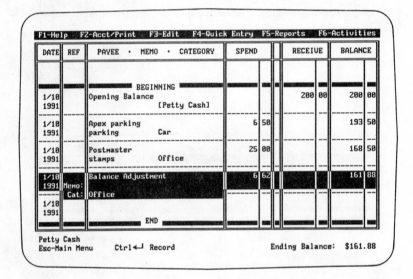

*Fig. 12.11.* The transaction recorded by the **Update Account Balance** option.

You often really don't know which category explains the difference between the old and new account balances. The reason is that the difference is explained by transactions that you either forgot to record or recorded incorrectly. In effect, what you are trying to do here is record or correct, using the Update Account Balance screen, erroneous or missing transactions. In a pinch, if you cannot figure out which category you should use, use the one that you use most frequently with this register. A warning needs to be issued here, however. You cannot guess or estimate tax deduction amounts. You therefore really shouldn't use this tip to increase tax deductions. The Internal Revenue Service disallows deductions that cannot be supported with evidence as to the type and amount.

# Dealing with Credit Card Accounts

The credit card account type is helpful if you want to keep track of the details of your credit card spending and pay off your account balance over time instead of on a monthly basis.

If you always pay your credit card in full every month, you do not need to use the credit card account type, unless you want to track exactly where and when charges are made. The reason you don't need to use the credit card account type is that you usually can record the details of your credit card spending when you record the check payment to the credit card company. What is more, because the credit card balance always is reduced to zero every month, you do not need to keep track of the balance. The steps involved in using the Credit Card account register to perform record keeping for your credit cards parallel the steps for using any other register. First, you set up the account and record the beginning balance. (Because you are working with a liability, the beginning balance is what you owe.) Second, you use the register to record credit card spending. As noted earlier in the chapter, you also are asked for the credit limit on the credit card so Quicken can track your available credit.

The check you write actually is recorded as a reduction in the amount owed on your credit card. You already have recorded the credit card spending by recording transactions in the Credit Card register.

As with the other asset and liability registers, some minor differences exist between the Bank Account register screen and menu options and the Credit Card register screen and menu options. The CHARGE field in the

Credit Card register is where you record each use of your credit card. The PAYMENT field is where you record payments made to the credit card company. If you fill in the Credit Limit field when you set up the credit card account, Quicken shows the credit remaining in the lower right corner of the screen above the Ending Balance field. Figure 12.12 shows the Credit Card register screen.

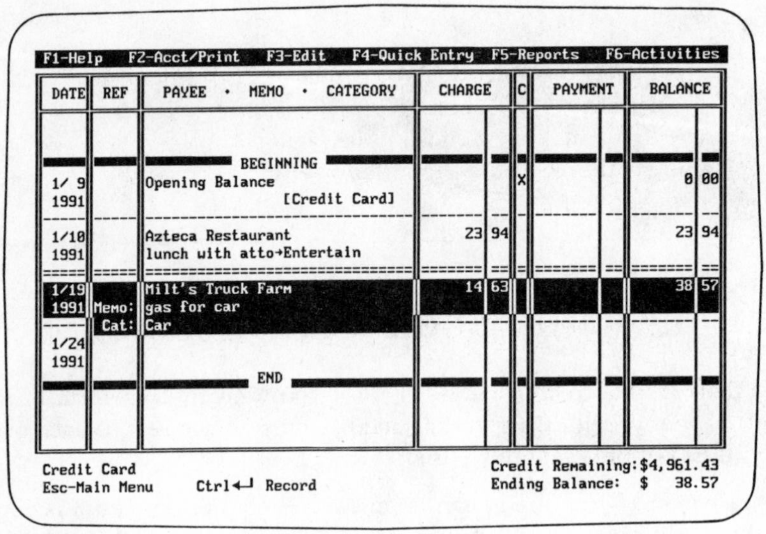

*Fig. 12.12. The Credit Card register screen.*

# Paying Credit Card Bills

The credit card Activities menu differs slightly from the standard Quicken Activities menu, replacing the **Reconcile** option with **Pay Credit Card Bill**, as shown in figure 12.13.

If you select **Pay Credit Card Bill**, Quicken displays the Credit Card Statement Information screen shown in figure 12.14.

Selecting **Pay Credit Card Bill** enables you to reconcile your credit card register balance with the monthly credit card statement, record finance charges, and record a handwritten check or set up a check to be printed by Quicken.

You fill in several fields to begin this process, but the process parallels the one you use for reconciling your bank account, which is described in

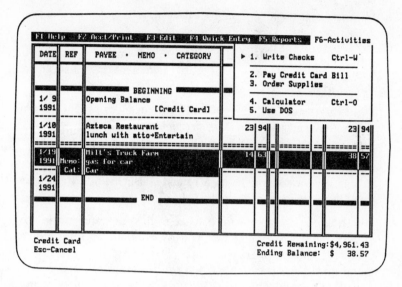

**Fig. 12.13.** *The credit card version of the Activities menu.*

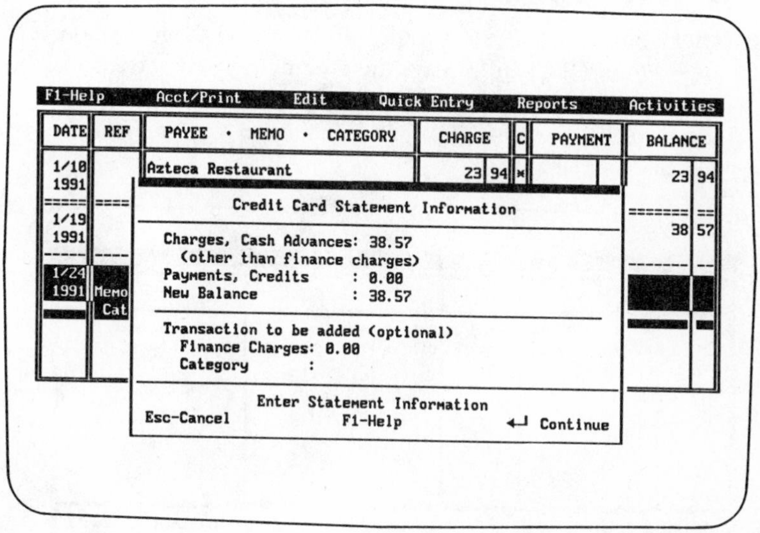

**Fig. 12.14.** *The Credit Card Statement Information screen.*

Chapter 8. In fact, the Credit Card Statement Information screen closely resembles the one used to start the bank account reconciliation process.

To use the **Pay Credit Card Bill** option, select the **Register** option, number 2, from the Main menu and follow these steps:

1. With the register for a credit card displayed, press F6 to access the Activities menu.

2. Select the **Pay Credit Card Bill** option from the Activities menu. Quicken displays the Credit Card Statement Information screen shown in figure 12.14.

3. Enter the credit card charges and cash advances as a positive number in the Charges, Cash Advances field.

4. Enter the total payments made in the Payments, Credits field also as a positive amount. If your statement shows credit slip transactions (because a store issued you a refund), also include these transactions in the Payments, Credits field.

5. Enter the ending credit card balance from your statement in the New Balance field. (Assuming that you owe money to the credit card company, the number you enter is a positive one.) Enter the monthly interest charges as a positive number in the Finance Charges field and enter the category to which you want finance charges assigned. (Quicken uses this information to record a transaction for the monthly interest you are charged on the credit card.)

6. After you complete the Credit Card Statement Information screen, press Enter. Quicken displays the credit card transactions list shown in figure 12.15. This screen and the abbreviated register screen, accessed by pressing F9, work like the reconciliation screens described in Chapter 8.

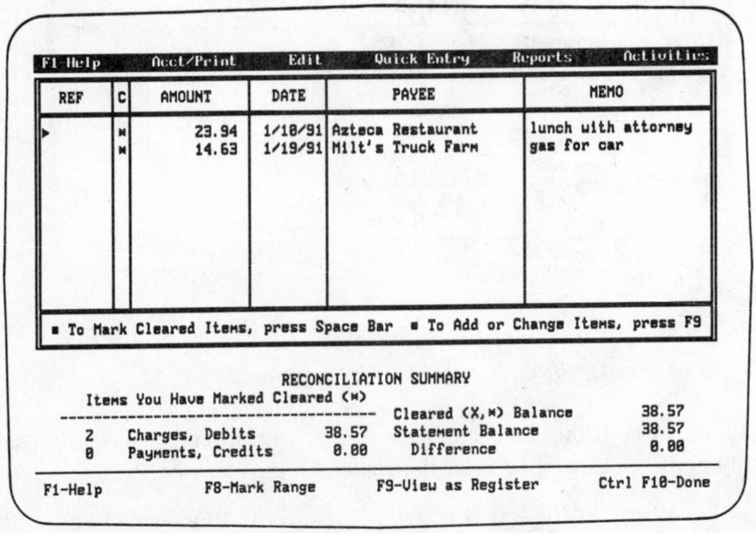

*Fig. 12.15. The credit card transactions list screen.*

7. Mark credit card transactions as cleared by pressing the space bar when the transaction is highlighted. A cleared credit card transaction is one that appears on the credit card statement. After you mark all the cleared credit card transactions, the cleared balance amount should equal the statement balance amount. If the two amounts do not equal each other, you missed recording a transaction or marking a transaction as cleared. (Chapter 8 gives tips on finding and correcting reconciliation errors for a bank account. These tips also apply to reconciling a credit card statement.)

8. When you finish the reconciliation process—the difference amount shows as zero—press Ctrl-F10. Quicken next displays the Make Credit Card Payment screen, shown in figure 12.16.

   If the reconciliation is not complete, Quicken displays a screen asking you to proceed or leave the reconciliation. At this time, Quicken displays an Adjusting Register To Agree with Statement screen. To accept Quicken's adjustments, press Enter; to cancel, press Esc.

   *Note:* If you press Ctrl-F10 prior to reconciling the balance to zero, Quicken makes the necessary adjustments to reconcile the balance. Refer to Chapter 8 for more information on this.

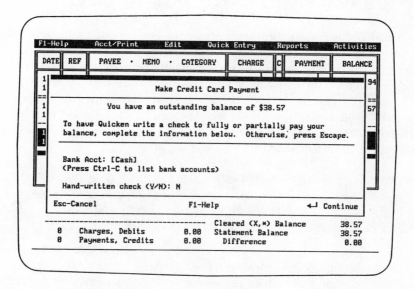

**Fig. 12.16.** *The Make Credit Card Payment screen.*

9. If you don't want to pay your credit card bill, press Esc from the Make Credit Card Payment screen. If you do want to pay your credit card bill, complete steps 10 and 11. Set the Hand-written check field to N if you want Quicken to move you to the Write Checks screen so that you can print a check to the credit card company on the specified bank account.

10. With the cursor positioned on the Bank account field, enter the name of the bank account on which you will write the check to pay the credit card bill. (Pressing Ctrl-C accesses the Category and Transfer List screen. At the end of the Category and Transfer List screen, Quicken shows account names.)

11. Move the cursor to the Hand-written check field. Set the Hand-written check field to Y if you want Quicken to move to the Register screen for the specified bank account so that you can record the check you wrote to the credit card company. In either case, Quicken enters the payment amount as the entire credit card balance. If you want to pay less than that amount, change the amount in the Payment amount field.

# Measuring Your Net Worth

A balance sheet is one of the traditional tools individuals and businesses can use to measure your net worth. A balance sheet lists the assets you own and the liabilities you owe. The difference between assets and liabilities is called owner's equity or net worth. Notice that a balance sheet is quite different from reports like income statements and cash-flow reports, which summarize what has happened over a period of time. A balance sheet provides a snapshot of your personal or business finances at a particular point in time.

*CPA Tip*

> Before you produce a balance sheet, make sure that all your assets and liability accounts are in the same account group.

Creating a balance sheet with Quicken is a two-step process. The first step is to set up an account for each of your assets, along with a beginning balance amount that equals the assets' cost or value. Assets generally are items you have paid for and that have lasting value. Personal assets include items like cash in your wallet, the surrender value of a life insurance policy, any investments, a home, and durable personal items like your car and furniture. Business assets usually include cash, accounts receivable, inventory, and other property and equipment.

The second step in creating a balance sheet is to set up an account for each of your liabilities, along with the balances owed. Liabilities are amounts you currently owe other people, banks, or businesses. Personal liabilities include items like credit card balances, income taxes owed, car loans, and a mortgage. Business liabilities usually include items like accounts payable, wages and salaries owed employees, income and payroll taxes, and bank credit lines and loans.

*CPA Tip*

Determine the cost or market value of all your assets and liabilities as of the same date. The cost or market value information needs to be accurate or your net worth calculation will not be accurate. Use only one method for valuing your assets or liabilities, such as historical cost or fair market value. Mixing the different methods does not yield beneficial results. You also should note on your opening balances whether you used historical cost or fair market value. If you do use fair market value, document where the fair market value estimate came from.

After you enter the costs or market values of all your assets and liabilities, Quicken calculates your net worth by subtracting your liabilities from your assets. Hopefully, the difference is a positive one. For businesses and individuals, you want the net worth amount to grow larger over time, because this amount acts as a financial cushion.

Figure 12.17 shows an example of a personal balance sheet, or net worth statement, created by Quicken. At the top of the page, Quicken lists each of the asset accounts along with their balances on the As of date. Below that, Quicken lists each of the liability accounts along with their balances on total—which is the same thing as net worth. In Figure 12.17, the net worth amount is $11,137.94.

A business balance sheet looks the same, although the assets and liabilities listed probably are different. Chapter 14 describes how to print a business balance sheet and each of Quicken's other reports.

# Chapter Summary

With the enhancements provided in Versions 3.0 and 4.0, you easily can use Quicken for almost all of your personal or small-business accounting

```
                              Personal Net Worth
                                As of 1/10/91
PERSONAL-All Accounts                                                    Page 1
1/10/91
                                                    1/10/91
                                 Acct                Balance
           ---------------------------------------  -----------
           ASSETS
             Cash and Bank Accounts
               Cash-Checking # 1987461               1,000.00
               Petty Cash-Business Petty Cash          161.88
                                                    -----------

               Total Cash and Bank Accounts          1,161.88

             Other Assets
               Real Estate-personal residence      100,000.00
                                                    -----------
               Total Other Assets                  100,000.00

                                                    -----------
             TOTAL ASSETS                          101,161.88

             LIABILITIES
               Credit Cards
                 Credit Card                            23.94
                                                    -----------
                 Total Credit Cards                     23.94

               Other Liabilities
                 Mortgage-Home mortgage             90,000.00
                                                    -----------
                 Total Other Liabilities            90,000.00

                                                    -----------
             TOTAL LIABILITIES                      90,023.94

                                                    -----------
             OVERALL TOTAL                          11,137.94
                                                    ===========
```

*Fig. 12.17. An example of a personal balance sheet.*

needs. This chapter described how to use Quicken to perform record keeping for assets like real estate or accounts receivable and for liabilities like credit card debts and loans. If you are interested, yet need a little more help, refer to Chapters 13, 17, and 18. Chapter 13 describes the new features Version 4.0 provides to help you monitor your investments. Chapter 17 describes how to use Quicken as a home accounting package. Chapter 18 describes how to use Quicken as business accounting package.

# 13

# Monitoring Your Investments

Quicken 4.0 provides features that enable you to monitor and report on your investments. Quicken provides a register specifically for investments, several menu options that make monitoring and managing your investments easier, and a series of investment reports. Together, these tools enable you to monitor investment transactions, measure performance, track market values, and create reports for income tax planning and preparation.

This chapter describes how to prepare to monitor your investments with Quicken and how to track mutual funds and other investments using the Quicken investment register. To save you from reviewing material you already know, the chapter will not describe the parts of the investment register that also are part of the regular Quicken register. If you are not well acquainted with the basics of Quicken, refer to the second section of this book, "Learning the Basics."

## Preparing To Monitor Investments

To monitor investments with Quicken, you need to set up an investment account. Quicken provides two investment account categories: the *mutual fund account* and the *investment and cash account*. The mutual fund account is a simplified investment account that you use for a single mutual fund. The investment and cash account is a more powerful investment account that you use for other investments and investment groups.

The basic difference between the two accounts is difficult to grasp. However, if you learn the difference now, you will find it much easier to decide when to set up mutual fund accounts and when to set up investment and cash accounts.

The mutual fund account keeps track of the market value and the number of shares you hold of a single investment. The investment and cash account keeps track of the market value of multiple securities, the shares, and the cash balance. (*Note:* The cash balance usually would represent the money with which you buy additional stocks, bonds, and so forth.)

Given these distinctions, the easiest approach is to set up a mutual fund account for each mutual fund investment you hold, set up an investment and cash account for each brokerage account you hold, and set up an investment and cash account for any collection of individual investments that you want to track and manage together in one register. As you work with the Quicken investment options, you will be able to fine-tune these suggestions.

To set up either type of investment account, follow these steps:

1. Choose the **Select Account** option from Quicken's Main menu. Quicken displays the Select Account to Use screen shown in figure 13.1.

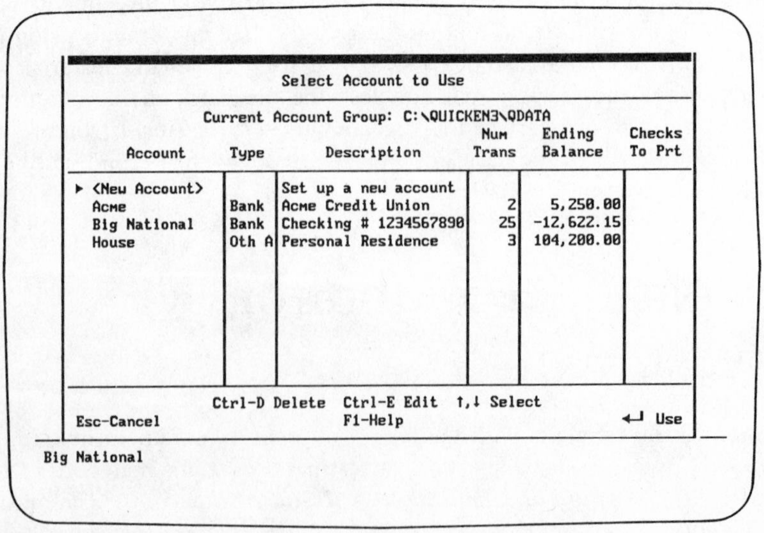

```
                      Select Account to Use

           Current Account Group: C:\QUICKEN3\QDATA
                                          Num     Ending    Checks
         Account      Type    Description Trans   Balance   To Prt

      ▶ <New Account>         Set up a new account
        Acme         Bank  Acme Credit Union     2    5,250.00
        Big National Bank  Checking # 1234567890 25  -12,622.15
        House        Oth A Personal Residence    3   104,200.00




           Ctrl-D Delete  Ctrl-E Edit  ↑,↓ Select
        Esc-Cancel              F1-Help                    ↵ Use

      Big National
```

*Fig. 13.1. The Select Account to Use screen.*

2. Select the New Account option from the list. Quicken displays the Set Up New Account screen shown in figure 13.2.

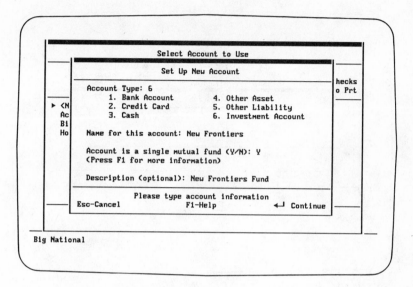

Big National

**Fig. 13.2.** *The Set up New Account screen.*

3. Press 6 in the Account Type field to indicate that this is an investment account.

4. Press Enter or Tab to move the cursor to the Name for this account field and enter a description of the account. The account name can be up to 15 characters long and can contain any characters except [, ], / and :. You can include spaces in the account name.

5. Press Enter or Tab to move the cursor to the Account is a single mutual fund field. If you want to set up a mutual fund account, set this field to Y for yes. If you want to set up an investment and cash account, press N for no.

6. Press Enter or Tab to move the cursor to the Description field. The Description field provides 21 spaces for additional investment description.

7. When you finish entering information for the new account, press Enter.

   If you are creating a mutual fund account and have set the Account is a single mutual fund field to Y, Quicken displays the Set Up Mutual Fund Security screen (see fig. 13.3). The account description appears in the Name field.

*Note:* If you set the Account is a single mutual fund field to N, you do not need to complete steps 8, 9, and 10.

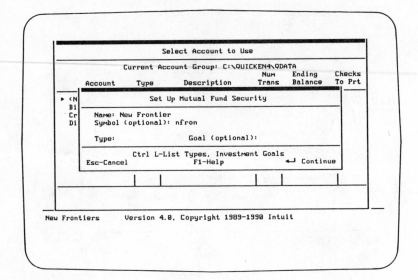

*Fig. 13.3. The Set Up Mutual Fund Security screen.*

8. (Optional) Enter the mutual fund symbol in the Symbol field if you plan to import price data from another file.

    *Note:* The symbol that you enter in the Symbol field should be whatever you use to identify the mutual fund in the other file. For more information on this process, refer to, "Updating Your Investment Records for Market Values," elsewhere in this chapter.

9. In the Type field, specify the type of mutual fund: Bond, CD, Mutual Fund, or Stock. Press Ctrl-L to see an on-screen list of the valid types, and select an item from the list (see fig. 13.4).

10. (Optional) Specify an investment goal: College Fund, Growth, Growth & Income, and Income. To see an on-screen list of valid goals, press Ctrl-L and select an item from the list. Figure 13.5 shows the list of valid investment goals.

    *Note:* The Type and Goal fields do not affect significantly the way Quicken processes information. (The Type field does dictate whether share prices are recorded using decimal or fractional numbers.) You can use the Type and Goal fields to sort and organize information on reports. How to define different investment types and goals will be discussed later in the chapter.

11. After you complete the Set Up Mutual Fund Security screen, press Enter while the cursor is on the Goal field. Alternatively, press Ctrl-Enter when the cursor is on one of the other fields. Quicken displays the Select Account to Use screen.

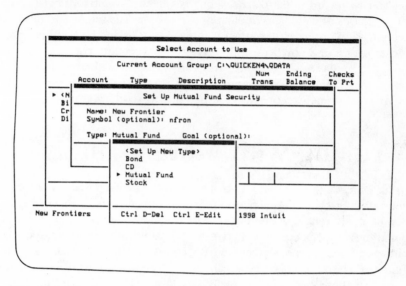

**Fig. 13.4.** *The Investment Types List screen.*

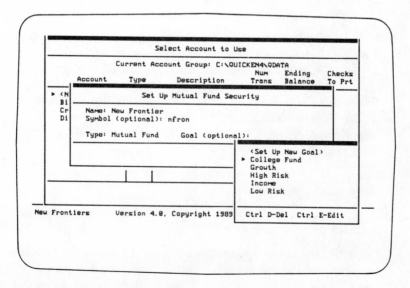

**Fig. 13.5.** *The Investment Goals List screen.*

Repeat steps 1 through 7 for each investment and cash account you choose to set up. For each mutual fund account you establish, repeat steps 1 through 10.

After you have created an investment account, you are ready to use the register to record initial balances, charges in the investment balance due to purchases or sales, and fluctuations in the market value. The next two sections—"Working With Mutual Funds" and "Working with Other Investments"—describe how to use the investment accounts you have created. Because mutual fund accounts are easier to work with than investment and cash accounts, consider starting with the next section—even if most of your investment record keeping pertains to stocks and bonds.

# Working with Mutual Funds

Using Quicken to monitor a mutual fund investment consists of recording your starting balance and periodically recording changes in the balance due to the purchase of additional shares or the redemption of shares. To put things in perspective, you record the same information that appears on your mutual fund statements. By recording the information in the Quicken register, however, you can use the information in several calculations that show you how you really are doing with your investments.

The first step in working with a mutual fund is to record the initial purchase. To record the initial purchase of a mutual fund, follow these steps:

1. With the Select Account to Use screen displayed, select the mutual fund investment account for which you want to record an initial balance. Quicken displays the Create Opening Share Balance screen (see fig. 13.6). The easiest way to set up a mutual fund balance is to follow steps 1, 2, 3, and 4. If you want reports that accurately summarize the complete history of a mutual fund investment, however, skip steps 2, 3, and 4, then enter each of the mutual fund transactions you make.

2. Enter the date that you want to begin recording the opening share balance and enter the price per share.

3. Move the cursor to the Number of shares field and enter the number of shares that you now own.

4. Move the cursor to the Price per share field and enter today's price per share for the mutual fund. You do not need to enter a dollar sign. If the price happens to be a whole number, you do not need to enter a decimal point and two zeros after the price. (You can

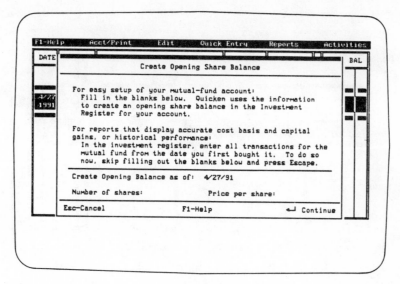

*Fig. 13.6. The Create Opening Share Balance screen.*

find price per share information in many local newspapers and in daily financial newspapers such as the *Wall Street Journal.*)

*Note:* By default, stock and bond prices use fractions. For example, a stock price might be 7 1/8 and a bond price might be 97 1/8. Other investment prices, such as mutual funds and certificates of deposit, use decimals. For example, a mutual fund price might be 14.02. You can use the + and − keys to increase and decrease the price of a security. The + key increases the price 1/8 or .125, and the − key decreases the price 1/8 or .125.

5. When the Create Opening Share Balance screen is complete, press Enter while the cursor is on the Price per share field. Alternatively, press Ctrl-Enter or F10 when the cursor is on any of the fields. Quicken displays the register into which you can record investment transactions (see fig. 13.7).

After you have set up the initial mutual fund investment balance, you are ready to record a wide variety of transactions: purchases, sales, dividends, and so forth. The basic process of recording each type of investment transaction is the same.

To record transactions in the mutual fund register, follow these steps:

1. Enter the date of the transaction in the Date field. You can use the + and − keys to change the date one day at a time.

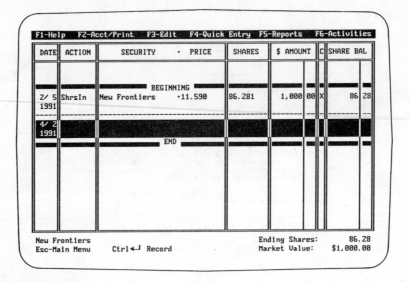

*Fig. 13.7. The mutual fund investment register with the opening mutual fund balance.*

2. Move the cursor to the Action field and choose the type of action that best describes the transaction you're recording.

To choose from a list of valid investment types, press Ctrl-L when the cursor is on the Action field. Alternatively, select **Action List** from the Quick Entry menu. The Action List screen shown in figure 13.8 appears. When you choose from the Action List, specific action descriptions appear in pop-up box menus. Table 13.1 summarizes the general actions shown in figure 13.8 and describes the specific actions that fall into the general category.

*Note:* After you learn the various mutual fund actions, consider using the auto-completion feature: Type just enough of the action for Quicken to uniquely identify it and then press Enter. Quicken completes the rest of the action for you.

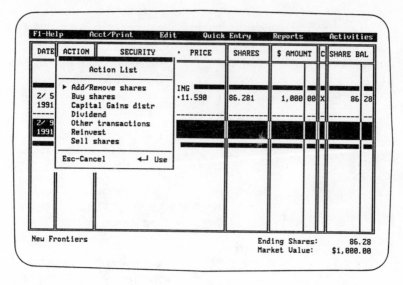

*Fig. 13.8. The Action List screen.*

**Table 13.1**
**Investment Actions for Mutual Fund Accounts**

| Action | Specific Action | Description |
|---|---|---|
| Add/Remove shares | ShrsIn | Investment shares transferred into the account |
| | ShrsOut | Investment shares transferred out of the account |
| Buy shares | BuyX | Purchase investment shares with cash transferred into the account |
| Capital Gains distr | CGLongX | Cash received from a long-term capital gain transferred out of the account |
| | CGShortX | Cash received from a short-term capital gain transferred out of the account |
| Dividend | DivX | Cash received from a dividend transferred out of the account |

*Table 13.1 continues*

**Table 13.1**—*continued*

| Action | Specific Action | Description |
|---|---|---|
| Other transactions | Reminder | Reminder note tied to future date (***Note:*** Billminder reminds you about these notes) |
| | StkSplit | Increase or decrease in number of shares because of a stock split |
| Reinvest | ReinvDiv | Reinvest cash dividends or interest by purchasing more investment shares |
| | ReinvLg | Reinvest long-term capital gains distribution by purchasing more investment shares |
| | ReinvSh | Reinvest short-term capital gains distribution by purchasing more investment shares |
| Sell Shares | SellX | Sell investment shares, but transfer cash received out of the investment account |

*Note:* You must enter an account for any action that involves transferring money into or out of an account (always indicated with an "X" at the end of the action name). If you do not want to record a transfer account, use ShrsIn or ShrsOut, because these options do not require you to enter an account.

If you have questions about transferring money between accounts, refer to Chapter 4, "Using Quicken's Register." Chapter 4 describes the logic and mechanics of transferring money between bank accounts. The same principles apply to transferring money between an investment account and a bank account.

3. Move the cursor to the Price field and enter the per share price of the mutual fund. When entering a price, you can use up to three decimal places (for example, $11.594). In the Price field, you can use the + key to increase the price by $.125 and the − key to decrease the price by $.125.

4. Move the cursor to the Shares field and enter the number of shares involved in the transaction. You can use up to four decimal places when entering the number of shares. Press Enter or Tab to leave the Shares field, and Quicken calculates the Amount field. (Quicken calculates the Amount field by multiplying the price times the number of shares.)

5. (Optional) Move the cursor to the Memo field and enter a further description of the transaction.

6. (Optional) When you enter a purchase or sale transaction (BuyX or SellX), Quicken displays the Comm/Fee field. Enter in the Comm/Fee field any commission or brokerage fee you paid to execute the transaction. When you press Tab or Enter, Quicken calculates the XferAmt field by adding the transaction amount to the commission or fee.

   *Note:* Quicken adjusts the dollar amount of the transaction to include the commission or fee amount. For a BuyX transaction, Quicken adds the commission or fee. For a SellX transaction, Quicken subtracts the commission or fee. If you enter the share price, number of shares, and dollar amount of the purchase, Quicken fills in the Comm/Fee field itself, if the Amount field doesn't equal the Price field times the Shares field. In this case, Quickens uses the Comm/Fee field to store the difference between what you entered as the dollar amount and the calculated result (price times the number of shares).

7. (Optional) Move the cursor to the Account field and record the bank account from which you withdrew the cash to purchase the mutual fund shares or the account in which you deposited cash from the sale of mutual fund shares, receipt of dividends, or receipt of capital gains distributions. Remember that you can display the Select Account to Use screen by pressing Ctrl-C. You also can use Quicken's auto-completion feature: type enough of the account name for Quicken to uniquely identify the account and then press Enter.

8. To record the transaction, press Enter when the cursor is on the XferAmt field. Alternatively, press Ctrl-Enter or F10 when the cursor is on any field in the investment register.

Figure 13.9 shows a sample transaction recording the purchase of additional shares of a mutual fund.

```
 F1-Help   F2-Acct/Print   F3-Edit   F4-Quick Entry   F5-Reports   F6-Activities

 DATE    ACTION      SECURITY    ·   PRICE     SHARES     $ AMOUNT   C  SHARE BAL


                         BEGINNING
 2/ 5  ShrsIn   New Frontiers    ·11.590    86.281     1,000 00  X       86 28
 1991

 2/ 9  BuyX     New Frontiers    ·11.810   101.609     1,200 00
 1991  Memo:    Sep/IRA contribution        Comm/Fee:
       Account: [Big National]              Xfer Amt:   1,200 00



 New Frontiers                              Ending Shares:      86.28
 Esc-Main Menu      Ctrl←┘  Record          Market Value:   $1,000.00
```

**Fig. 13.9.** *A sample transaction recorded in the mutual fund version of the investment register.*

Although the preceding eight steps illustrate only one type of investment transaction, the steps for recording other kinds of investment transactions are identical. The key is to choose the correct action description (see table 13.1). The following paragraphs describe when to choose particular actions when executing mutual fund transactions.

The action descriptions of the mutual fund transactions you most often execute are BuyX for purchases or SellX for sales. If you invest in an income-oriented fund, you probably have monthly dividend or income payments. Record the monthly dividend or income payments as DivX if you withdraw the money from the fund. If you reinvest the dividends by buying more fund shares, record the dividend payments as ReinvDiv.

At the end of the year, the fund will make a capital gain distribution, which you record as CGLongX or CGShortX if you withdraw the money and as ReinvLg or ReinvSh if you reinvest the capital gains by buying more shares. (*Note:* At this time, the income tax treatment for long- and short-term capital gains is identical; however, this may change.) When the mutual fund reports the capital gain, the statement should indicate whether the gain is long-term or short-term.

Occasionally, you may need to choose the StkSplit action, which adjusts the number of shares without changing the dollar amount. A StkSplit transaction does not require entries in the Price, Shares, or Amount fields. StkSplit records the date on which a certain number of new shares equals a certain number of old shares. The first number equals the number of new shares; the second number equals the number of old shares.

For example, suppose that the New Frontiers mutual fund declares a stock split in which each old share is converted into two new shares. Figure 13.10 shows just such a stock split transaction in which you receive two new shares for every old share. You also can use this approach to record non-taxable stock dividends. For example, when you receive a 10 percent stock dividend, record the stock dividend as a 1.1:1 stock split.

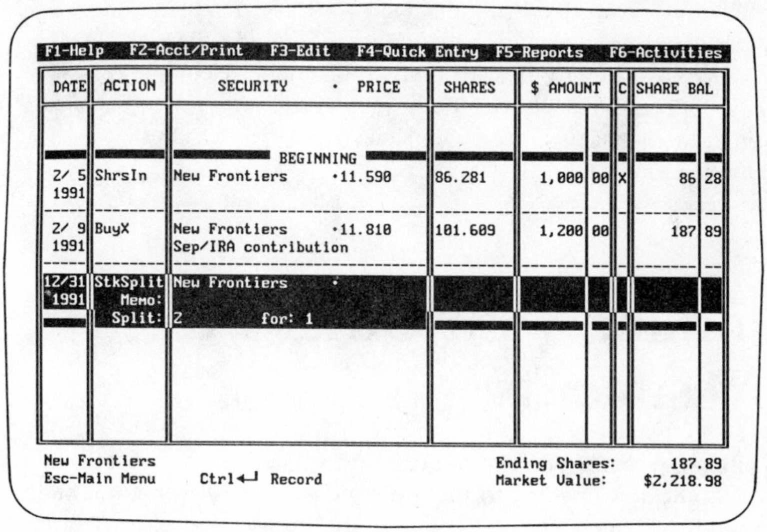

**Fig. 13.10.** *A stock split transaction.*

The last action description that is used with mutual fund transactions is the Reminder option. Reminder transactions do not have a share or dollar amount—only the Security and Memo fields are filled. You can use the Reminder option in two ways: to make notes in your investment register and to remind yourself about certain transactions through the Quicken Billminder feature. The Billminder feature will display messages that alert you to Reminder transactions (just as Billminder will display messages that alert you to unprinted checks). To turn off a reminder transaction, mark the transaction as cleared by entering an * or X in the C field.

*CPA Tip*

If you buy mutual fund shares, you should know the difference between *load funds* and *no load funds.* You usually purchase load funds through a broker, who charges a commission that can run from three to ten percent. The commission is compensation for the salesperson who placed the order and helped you select the fund. Even though you may need the help of a broker in selecting a fund and placing an order, you should be aware that you can save yourself the commission (which means you're ahead from the start) by choosing a no-load mutual fund.

Research shows that on the average, load funds perform no better than no-load funds. Therefore, many investors see no reason to choose a load fund over a no-load fund. No-load funds deal directly with their customers, which means the customer pays no commission. To find a no-load mutual fund, flip through the *Wall Street Journal* and look for mutual fund advertisements that specify "no load." T. Rowe Price, Vanguard, and Scudder are large investment management companies that offer families of no-load mutual funds.

# Working with Other Investments

If you have worked with the mutual fund version of the investment register, you quickly can adapt to the investment and cash version. The investment and cash account register tracks the number of shares you hold in the account of each individual security and any extra cash you are holding because you have just sold (or plan to purchase) a security. This process mirrors the way many brokerage accounts work: your account can have a cash component and a component detailing stock, bond, and certificate of deposit investments.

The steps for using the investment and cash account register mirror those for using the mutual fund register. To use the investment and cash account register, follow these steps:

1. With the Select Account to Use screen displayed, select the investment and cash account for which you want to record an initial balance. (You have to define an investment and cash account prior to selecting the account.)

Quicken displays the regular version of the investment register screen with the First Time Setup screen displayed (see fig. 13.11). The First Time Setup screen informs you that you need to add shares by entering a `ShrsIn` transaction. You will enter a `ShrsIn` transaction later in this process.

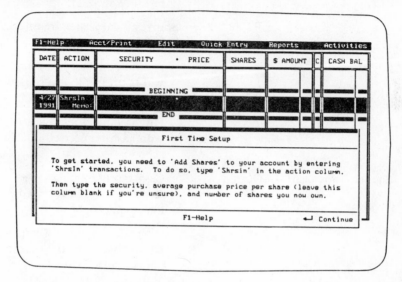

*Fig. 13.11. The First Time Setup screen.*

2. To continue past the First Time Setup screen, press Enter. Quicken displays the investment and cash account register. Position the cursor on the `Date` field and enter the purchase date of the first security you want to record in the register.

3. Move the cursor to the `Action` field and press Ctrl-L to display the Action List (see fig. 13.8). Alternatively, choose **Action List** from the Quick Entry menu. Choose the action that best describes the transaction you are recording. When Quicken lists the specific actions that fall into the general category, choose the appropriate action.

Table 13.2 summarizes the general and specific actions for the investment and cash account version of the investment register. In essence, this list is an expanded version of the investment actions available for mutual fund accounts. The list is expanded because you can hold cash in an investment and cash account. When a transaction involves cash, you need to tell Quicken whether you are transferring the cash out of the account or leaving the cash in the account.

**Table 13.2**
**Investment Actions for Investment and Cash Accounts**

| Action | Specific Action | Description |
|--------|-----------------|-------------|
| Add/Remove shares | ShrsIn | Investment shares transferred into the account |
| | ShrsOut | Investment shares transferred out of the account |
| Buy shares | Buy | Purchase investment shares with cash in the investment account |
| | BuyX | Purchase investment shares with cash transferred into the account |
| Capital Gains distr | CGLong | Cash representing a long-term capital gain received into the account |
| | CGLongX | Cash received from a long-term capital gain transferred out of the account |
| | CGShort | Cash representing a short-term capital gain received into the account |
| | CGShortX | Cash received from a short-term capital gain transferred out of the account |
| Dividend | Div | Cash received representing a dividend |
| | DivX | Cash received from a dividend transferred out of the account |
| Interest | IntInc | Cash received representing interest income |
| | MargInt | Cash paid on margin loan interest using cash in account |

| Action | Specific Action | Description |
|---|---|---|
| Other transactions | MiscExp | Pay for expenses, using cash from the account |
| | Reminder | Reminder note tied to future date (*Note:* Billminder reminds you about these notes) |
| | RtrnCap | Cash received that represents return of initial capital investment |
| | StkSplit | Increase or decrease in number of shares because of a stock split |
| Reinvest | ReinvDiv | Reinvest cash dividends or interest by purchasing more investment shares |
| | ReinvLg | Reinvest long-term capital gains distribution by purchasing more investment shares |
| | ReinvSh | Reinvest short-term capital gains distribution by purchasing more investment shares |
| Sell Shares | Sell | Sell investment shares and leave cash received in the investment account |
| | SellX | Sell investment shares, but transfer cash received out of the investment account |
| Transfer Cash | XIn | Cash transferred into the investment account |
| | XOut | Cash transferred out of the investment account |

*Note:* If you do not want to record a transfer account, use ShrsIn or ShrsOut, because these options do not require you to enter an account.

4. Move the cursor to the Security field and enter the name of the security you are recording. If you have not used the security name before (which is the case the first time you record the security), Quicken displays the Security Not Found screen (see fig. 13.12). The Security Not Found screen lists two options: Add to Security List and Select from Security List.

*Note:* After you define a security, you can use Quicken's auto-completion feature. To use the auto-completion feature, type enough of the security name to uniquely identify the security and press Enter. Quicken completes the security name for you.

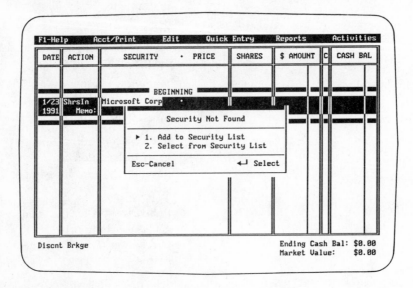

*Fig. 13.12. The Security Not Found screen.*

5. If you entered a new security in step 4, press 1 (or highlight Add to Security List) to add the new security. Quicken displays the Set Up Security screen shown in figure 13.13. Entering the security symbol in the Symbol field is optional. (You use security symbols for importing price data from a separate ASCII file, a process described later in this chapter.) Define the type of investment by moving the cursor to the Type field, pressing Ctrl-L, highlighting the current investment type (see fig. 13.4), and pressing Enter. Define the investment goal by moving the cursor to the Goal field, pressing Ctrl-L, highlighting the investment goal (see fig. 13.5), and pressing Enter. (You also can use the auto-completion feature to fill the Type

and Goal fields.) When the Set Up Security screen is complete, press Enter when the cursor is on the Goal field.

If the security name you entered in step 4 has been defined, press 2 to choose the Select from Security List option. Quicken displays the Securities List screen, shown in figure 13.14. The Securities List shows the securities you have previously defined. Highlight the security you want and press Enter.

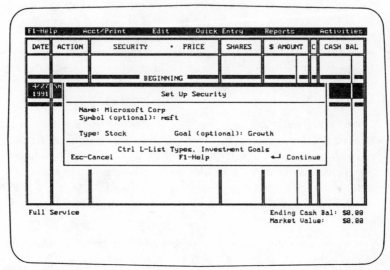

***Fig. 13.13.*** *The Set Up Security screen.*

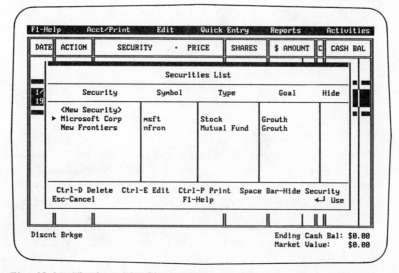

***Fig. 13.14.*** *The Securities List screen.*

6. Move the cursor to the Price field and enter the per share price of the security.

For investments without an actual share price, you can enter the Price field value as 1 (representing one dollar) and subsequently enter the number of shares as the number of dollars of the investment. For investments that have a share or unit price, enter that figure in the Price field.

By default, stock and bond prices use fractions. A stock price might be 6 7/8. A bond price might be 98 1/8. Other prices, such as mutual funds and certificates of deposit, use decimals. A mutual fund price, for example, might be 13.02. As noted earlier in the chapter, you can use the + and − keys to increase and decrease the price of a security. The + key increases the price 1/8, or .125, and the − key decreases the price 1/8, or .125.

*Note:* You easily can find stock share prices in the newspaper. Other securities' prices, however, can be more difficult to determine. Some securities, such as money market funds and nonnegotiable certificates of deposit, do not have a share price. In these cases, enter the price as 1 (representing one dollar). The number of shares will equal the number of dollars' worth of the security you hold.

For other investments, such as bonds and negotiable certificates of deposit, the price shows as a percent. A bond price might be 98 3/8, which indicates the bond is 98 3/8 percent of its face value. (Usually the face value of a bond is $1,000.) A negotiable certificate of deposit price might be 100.971, which indicates that the certificate of deposit is worth 100.971 percent of its face value. (Negotiable certificates of deposit are available in a wide variety of denominations less than $100,000.)

As a general rule, enter the security price using whatever form appears in the newspaper or on your brokerage statement. Then enter the number of shares as the value that, when multiplied by the share price, equals the total dollar value of the investment.

7. Move the cursor to the Shares field and enter the number of shares or units of the transaction. You can use up to four decimal places when entering the number of shares. When you press Enter or Tab to leave the Shares field, Quicken calculates the Amount field.

*Note:* You can enter any two of the three fields—Price, Shares, and Amount—and Quicken will calculate the third field. If you enter all three fields and the price times the number of shares does not equal the amount, Quicken puts the difference in the Comm/Fee field.

8. (Optional) Move the cursor to the Memo field and enter a further description of the transaction.

9. (Optional) If you enter a purchase and sales transaction, Quicken displays the Comm/Fee field. Move the cursor to the Comm/Fee field and enter any commission or brokerage fee you paid to execute the transaction. When you press Tab or Enter, Quicken calculates the XferAmt field by adding the transaction amount and the commission or fee.

10. If the action isn't ShrsIn or ShrsOut, move the cursor to the Account field and record the bank account you tapped for cash to purchase the investment. Remember that you can display the Select Account to Use screen by pressing Ctrl-C. Alternatively, you can use Quicken's auto-completion feature: type enough of the account name to uniquely identify the account and press Enter. Quicken finishes typing the name for you.

11. Record the transaction by pressing Enter when the cursor is on the XferAmt field. Alternatively, press Ctrl-Enter or F10 when the cursor is on any of the fields on the investment register. Quicken displays the standard message box and asks whether you want to record the transaction. Press Enter to record the transaction.

Figure 13.15 shows several sample transactions. The first transaction records the initial purchase of stock shares. The second transaction

```
F1-Help   F2-Acct/Print   F3-Edit   F4-Quick Entry   F5-Reports   F6-Activities
┌────┬──────┬─────────────────────────┬────────┬──────────┬──┬──────────┐
│DATE│ACTION│ SECURITY      ·  PRICE   │ SHARES │ $ AMOUNT │C │ CASH BAL │
├────┼──────┼─────────────────────────┼────────┼──────────┼──┼──────────┤
│1/23│ShrsIn│Microsoft Corp    ·87 7/8 │100     │ 8,787 50 │  │      0 00│
│1991│      │initial purchase         │        │          │  │          │
├────┼──────┼─────────────────────────┼────────┼──────────┼──┼──────────┤
│1/31│XIn   │                 ·        │        │15,000 00 │  │15,000 00 │
│1991│      │deposit                  │        │          │  │          │
├────┼──────┼─────────────────────────┼────────┼──────────┼──┼──────────┤
│2/13│BuyX  │Trump's Taj Mahal ·96 5/8 │100     │ 9,708 50 │  │15,000 00 │
│1991│      │                         │        │          │  │          │
├────┼──────┼─────────────────────────┼────────┼──────────┼──┼──────────┤
│2/13│IntInc│Trump's Taj Mahal ·       │        │   65 00  │  │15,065 00 │
│1991│      │semi annual interest     │        │          │  │          │
├────┼──────┼─────────────────────────┼────────┼──────────┼──┼──────────┤
│2/13│SellX │Microsoft Corp    ·95 1/8 │50      │ 4,756 25 │  │15,065 00 │
│1991│ Memo:│sell half of Microsoft   │Comm/Fee│          │  │          │
│    │Account:│[Discnt Brkge]          │Xfer Amt│ 4,756 25 │  │          │
├────┼──────┼─────────────────────────┼────────┼──────────┼──┼──────────┤
│2/13│      │                         │        │          │  │          │
│1991│      │          END            │        │          │  │          │
└────┴──────┴─────────────────────────┴────────┴──────────┴──┴──────────┘
Discnt Brkge                        Ending Cash Bal: $15,065.00
Esc-Main Menu    Ctrl↵ Record       Market Value:    $38,271.25
```

**Fig. 13.15.** *Sample transactions recorded in the investment and cash account version of the register.*

records the initial deposit of cash into the brokerage account. The third transaction shows the purchase of a bond, the fourth transaction shows the receipt of interest income from the bond, and the fifth transaction shows the sale of a portion of the stock purchased in the first transaction.

To record each transaction, follow the steps listed in the preceding paragraphs. Notice that the investment and cash account version of the register (as compared to the mutual fund version) does not track share balances. However, the investment and cash account version of the register tracks the cash you have available to purchase additional investments.

# Working with the Investment Register

The preceding sections of this chapter describe the fundamentals of working with the Quicken investment registers. You can set up mutual fund accounts, create investment and cash accounts, and record transactions in the register.

The remaining sections of this chapter describe how to work with the Quicken securities lists. You learn how to define your own investment types and goals; how to update your investment records because of changes in market values; and how to reconcile your investment records with those provided by the mutual fund company, brokerage house, or bank. The last section in the chapter offers tips on investments and investment record keeping that may save you headaches and money.

## Working with the Securities Lists

When working with the investment and cash account register, you can add securities to the list that Quicken maintains. Although this approach may be all you ever need, Quicken's **Security List** option enables you to work with the securities list before entering transactions in the register. This option is helpful when, for example, you know that over the coming months you will be purchasing shares of several companies. The **Security List** option saves you time by enabling you to define the securities before you purchase them.

You can access the **Security List** option by pressing F4 and then selecting **Security List** from the Quick Entry menu (see fig. 13.16). Alternatively, you can press Ctrl-Y. Either method produces the Securities List screen shown in figure 13.17. From this screen, you can add, edit, delete, and print lists of securities. You also can use the Securities List screen to access screens that enable you to add, edit, and delete investment types and goals.

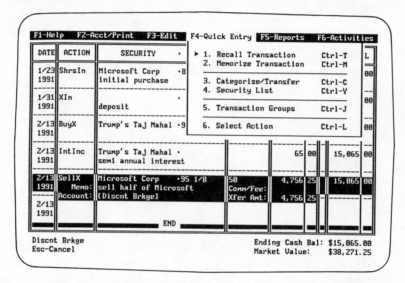

**Fig. 13.16.** *The investment register version of the Quick Entry menu.*

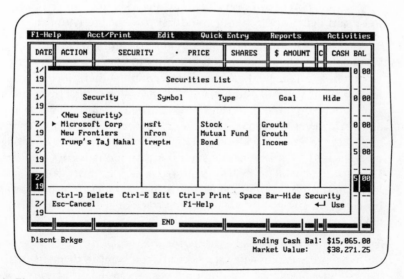

**Fig. 13.17.** *The Securities List screen.*

To add a security to the securities list, follow these steps:

1. Press Ctrl-Y to display the Securities List screen.

2. Use the up- and down-arrow keys to highlight New Security and then press Enter. Quicken displays the Set Up Security screen shown in figure 13.13.

3. Enter the security name in the Name field. You can enter a maximum of 18 characters.

4. (Optional) Enter the security symbol in the Symbol field. (You use security symbols for importing price data from a separate ASCII file, a process described later in the chapter.) You can enter a maximum of 12 characters.

5. To define the investment type, move the cursor to the Type field, press Ctrl-L, highlight the investment type in the Type List box, and press Enter. You also can use the auto-completion feature to fill the Type field.

   Alternatively, if you want to define a new investment type, move the cursor to the Type field, press Ctrl-L, and select the **Set Up New Type** option from the Type List box. Quicken displays the Set Up Security Type screen (see fig. 13.18). To define a new security type, describe the security type in the Type field and indicate whether you want the price calibrated in fractional or decimal units. You can have up to eight types. Only six security types fit in the Type List box at one time, so if you use more than six security types, use PgUp and PgDn to see the first and last parts of the type list.

   *Note:* The Type field is optional and has no effect on record keeping, other than determining the form in which a security price is shown. The Type field enables you to enter another piece of information about your investment. Quicken provides several investment types that you may find valuable: Bond, CD, Mutual Funds, and Stock. However, you may have another piece of data that is more important to collect and store. For example, if you are investing money based on the advice of several investment advisors, you can keep track of which advisor suggested which security. Or, if you invest in several different industries, such as utilities, transportation, banking, and computers, you can keep track of the industry of individual issuers.

   *Note:* You also can edit and delete security types. To delete a security type, press Ctrl-D when the security you want to delete is highlighted in the Type List box. Quicken warns you that a security type

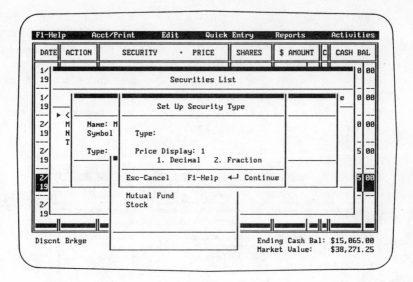

**Fig. 13.18.** *The Set Up Security Type screen.*

is about to be deleted and alerts you if the type is in use. If you want to delete the security type, press Enter. Press Esc if you do not want to delete the security type.

To edit a security type, press Ctrl-E when the security you want to edit is highlighted in the Type List box. Quicken displays the Set Up Security Type screen (see fig. 13.18), which you use as described in the preceding paragraph to change the security type name or the price calibration.

6. To define the investment goal, move the cursor to the Goal field, press Ctrl-L, highlight the current investment type from the Goal List box, and press Enter. You also can use the auto-completion feature to fill the Goal field.

To define a new investment goal, move the cursor to the Goal field, press Ctrl-L, and select the **Set Up New Goal** option. Quicken displays the Set Up Investment Goal screen (see fig. 13.19). To define a new investment goal, describe the goal in the Goal field. You can have up to eight goals. As is the case with the Type List box, only six goals fit on the Goal List screen at one time. Use the PgUp and PgDn keys to view the first and last parts of the goal list.

*Note:* The Goal field is optional and has no effect on the way that you track or monitor a particular investment. Like the Type field, the Goal field enables you to record another piece of information about your investment. Quicken provides several investment goals that you may find valuable: College Fund, Growth, High Risk, Income, and Low Risk. However, you may have another piece of information that is more important to collect and store. For example, rather than using the Goal field to describe the investment, you can use the Goal field to categorize how you want to spend the money you make on the investment. In that case, you can choose other goals, such as Retirement, Vacation, Emergency, and so on.

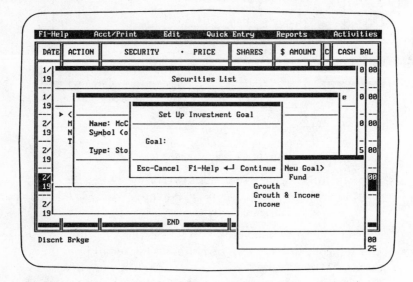

*Fig. 13.19. The Set Up Investment Goal screen.*

*Note:* You also can edit and delete investment goals. To delete an investment goal, press Ctrl-D when the goal you want to delete is highlighted on the Goal List screen. Quicken warns you that a goal is about to be deleted and alerts you if the goal is in use.

To edit a goal (to change the goal's name), press Ctrl-E when the goal is highlighted in the Goal List box. Quicken displays the Set Up Investment Goal screen, which you use to edit the name (see fig. 13.19). After you enter the goal, press Enter to return to the Set Up Security screen.

7. When the Set Up Security screen is complete, press Enter while the cursor is on the Goal field.

Even if you are a long-term investor, you eventually will decide to sell a certain stock or bond and never purchase that security again. Because there is no reason to clutter your securities list, Quicken enables you to delete securities in which you no longer invest.

To delete a security from the Securities List screen, follow these steps:

1. To display the Securities List screen, press Ctrl-Y.

2. Use the up- and down-arrow keys to mark the security you want to delete.

3. With the security you want to remove highlighted, press Ctrl-D. Quicken alerts you the security is about to be deleted permanently. Press Enter to delete the security or press Esc if you do not want to delete the security.

   *Note:* When a security is in use, Quicken will present a message that the security is in use and cannot be deleted at this time.

As you know, Quicken stores four pieces of information about a security on the Securities List: name, symbol, type, and goal. Over time, one or more of these elements may change. When changes in the name, symbol, type, or goal occur, you can edit the security.

To edit a security on the securities list, follow these steps:

1. Press Ctrl-Y to display the Securities List screen.

2. Use the up- and down-arrow keys to mark the security you want to modify.

3. With the security you want to modify highlighted, press Ctrl-E. Quicken displays the Set Up Security screen. The process for editing a security mirrors the process of adding a new security. If you have questions about how to complete the Set Up Security screen, refer to the steps that describe how to add a new security.

To print a list of the securities on the securities list, follow these steps:

1. Press Ctrl-Y to display the Securities List screen.

2. Press Ctrl-P when the securities list is displayed. Quicken displays the Print Securities List screen, which is similar to the Print Register screen.

3. Complete the Print Securities List screen as you would the Print Register screen: Indicate which printer setting you want to use and then press Enter.

You also can hide certain securities so that they do not appear on Quicken's investment reports. For example, suppose that you do not want your children (who print out reports of investments for their college education) to see your retirement savings balance. You can hide the investments that you do not want them to see.

To hide a security, follow these steps:

1. Press Ctrl-Y to display the Securities List screen.

2. Highlight the security you want to hide and press the space bar.

Follow the same process to "unhide" the security. The space bar acts as a toggle between yes/no choices.

## Updating Your Investment Records for Market Values

One of the most common investment record keeping activities is tracking the market value of your investments. Quicken provides several tools that enable you to update your investment records and determine the overall market value of your investments.

To record manually the market value of an investment, follow these steps:

1. Access the register that records the transactions for an investment. (The register may be a mutual fund account register or a investment and cash account register, depending on the investment.)

2. Press F6 to access the Activities menu. Figure 13.20 shows the investment register version of the Activities menu.

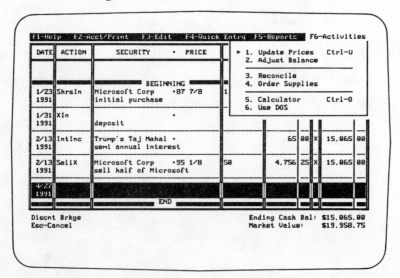

*Fig. 13.20. The investment register version of the Activities menu.*

3. Select the **Update Prices** option or press Ctrl-U. Quicken displays the Update Prices and Market Value screen shown in figure 13.21.

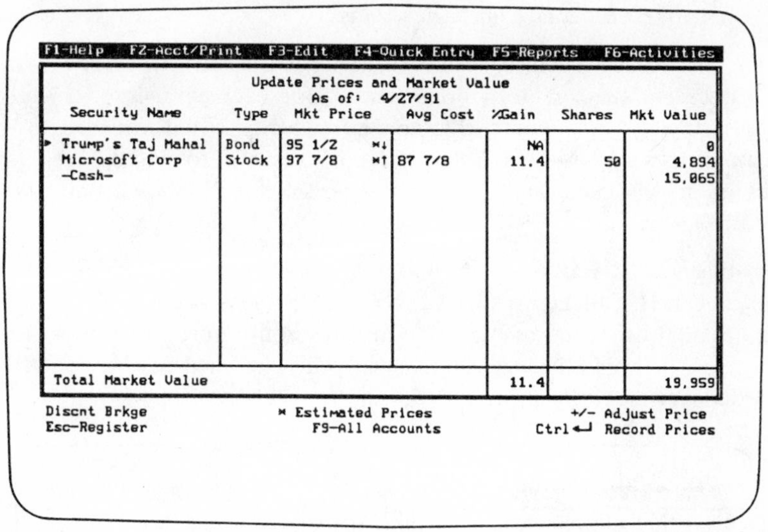

```
F1-Help   F2-Acct/Print   F3-Edit   F4-Quick Entry   F5-Reports   F6-Activities

                        Update Prices and Market Value
                              As of:  4/27/91
            Security Name      Type  Mkt Price   Avg Cost   %Gain   Shares  Mkt Value

    ► Trump's Taj Mahal       Bond   95 1/2  ↓              NA                      0
      Microsoft Corp          Stock  97 7/8  ↑    87 7/8   11.4        50      4,894
      —Cash—                                                                  15,065




      Total Market Value                                   11.4               19,959

      Discnt Brkge                  ↦ Estimated Prices           +/- Adjust Price
      Esc-Register                    F9-All Accounts        Ctrl↵ Record Prices
```

*Fig. 13.21. The Update Prices and Market Value screen.*

4. Use the up- and down-arrow keys to highlight the security whose price you want to update.

5. With the cursor positioned on the Mkt Price field, enter the current market price. You also can use the + and − keys to increase or decrease the price by 1/8 or .125.

6. Repeat steps 3 and 4 for each security on the screen. If you want to update investments in your other accounts, press F9 to display a complete list of your securities.

   After you record the change in the market price, Quicken asks you whether it is OK to record the new prices and if the system date is appropriate. If this is the case, press Enter. To change the date, use the + and − keys to change to the date of record. Otherwise, F9 acts as a toggle between the current investment register and all accounts.

   *Note:* The Update Prices and Market Value screen shows several pieces of data with which you are familiar: the security name, the type, the market price, the number of shares, and the total market value. However, two additional fields appear: Avg Cost and %Gain. The Avg Cost field shows the average unit cost of all the shares or units of a particular security that you currently hold. The %Gain field shows the percentage difference between the total cost and the total market value of all the shares you currently hold. A negative percentage indicates a loss.

When you record security prices using the Update Prices and Market Values screen, you create a price history for each security. To see the price history for the currently selected security when you are on the Update Prices and Market Value screen, press F4 to access the Quick Entry menu. Quicken displays a special version of the Quick Entry menu (see fig. 13.22).

From this special version of the Quick Entry menu, select **Price History** or press Ctrl-H. Quicken displays the Price History screen shown in figure 13.23, which lists each of the price updates you entered for the security. The dates shown in the price history are the system dates on which you recorded new security prices.

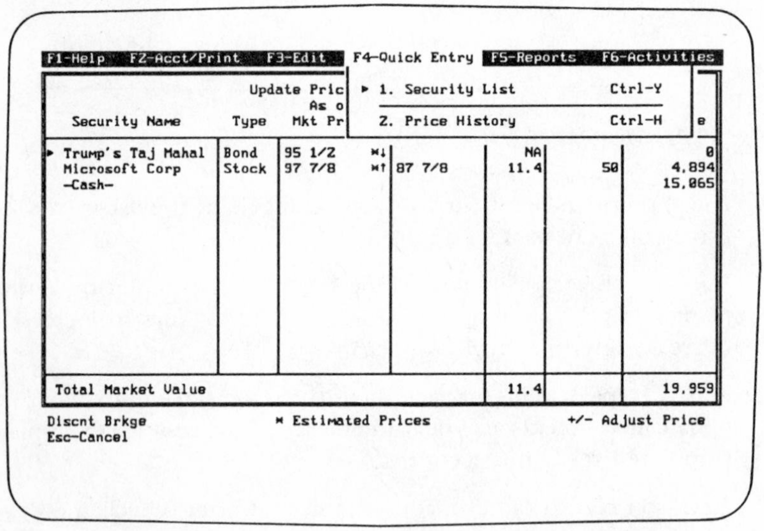

*Fig. 13.22. The Update Prices and Market Value screen's version of the Quick Entry menu.*

You can request reports that show the market value of your investments on different dates. (Chapter 14 discusses Quicken's reports in detail.) Quicken uses the security prices from the price history to prepare these reports. For example, if you want to see market values as of June 1, Quicken uses the securities prices from the price history that are on or before June 1. For this reason, you may want to update security prices

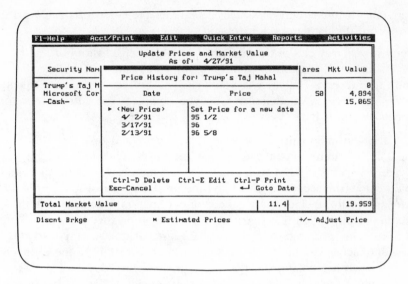

***Fig. 13.23.*** *The Price History screen.*

regularly. However, with the Update Prices and Market Value screen, you add a price to the price history for the current date.

To add to the price history a price for some date other than the current system date, select the New Price item from the Price History screen. Quicken displays the New Price screen shown in figure 13.24, with the

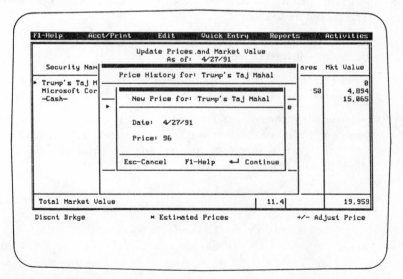

***Fig. 13.24.*** *The New Price screen.*

date filled in as the current system date. Enter the correct date and price. To record the date and price combination, press Enter.

You likewise may edit or delete a price from the price history of a particular investment. Use Quicken's standard key combinations: Ctrl-D to delete and Ctrl-E to edit. The changes you make will be reflected on the Update Prices and Market Value screen after you complete the entry of new or updated information.

You also can import price history data from an ASCII text file. The steps for doing so aren't difficult, as long as the ASCII text file looks the way Quicken expects it to. The file needs to contain at least two pieces of information: the security symbol and the price in decimal form. You also can (optionally) include a third piece of information—the date. The three pieces of information that make up a price must be together on a single line, must be separated by commas, and must not contain any embedded spaces. Quicken can import the data even if one or more of the elements are enclosed in quotation marks. If the price history does not include a date, Quicken uses a default date that you specify as part of the import operation. All of the following, for example, can be imported as price history data:

    MSFT,87.125,6/30/91
    MSFT,87.125
    "MSFT",87.125,"6/30/91"
    "MSFT","87.125","6/30/91"

To import price history data, access the Update Prices and Market Values screen and follow these steps:

1. Press F2 to display the Update Prices and Market Values version of the Acct/Print menu (see fig. 13.25).

2. Select the **Import Prices** option or press Ctrl-I. Quicken displays the Import Price Data screen (see fig. 13.26).

3. Enter the file name and extension of the ASCII text file that contains the price history information you want to import. If the ASCII file is not in the current directory, also specify the drive and directory where the ASCII file can be found.

4. Enter the date that should be used as the default price date in case a date is not specified in the ASCII text file.

5. When the Import Price Data screen is complete, press Enter. Quicken imports the price history data contained in the ASCII text file and updates the appropriate security price histories.

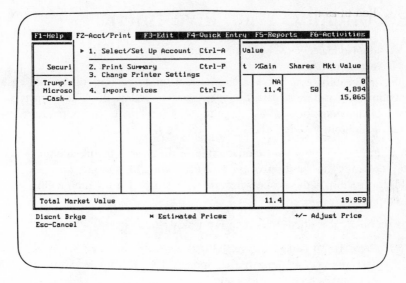

**Fig. 13.25.** *The Update Prices and Market Value screen's version of the Acct/Print menu.*

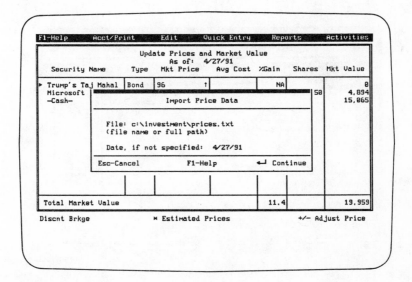

**Fig. 13.26.** *The Import Price Data screen.*

# Reconciling Your Investment Accounts

Quicken enables you to reconcile mutual fund and investment and cash accounts. For the most part, the steps for reconciling these account types parallel the steps for reconciling other Quicken accounts. There are, however, a few minor differences.

In a mutual fund account, you reconcile the shares in the account—not the dollars. The basic process of reconciling a mutual fund account closely resembles the process described in Chapter 8 for reconciling bank accounts.

To reconcile a mutual fund account, follow these steps:

1. Press F6 to access the Activities menu on the investment register and select the **Reconcile** option. The Reconcile Mutual Fund Account screen appears (see fig. 13.27).

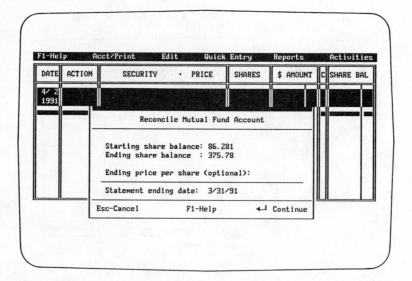

**Fig. 13.27.** *The Reconcile Mutual Fund Account screen.*

2. Enter the starting and ending shares balance from your mutual fund statement.

3. Mark the transactions that appear on the mutual fund statement in your register, using an abbreviated transaction list (see fig. 13.28).

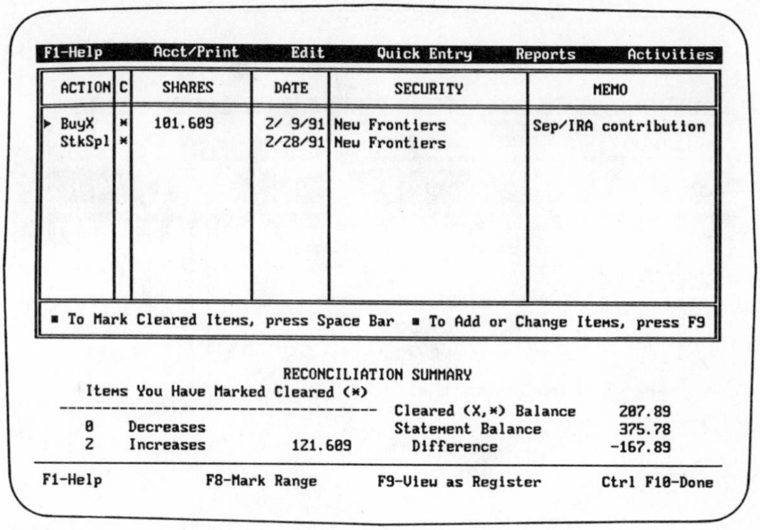

```
┌─────────────────────────────────────────────────────────────────────┐
│ F1-Help      Acct/Print      Edit      Quick Entry    Reports    Activities │
│ ┌──────┬─┬─────────┬───────┬──────────────┬──────────────────────┐ │
│ │ACTION│C│ SHARES  │ DATE  │  SECURITY    │       MEMO           │ │
│ ├──────┼─┼─────────┼───────┼──────────────┼──────────────────────┤ │
│ │►BuyX │*│ 101.609 │2/ 9/91│New Frontiers │Sep/IRA contribution  │ │
│ │ StkSpl│*│        │2/28/91│New Frontiers │                      │ │
│ │      │ │         │       │              │                      │ │
│ │      │ │         │       │              │                      │ │
│ │      │ │         │       │              │                      │ │
│ │      │ │         │       │              │                      │ │
│ │      │ │         │       │              │                      │ │
│ │      │ │         │       │              │                      │ │
│ ├──────┴─┴─────────┴───────┴──────────────┴──────────────────────┤ │
│ │ ▪ To Mark Cleared Items, press Space Bar ▪ To Add or Change Items, press F9 │ │
│ └─────────────────────────────────────────────────────────────────┘ │
│                      RECONCILIATION SUMMARY                          │
│     Items You Have Marked Cleared (*)                               │
│     ──────────────────────────────── Cleared (X,*) Balance   207.89 │
│        0    Decreases                 Statement Balance      375.78  │
│        2    Increases      121.609    Difference           -167.89  │
│                                                                     │
│ F1-Help          F8-Mark Range      F9-View as Register   Ctrl F10-Done │
└─────────────────────────────────────────────────────────────────────┘
```

*Fig. 13.28. The mutual fund account Transaction List screen.*

You can mark transactions individually by using the space bar to toggle the * character in the C field. Alternatively, press F8, and Quicken asks you to indicate cleared transactions between two dates. Pressing F9 toggles you between the **Reconcile** option and the investment register that you are reconciling. Quicken records a balance adjustment in the investment register to balance the account.

As with the process of reconciling bank accounts, the basic idea is that the difference in shares between your records and the mutual fund's record should stem only from transactions that (for reasons of timing) have not yet appeared on the mutual fund statement.

In an investment and cash account, you reconcile the cash balance. Predictably, this process parallels that for reconciling a bank account. (The cash balance in an investment and cash account also may be a bank account.) To reconcile the cash balance, enter the beginning and ending statement balances on the Reconcile Investment Account screen (see fig. 13.29). Just as for a bank account, mark the transactions that have cleared the cash account, using an abbreviated transaction list (see fig. 13.30). Use the space bar to toggle, and mark transactions that have cleared with an *.

If you want to reconcile an account but have questions about the mechanics of the reconciliation process, refer to Chapter 8. The basic principles described there also apply to investment accounts.

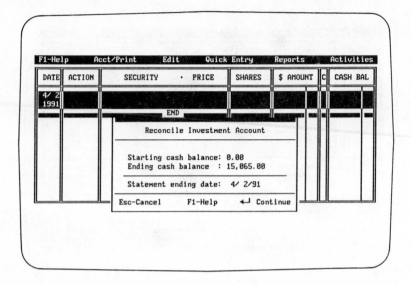

**Fig. 13.29.** *The Reconcile Investment Account screen.*

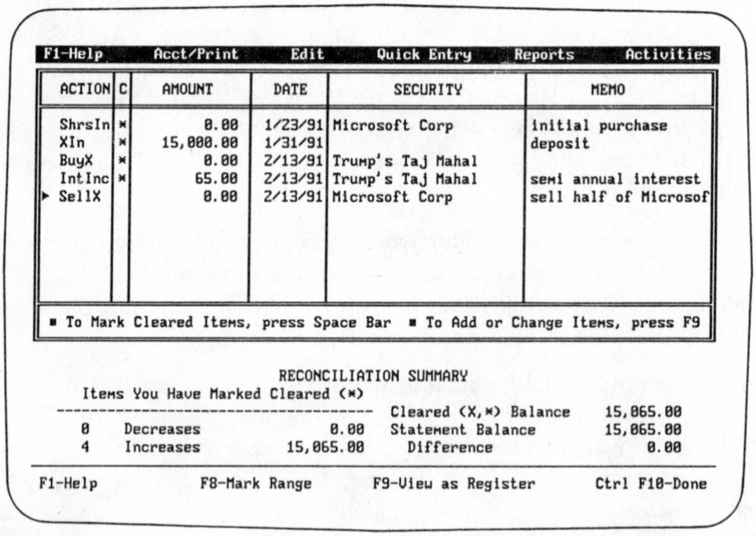

**Fig. 13.30.** *The investment and cash account Transaction List screen.*

If you do not want to reconcile your account, you may want to use the **Adjust Balance** option that appears on the investment register version of the Activities menu. If the investment is an investment and cash account, Quicken displays the Adjust Balance menu (see fig. 13.31), which lists

better understand investments, read *A Random Walk Down Wall Street*, by Burton G. Malkiel, a Princeton economics professor. You should be able to find the most recent edition (1990) in any good bookstore.

# Chapter Summary

This chapter described how to monitor your investments using Quicken's new investment versions of the register. The chapter listed the steps for tracking mutual funds with Quicken and the steps for tracking other investments, such as stocks, bonds, and certificates of deposit. The next chapter describes Quicken's investment report capabilities.

# 14

# Tapping the Power of Quicken's Reports

When you collect information about your financial affairs in a Quicken register, you essentially construct a database. With a database, you can arrange, retrieve, and summarize the information that database contains. With a financial database, you can determine your cash flows, profits, tax deductions, and net worth. You do need a way to arrange, retrieve, and summarize the data, however, and within Quicken, this need is met with the Reports menu.

This chapter describes the eight options available on the Reports menu, accessed by selecting **Reports** from the Main menu or from the Activities menu on the Write Checks and Register screens. Figure 14.1 shows the Reports menu.

The first three options on the Reports menu display menus of additional choices. Figure 14.2 shows the Personal Reports menu. Figure 14.3 shows the Business Reports menu. Figure 14.4 shows the Investment Reports menu.

The fourth option, **Memorized Reports**, enables you to use report descriptions you have created. The final four options on the Reports menu enable you to create custom reports as discussed later in this chapter.

**301**

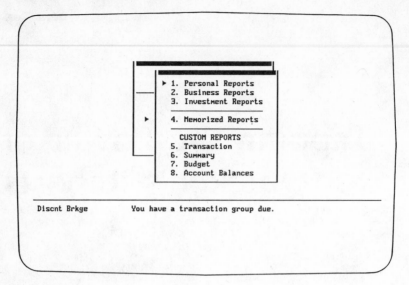

**Fig. 14.1.** *The Reports menu.*

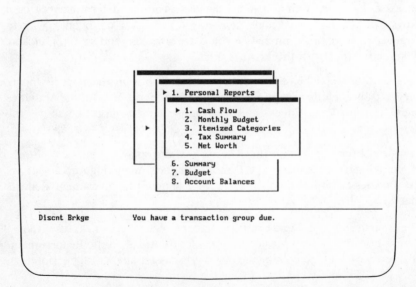

**Fig. 14.2.** *The Personal Reports menu.*

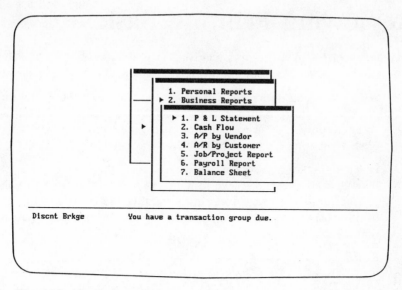

**Fig. 14.3.** *The Business Reports menu.*

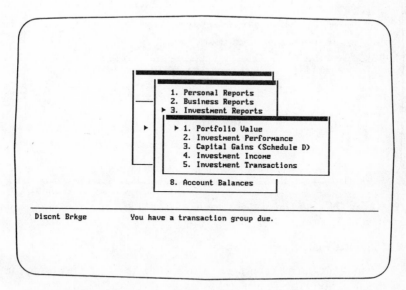

**Fig. 14.4.** *The Investment Reports menu.*

# Reviewing Printing Basics

No matter which Quicken report you want to print, you need to take the same basic steps. To print any report, you complete the following steps:

1. Select the menu option for the report you want to print. For example, if you want to print a personal cash flow report, select the **Personal Reports** option from the Reports menu and then select the **Cash Flow** option from the Personal Reports menu.

   Quicken displays the screen you use to create the report. The Cash Flow Report screen is shown in figure 14.5, but this screen closely resembles the screens you use for several of the reports. (The rest of this chapter describes how you complete the individual create report screens.)

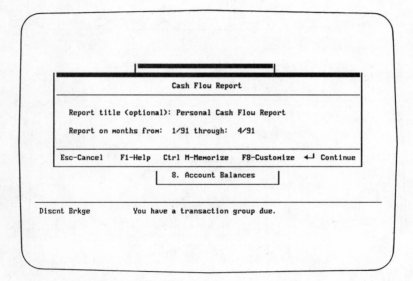

**Fig. 14.5.** *The Cash Flow Report screen.*

2. (Optional) Enter a report title.

   If you don't enter a report title, Quicken names the report using the menu option. The report produced by the **Cash Flow** option, for example, is named "Cash Flow Report." The report produced by the **Monthly Budget** option is named "Monthly Budget Report."

3. (Optional) Press Enter or Tab to move the cursor to the Report on months from and through fields. Set up the time frame the report

should cover by entering the starting month and year and the ending month and year you want included in the report. If you don't enter these dates, the report covers January of the current year through the current date. (*Note:* The + and − keys move the date forward and backward a month at a time.)

4. Press Enter when the cursor is on the Report on months through field. You also can press F10 or Ctrl-Enter when the cursor is on any of the other fields. Quicken generates and displays the report on-screen.

   You can use the cursor-movement keys to see different portions of the report. You also can use the Home and End keys to see the first and last pages of the report. When working with reports too wide to fit on-screen, you can use F9 to toggle between a full column-width and a half column-width version of the report.

5. When you are ready to print the report, press F8 or Ctrl-P. Either approach displays the Print Report screen shown in figure 14.6. This screen enables you to specify where you want the report printed to.

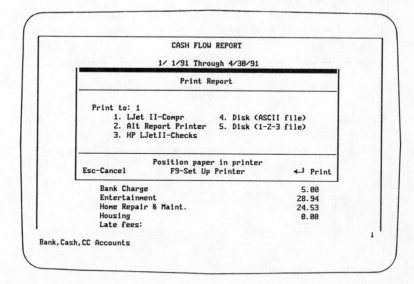

*Fig. 14.6. The Print Report screen.*

6. In the Print to field, press 1 for printer 1, 2 for printer 2, and so on. If you use printer names on the Printer Settings screen, you also see those printer names on the Print Report screen. Figure 14.6 shows, for example, that the third printer is called HP LJetII-Checks.

If you select 4 in the Print to field, Quicken prints an ASCII file. *ASCII files* are standardized text files that you can use to import a Quicken report into a word processing program, such as WordPerfect or Microsoft Word. Before creating the ASCII file, Quicken uses the Print To Disk screen to request three pieces of information (see fig. 14.7). Complete the following steps:

1. (Optional) In the File field, enter a name for Quicken to use for the ASCII file. To use a data directory other than the Quicken data directory, QUICKEN3, you can specify a path name. (See your DOS user's manual for information on path names.)

2. (Optional) In the Lines per page field, set the number of report lines between page breaks. If you are using 11-inch paper, the page length usually is 66 lines.

3. (Optional) In the Width field, set the number of characters (including blanks) that Quicken prints on a line. If you are using 8 1/2-inch paper, the characters per line usually is 80. Figure 14.7 shows the completed Print To Disk screen with the filename printer.txt.

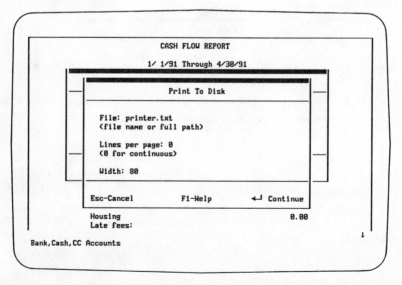

**Fig. 14.7.** *The completed Print To Disk screen.*

If you select 5 at the Print to field on the Print Report screen, Quicken displays the Print to Lotus File screen (see fig. 14.8). (1-2-3 is a popular spreadsheet program manufactured by Lotus Development Corporation.) You need to complete one more step.

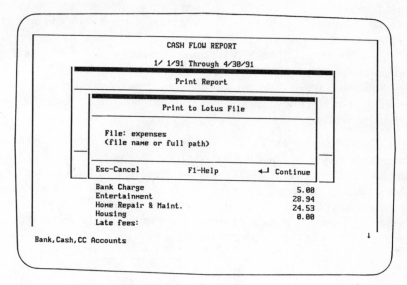

*Fig. 14.8. The Print to Lotus File screen.*

To create a 1-2-3 file, Quicken requests the name of the file you want to create using the Print to Lotus File screen. As with the ASCII file creation option, if you want to use a data directory other than QUICKEN3, you also can specify a path name. Figure 14.8 shows the completed Print to Lotus File screen with the file specified as expenses. (***Note:*** You don't have to worry about the correct file extension. Quicken adds the extension for you.)

# Tracking Personal Finances with Personal Reports

On the Personal Reports menu, you have five choices. To create any of the five reports, you need to complete the screen that appears when you select a report from the Personal Reports menu.

# Cash Flow

Figure 14.5 shows the Cash Flow Report screen completed so that the report title is Personal Cash Flow Report and the report includes transactions between 1/91 and 4/91. The screen also provides two function keys, F8-Customize and F9-Filter, that you can use to modify the appearance of the report produced. (The F9-Filter key does not always appear on-screen, but it is available. This chapter often refers to this key as if it appears on-screen.) Because these two function keys apply to all the personal, business, and investment reports, they are described in the "Customizing and Filtering Reports" section following the discussion of investment reports.

Figure 14.9 shows an example of a personal cash flow report. The cash flow report shows the total money you have received and expended by category. The report also shows transfers. The last two lines of the outflows section of the report show transfers to the two investment accounts used in the sample figures in Chapter 13: Discnt Brkge and New Frontiers. The report includes transactions from all the bank, cash, and credit card accounts in the current account group.

```
                              Personal Cash Flow Report
                                 1/ 1/91 Through 4/30/91
   Bank,Cash,CC Accounts                                                    Page 1
   4/ 2/91
                                                      1/ 1/91-
                       Category Description            4/30/91
   -----------------------------------------------   ------------------------

   INFLOWS
     Interest Income                                     10.75
     Salary Income                                    2,000.00
                                                     -----------
   TOTAL INFLOWS                                      2,010.75

   OUTFLOWS
     Automobile Service                                  34.91
     Bank Charge                                          5.00
     Entertainment                                       28.94
     Home Repair & Maint.                                24.53
     Housing                                              0.00
     Late fees:
       Late payment fees-credit          11.59
       Late payment fees-mortg.          28.73
                                       -----------
     Total Late fees                                     40.32
     Office Expenses                                     34.56
     Water, Gas, Electric                                75.39
     Outflows - Other                                16,082.88
     TO Discnt Brkge                                 24,708.50
     TO New Frontiers                                 1,200.00
                                                     -----------
   TOTAL OUTFLOWS                                     42,235.03

                                                     -----------
   OVERALL TOTAL                                     -40,224.28
                                                     ===========
```

*Fig. 14.9. The personal cash flow report.*

The cash report can be extremely valuable. The cash report shows the various categories of cash flowing into and out of your personal banking accounts. If you question why you seem to have a bigger bank balance than usual or you always seem to run out of money before the end of the month, for example, this report provides the answers.

## Monthly Budget Report

The monthly budget report shows the total money you have received and expended by category and the amounts you budgeted to spend. The report also calculates the difference between what you budgeted and what you actually spent. This report includes transactions from all the bank, cash, and credit card accounts within the account group. Figure 14.10 shows the Monthly Budget Report screen.

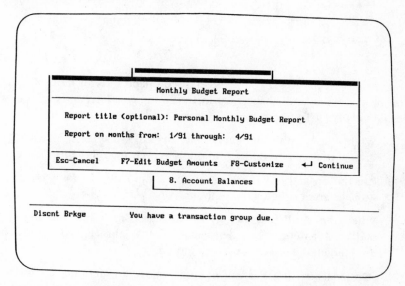

**Fig. 14.10.** *The Monthly Budget Report screen.*

The Monthly Budget Report screen provides two special function keys: F7-Edit Budget Amounts and F8-Customize. The "Customizing and Filtering Reports" section of this chapter describes how to use the F8-Customize function key. Pressing F7 enables you to change or enter the budgeted amounts for categories using the Specify Budget Amounts screen (see fig. 14.11).

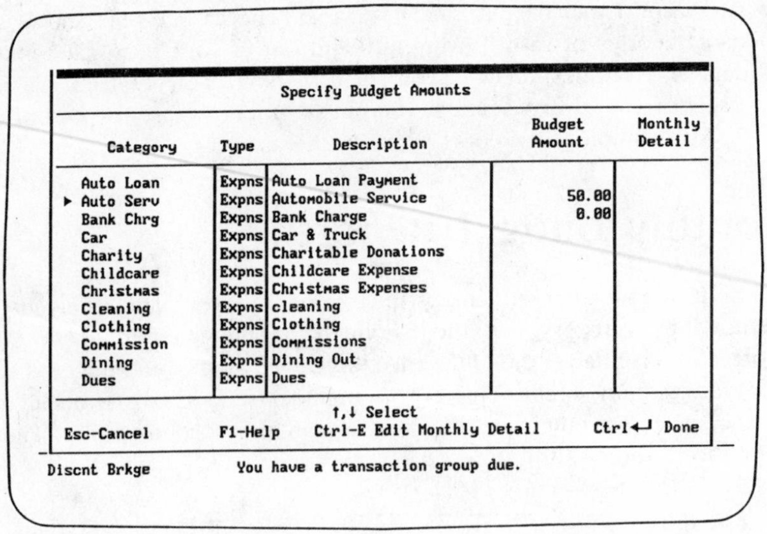

```
                    Specify Budget Amounts

                                              Budget      Monthly
        Category      Type      Description    Amount      Detail

      Auto Loan     Expns  Auto Loan Payment
   ▶  Auto Serv     Expns  Automobile Service           50.00
      Bank Chrg     Expns  Bank Charge                   0.00
      Car           Expns  Car & Truck
      Charity       Expns  Charitable Donations
      Childcare     Expns  Childcare Expense
      Christmas     Expns  Christmas Expenses
      Cleaning      Expns  cleaning
      Clothing      Expns  Clothing
      Commission    Expns  Commissions
      Dining        Expns  Dining Out
      Dues          Expns  Dues

                            ↑,↓ Select
     Esc-Cancel     F1-Help    Ctrl-E Edit Monthly Detail    Ctrl↵ Done

   Discnt Brkge        You have a transaction group due.
```

*Fig. 14.11. The Specify Budget Amounts screen.*

You use this screen to set your budget. (See Chapter 16 for more information on budgeting and Chapter 10 for more information on using categories and classes.) To complete the screen, execute the following steps:

1. While the Monthly Budget Report screen is displayed, press F7 to
   display the Specify Budget Amounts screen (see fig. 14.11).

2. Use the up and down arrows to mark the category for which you
   want to enter a budgeted amount.

3. When the small triangle marks the category, enter the monthly
   budgeted amount. Quicken assumes that this figure represents
   the budgeted amount for every month.

4. (Optional) To use varying monthly budgeted amounts for a category, press Ctrl-E when the small triangle marks the category.
   Quicken displays the Monthly Budget for Category screen (see fig.
   14.12).

5. (Optional) While on the Monthly Budget for Category screen, use
   the up and down arrows to mark the month for which you want to
   enter a budgeted amount and then enter the amount. To copy the
   marked month's budgeted amount to the subsequent months of the
   year, press F9.

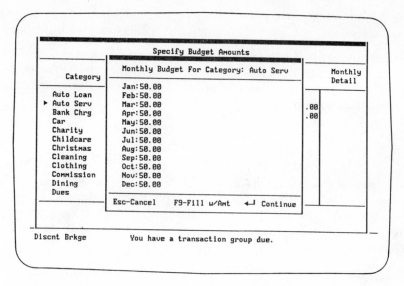

*Fig. 14.12. The Monthly Budget for Category screen.*

6. (Optional) To leave the Monthly Budget for Category screen, press Enter when the cursor is on the Dec field. You also can press F10 or Ctrl-Enter when the cursor is on any of the month fields.

7. To leave the Specify Budget Amounts screen, press Enter when the cursor is on the last category, or press F10 or Ctrl-Enter when the cursor is on any of the category fields. Figure 14.13 shows a sample monthly budget report.

```
                                   Personal Monthly Budget Report
                                      1/ 1/91 Through 4/30/91
Bank,Cash,CC Accounts                                                                          Page 1
4/ 2/91
                      1/ 1/91    -    1/31/91   2/ 1/91    -    2/28/91   3/ 1/91    -    3/31/91
Category Description  Actual   Budget   Diff    Actual   Budget   Diff    Actual   Budget   Diff
------------------
INFLOWS
  Salary Income       2,000.00 2,000.00  0.00    0.00   2,000.00 -2,000.00  0.00   2,000.00 -2,000.00
                      --------- -------- -------- -------- -------- -------- -------- -------- --------
TOTAL INFLOWS         2,000.00 2,000.00  0.00    0.00   2,000.00 -2,000.00  0.00   2,000.00 -2,000.00

OUTFLOWS
  Automobile Service    34.91    50.00  -15.09    0.00     50.00   -50.00    0.00     50.00   -50.00
  Bank Charge            5.00     5.00    0.00    0.00      0.00     0.00    0.00      0.00     0.00
  Entertainment         28.94    50.00  -21.06    0.00     50.00   -50.00    0.00     50.00   -50.00
  Home Repair & Maint.  24.53     0.00   24.53    0.00      0.00     0.00    0.00      0.00     0.00
  Late Payment Fees      0.00     0.00    0.00    0.00      0.00     0.00    0.00      0.00     0.00
  Office Expenses       34.56    25.00    9.56    0.00     25.00   -25.00    0.00     25.00   -25.00
  Water, Gas, Electric  75.39    60.00   15.39    0.00     60.00   -60.00    0.00     60.00   -60.00
                      --------- -------- -------- -------- -------- -------- -------- -------- --------
TOTAL OUTFLOWS        203.33   185.00   18.33    0.00    185.00  -185.00    0.00    185.00  -185.00

                      --------- -------- -------- -------- -------- -------- -------- -------- --------
OVERALL TOTAL        1,796.67 1,815.00  -18.33   0.00   1,815.00 -1,815.00  0.00   1,815.00 -1,815.00
                      ========= ======== ======== ======== ======== ======== ======== ======== ========
```

*Fig. 14.13. A sample monthly budget report.*

The monthly budget report shows only categories for which amounts have been spent or budgeted. Transfers are not included on the report.

Budget reports gauge whether you are following the budget you have specified. Your budget is, in essence, your financial game plan. The budget report is the tool you use to increase your chances for financial success. Chapter 16 discusses budgeting in detail.

## Itemized Category Report

The itemized category report shows each transaction in an account group sorted and subtotaled by category. This type of report provides a convenient way to see the detailed transactions that add up to a category total. The Itemized Category Report screen, shown in figure 14.14, works like the other report request screens.

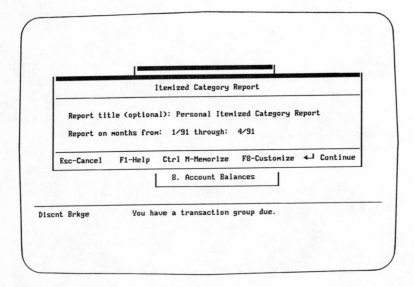

**Fig. 14.14.** *The Itemized Category Report screen.*

You can replace the default report title, Itemized Category Report, with a more specific title, such as Personal Itemized Category Report, by using the optional Report title field. You also can specify a range of months to be included on the report and use the F8-Customize and F9-Filter function keys to change the appearance of the data. Figure 14.15 shows a page of a sample of the itemized category report. (The defaults have been changed in this figure to customize the report titles.)

```
                              Personal Itemized Category Report
                                  1/ 1/91 Through 4/30/91
  All Accounts
  4/ 2/91                                                                            Page 2


       Date   Acct    Num    Description      Memo    Category   Clr  Amount
       -----  ------- ------ ---------------- ------- ---------- --- ----------
                                                                      ----------
              Total Entertainment                                      -28.94

              Home Repair & Maint.
              --------------------
       1/ 9 Big Nati     S Big National Ban          Home Rpair        -24.53
                                                                      ----------
              Total Home Repair & Maint.                               -24.53

              Housing
              -------
       1/15 Big Nati        VOID Puget Sound January  Housing      X     0.00
                                                                      ----------
              Total Housing                                              0.00

              Late fees:
              ----------

                 Late payment fees-credit
                 ------------------------
       1/ 9 Big Nati     S Big National Ban          Latefees:LCred    -11.59
                                                                      ----------
                 Total Late payment fees-credit                        -11.59

                 Late payment fees-mortg.
                 ------------------------
       1/ 9 Big Nati     S Big National Ban          Latefees:LMort    -28.73
                                                                      ----------
                 Total Late payment fees-mortg.                        -28.73
                                                                      ----------
              Total Late fees                                          -40.32

              Office Expenses
              ---------------
       1/ 3 Big Nati 767  Sammamish Cleani            Office       X   -34.56
                                                                      ----------
              Total Office Expenses                                    -34.56

              Water, Gas, Electric
              --------------------
       1/ 2 Big Nati 765  Seattle Power Co December   Utilities    X   -75.39
                                                                      ----------
              Total Water, Gas, Electric                              -75.39

              Expenses - Other
              ----------------
       1/ 3 Big Nati 766  National Motors  car payment             X  -200.08
       1/23 Big Nati                       money for m              -8,821.00
       2/ 9 Big Nati                       employer co              -1,200.00
       3/ 1 Big Nati                       employer co              -1,000.00
       3/ 8 Big Nati                                                -2,546.00
       3/ 8 Big Nati                                                  -815.79
```

**Fig. 14.15.** *A sample itemized category report.*

The itemized category resembles the cash-flow report in purpose and information, except that the itemized category does not include account transfers. If you want to see your cash inflows and outflows grouped and summarized by category, this is the report you want.

# Tax Summary

The tax summary report shows all the transactions assigned to categories you marked as tax-related. Transactions are sorted and subtotaled by category. The Tax Summary Report screen, shown in figure 14.16, works like the other request screens, enabling you to give the tax summary report a more specific title or to include only transactions from specified months.

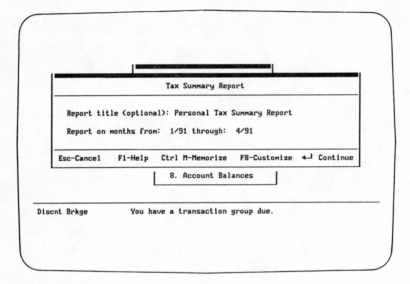

*Fig. 14.16. The Tax Summary Report screen.*

The F8-Customize and F9-Filter function keys are available so that you can produce a custom-tailored version of the report. (See "Customizing and Filtering Reports" later in this chapter.) Figure 14.17 shows a page from a sample tax summary report.

The tax summary report is a handy tax preparation tool to use at the end of the year. This report summarizes the tax deductions you need to report on your federal and state income tax returns. (***Note:*** The report, however, summarizes only tax deductions paid with those bank accounts and cash accounts you choose to track with Quicken. If you have two checking accounts, write tax-deductible checks using both accounts, and track only one of the accounts with Quicken, you are missing half of your deductions.)

```
                              Personal Tax Summary Report
                                 1/ 1/91 Through 4/30/91
 All Accounts
 4/ 2/91                                                                    Page 1


        Date   Acct     Num    Description      Memo      Category   Clr Amount
        -----  -------- ------ ---------------- --------- ---------- - --------

              Note: Investment transaction amounts represent changes in cash
                      and the value of your investments.  See Chapter 20.


              INCOME/EXPENSE
                INCOME
                  Interest Income
                  ---------------
        1/ 2 Big Nati      Interest        October    Int Inc    X    5.75
        1/ 6 Big Nati      Interest Earned            Int Inc    X    4.50
        1/ 6 Big Nati      Balance Adjustme           Int Inc    X    0.50
                                                                   ----------
                    Total Interest Income                             10.75

                  Investment Interest Inc
                  -----------------------
        2/13 Discnt B IntInc Trump's T     semi annual _IntInc   X   65.00
                                                                   ----------
                    Total Investment Interest Inc                    65.00

                  Realized Gain/Loss
                  ------------------
        2/13 Discnt B SellX  50 Microsoft             _RlzdGain  X  362.50
                                                                   ----------
                    Total Realized Gain/Loss                        362.50

                  Salary Income
                  -------------
        1/24 Big Nati      Washington Manuf payroll che Salary      2,000.00
                                                                   ----------
                    Total Salary Income                            2,000.00
                                                                   ----------
                  TOTAL INCOME                                     2,438.25


                EXPENSES
                  Late fees:
                  ----------

                  Late payment fees-credit
                  ------------------------
        1/ 9 Big Nati     S Big National Ban        Latefees:LCredi    -11.59
                                                                   ----------
                    Total Late payment fees-credit                    -11.59

                  Late payment fees-mortg.
                  ------------------------
        1/ 9 Big Nati     S Big National Ban        Latefees:LMortg    -28.73
                                                                   ----------
                    Total Late payment fees-mortg.                    -28.73
                                                                   ----------
```

*Fig. 14.17. A sample tax summary report.*


# Net Worth Reports

A net worth report shows the balance in each of the accounts in an account group on a particular date. If the account group includes all your assets and liabilities, the resulting report is a balance sheet and provides one estimate of your financial net worth. (Balance sheets are described in Chapter 12, "Tracking Your Net Worth, Other Assets, and Liabilities.") Figure 14.18 shows the Net Worth Report screen.

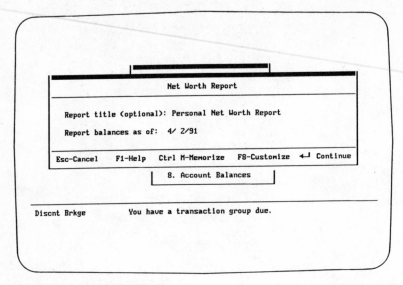

*Fig. 14.18. The Net Worth Report screen.*

The Net Worth Report screen differs from other personal report screens because you cannot enter a range of dates; you can enter only one date. The net worth report does not report on activity for a period of time but provides a snapshot of certain aspects of your financial condition—the account balances in your account group—at a point in time. Figure 14.19 shows a sample net worth report.

Monitoring your financial worth probably is more important than most people realize. Over the years that you work, one of your financial goals may be to increase your net worth. During your retirement years, you probably will look to your net worth to provide income and security. Your net worth, for example, may include investments that produce regular interest or dividend income. Your net worth also may include your personal residence, completely paid for by the time you retire.

```
                              Personal Net Worth Report
                                  As of 4/ 2/91
    All Accounts                                                          Page 1
    4/ 2/91
                                                  4/ 2/91
                               Acct                Balance
    --------------------------------------------  ------------
    ASSETS
      Cash and Bank Accounts
        Acme-Acme Credit Union                      5,250.00
        Big National-Checking # 1234567890        -42,174.27
                                                  ------------
        Total Cash and Bank Accounts              -36,924.27

      Other Assets
        House-Personal Residence                  104,200.00
                                                  ------------
        Total Other Assets                        104,200.00

      Investments
        Discnt Brkge-Discount Brokers, Inc         29,508.75
        New Frontiers-New Frontiers Fund            6,420.74
                                                  ------------
        Total Investments                          35,929.49

                                                  ------------
      TOTAL ASSETS                                103,205.22

    LIABILITIES
      Other Liabilities
        Home mortgage                              75,000.00
                                                  ------------
        Total Other Liabilities                    75,000.00

                                                  ------------
      TOTAL LIABILITIES                            75,000.00

                                                  ------------
      OVERALL TOTAL                                28,205.22
                                                  ============
```

**Fig. 14.19.** *A sample net worth report.*

# Tracking Your Business Finances with Business Reports

The Business Reports menu, shown in figure 14.3, provides seven reports. To request any of the reports, complete the report request screen with an optional title and the period of time you want the report to cover.

## Profit and Loss Statement

A profit and loss statement shows the total income and expense transactions by category for all accounts on a monthly basis. Transactions from any of the accounts in the account groups are included, but transfers between accounts are not. Figure 14.20 shows the Profit & Loss Statement screen. Like most of the report request screens, you have two options: to use your own report title or the default title and to specify the months to be included on the report or to use the default (from January of the current year to the current date). Figure 14.21 shows a sample profit and loss statement.

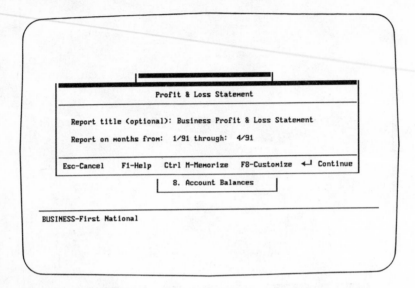

**Fig. 14.20.** *The Profit & Loss Statement screen.*

```
                          Business Profit & Loss Statement
                             1/ 1/91 Through 4/30/91
BUSINESS-All Accounts                                                        Page 1
4/ 2/91
                                              1/ 1/91-
                         Category Description   4/30/91
                         ------------------------ -----------
                         INCOME/EXPENSE
                           INCOME
                             Gross Sales       106,000.00
                                               ------------
                             TOTAL INCOME      106,000.00

                           EXPENSES
                             Advertising           135.72
                             Building Lot            0.00
                             Building Materials      0.00
                             Cost of Goods Sold  90,000.00
                             Late Payment Fees      23.85
                             Legal & Prof. Fees     75.89
                             Office Expenses       584.68
                             Subcontractor Labor     0.00
                             Expenses - Other      400.00
                                               ------------
                             TOTAL EXPENSES     91,220.14

                                               ------------
                           TOTAL INCOME/EXPENSE 14,779.86
                                               ============
```

**Fig. 14.21.** *A sample profit and loss statement.*

Unless a business makes money, the business cannot keep operating for very long. Accordingly, business owners and managers must monitor profits. The profit and loss statement provides the means to do so.

# Cash Flow Report

A cash flow report resembles a profit and loss statement. This report includes all bank, cash, and credit card accounts and shows the money received (inflows) and the money spent (outflows) by category for each month. The cash flow report also shows transfers between accounts. Figure 14.22 shows the Cash Flow Report screen.

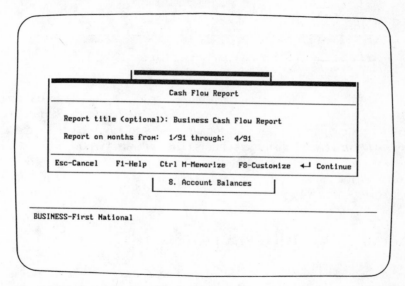

*Fig. 14.22. The Cash Flow Report screen.*

Like the Profit & Loss Statement screen, the Cash Flow Report screen provides fields for you to enter the range of months for which you want the cash flow report prepared. You can enter your own report title for Quicken to print on the cash flow report in place of the default title, Cash Flow Report. You also can use the F8-Customize and F9-Filter keys to fine-tune the report produced.

Figure 14.23 shows a sample cash flow report. The major difference between this report and the profit and loss statement is that transfers to other accounts are shown on the cash flow report. The transfer to Inventory is the last outflow listed.

```
                              Business Cash Flow Report
                               1/ 1/91 Through 4/30/91
  BUSINESS-First National                                                    Page 1
  4/ 2/91
                                                1/ 1/91-
                           Category Description   4/30/91
                           ---------------------  -----------

                           INFLOWS
                             Gross Sales         105,000.00
                                                 -----------
                           TOTAL INFLOWS         105,000.00

                           OUTFLOWS
                             Advertising            135.72
                             Building Lot        30,400.00
                             Building Materials  23,456.00
                             Late Payment Fees       23.85
                             Legal & Prof. Fees      75.89
                             Office Expenses        584.68
                             Subcontractor Labor 16,753.00
                             TO Inventory       100,000.00
                                                 -----------
                           TOTAL OUTFLOWS        171,429.14


                                                 -----------
                           OVERALL TOTAL         -66,429.14
                                                 ===========
```

**Fig. 14.23.** *A sample business cash flow report.*

Cash flow is just as important as profits—particularly over shorter time periods. Besides making money, businesses need to have cash to purchase inventory or equipment, to wait for customers to pay their bills, and to pay back loans from banks and vendors. The cash flow report, which summarizes your cash inflows and outflows by category and account, provides a method for monitoring your cash flow—and for pinpointing problems that arise.

# A/P by Vendor Report

Because Quicken uses what is called cash-basis accounting, expenses are recorded only when you actually pay the bill. By not paying bills, or even paying bills late, you can improve profits or cash flows. The problem, of course, is that this concept is clearly illogical. Just because you haven't paid a bill by the end of the month doesn't mean the bill shouldn't be considered in assessing the month's financial performance. To partially address this shortcoming, Quicken provides the A/P (unprinted checks) by vendor report, which enables you to see which bills have not been paid.

The A/P by vendor report lists all the unprinted checks, sorted and subtotaled by payee. (A/P is an abbreviation for accounts payable, the unpaid bills of a business.) Figure 14.24 shows the A/P (Unprinted Checks) by Vendor screen. You do not enter a date or a range of dates on this screen.

You can enter a substitute report title for Quicken to use instead of the default report title, A/P by Vendor Report. You also can use the F8-Customize and F9-Filter function keys as described later in the chapter to change the appearance of the report and the data used.

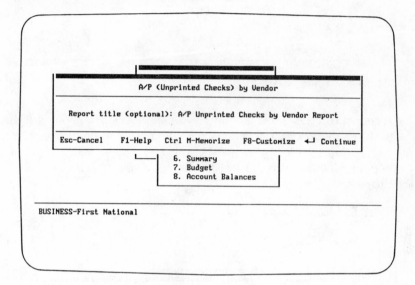

*Fig. 14.24. The A/P (Unprinted Checks) by Vendor screen.*

Figure 14.25 shows a sample A/P by vendor report. Two vendor totals appear: one for Hugh D. James and another for Stouffer's Office Supplies. Quicken subtotals unprinted checks with the exact payee names. If you type the payee name differently for different checks, the payee is not recognized by Quicken as the same payee, and the amounts are not subtotaled. If you plan to use this report (or the A/R by customer report described next), use the memorized transactions feature. When you use this feature, the payee name is identical for each transaction.

## A/R by Customer Report

The A/R by customer report shows the transactions in all of the other asset accounts, sorted and subtotaled by payee. The report, however, does not include transactions marked as cleared—those transactions marked with an asterisk or X in the C field of the register. (A/R is an abbreviation

```
                        A/P Unprinted Checks by Vendor Report
                               4/ 1/91 Through 4/30/91
   BUSINESS-First National                                                    Page 1
   4/ 2/91


                               Payee              4/91
                        ---------------------------  ----------
                        Hugh D. James                   -820.00
                        Stouffer's Office Supplies      -944.90
                                                     ----------
                        OVERALL TOTAL                -1,764.90
                                                     ==========
```

*Fig. 14.25. A sample A/P by vendor report.*

for accounts receivable, the amounts a business's customers owe.) Figure 14.26 shows the A/R by Customer screen. You can enter a title to replace the default report title Quicken uses, A/R by Customer Report. You also can use the F8-Customize and F9-Filter function keys as described later in the chapter.

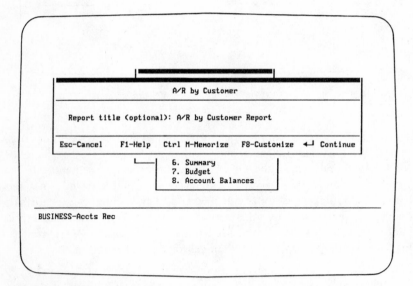

```
                        A/R by Customer

   Report title (optional): A/R by Customer Report

   Esc-Cancel    F1-Help   Ctrl M-Memorize   F8-Customize   ← Continue

                          6. Summary
                          7. Budget
                          8. Account Balances


   BUSINESS-Accts Rec
```

*Fig. 14.26. The A/R by Customer screen.*

After you complete the request screen, press Enter. Quicken displays the Select Accounts to Include screen (see fig. 14.27).

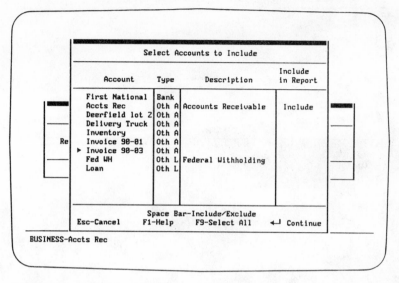

*Fig. 14.27.* *The Select Accounts to Include screen.*

Quicken initially selects all asset account types for inclusion on the A/R by customer report. If you have other asset accounts besides accounts receivable, exclude these accounts. For example, figure 14.27 shows one account marked for inclusion, Accts Rec. To exclude or include accounts, follow these steps:

1. Use the up- and down-arrow keys to move the selection triangle to the left of the account you want to exclude or include.

2. Press the space bar. The space bar acts as a toggle switch, alternately marking the account for inclusion or exclusion.

3. (Optional) To select all the accounts, press F9.

Figure 14.28 shows a sample A/R by customer report.

For businesses that extend customer credit—which is what you do anytime you allow a customer to "buy now, pay later"—monitoring the amounts the customers owe is essential to profits and cash flows. Unfortunately, some customers don't pay unless you remind them several times, some customers frequently lose invoices and then forget that they owe you, and sometimes customers never receive your bill. To make sure that these small problems don't become big cash flow problems, you can use the A/R by customer report.

**Fig. 14.28.** *A sample A/R by customer report.*

**CPA Tip**   Good collection procedures usually improve cash flows dramatically, so consider using the customer aging report as a collection guide. You may, for example, want to telephone any customer with an invoice 30 days past due, and you may want to stop granting additional credit to any customer with invoices more than 60 days past due, and—in the absence of special circumstances—you may want to initiate collection procedures for any customer with invoices more than 90 days past due.

# Job/Project Report

The job/project report shows category totals by month for each month in the specified date range. The report also shows account balances at the end of the last month. (If you are using classes, the report shows category totals by classes in separate columns across the report page.) Figure 14.29 shows the Job/Project Report screen. Figure 14.30 shows a sample job/ project report. (*Note:* Refer to Chapter 18 for more information on job costing.)

# Payroll Report

The payroll report shows the total amounts paid to individual payees when the transaction category starts with payroll. (The search argument used is payroll.... See the discussions of exact and key-word matches in Chapters 5 and 7 for more information.) This report type includes transactions from all accounts. Figure 14.31 shows the Payroll Report screen.

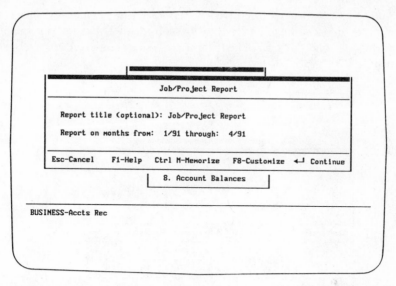

**Fig. 14.29.** *The Job/Project Report screen.*

```
                                    Job/Project Report
                                    1/ 1/91 Through 4/30/91
BUSINESS-All Accounts                                                              Page 1
4/ 2/91

                                                                       OVERALL
        Category Description    California    Oregon   Washington    Other      TOTAL
        --------------------    ----------   -------   ----------   -------   --------
        INCOME/EXPENSE
          INCOME
            Gross Sales           3,634.74   5,811.00    7,600.00  106,000.00  123,045.74

          TOTAL INCOME           3,634.74    5,811.00    7,600.00  106,000.00  123,045.74

          EXPENSES
            Advertising              0.00      135.72        0.00        0.00      135.72
            Building Lot             0.00        0.00        0.00        0.00        0.00
            Building Materials       0.00        0.00        0.00        0.00        0.00
            Cost of Goods Sold       0.00        0.00        0.00   90,000.00   90,000.00
            Late Payment Fees        0.00        0.00       23.85        0.00       23.85
            Legal & Prof. Fees     125.89      120.00      650.00        0.00      895.89
            Office Expenses        584.68        0.00      124.76        0.00      709.44
            Subcontractor Labor      0.00        0.00        0.00        0.00        0.00
            Expenses - Other         0.00        0.00        0.00      400.00      400.00

          TOTAL EXPENSES          710.57      255.72      798.61   90,400.00   92,164.90


        TOTAL INCOME/EXPENSE     2,924.17    5,555.28    6,801.39   15,600.00   30,880.84

        TRANSFERS
          TO Inventory              0.00        0.00        0.00 -100,000.00 -100,000.00
          FROM First National       0.00        0.00        0.00  100,000.00  100,000.00

        TOTAL TRANSFERS            0.00        0.00        0.00        0.00        0.00

        BALANCE FORWARD
          Deerfield lot 2          0.00        0.00        0.00        0.00        0.00
          Delivery Truck           0.00        0.00        0.00   12,000.00   12,000.00
          Fed WH                   0.00        0.00        0.00        0.00        0.00
          Inventory                0.00        0.00        0.00   30,000.00   30,000.00
          Invoice 90-03            0.00        0.00        0.00    3,000.00    3,000.00
          Loan                     0.00        0.00        0.00  -12,000.00  -12,000.00

        TOTAL BALANCE FORWARD      0.00        0.00        0.00   33,000.00   33,000.00


        OVERALL TOTAL           2,924.17    5,555.28    6,801.39   48,600.00   63,880.84
                             ===========  =========  ==========  =========  ==========
```

**Fig. 14.30.** *A sample job/project report.*

Figure 14.32 shows a sample payroll report. (***Note:*** Refer to Chapter 18 for more information on preparing payrolls with Quicken. For specific information on using Quicken for processing employee payroll, see Chapter 17.)

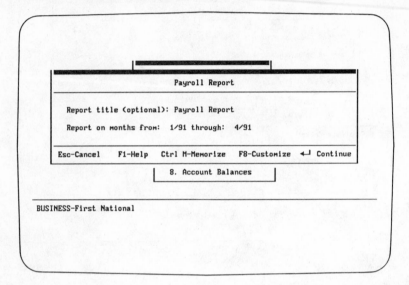

**Fig. 14.31.** *The Payroll Report screen.*

**Fig. 14.32.** *A sample payroll report.*

# Balance Sheet

The balance sheet report shows the account balances for all the accounts in the account group at a specific point in time. If the account group includes accounts for all of your assets and liabilities, the resulting report is a balance sheet and shows the net worth of your business. (Chapter 12, "Tracking Your Net Worth, Other Assets, and Liabilities," describes balance sheets in more detail.) Figure 14.33 shows the Balance Sheet screen. Figure 14.34 shows an example of a business balance sheet.

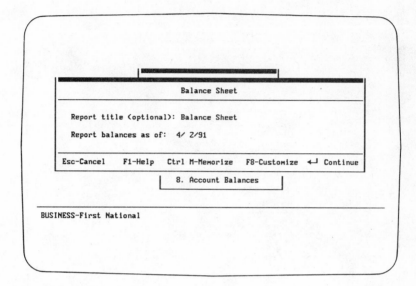

**Fig. 14.33.** *The Balance Sheet screen.*

Even for small businesses, balance sheets are important reports. Because a balance sheet shows what a business owns and what it owes, balance sheets give an indication of the financial strength or weakness of a business. For example, the smaller the total liabilities amount in relation to the total assets amount, the stronger the business. Alternatively, the larger the total liabilities in relation to the total assets, the weaker the business. As a result of these and similar financial insights, banks usually require a balance sheet in order to evaluate loan applications from businesses.

```
                              Balance Sheet
                              As of 4/ 2/91

BUSINESS-All Accounts                                              Page 1
4/ 2/91

                                           4/ 2/91
                           Acct              Balance
-------------------------------------- ------------------
ASSETS

   Cash and Bank Accounts
     First National
       Ending Balance           180,776.10
       plus: Checks Payable       1,764.90
                                ------------
       Total First National                  182,541.00
                                             ------------
     Total Cash and Bank Accounts            182,541.00

   Other Assets
     Accts Rec-Accounts Receivable            17,045.74
     Deerfield lot 2                          70,609.00
     Delivery Truck                           12,000.00
     Inventory                                40,000.00
     Invoice 90-01                             1,000.00
     Invoice 90-03                             3,000.00
                                             ------------
     Total Other Assets                      143,654.74

                                             ------------
   TOTAL ASSETS                              326,195.74
                                             ============
   LIABILITIES & EQUITY

     LIABILITIES
       Checks Payable                          1,764.90

     Other Liabilities
       Fed WH-Federal Withholding               400.00
       Loan                                   12,000.00
                                             ------------
       Total Other Liabilities               12,400.00

                                             ------------
     TOTAL LIABILITIES                        14,164.90

     EQUITY                                  312,030.84
                                             ------------
     TOTAL LIABILITIES & EQUITY             326,195.74
                                             ============
```

*Fig. 14.34.* *An example of a business balance sheet.*

# Tracking Your Investments with Quicken's Investment Reports

The Investment Reports menu provides five report options (see fig. 14.4). As with personal and business reports, the basic steps for printing an investment report are straightforward. To print any of the five reports, you complete the appropriate report request screen and then print the report.

*Note:* If you haven't reviewed the material in Chapter 13, "Monitoring Your Investments," you may need to skim that chapter before trying to print investment reports.

# Portfolio Value Reports

A portfolio value report shows the estimated market values of each of the securities in your Quicken investment accounts on a specific date. To estimate the market values, Quicken uses each security's individual price history (a list of prices on certain dates). Quicken determines which price to use by comparing the date in the Report value as of field to the dates that have prices in the price history. Ideally, Quicken uses a price for the same date as the Report value as of field date. When the price history does not contain a price for the same date as the field entry, Quicken uses the price for the date closest to the field entry.

To request a portfolio value report, you use the screen shown in figure 14.35. You can enter a report title, and you need to enter a date in the Report value as of field. You can specify that the information on the report be summarized by account, investment type, and investment goal. You also can specify whether the report should include the current account, all accounts, or only selected accounts, by using a screen that mirrors the one shown in figure 14.27. Figure 14.36 shows an example of the portfolio value report.

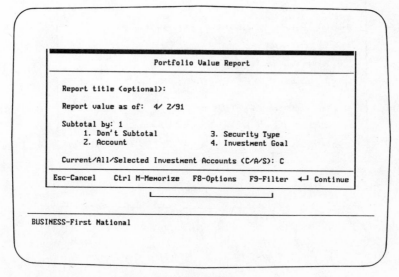

```
                          Portfolio Value Report

    Report title (optional):

    Report value as of:  4/ 2/91

    Subtotal by: 1
        1. Don't Subtotal              3. Security Type
        2. Account                     4. Investment Goal

    Current/All/Selected Investment Accounts (C/A/S): C

   Esc-Cancel    Ctrl M-Memorize    F8-Options    F9-Filter   ◄┘ Continue


BUSINESS-First National
```

*Fig. 14.35. The Portfolio Value Report screen.*

```
                                  Portfolio Value Report
                                      As of 4/ 2/91
 Discnt Brkge                                                                              Page 1
 4/ 2/91


                        Security    Shares  Curr Price  Cost Basis  Gain/Loss  Balance
                   --------------------  -------  ----------  ----------  ---------  ---------
                   Microsoft Corp        50.00    97 7/8     4,393.75    500.00    4,893.75
                   Trump's Taj Mahal    100.00    95 1/2     9,708.50   -158.50    9,550.00
                   -Cash-            15,065.00         1    15,065.00      0.00   15,065.00
                                                          ----------  ---------  ---------
                   Total Investments                       29,167.25    341.50   29,508.75
                                                          ==========  =========  =========
```

**Fig. 14.36.** *A sample of the portfolio value report.*

# Investment Performance Reports

Investment performance reports help you measure how well or how poorly your investments are doing. These reports look at all the transactions for a security and calculate an annual rate of return—in effect, the interest rate—an investment has paid you. To generate an investment performance report, you use the report request screen shown in figure 14.37.

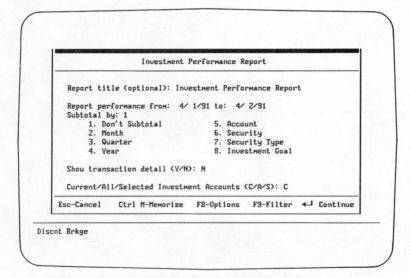

```
                  Investment Performance Report


     Report title (optional): Investment Performance Report

     Report performance from:  4/ 1/91 to:  4/ 2/91
     Subtotal by: 1
             1. Don't Subtotal        5. Account
             2. Month                 6. Security
             3. Quarter               7. Security Type
             4. Year                  8. Investment Goal

     Show transaction detail (Y/N): N

     Current/All/Selected Investment Accounts (C/A/S): C

    Esc-Cancel    Ctrl M-Memorize   F8-Options   F9-Filter  ← Continue

 Discnt Brkge
```

**Fig. 14.37.** *The Investment Performance Report screen.*

The report request screen enables you to use a custom title for the report. The screen also requires that you enter dates into the `Report performance from` and `to` fields. These dates tell Quicken for which time frame you want to calculate returns. The report request screen also enables you to subtotal rates of return by different time periods, by account, by security, by investment type, or by investment goals. You also can specify whether you want rates of return calculated for just the current account, for all accounts, or for selected accounts. Quicken notifies you if one or more of the total return calculations cannot be completed and displays the value as `NA`. Figure 14.38 shows an example of the investment performance report.

```
                         Investment Performance Report
                           1/ 1/91 Through 4/30/91
All Investment Accounts                                                  Page 1
4/ 2/91
                                                          Avg. Annual
                          Description                     Tot. Return
             ---------------------------------------- -------------

             Total Microsoft Corp                              79.5%

             Total New Frontiers                              -15.2%

             Total Trump's Taj Mahal                           -4.5%
```

***Fig. 14.38.*** *A sample investment performance report.*

# Capital Gains (Schedule D) Reports

The capital gains report attempts to print all the information you need to complete the federal income tax form, Schedule D. Taxpayers use Schedule D to report capital gains and losses. To generate a capital gains report, use the Capital Gains (Schedule D) Report screen shown in figure 14.39.

Most of the fields on the Capital Gains Report screen should be familiar to you, and the fields that also appear on the other investment report screens are not described here. Two fields do deserve mention, however: the `Subtotal by Short- vs Long-Term` and the `Maximum short-term gain holding period (days)` fields. Although income tax laws currently in effect treat short-term capital gains the same as long-term capital gains, Congress may change this treatment. Accordingly, Quicken enables you to subtotal by short-term and long-term gains and losses.

Currently, gains and losses that stem from the sale of capital assets held for more than one year are considered long-term. However, the `Maximum` short-term gain holding period field enables you to change the default number of days Quicken uses to determine whether a gain or loss is long-term. Figure 14.40 shows an example of a capital gains report.

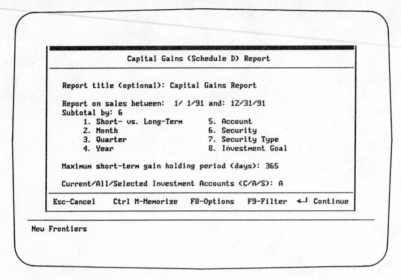

*Fig. 14.39. The Capital Gains (Schedule D) Report screen.*

Capital Gains Report
1/ 1/91 Through 12/31/91

All Investment Accounts    Page 1
4/ 2/91

| Acct | Security | Shares | Bought | Sold | Sales Price | Cost Basis | Gain/Loss |
|---|---|---|---|---|---|---|---|
| | Microsoft Corp | | | | | | |
| Discn | Microsof | 50 | 1/23/91 | 2/13/91 | 4,756.25 | 4,393.75 | 362.50 |
| | Total Microsoft Corp | | | | 4,756.25 | 4,393.75 | 362.50 |

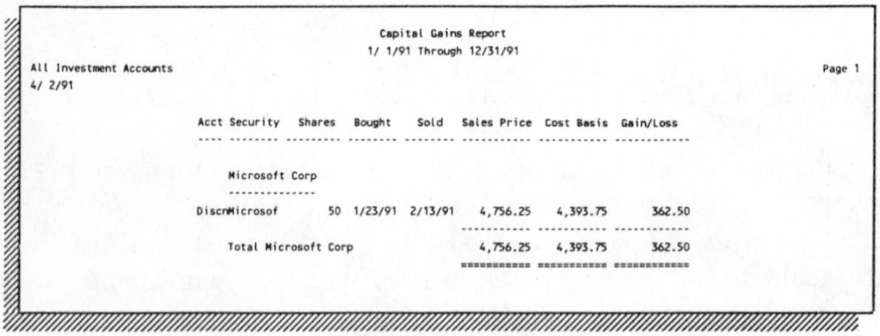

*Fig. 14.40. A sample capital gains report.*

# Investment Income Reports

The investment income report summarizes all the income transactions you recorded in one or more of the investment accounts. To generate the report, use the report request screen shown in figure 14.41. Figure 14.42 shows an example of the report.

Realized gains and losses are calculated when the investment is actually sold and cash is received, by comparing the cash received with the original cost. Unrealized gains and losses are calculated when the cost of the investment is compared with the market value to determine what the gain or loss would have been if the investment had been sold.

```
Investment Income Report

Report title (optional): Investment Income Report

Restrict to transactions from:  1/ 1/91 through:  3/31/91
Subtotal by: 6
     1. Don't Subtotal              5. Account
     2. Month                       6. Security
     3. Quarter                     7. Security Type
     4. Year                        8. Investment Goal

Current/All/Selected Investment Accounts (C/A/S): A

Esc-Cancel   Ctrl M-Memorize   F8-Options   F9-Filter   ↵ Continue

New Frontiers
```

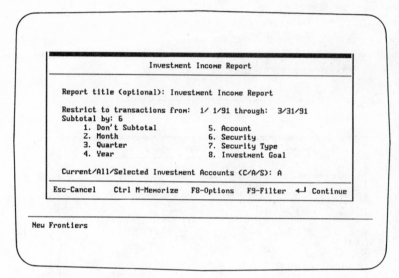

*Fig. 14.41.* *The Investment Income Report screen.*

Investment Income Report
1/ 1/91 Through 3/31/91

All Investment Accounts
4/ 2/91

Page 1

| Category Description | Microsoft C | New Frontie | Trump's Taj | OVERALL TOTAL |
|---|---|---|---|---|
| INCOME/EXPENSE | | | | |
| INCOME | | | | |
| Investment Interest Inc | 0.00 | 0.00 | 65.00 | 65.00 |
| Realized Gain/Loss | 362.50 | 0.00 | 0.00 | 362.50 |
| Unrealized Gain/Loss | 362.50 | 2,237.96 | -108.50 | 2,491.96 |
| TOTAL INCOME | 725.00 | 2,237.96 | -43.50 | 2,919.46 |
| EXPENSES | | | | |
| Expenses - Other | 0.00 | 0.00 | 0.00 | 0.00 |
| TOTAL EXPENSES | 0.00 | 0.00 | 0.00 | 0.00 |
| TOTAL INCOME/EXPENSE | 725.00 | 2,237.96 | -43.50 | 2,919.46 |

*Fig. 14.42.* *A sample investment income report.*

# Investment Transactions Reports

The investment transactions report lists each of the investment transactions in the register. To request the report, use the Investment Transactions Report screen shown in figure 14.43. As with many of the other report request screens, Quicken enables you to enter an optional title, specify the time frame the report should cover, indicate whether you want transactions subtotaled according to some convention, and which accounts you want included on the report. Figure 14.44 shows an example of the investment transactions report.

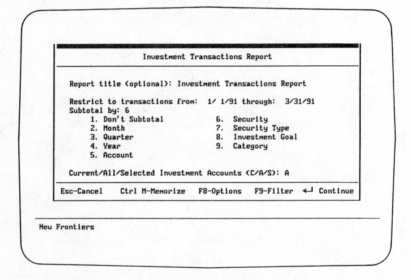

**Fig. 14.43.** *The Investment Transactions Report screen.*

# Customizing and Filtering Reports

Personal reports (except the monthly budget report), business reports, and investment reports provide two special function keys: F8-Customize and F9-Filter. (The F9-Filter key often isn't shown on-screen, but is available.) F8-Customize enables you to modify the way data is organized and presented on a report. F9-Filter enables you to include or exclude certain

Investment Transactions Report
1/ 1/91 Through 3/31/91

All Investment Accounts
4/ 2/91

Page 1

| Date | Acct | Action | Secur | Categ | Price | Shares | Commssn | Cash | Invest. Value | Cash + Invest. |
|---|---|---|---|---|---|---|---|---|---|---|
| | Microsoft Corp | | | | | | | | | |
| 1/23 | Discnt | ShrsIn | Micros | | 87 7/8 | 100 | | -8,787.50 | 8,787.50 | |
| | | | | [Discn | | | | 8,787.50 | | 8,787.50 |
| 2/13 | Discnt | SellX | Micros | | 95 1/8 | 50 | | 4,393.75 | -4,393.75 | |
| | | | | [Discn | | | | -4,756.25 | | -4,756.25 |
| | | | | Realized Gain/Loss | | | | 362.50 | | 362.50 |
| 2/13 | | UnrlzGn | Micros | Unreal | 95 1/8 | | | | 362.50 | 362.50 |
| | Total Microsoft Corp | | | | | | | 0.00 | 4,756.25 | 4,756.25 |
| | New Frontiers | | | | | | | | | |
| 2/ 5 | New Fr | ShrsIn | New Fr | | 11.590 | 86.281 | | -1,000.00 | 1,000.00 | |
| | | | | [New F | | | | 1,000.00 | | 1,000.00 |
| 2/ 5 | | UnrlzGn | New Fr | Unreal | 11.590 | | | | -22.35 | -22.35 |
| 2/ 9 | New Fr | BuyX | New Fr | | 11.810 | 101.609 | | -1,200.00 | 1,200.00 | |
| | | | | [Big N | | | | 1,200.00 | | 1,200.00 |
| 2/ 9 | | UnrlzGn | New Fr | Unreal | 11.810 | | | | 2,260.31 | 2,260.31 |
| 2/28 | New Fr | StkSpli | New Fr | | | 2:1 | | | | |
| | Total New Frontiers | | | | | | | 0.00 | 4,437.96 | 4,437.96 |
| | Trump's Taj Mahal | | | | | | | | | |
| 2/13 | Discnt | BuyX | Trump' | | 96 5/8 | 100 | 46.00 | -9,708.50 | 9,708.50 | |
| | | | | [Big N | | | | 9,708.50 | | 9,708.50 |
| 2/13 | Discnt | IntInc | Trump' | Investment Interest Inc | | | | 65.00 | | 65.00 |
| 2/13 | | UnrlzGn | Trump' | Unreal | 96 5/8 | | | | -46.00 | -46.00 |
| 3/17 | | UnrlzGn | Trump' | Unrealized | 96 | | | | -62.50 | -62.50 |
| | Total Trump's Taj Mahal | | | | | | | 65.00 | 9,600.00 | 9,665.00 |
| | -Cash- | | | | | | | | | |
| 1/31 | Discnt | XIn | -Cash- | [Big N | | | | 15,000.00 | | 15,000.00 |
| | Total -Cash- | | | | | | | 15,000.00 | 0.00 | 15,000.00 |
| | OVERALL TOTAL | | | | | | | 15,065.00 | 18,794.21 | 33,859.21 |

*Fig. 14.44.* *A sample investment transactions report.*

transactions from a report. These two function keys give you complete flexibility over the way Quicken generates personal, business, and investment reports. The F9-Filter function key also enables you to change the way Quicken prepares custom reports.

# Customizing a Report

If you press F8-Customize from one of the report screens, Quicken displays the Create Summary Report screen shown in figure 14.45. Quicken fills out the Create Summary Report screen to generate the report default type.

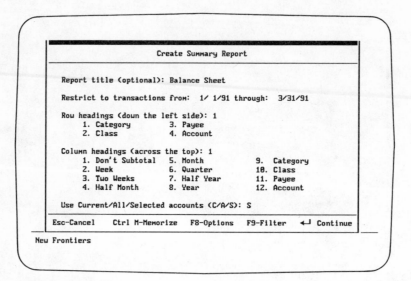

                          Create Summary Report

    Report title (optional): Balance Sheet

    Restrict to transactions from:  1/ 1/91 through:  3/31/91

    Row headings (down the left side): 1
         1. Category       3. Payee
         2. Class          4. Account

    Column headings (across the top): 1
         1. Don't Subtotal  5. Month          9.  Category
         2. Week            6. Quarter        10. Class
         3. Two Weeks       7. Half Year      11. Payee
         4. Half Month      8. Year           12. Account

    Use Current/All/Selected accounts (C/A/S): S

    Esc-Cancel    Ctrl M-Memorize    F8-Options    F9-Filter    ↵ Continue

    New Frontiers

**Fig. 14.45.** *The Create Summary Report screen.*

Not all of the fields on the Create Summary Report screen are displayed every time—only those fields that make sense for the report you are generating. You can fill in a combination or perhaps all of the fields shown in figure 14.45. Complete the following basic steps:

1. From the Create Summary Report screen shown in figure 14.45, press F8 to access the Create Summary Report screen options.

2. Press the Enter or Tab key to move through the fields on-screen and then enter the appropriate values or figures. These fields are described in the following paragraphs.

3. When you complete the Create Summary Report screen, press Enter when the cursor is on the last field on-screen. You also can press F10 or Ctrl-Enter when the cursor is on any field.

## Entering a Report Title

You can use the Report title field to substitute a more specific title for the default report title. The Report title field provides space for up to 39 characters.

*Note:* The default report title that Quicken uses to identify a report corresponds to the report screen title. For example, if you press F8-Customize from the Cash Flow Report screen, the default report title is "Cash Flow Report."

## Restricting Transactions

You may want to see account transactions for a specific period of time. For example, when assessing your cash flows for the month of June, you want account transactions for only that month. Use the Restrict to transactions from and through fields for this purpose. By entering from and through dates in these fields, you limit the transactions included on a report to those transactions with dates falling between the from and through dates.

Both date fields need to be filled using the standard date format. As with the date fields found elsewhere in the Quicken system, you can move the date ahead one day at a time by pressing the + key and back one day at a time by pressing the − key.

## Sorting Transactions

The Row headings field enables you to select the order in which transactions are sorted and the subtotals that are calculated. You generally have four choices: Category, Class, Payee, or Account. The names of the row headings you select appear down the left side of the printed report.

## Segregating Transactions

The Column headings field enables you to select the order in which transactions are segregated and subtotaled in columns across the report page. You generally have twelve options:

```
Don't Subtotal
Week
Two Weeks
Half Month
Month
Quarter
Half Year
Year
Category
Class
Payee
Account
```

You select the heading you want to use by typing the number that appears to the left of the column heading you want.

## Selecting Accounts

The Use Current/All/Selected accounts field enables you to specify which accounts from the selected account group should be included on the report:

C          Designates just the current account
A          Designates all accounts
S          Designates only the selected accounts

If you choose only selected accounts, Quicken displays the Select Accounts to Include screen shown in figure 14.27. To include an account, use the up- and down-arrow keys to move the selection triangle to the left of the account you want to include and press the space bar. The space bar acts as a toggle switch, alternately marking the account for inclusion and exclusion. To select all the accounts, press F9.

*Note:* For the net worth and balance sheet reports, you have three choices that the space bar toggles. You can include an account, exclude an account, and show any class detail. Pressing the space bar alternately displays Include, Detail, or nothing next to the option.

# Filtering a Report

If you press F9-Filter from one of the report request screens, Quicken displays the Filter Report Transactions screen shown in figure 14.46.

As on the Create Summary Report screen, you can use a variety of fields to include or exclude transactions from a report. Complete the following basic steps:

1. From the report screen, press F9 to access the Filter Report Transactions screen shown in figure 14.46.

2. Use the Enter or Tab key to move through the various fields on-screen and then enter the appropriate values or figures. These fields are described in the following paragraphs.

3. (Optional) If you start modifying these fields and then want to reset them to the original values, press Ctrl-D.

4. When you complete the screen, press Enter when the cursor is on the last field. You also can press F10 or Ctrl-Enter when the cursor is on any of the fields.

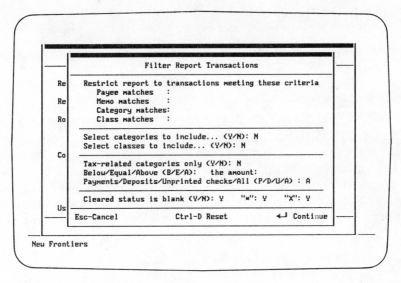

```
                    Filter Report Transactions
Re      Restrict report to transactions meeting these criteria
                 Payee matches    :
Re               Memo matches     :
                 Category matches:
Ro               Class matches    :

        Select categories to include... (Y/N): N
        Select classes to include... (Y/N): N
Co
        Tax-related categories only (Y/N): N
        Below/Equal/Above (B/E/A):    the amount:
        Payments/Deposits/Unprinted checks/All (P/D/U/A) : A

        Cleared status is blank (Y/N): Y      "*": Y    "X": Y
Us
        Esc-Cancel           Ctrl-D Reset           ↵ Continue

New Frontiers
```

**Fig. 14.46.** *The Filter Report Transactions screen.*

## Matching Payees

The Payee matches field enables you to instruct Quicken to include or exclude a certain payee or transaction description from a transaction report based on exact or key-word matches. (Chapters 5 and 7 describe in detail the mechanics of exact and key-word matches.) If you leave this field blank, you do not affect transactions being included or excluded from the report.

## Matching Memos

The Memo matches field works like the Payee matches field, except that Quicken compares the Memo matches field entry to the transactions' Memo field entries. This field affects the transactions included or excluded on the report, as does the Payee matches field. Using this field is optional.

## Matching Categories

The Category matches field enables you to instruct Quicken to include or exclude transactions assigned to certain categories based on exact or key-word matches. If you leave this field blank, the transactions being included or excluded from the report are not affected.

## Matching Classes

The Class matches field works like the Category matches field, except that Quicken compares the Class matches field entry to entries in the transactions' Category field. Like the Category matches field, this optional field affects the transactions included or excluded on the report.

## Selecting Categories

The Select categories to include field enables you to specify an entire set of categories to be included on a report. If you set this field to Y for yes, Quicken displays the Select Categories To Include screen that you can use to mark the categories you want included on a report (see fig. 14.47).

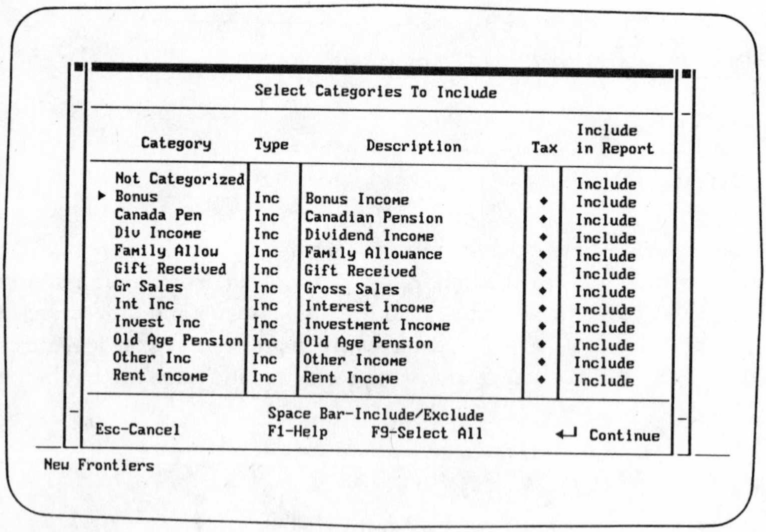

```
                    Select Categories To Include

                                                         Include
        Category     Type      Description        Tax   in Report

       Not Categorized                                   Include
     ▶ Bonus         Inc    Bonus Income           •      Include
       Canada Pen    Inc    Canadian Pension       •      Include
       Div Income    Inc    Dividend Income        •      Include
       Family Allow  Inc    Family Allowance       •      Include
       Gift Received Inc    Gift Received          •      Include
       Gr Sales      Inc    Gross Sales            •      Include
       Int Inc       Inc    Interest Income        •      Include
       Invest Inc    Inc    Investment Income      •      Include
       Old Age Pension Inc  Old Age Pension        •      Include
       Other Inc     Inc    Other Income           •      Include
       Rent Income   Inc    Rent Income            •      Include

                      Space Bar-Include/Exclude
     Esc-Cancel       F1-Help      F9-Select All       ↵ Continue

 New Frontiers
```

*Fig. 14.47. The Select Categories To Include screen.*

To include a category, use the up- and down-arrow keys to move the selection triangle to the left of the category and press the space bar. The space bar acts as a toggle switch, alternately marking the category for inclusion or exclusion. To select all the categories, press F9.

## Selecting Classes

The Select classes to include field enables you to specify an entire set of classes to be included on a report. If you set this field to Y for yes, Quicken displays the Select Classes To Include screen that you can use to mark individual categories you want included on a report (see fig. 14.48).

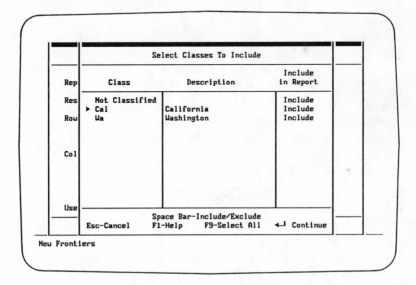

**Fig. 14.48.** *The Select Classes To Include screen.*

To include a class, use the up- and down-arrow keys to move the selection triangle to the left of the class and then press the space bar. The space bar acts as a toggle switch, alternately marking the class for inclusion and exclusion. To select all classes, press F9.

## Including Only Tax-Related Categories

The Tax-related categories only field enables you to include each of the categories you marked as tax-related when initially defining the category. (Chapter 10 describes how you identify a category as tax-related.)

## Matching Transaction Amounts

The Below/Equal/Above and amount fields enable you to include transactions on a report based on the transaction amount. By using these two fields, you tell Quicken that you want transactions included on your report only when the transaction amount is less than, equal to, or greater than some amount. Type *b* to indicate below, *e* to indicate equal, or *a* to indicate above. Enter the amount you want transaction amounts compared to in the amount field.

## Specifying Certain Types of Transactions

The Payments/Deposits/Unprinted checks/All field enables you to include only certain types of transactions. To include only payments, enter a *p*; to include only deposits, enter a *d*; to include only unprinted checks, enter a *u*; to include all transactions, enter an *a*.

You can use this report to determine your cash flow requirements. If you have entered all of your bills and want to know the total, press U for unprinted checks. Your report tells you the total cash required for all unpaid bills.

## Specifying Cleared/Uncleared Transactions

The Cleared status is blank field enables you to include transactions on a report based on the contents of the C field in the register. The C field shows whether or not a transaction has been marked as cleared. Three valid entries exist for the C field: *, X, and nothing. As the Filter Report Transactions screen shows, you can include transactions on a report by entering a Y for yes next to the is blank, *, or X fields. You also can exclude transactions by entering a N for no next to the same three fields.

## Setting Report Options

You can access the Create Summary Report screen, shown in figure 14.45, in one of two ways: by pressing F8-Customize from one of the personal or business report screens or by selecting one of the custom report options. From the Create Summary Report screen, you also can use the F8-Options function key. Like the F8-Customize and F9-Filter keys, the screen that F8-Options displays varies depending on which you report you are preparing. Figure 14.49 shows the Report Options screen for creating a transaction report. Mechanically, however, the Report Options screen works the same for each of the Quicken reports.

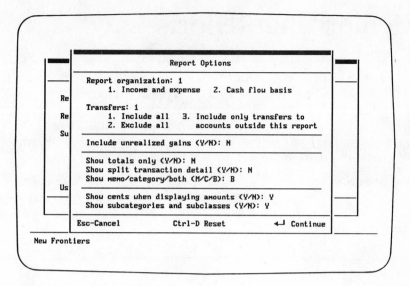

**Fig. 14.49.** *The Report Options screen.*

You can have as many as five additional fields that are similar to the F8-Customize function key's effect on the appearance and organization of a report. Using the Report organization field determines whether the report includes only transactions assigned to categories (income and expense transactions, cashflow, net worth, or balance sheet) or transactions assigned to categories and transactions representing transfers. Using the Transfers field determines whether all transfers are included or excluded or whether only transfers including an account outside of the set of selected accounts are included. Using the Show totals only field determines whether a report shows the detail transactions that make up a total along with the actual total. Show Split Transaction Detail applies only when the Show totals only field is set to N for no and determines whether split transaction detail is printed on the report.

Using the Show memo/category/both field determines whether just the memo, just the category, or the memo and category entries appear on the report. By using Show cents when displaying amounts, you can have Quicken round cents or show cents when displaying amounts. You also can specify the report to show subcategories and subclasses by setting the Show subcategories and subclasses field to Y for yes.

# Memorizing Reports

One of the Ctrl-key combinations that appears at the bottom of each of the report request screens is Ctrl-M Memorize. Ctrl-M Memorize enables you to record and add a title to a set of report descriptions. These report descriptions include what you enter on the report request screen, the F8-Options screen, and the F9-Filter screen. You can use this feature to customize a special report so that you do not have to re-invent the wheel every time you need the report.

To memorize a report, press Ctrl-M after you complete the descriptions of the report you want to print. Quicken displays the Memorizing Report screen shown in figure 14.50. Enter a unique title for the report description and then press Enter.

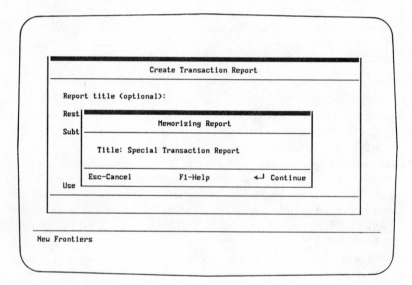

***Fig. 14.50.*** *The Memorizing Report screen.*

To later use the memorized report description, select the **Memorized Reports** option from the Reports menu and use the arrow keys to mark the memorized report you want to print on the Memorized Reports List and press Enter (see fig. 14.51). Quicken displays the Memorized Report screen (see fig. 14.52). To generate the report, press Enter.

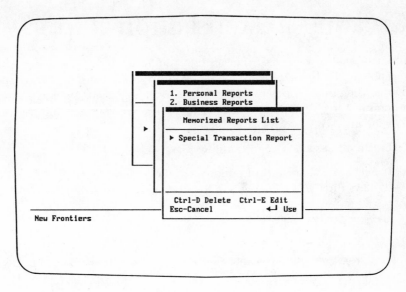

**Fig. 14.51.** *The Memorized Reports List.*

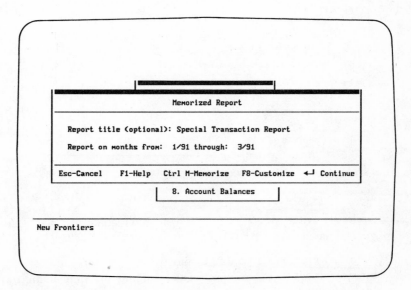

**Fig. 14.52.** *The Memorized Report screen.*

# Creating a Transaction Report

You may want to view your register transactions in some order other than chronologically by date. For example, you may find value in sorting and summarizing transactions by the payee or for time periods such as a week or month. The transaction report enables you to see your account transactions in any of these ways.

To create a transaction report, follow these steps:

1. Select the **Transaction** option from the Reports menu. Quicken displays the Create Transaction Report screen (see fig. 14.53.)

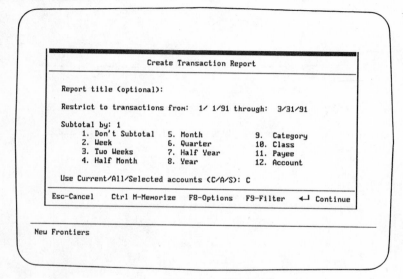

```
                    Create Transaction Report

    Report title (optional):

    Restrict to transactions from:  1/ 1/91 through:  3/31/91

    Subtotal by: 1
         1. Don't Subtotal   5. Month          9.   Category
         2. Week             6. Quarter        10.   Class
         3. Two Weeks        7. Half Year      11.   Payee
         4. Half Month       8. Year           12.   Account

    Use Current/All/Selected accounts (C/A/S): C

   Esc-Cancel    Ctrl M-Memorize   F8-Options   F9-Filter   ↵ Continue

   New Frontiers
```

*Fig. 14.53. The Create Transaction Report screen.*

2. (Optional) Enter a report title. If you don't enter a report title, Quicken names the report "Transaction Report."

3. (Optional) Press Enter or Tab to move the cursor to the Restrict to transactions from and through fields. Enter the time frame the report should cover by entering the starting and the ending dates you want included in the report. If you don't enter these dates, the report covers from January of the current year through the current date.

4. (Optional) Press Enter or Tab to move the cursor to the Subtotal by field. Pick one of the twelve subtotal choices by typing the number that appears to the left of the choice.

5. (Optional) Press Enter or Tab to move the cursor to the Use Current/All/Selected accounts field. You can use the Use Current/All/Selected accounts field to determine whether just the current account's transactions are included, just the selected account's transactions are included, or all the accounts' transactions are included. If you choose just selected accounts, Quicken displays the Select Accounts to Include screen. (The Use Current/All/Selected accounts field is described in more detail in the earlier chapter section called "Customizing a Report.")

6. (Optional) Press F8-Options to access the Report Options screen. Complete the Report Options screen as described earlier in the chapter.

7. (Optional) Press F9-Filter to access the Filter Report Transactions screen. Complete the Filter Report Transactions screen as described earlier in the chapter.

8. When the Create Transaction Report screen is complete, press Enter when the cursor is on the Use Current/All/Selected accounts field. You also can press F10 or Ctrl-Enter when the cursor is on any of the other fields. Quicken generates and displays the report on-screen.

   You can use the arrow keys, PgUp, and PgDn to see different portions of the report. You also can use the Home and End keys to see the first and last pages of the report. On reports too wide to fit comfortably on-screen, you can use F9 to toggle between a full column-width and a half column-width version of the report.

9. When you are ready to print the report, press F8 or Ctrl-P. Either approach displays the Print Report screen shown in figure 14.6. This screen enables you to specify to where you want the report printed.

10. Answer the Print to field by pressing a 1 for printer 1, 2 for printer 2, and so on.

If you select 4 at the Print to field, Quicken prints an ASCII file. To create an ASCII file, Quicken requests three pieces of information, using the Print to Disk screen. Follow these steps:

1. In the Print to Disk screen's File field, enter a name for Quicken to use for the ASCII file. To use a data directory other than the

Quicken data directory, QUICKEN3, you also can specify a path name. (See your DOS user's manual for information on path names.)

2. In the Print to Disk screen's Lines per page field, set the number of report lines between page breaks. If you are using 11-inch paper, the page length usually is 66 lines.

3. In the Print to Disk screen's Width field, set the number of characters, including blanks, that Quicken prints on a line. If you are using 8 1/2-inch paper, the characters per line number usually is 80.

If you select 5 at the Print to field on the Print Report screen, Quicken displays the Print to Lotus File screen. To create a 1-2-3 file, Quicken requests the name of the file you want to create. As with the ASCII file creation option, to use a data directory other than QUICKEN3, you also can specify a path name.

# Creating a Summary Report

Like a transaction report, a summary report extracts information from the financial database you create using Quicken's registers. A summary report, however, gives you totals by category, class, payee, or account, in addition to any of the other subtotals you request. With this type of report, you also can select the accounts to include.

To print a summary report, you follow essentially the same steps as for creating a transaction report, except that you select the **Summary** option from the Custom Reports menu. Quicken then displays the Create Summary Report screen, shown in figure 14.54, which you use to specify how the custom report should appear. The five fields you use to create custom summary report are described earlier in the chapter.

# Creating a Budget Report

Chapter 16 describes budgeting as a fundamental tool that businesses and individuals can use to better manage their finances. One of the on-going steps in using a budget as a tool is to compare the amount you spent with the amount you planned to spend, or budgeted. Quicken's **Budget** option on the Reports menu enables you to create customized budget reports tailored to your business or personal needs.

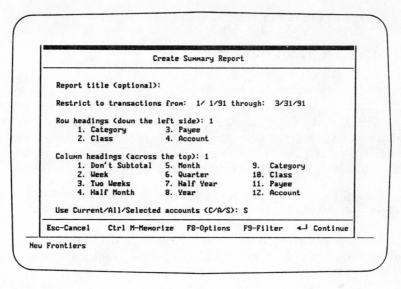

```
                    Create Summary Report

    Report title (optional):

    Restrict to transactions from:  1/ 1/91 through:  3/31/91

    Row headings (down the left side): 1
         1. Category      3. Payee
         2. Class         4. Account

    Column headings (across the top): 1
         1. Don't Subtotal  5. Month        9.  Category
         2. Week            6. Quarter      10. Class
         3. Two Weeks       7. Half Year    11. Payee
         4. Half Month      8. Year         12. Account

    Use Current/All/Selected accounts (C/A/S): S

  Esc-Cancel   Ctrl M-Memorize   F8-Options   F9-Filter   ↵ Continue

New Frontiers
```

***Fig. 14.54.*** *The Create Summary Report screen.*

To print a budget report, you follow the same steps you use when creating any other custom report. Select the **Budget** option from the Reports menu. Quicken then displays the Create Budget Report screen, shown in figure 14.55, which you use to specify how the custom report should appear. The five fields you use to create a custom summary report are described earlier in the chapter.

```
                    Create Budget Report

    Report title (optional):

    Restrict to transactions from:  1/ 1/91 through:  3/31/91

    Column headings (across the top): 5
         1. None           5. Month
         2. Week           6. Quarter
         3. Two Weeks      7. Half Year
         4. Half Month     8. Year

    Use Current/All/Selected accounts (C/A/S): S

  Esc-Cancel  F7-Budget Amts   Ctrl M-Memorize   F9-Filter  ↵ Continue


New Frontiers
```

***Fig. 14.55.*** *The Create Budget Report screen.*

# Creating an Account Balances Report

You can use the eighth and final option on the Reports menu to create customized account balances reports. If you have extensive investments with several brokers, for example, and you want a report that specifies only those accounts, you can create this report (or a specialized version of this report). Figure 14.56 shows the Create Account Balances Report screen that you use to construct customized account balances reports.

The basic steps you follow for creating an account balances report are the same as for any of the other reports. You select the **Account Balances** option from the Reports menu, and Quicken displays the Create Account Balances Report screen. You complete this screen like the other custom report creation screens. However, some of the fields differ from those you use on other report creation screens.

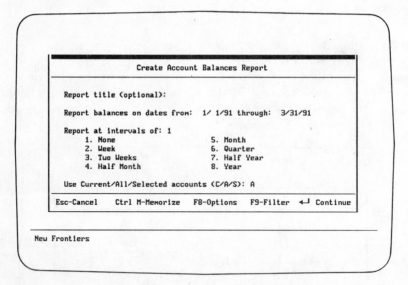

**Fig. 14.56.** *The Create Account Balances Report screen.*

# Using the Report Title Field

You can use the optional, 34-character Report title field to label reports. If you leave this field blank, Quicken supplies the title "Account Balances Report."

# Using the Report Balances on Dates from and through Fields

The Report balances on dates from and through fields are slightly different from the Restrict to transactions from and through fields on other report creation screens. The account balances report shows the account balances at a specific point in time. This field sets a boundary around the points in time for which an account balances report is generated.

# Using the Report at Intervals of Field

The Report at intervals of field determines the points in time for which an account balances report is generated. The start of the first interval is the first day of the year. Assuming that the Report balances on dates from field is 1/1/91, the first account balances column is for 1/1/91. The next date depends on the interval. If the interval is weekly, the second column is 1/7/91. If the interval is biweekly, the second column is for 1/14/91. If the interval is by half month, the second column is for 1/15/91, and so on. The report shows account balances for each interval between the from and through dates. The last column of the report shows the account balances on the through date.

If the Report at intervals of field is set to 1 for None, the only point in time for which the account balances report is generated is the Report balances on dates through field.

# Using the Use Current/All/Selected Accounts Field

As with the other Quicken reports, the Use Current/All/Selected accounts field enables you to determine which account balances are reported on the account balances report. A C designates just the current account; an S designates only the selected accounts; an A designates all accounts. If you choose only selected accounts, Quicken displays the Select Accounts to Include screen shown in Figure 14.27.

# Chapter Summary

This chapter reviewed the basics of printing any Quicken report and detailed the steps and tricks for printing each of Quicken's personal, business, investment, and custom reports. These reports use the information stored in your account register to provide you with a wealth of financial information that you can use to better manage your personal or business finances.

# 15

# Paying Bills
# Electronically

Quicken Version 4.0 enables you to use CheckFree, an electronic bill payment service, to pay bills. By using Quicken and a modem, you can send payment instructions to CheckFree Corporation. Your payment instructions include all the information CheckFree needs to actually pay the bill: who you owe the money to, when the bill needs to be paid, how much you owe, and so forth. CheckFree Corporation then either draws a check on or electronically transfers funds from your bank account to whomever you owe the money.

Paying bills electronically isn't for everybody. By getting one more party involved in the bill-paying process, you may just make things more complicated. However, for those Quicken users who have a modem and who want to stop printing checks, electronic payment is appealing. This chapter explains how to set up your system for electronic payment using the CheckFree service, how to identify the people you will pay, and how to actually pay bills.

## Setting Up Your System for Electronic Payment

To begin using electronic bill paying, you need to complete three steps. First, you need to complete the paperwork. Second, you need to tell Quicken you want to use CheckFree. Third, you may need to spend a few minutes telling Quicken about your modem. None of the three steps is difficult. Completing your part of the work should take you no more than a few minutes.

## Completing the CheckFree Paper Work

Before you begin using the CheckFree service, you need to complete the CheckFree Service Form (see fig. 15.1). The form is not particularly confusing. You need to tell CheckFree Corporation how much memory your computer has, give CheckFree some personal information, including your social security number, name, address, and so on, and provide CheckFree with a credit card account number so that CheckFree can charge your credit card account if they—acting on your payment instructions—overdraw your account. (*Note:* For security reasons, use a security code —similar to what you use for automated teller machines—to gain access to your account.)

After you provide that basic information, you also need to tell CheckFree which telephone phone lines you will be using, specify which account number/security code you will use to gain access to the CheckFree system, and sign an authorization so that CheckFree can deduct funds from your bank account. (*Note:* If you don't choose an account number/security code, CheckFree creates one for you.)

After you complete the CheckFree Service Form, attach a voided check to the form and then mail the form to Intuit. To mail the form, use the business reply envelope that's specifically included for returning the Check-Free Service Form. Intuit forwards the service form to CheckFree Corporation. In a few days, CheckFree sends you a confirmation letter that confirms or assigns the account number/security code, gives you the telephone number you will use for CheckFree transmissions, and the baud rate, or transmission speed, you will use for sending payment information.

## Telling Quicken You Will Use Electronic Bill Paying

After you receive the confirmation letter from CheckFree, you are ready to tell Quicken you are going to use the CheckFree service. Select the **Change Settings** option from the Main menu. Quicken then displays the Change Settings menu shown in figure 15.2. From the Change Settings

FORMSERVE • (614) 442-8980

# CheckFree®

CONFIDENTIAL
## CHECKFREE SERVICE FORM

(To receive CheckFree service, please complete this form and return the top copy in the enclosed postage paid envelope as soon as possible. As with all CheckFree data, the information on this form is handled with the strictest security. Please print all information.)

### IMPORTANT
**PLEASE ATTACH A VOIDED CHECK FROM YOUR PAYMENT ACCOUNT TO THE TOP OF THIS FORM.**

### YOUR EQUIPMENT
How much RAM does your computer have? _____ 384 _____ 512 _____ more than 512
What disk size do you require? _____ 3 1/2 _____ 5 1/4

### PERSONAL IDENTIFICATION
Your social security number _____ _____ _____ - _____ - _____ _____ _____ _____

Name _____
            Last                    First                    Middle

Current Address _____
            Street              City              State         Zip

### CREDIT CARD INFORMATION
CheckFree requires an account number for at least one credit card, should an overdraft occur. CheckFree reserves the right to charge the account only for the purpose of overdraft protection.

MasterCard or Visa Account Number _____ Exp. _____

### COMMUNICATIONS INFORMATION
Home Phone (_____) _____ - _____     Work Phone (_____) _____ - _____
            Circle number from which you will be transmitting.

### CHECKFREE ACCOUNT NUMBER
Your CheckFree account number/security code is a four digit number which you may choose yourself. You will need to enter this number in your Quicken software and use it as a password to run your software. My number is |___|___|___|___|. If you have no number preference, leave the space provided blank and CheckFree will assign a number for you. You will be given this number at the same time you receive your CheckFree network access telephone number.

Date _____ Signature _____
            Your use of the CheckFree service signifies that you have read and accepted all of the terms and conditions of the CheckFree service contained in the Quicken 3.0 EP package.

### CHECKFREE BANK REGISTRATION

I, _____
    (Last Name)              (First Name)              (Middle Initial)
    authorize my bank to post my bill payment transactions from CheckFree to my account as indicated below.
    I understand that I am in full control of my account. If at any time I decide to discontinue service,
    I will simply call or write CheckFree to cancel service.

_____
            (Bank Name)

_____
            (Street Address)

_____
    (City)              (State)              (Zip)

_____
    Customer Signature

Return the top copy of this entire form to Intuit in the postage paid envelope provided and retain the bottom copy for your records. Also,

## DON'T FORGET TO PROVIDE A VOIDED CHECK WITH THE INFORMATION YOU RETURN TO INTUIT.

X

Return to Intuit in the enclosed postage paid envelope with your order form. Intuit 66 Willow Place, Menlo Park, CA 94025.

# CheckFree®

**Fig. 15.1.** *The CheckFree Service Form.*

menu, select the **Electronic Payment** option. Quicken displays the Electronic Payment menu (see fig. 15.3).

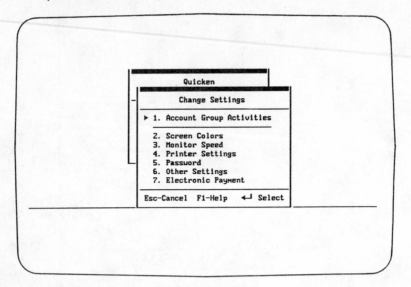

**Fig. 15.2.** *The Change Settings menu.*

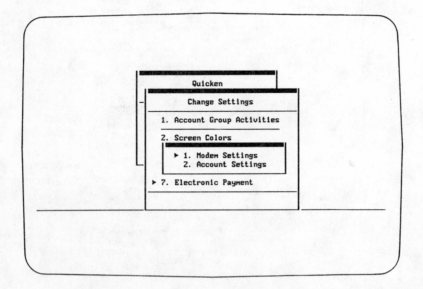

**Fig. 15.3.** *The Electronic Payment menu.*

You need to do two things when telling Quicken you will use electronic bill paying. One is to configure your modem. The other is to set up the bank accounts you will use to make the payments.

To configure your modem, complete these steps:

1. Select the **Modem Settings** option from the Electronic Payment menu. Quicken next displays the Electronic Payment Settings screen shown in figure 15.4.

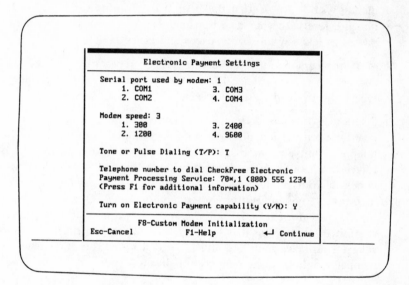

```
                 Electronic Payment Settings

        Serial port used by modem: 1
             1. COM1              3. COM3
             2. COM2              4. COM4

        Modem speed: 3
             1. 300               3. 2400
             2. 1200              4. 9600

        Tone or Pulse Dialing (T/P): T

        Telephone number to dial CheckFree Electronic
        Payment Processing Service: 70x,1 (800) 555 1234
        (Press F1 for additional information)

        Turn on Electronic Payment capability (Y/N): Y

                 F8-Custom Modem Initialization
        Esc-Cancel          F1-Help          ↵ Continue
```

*Fig. 15.4. The Electronic Payment Settings screen.*

2. With the cursor positioned on the Serial port field, enter the number of the serial port that your modem uses: 1 for serial communications port 1; 2 for serial communications port 2; and so on. If you don't know which serial communications port your modem uses, follow the cable that connects your modem to your computer and see whether the socket into which the modem cable plugs is labeled. The socket should be labeled with something like "COM1" or "Serial 1."

3. Move the cursor to the Modem speed field. Pick the fastest modem speed setting that CheckFree supports and your modem can handle. The CheckFree confirmation letter gives the modem speed settings that CheckFree supports. Your modem user's manual indicates which transmission speeds your modem is capable of running.

4. Move the cursor to the Tone or Pulse field. Press T if your telephone service is tone; press P if your telephone service is pulse. If you aren't sure, refer to your monthly telephone bill or call the telephone company.

5. Move the cursor to the Telephone number field. Enter the telephone number given in the confirmation letter you receive from Check-Free. Include any special characters you want to dial. For example, if you have call waiting, "*70" may turn it off. You can start the dialing with "*70" so that the beep a call-waiting call makes does not interfere with your data transmission. You can use a comma to pause. Quicken ignores any spaces and parentheses you enter.

6. Move the cursor to the Turn on Electronic Payment capability field and press Y for yes. Figure 15.4 shows an example of the completed Electronic Payment Settings screen.

7. (Optional) If your modem is not Hayes-compatible, you need to give Quicken the initialization codes the modem uses to access the telephone line and get a dial tone. The odds are that your modem is Hayes-compatible, so you probably don't have to worry about the codes. If your modem isn't Hayes-compatible, press F8 when the Electronic Payment Settings screen is displayed. Quicken displays the Custom Modem Initialization screen shown in figure 15.5. Enter the initialization code that Quicken should send to the modem to access your telephone line and get a dial tone. The modem user's manual should give the needed initialization code.

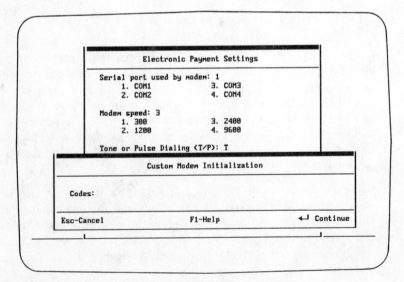

*Fig. 15.5. The Custom Modem Initialization screen.*

# Identifying CheckFree Bank Accounts

After you complete the Electronic Payment Settings screen, you are ready to identify the CheckFree bank account or accounts. Essentially, all you do here is identify which bank accounts will be used for electronic payment. You cannot use a credit card, other asset, other liability, or investment account for electronic payment—only bank accounts.

*Note:* Quicken does not enable you to select an account to use for electronic payment until the modem settings menu has been filled out and the Turn on Electronic Payment capability field has been set to Y.

To set up a bank account for electronic payment, follow these steps:

1. Select the **Account Settings** option from the Electronic Payment menu. Quicken next displays the Set Up Account for Electronic Payment screen shown in figure 15.6. Because you can set up only bank accounts for electronic payment, Quicken only lists bank accounts on the screen.

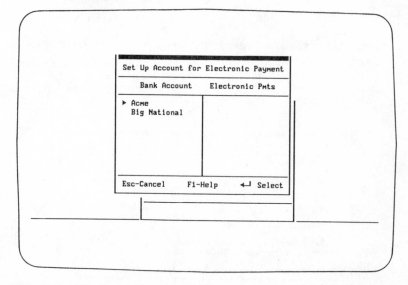

*Fig. 15.6. The Set Up Account for Electronic Payment screen.*

2. To indicate that you may pay bills electronically using the money in an account, use the arrow keys to mark the account you want to pay electronically. Press Enter.

Quicken next displays a message box that asks whether you want to set up the account for electronic payment (see fig. 15.7).

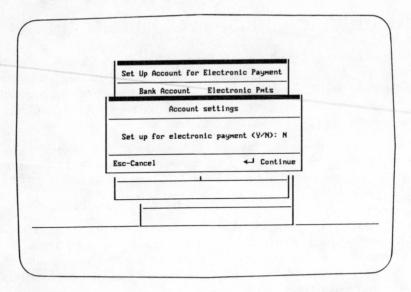

**Fig. 15.7.** *Quicken asks you to confirm that you want to set up the account for electronic payment.*

3. Press Y for yes and press Enter. Quicken next displays the Electronic Payment Account Settings screen (see fig. 15.8).

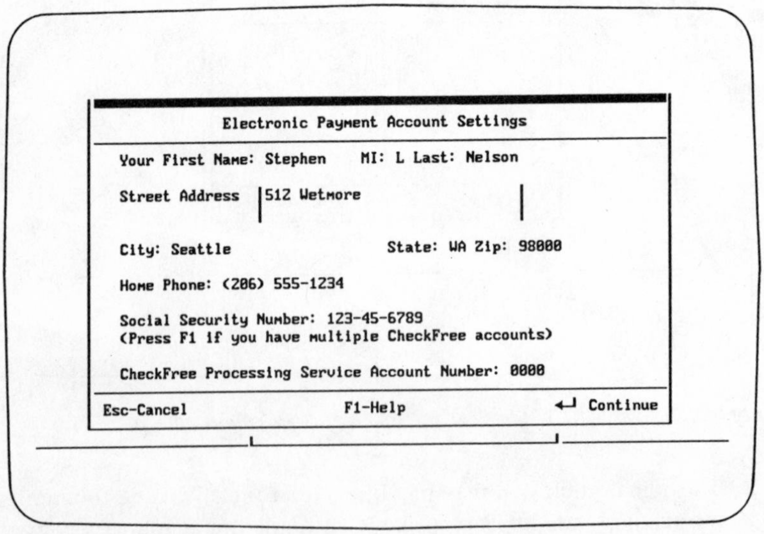

**Fig. 15.8.** *The Electronic Payment Account Settings screen.*

4. With the cursor positioned on the Your First Name field, enter your first name.

5. Move the cursor to the MI field and enter your middle initial.

6. Move the cursor to the Last field and enter your last name.

7. Move the cursor to the Street Address field and enter the appropriate information.

8. Move the cursor to the City field and enter the name of the city or town in which you live.

9. Move the cursor to the State field and enter the two-character abbreviation for your state. If you don't know the two-character abbreviation, enter the first letter of the state name and press Enter. Quicken displays a list of valid state abbreviations from which you choose your state's abbreviation.

10. Move the cursor to the Zip field and enter your ZIP code. Quicken validates your entry against a list of valid ZIP codes. If Quicken doesn't recognize what you enter, but you know the code is correct anyway, press Ctrl-Z to force Quicken to accept the ZIP code.

11. Move the cursor to the Home Phone field and enter your home phone number, including the area code. You don't have to include the punctuation characters like hyphens and parentheses; Quicken adds these automatically when you press Enter.

12. Move the cursor to the Social Security Number field and enter your social security number, or the alternative identification number assigned by CheckFree. (*Note:* If you have more than one bank account set up for electronic bill paying—meaning you filled out more than one CheckFree Service Agreement Form—CheckFree gives you identifying numbers based on your social security account for each account. That identifying number is what you should enter here.)

13. Move the cursor to the CheckFree Processing Service Account Number field and enter your account number/security number. Figure 15.8 shows an example of a completed screen.

14. When the Electronic Payment Account Settings screen is complete, press Enter. Quicken redisplays the Set Up Account for Electronic Payment screen. The account you set up now is marked as "enabled" for electronic payment. When the account is the one selected, Quicken adds several additional menu options that you can use for processing electronic payments.

# Identifying the People You Will Pay

To pay a bill electronically, you need to collect and store information about each person or company you will pay so that CheckFree Corporation can process payments to the person or business. To collect and store this information, follow these steps:

1. From the Main menu, select the **Write/Print Checks** option. Quicken displays the electronic payment version of the screen (see fig. 15.9).

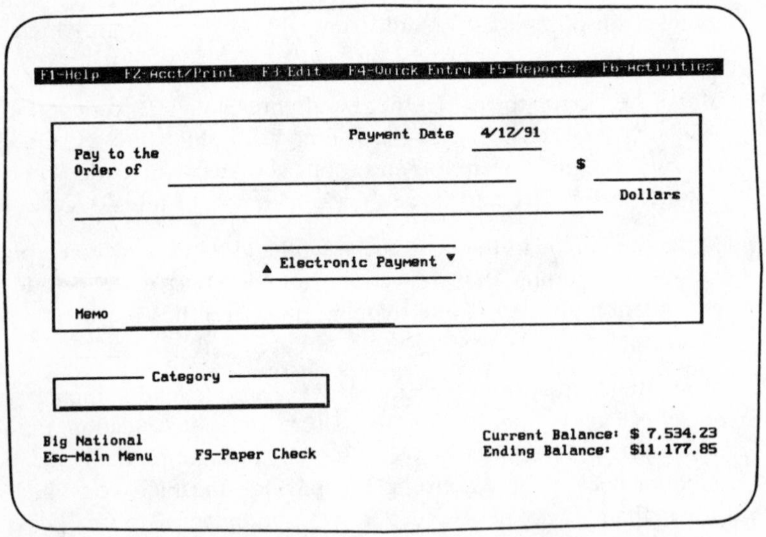

```
 F1-Help  F2-Acct/Print   F3-Edit   F4-Quick Entry  F5-Reports   F6-Activities


     Pay to the              Payment Date   4/12/91
     Order of  _____  $ _____
                                                         Dollars
           _____

                     ▲ Electronic Payment ▼


     Memo  _____


         ___ Category ___
        |                  |
        |_____|

     Big National                          Current Balance: $ 7,534.23
     Esc-Main Menu     F9-Paper Check      Ending Balance:  $11,177.85
```

*Fig. 15.9. The electronic payment version of the Write/Print Checks screen.*

2. Press Ctrl-Y to access the Electronic Payee List. Alternatively, press F4 to access the Quick Entry menu and then choose the **Electronic Payee** option from that menu. Either way, Quicken displays the Electronic Payee List screen shown in figure 15.10.

3. To set up your first electronic payee, select Set Up New Payee on the list. Quicken displays the Set Up Electronic Payee screen (see fig. 15.11).

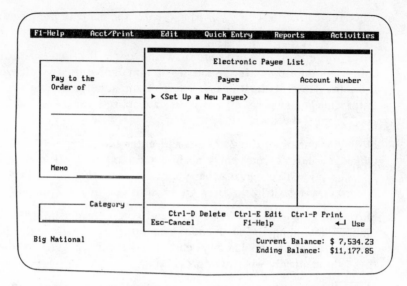

**Fig. 15.10.** *The Electronic Payee List.*

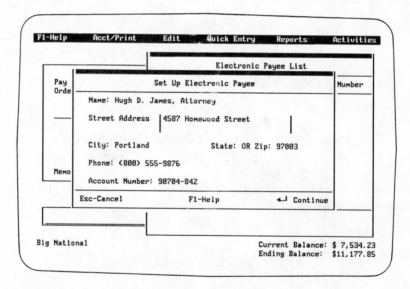

**Fig. 15.11.** *The Set Up Electronic Payee screen.*

4. Move the cursor to the Name field and enter the complete name of the person or company you want to pay. You have up to 28 characters of space.

5. Move the cursor to the Street Address field and enter the mailing address for sending payments to the payee.

6. Move the cursor to the City field and enter the name of the payee's city or town.

7. Move the cursor to the State field and enter the two-character abbreviation for the payee's state. If you don't know the two-charac-ter abbreviation, enter the first letter of the state name and press Enter. Quicken displays a list of valid state abbreviations from which you can pick the correct one.

8. Move the cursor to the Zip field and enter the payee's ZIP code. Quicken validates your entry against a list of valid ZIP codes. If Quicken doesn't recognize what you enter but you know the code is correct, press Ctrl-Z to force Quicken to accept the ZIP code.

9. Move the cursor to the Phone field and enter the person's phone number, including the area code. You don't have to include the punctuation characters like hyphens and parentheses; Quicken adds these automatically when you press Enter.

10. Move the cursor to the Account Number field and enter the account number the person or business uses to identify you.

11. When the Set Up Electronic Payee screen is complete, press Enter. Quicken returns you to the Electronic Payee List screen. Figure 15.11 shows an example of a completed Set Up Electronic Payee screen. If you want to define additional electronic payees, repeat steps 3 through 11.

*Note:* As on other lists in the Quicken system, you can use Ctrl-D to delete a payee from the Electronic Payee List and you can use Ctrl-E to edit a payee on the Electronic Payee List. The only difference in working with electronic payees as compared to accounts, categories, classes, and so on is that you cannot edit or delete an electronic payee if an untransmitted transaction exists for that payee. The next section explains more about untransmitted transactions.

# Paying Bills with CheckFree

Paying bills electronically closely resembles the process of writing and printing checks with Quicken. For that reason, this chapter doesn't repeat the discussions of Chapters 6 and 7, which cover how you write and print checks with Quicken. Instead, this section concentrates on those parts of the process that are different. (*Note:* If you haven't used the Quicken Write/Print Checks feature, you may want to review Chapters 6 and 7 before going further in this chapter.)

After you set up for electronic payment and identify the people you will pay, you are ready to begin paying bills electronically. For each bill you want to pay, follow these steps:

1. From Quicken's Main menu, select the **Write/Print Checks** option. Quicken displays the electronic payment version of the Write Checks screen (see fig. 15.9).

2. Complete the electronic payment version of the Write Checks screen in the same way you complete the regular version of the screen, except for the following differences.

   Rather than typing in the payee's name, you select the payee from the electronic payee list. To display the electronic payee list, press Ctrl-Y. To use one of the electronic payees shown on the list, use the arrow keys to select the payee and then press Enter. You also can use Quicken's auto-completion feature to enter an electronic payee.

   Rather than track unprinted checks, Quicken shows you the Checks to Xmit (transmit) in the lower right corner of the screen.

3. When the Write Checks screen is complete, press Enter when the cursor is on the Category field, or you can press Ctrl-Enter or F10 when the cursor is on one of the other fields.

The check containing the electronic payment scrolls off the screen, leaving behind an empty check that you can use to complete another electronic payment. Until the time you transmit the electronic payments, you can edit the electronic payments just like those for a check.

*Note:* You also can enter and edit electronic payments using the Quicken register. Quicken identifies electronic payment transactions in the Quicken register with ›››› in the Num field.

After you enter the electronic payments, you are ready to transmit the electronic payments to CheckFree Corporation so that they can be paid. To transmit the electronic payments, follow these steps:

1. Turn on your modem.

   Quicken first attempts to initialize the modem and then retries the modem twice before Quicken informs you that it is unable to initialize the modem.

2. Press Ctrl-I to initiate the electronic payment transmission, or press F2 to access the Acct/Print menu (see fig. 15.12) and select the **Transmit Payments** option.

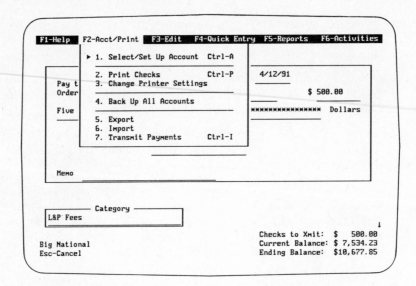

*Fig. 15.12. The electronic payment version of the Acct/Print menu.*

Quicken displays the message box shown in figure 15.13, which tells you how many payments you have to transmit.

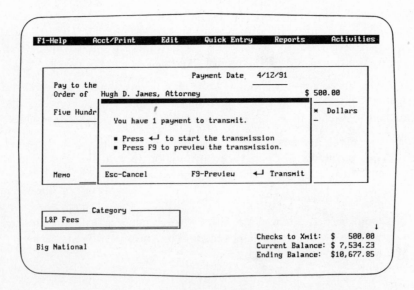

*Fig. 15.13. The message box that tells you how many payments you have to transmit.*

3. If you are ready to transmit, press Enter. Alternatively, if you want to review the payments that are ready to be transmitted, press F9, and Quicken displays the Preview Transmission to CheckFree screen (see fig. 15.14). The screen lists the payments Quicken will transmit. After you do transmit, CheckFree sends confirmation numbers back to Quicken for each of the transmitted payments. Confirmation numbers are stored in the Memo field.

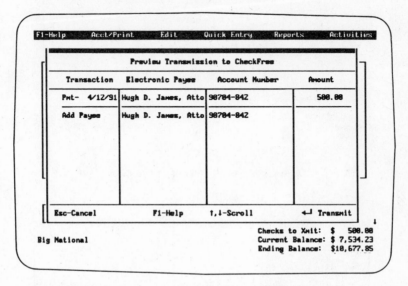

*Fig. 15.14. The Preview Transmission to CheckFree screen.*

# Using the Special CheckFree Functions

Quicken adds a couple of menu options to the Edit menu and one menu option to the Activities menu for processing electronic payments (see figs. 15.15 and 15.16). The Edit menu has a **Transmit Stop Payment Request** feature and an **Electronic Payment Inquiry** feature. The Activities menu has a **Send Electronic Mail** option. If you use the CheckFree service, you have the opportunity to use all three of these features.

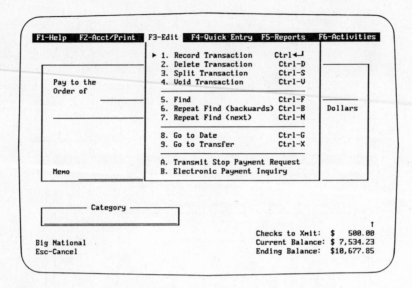

**Fig. 15.15.** *The electronic payment version of the Edit menu.*

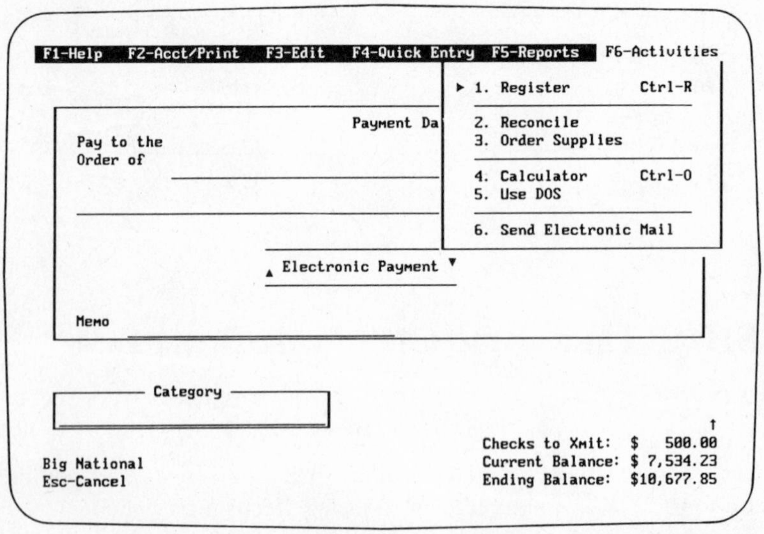

**Fig. 15.16.** *The electronic payment version of the Activities menu.*

# Issuing a Stop Payment Request

You can use Quicken to issue stop payment requests on electronic payments you transmitted previously. To do so, first turn on your modem. Highlight the payment in the register, press F3 to access the Edit menu, and then press A to initiate the stop payment request. Quicken asks you to confirm that you want to stop payment. Press Y for yes. Quicken immediately transmits your request to CheckFree. If the transmission is successful, Quicken marks the transaction as "Void." Obviously, as with stop payment requests issued directly to the bank, you need to make the request before the transaction is processed.

# Making an Electronic Payment Inquiry

You can inquire about a payment you transmitted previously. Say, for example, that you receive a telephone call from someone who wants to know whether you have sent a check yet. First turn on your modem. Highlight the payment in the register, press F3 to access the Edit menu, and press B to initiate the payment inquiry. Quicken displays the Payment Information screen, which gives all the details of the transmitted payment, including the payee, the scheduled payment date, the amount, the account number, and the confirmation number you received from Check-Free. The screen also indicates whether you can stop payment. Finally, Quicken also asks whether you want to send a message to CheckFree regarding the transaction.

# Sending Electronic Mail

You also can send an electronic message to CheckFree. To do so, use the **Send Electronic Mail** option on the electronic payment version of the Activities menu. To send a mail message, first turn on your modem. Press F6 to access the Activities menu and select the **Send Electronic Mail** option. Quicken displays the Transmit Inquiry to CheckFree screen (see fig. 15.17). Type the message you want to send and then press Enter. When you press Enter, Quicken sends the message.

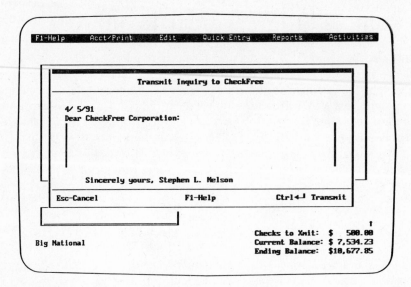

**Fig. 15.17.** *The Transmit Inquiry to CheckFree screen.*

# Chapter Summary

This chapter described Quicken Version 4.0's electronic payment capability. The chapter described what you need to do to set up your system for electronic payment, how to identify the people you will pay electronically, and how to actually transmit payments to those people. The chapter also gave an overview of the three special menu options that Quicken adds for supporting the electronic payment feature: transmitting stop payment requests, making electronic payment inquiries, and sending electronic mail messages to CheckFree Corporation.

# IV

# Putting Quicken To Work

## Includes

Budgeting with Quicken

Using Quicken for Home Accounting

Using Quicken in Your Business

Preparing for Income Taxes with Quicken

# 16

# Budgeting with Quicken

**B**udgeting has an undeserved bad reputation. People tend to think of a budget as something like financial handcuffs—an obstacle to enjoyment and a drag on financial freedoms. Actually, nothing could be further from the truth. Budgeting is a simple tool with astonishingly positive benefits for businesses and households. Essentially, budgets represent game plans that calibrate, or specify, what you need to do to succeed in your business or personal financial life.

Because one of Quicken's most significant benefits is that you can monitor your success in achieving a budget, this chapter reviews the three steps of budgeting, describes how Quicken helps, and provides some tips on how to budget successfully.

## Defining Budgeting

Budgeting consists of the following three steps:

1. Setting your business or personal financial goals.

2. Using your list of goals as a guide to developing a financial game plan, or budget.

3. Using the budget to monitor your spending to determine how closely you are progressing toward your business or personal goals.

**373**

# Setting Your Goals

Budgeting begins with identifying your goals in business or life. You are on your own here. When building a list of your goals, however, keep the following two things in mind:

❏ Keep your goals general.

❏ Involve other people—particularly those who have to live within the budget—in setting the goals.

By stating your goals in more general terms, you don't start with built-in constraints and conflicts. Suppose that your goal is to live in an opulent fashion where the weather is warm and sunny. With this goal, you have a world of choices and an incredible range of prices. If your goal is to live in a mansion in Beverly Hills, you have limited yourself. Living in a Beverly Hills mansion is one way to live in an opulent fashion where the weather is warm and sunny, but it is not the only way. Keep your options open as you build a list of life goals, and you are more likely to get more of the things you want out of life and to achieve more in your business.

A second point about setting goals is to involve other people. The often stated and obvious reason for this rule is that people who work together to build a list of goals later work together to achieve the goals. But working together also produces better goal lists.

The United States Air Force and many businesses play a game called Desert Survival that demonstrates the results of a group working to make a decision. You pretend that a plane on which you are a passenger crashes in the desert. You are 30 miles off course and at least that far from civilization; it's more than 100 degrees in the shade, and you can salvage about 15 or 20 items before the plane bursts into flames. First, you decide by yourself whether you stay with the wreckage or start towards civilization and which of the items you keep. Next, you repeat the analysis in groups of four or five people, and this time the entire group must agree on the plan and which items to keep. The interesting thing about the game and the reason that this whole issue applies to budgeting is that in almost every case, when people make the decisions together, they dramatically increase their chances of survival.

Making the wrong budgeting decision may not cost you your life or your business, but the moral of the desert survival game still applies. Whether you are budgeting your personal or business finances, you build better goal lists when you get more people involved. Your spouse may end up discovering some option you did not consider. A daughter may admit that she is not interested in piano lessons or charm school. Your partner may point out a subtle flaw you overlooked.

When you finish setting your goals, write them down. Do not limit yourself to just financial goals. You may have financial goals, such as accumulating the down payment for a new car or taking a special vacation. You also may have nonfinancial goals, such as spending more time with your family or beginning some recreational or charitable activity.

# Designing a Game Plan

After you build a list of goals, you are ready to create a game plan for achieving them. As you work through the details, you will undoubtedly modify your goals and make compromises. If you describe your goals in general terms and include everybody's good ideas, you should be able to come up with a detailed list of the costs of pursuing and achieving your business or personal goals.

At this stage, you decide what you are going to spend on entertainment or a vacation, how much you can spend on housing, and other such issues. As a rough yardstick to use to build your own detailed game plan, table 16.1 summarizes what most people spend on the average as a percent of their income. (This list comes from a survey made by *Consumer Reports* magazine. The survey data are a few years old, but because the results show as percentages of total income, the data are still valid for planning and comparison purposes.)

**Table 16.1**
**Average Spending Based on Income**

| Spending category | Percent spent, by income level | | |
| --- | --- | --- | --- |
| | $15,000-30,000 | $30,000-50,000 | $50,000-150,000 |
| Taxes | | | |
|     Federal income | 7% | 11% | 15% |
|     Social security | 7% | 8% | 7% |
|     State and local | 6% | 6% | 7% |
| Housing | | | |
|     Mortgage or rent | 11% | 11% | 9% |
|     Other housing costs | 13% | 12% | 11% |
| Food | 20% | 15% | 10% |
| Transportation | 12% | 10% | 7% |
| Vacation, recreation | 5% | 4% | 5% |

*Table 16.1 continues*

**Table 16.1—***continued*

| Spending category | Percent spent, by income level | | |
|---|---|---|---|
| | $15,000-30,000 | $30,000-50,000 | $50,000-150,000 |
| Health care, insurance | 5% | 4% | 3% |
| Clothing | 3% | 3% | 3% |
| Savings and investments | 5% | 8% | 12% |
| Other, specified* | 5% | 4% | 5% |
| Other, unspecified | 1% | 4% | 8% |

\* Includes tuition, educational supplies, books, magazines, contributions and gifts, finance charges other than mortgage and auto loans, day-care, child support, alimony

Copyright © 1986 by Consumers Union of the United States, Inc., Mount Vernon, NY 10553. Reprinted by permission from CONSUMER REPORTS, September, 1986.

If you are budgeting for a business, you can visit your local public library to obtain similar information. Dun and Bradstreet and Robert Morris Associates annually publish financial information on businesses grouped by industry and business size. For business or personal budgeting, however, do not interpret the averages as anything other than general guidelines. Seeing other people's spending provides a useful perspective on your own spending, but your goals should determine the details of your financial game plan.

*CPA Tip*  When budgeting for taxes, you should be able to estimate the amount fairly precisely. You can pick up one of the personal income tax guides to give you all the details, but the following general rules apply: social security amounts to 7.65 percent of your earnings up to a maximum amount of $51,300 of taxable income for 1990. Federal income taxes depend on your filing status and your taxable income. Generally, you can calculate your taxable income as:

(Total income) − (your deductions) − (your personal exemptions)

Your income includes wages, salaries, interest, dividends, and so on. Deductions include individual retirement accounts, alimony, and your itemized deductions or your standard deduction. Personal exemptions are $2,050 allowances you get to subtract from your total income for each person in your family. Your filing status relates to whether you are single, married, or have dependents. The standard deductions for the various filing statuses for 1990 are shown in table 16.2. The tax-rate schedules for the various filing statuses that show the taxes you pay on your taxable income are shown in table 16.3. For 1991, the dollar amounts for personal exemptions, the standard deduction amounts, and the tax-rate schedules are adjusted for inflation.

### Table 16.2
### Standard Deduction for 1990

| Filing status | Standard deduction |
| --- | --- |
| Married filing joint return and qualifying widow(er) | $5,450* |
| Head of household | $4,750* |
| Single | $3,250* |
| Married filing separately | $2,725* |

\* To these amounts, you can add the following amounts:

*Additional amount for the elderly or blind*—An additional standard deduction amount of $650 is allowed for a married individual (whether filing jointly or separately) or a qualifying widow(er) who is 65 or older or blind ($1,300 if the individual is 65 or older and blind, $2,600 if both spouses are 65 or older and blind). An additional standard deduction amount of $800 is allowed for an unmarried individual (single or head of household) who is 65 or older or blind ($1,600 if the individual is 65 or older and blind).

*Limited standard deduction for dependents*—If you can be claimed as a dependent on another person's return, your standard deduction is the greater of (a) $500 or (b) your earned income, up to the standard deduction amount. To this amount add any additional amount for the elderly or blind as discussed in the preceding paragraph.

When you finish setting your goals, write down your spending game plan. Now that you know how much time and money you can allocate to each of your goals, you often can expand your list of goals to include estimates of costs and time. Table 16.4 lists a set of sample personal goals, and table 16.5 lists a set of sample business goals. Table 16.6 shows an example of an annual personal budget with monthly breakdowns supporting the goals from table 16.4. Table 16.7 shows an example of an annual business budget that supports the goals from table 16.5.

## Table 16.3
## 1990 Tax Rate Schedules

**1990 Tax Rate Schedules**
Caution: *Do not use these Tax Rate Schedules to figure your 1989 taxes. Use only to figure your 1990 estimated taxes.*

**Schedule X—Single**

| If line 5 is: Over— | But not over— | The tax is: | of the amount over— |
|---|---|---|---|
| $0 | $19,450 | . . . . . . .15% | $0 |
| 19,450 | 47,050 | $2,917.50 + 28% | 19,450 |
| 47,050 | 97,620 | 10,645.50 + 33% | 47,050 |
| 97,620 | . . . . . . . | Use Worksheet below to figure your tax. | |

**Schedule Z— Head of household**

| If line 5 is: Over— | But not over— | The tax is: | of the amount over— |
|---|---|---|---|
| $0 | $26,050 | . . . . . . .15% | $0 |
| 26,050 | 67,200 | $3,907.50 + 28% | 26,050 |
| 67,200 | 134,930 | 15,429.50 + 33% | 67,200 |
| 134,930 | . . . . . . . | Use Worksheet below to figure your tax. | |

**Schedule Y-1—Married filing jointly or Qualifying widow(er)**

| If line 5 is: Over— | But not over— | The tax is: | of the amount over— |
|---|---|---|---|
| $0 | $32,450 | . . . . . . .15% | $0 |
| 32,450 | 78,400 | $4,867.50 + 28% | 32,450 |
| 78,400 | 162,770 | 17,733.50 + 33% | 78,400 |
| 162,770 | . . . . . . . | Use Worksheet below to figure your tax. | |

**Schedule Y-2— Married filing separately**

| If line 5 is: Over— | But not over— | The tax is: | of the amount over— |
|---|---|---|---|
| $0 | $16,225 | . . . . . . .15% | $0 |
| 16,225 | 39,200 | $2,433.75 + 28% | 16,225 |
| 39,200 | 123,570 | 8,866.75 + 33% | 39,200 |
| 123,570 | . . . . . . . | Use Worksheet below to figure your tax. | |

## Table 16.4
## Sample Personal Budget Goals

| Goal | Cost | Timing |
|---|---|---|
| Visit Egypt | $5,000 | 1995 |
| Start fishing again | $50 | ASAP |
| Prepare for retirement | $100,000 | 2025 |
| Spend time with family | $0 | ASAP |

## Table 16.5
## Sample Business Budget Goals

| Goal | Cost | Timing |
|---|---|---|
| Generate 20% more annual sales | $20,000 | over year |
| Pay down credit line | $5,000 | year-end |
| Make profits of $25,000 | $25,000 | over year |
| Provide better quality service | $0 | ASAP |

**Table 16.6**
**Sample Budget To Support Personal Goals**

| Personal budget | Annual | Monthly |
|---|---|---|
| Income | $25,000 | $2,083 |
| Outgo | | |
| Income taxes | $1,750 | $146 |
| Social security | 1,878 | 156 |
| Rent | 6,000 | 500 |
| Other housing | 3,000 | 250 |
| Food | 4,800 | 400 |
| Transportation | 2,500 | 208 |
| Vacation, recreation | 1,200 | 100 |
| Fishing gear | 50 | 4 |
| Clothing | 1,250 | 104 |
| Savings—IRA | 500 | 42 |
| Other | 1,200 | 100 |
| Total Expenses | 24,628 | 2,052 |
| Leftover/Contingency | 373 | 31 |

**Table 16.7**
**Sample Budget To Support Business Goals**

| Business budget | Annual | Monthly |
|---|---|---|
| Sales | $125,000 | $10,417 |
| Expenses | | |
| Materials | $30,000 | 2,500 |
| Labor | 30,000 | 2,500 |
| Rent | 12,000 | 1,000 |
| Transportation | 12,500 | 1,042 |
| Supplies | 12,000 | 1,000 |
| Legal/Accounting | 1,200 | 100 |
| Other | 2,100 | 175 |
| Total expenses | 99,800 | 8,317 |
| Profits | 25,200 | 2,100 |

Notice a few things about the relationships between the goals and budget. First, some of your goals represent things you can achieve almost immediately, and others may take much longer. Second, some goals on your list do not directly affect your budget. Third, some expenditures do not tie to formal, or stated, goals, but still represent implied goals. For example, you do not list feeding the children or staying in business as goals, but these goals may be your most important ones.

## Monitoring Your Progress

The third and final step in budgeting relates to monitoring your progress in achieving your personal or business goals. On a periodic basis—every month or quarter—compare the amount you budgeted to spend with the amount you actually spent. Sometimes, people view these comparisons as negative, but the idea is that if you are following your budget, you are moving toward your goals. For example, if you get through the first month of the year and are operating under the budget shown in table 16.6, you can compare what you spent with your budget. If you see that you are having difficulty salting away extra money for the trip to Egypt and into your individual retirement account, you know that your spending or your goals need to change.

# Using Quicken for Budgeting

Quicken provides two related features that enable you to budget more effectively for your personal finances and for small businesses: categories and reporting.

## Using Categories

With categories, you can distribute each of the checks you record into a spending category such as housing, contribution, entertainment, or taxes. You also can identify each of the deposits you record as falling into a revenue category such as wages, gross sales, or interest income. The steps and benefits of using categories are discussed in more detail in Chapter 10. By noting the category into which every check and deposit you record belongs, you can produce reports that summarize and total the amounts spent for each category. Figure 16.1 shows an example of a Quicken spending report.

If you decide to tap the power of budgeting, reports such as the report shown in figure 16.1 are invaluable. The report shows what you actually spend. What you actually spend can be compared to what you budgeted. When your actual spending matches your budgeted spending, you know

```
                                   Example Category Report
                                    1/ 1/91 Through 1/31/91

     Bank,Cash,CC Accounts                                                    Page 1
     1/10/91

                                                    1/ 1/91-
                          Category Description       1/31/91
                         ------------------------    ----------

                         INFLOWS
                            Interest Income             10.75
                            Salary Income            2,000.00
                                                     ----------

                         TOTAL INFLOWS               2,010.75


                         OUTFLOWS
                            Automobile Service          34.91
                            Bank Charge                  5.00
                            Entertainment               28.94
                            Home Repair & Maint.        24.53
                            Housing                      0.00
                            Late fees:
                               Late payment fees-credit    11.59
                               Late payment fees-mortg.    28.73
                                                         ----------

                               Total Late fees           40.32
                            Office Expenses              34.56
                            Water, Gas, Electric         75.39
                            Outflows - Other            200.08
                                                        ----------

                         TOTAL OUTFLOWS               443.73

                                                     ----------

                         OVERALL TOTAL              1,567.02
                                                     ==========
```

*Fig. 16.1.* *A sample category report.*

you are following your financial game plan. When your spending doesn't match your budget, you know you are not following your game plan.

# Creating Budgeting Reports

Quicken also enables you to enter any amount budgeted for a category. With this information, Quicken calculates the difference, called a variance, between the total spent on a category and the budgeted amount for a category. Quicken does the arithmetic related to monitoring how closely you follow your budget and how successfully you are marching toward your life goals. Figure 16.2 shows an example of a Quicken budget report. (*Note:* Chapter 14 describes in detail the process of creating and printing a budget report.)

```
                           Example Budget Report
                           1/ 1/91 Through 1/31/91

 Bank,Cash,CC Accounts                                          Page 1
 1/10/91
                                     1/ 1/91         1/31/91
                  Category Description   Actual    Budget    Diff
                  --------------------  ---------------------------

                  INFLOWS
                    Salary Income       2,000.00  2,000.00    0.00
                                        ---------- ---------- ----------
                  TOTAL INFLOWS         2,000.00  2,000.00    0.00

                  OUTFLOWS
                    Automobile Service     34.91     50.00  -15.09
                    Bank Charge             5.00      0.00    5.00
                    Entertainment          28.94     50.00  -21.06
                    Home Repair & Maint.   24.53      0.00   24.53
                    Late Payment Fees       0.00      0.00    0.00
                    Office Expenses        34.56     25.00    9.56
                    Water, Gas, Electric   75.39     60.00   15.39
                                        ---------- ---------- ----------
                  TOTAL OUTFLOWS        203.33    185.00   18.33

                                        ---------- ---------- ----------
                  OVERALL TOTAL       1,796.67  1,815.00  -18.33
                                        ========== ========== ==========
```

**Fig. 16.2.** *A sample budget report.*

# Reviewing Tips for Successful Budgeting

Even if you started out listing your personal or business goals, involved the entire family or company in the process, and created a budget compatible with your stated and implied goals, you can take other precautions to succeed in budgeting. These precautions include paying yourself first, recognizing after-tax shares, providing for unplanned or emergency events, and using zero-based budgeting.

## Paying Yourself First

Families need savings to provide cushions for financial emergencies, money for major expenditures such as a home or a child's education, and the means for financial support during retirement. Small businesses need savings to provide funds for growing the business, for replacing assets, and for unexpected delays in collecting from customers.

You always have bills to pay, however, and you have to resist a lot of financial temptations. Getting to the end of the month with extra money is difficult—which is why you need to pay yourself first. For many people, paying yourself first is the only way to successfully save money.

Figure 16.3 shows the amount you ultimately accumulate if you put away $25 a month and earn 10 percent interest, assuming various income tax rates. (The logic behind including income taxes is that if you earn $100 in interest and are taxed on the money at, say, the 33 percent tax rate, you need to withdraw $33 of the $100 to pay income taxes.)

QCKN0110.XLS

Ultimate Savings Accumulated:
$25 dollars a month
10% interest rate

| Years of Savings | 0% Tax rate | 15% Tax rate | 28% Tax rate | 33% Tax rate |
|---|---|---|---|---|
| 5 | $1,936 | $1,861 | $1,799 | $1,776 |
| 10 | 5,121 | 4,703 | 4,375 | 4,256 |
| 15 | 10,362 | 9,045 | 8,063 | 7,721 |
| 20 | 18,984 | 15,675 | 13,344 | 12,559 |
| 25 | 33,171 | 25,801 | 20,905 | 19,316 |
| 30 | 56,512 | 41,268 | 31,731 | 28,754 |
| 35 | 94,916 | 64,889 | 47,231 | 41,935 |

**Fig. 16.3.** *Saving $25 a month adds up.*

If you save $50 a month, double the amounts shown in the figure. If you save $100, quadruple the amounts shown in the table, and so on.

*CPA Tip*

If you save money for retirement, try to use options like individual retirement accounts (IRA) and 401(k) plans. Figure 16.3 shows that when you save $25 a month for 35 years in one of these investment vehicles where you pay 0 percent income tax, you end up with roughly twice as much as you would if you were paying a 28 or 33 percent income tax on your interest income. (If you are saving for retirement, refer to Appendix C, which discusses how to estimate how much you should save for retirement.)

# Recognizing After-Tax Shares of Bonuses and Raises

A second important budgeting consideration in personal and business situations is that you need to recognize that if you receive an extra $1,000 as a bonus, raise, or windfall, you cannot spend the entire $1,000. For 1990, a 7.65 percent social security tax and a 15.3 percent self-employment tax is levied on up to $51,300 of earned income. You also have to pay any federal income taxes of 15, 28, or 33 percent, plus any state income taxes. You may even have other expenses that, like income taxes, decrease your take-home share of any bonus or windfall, such as an automatic contribution to a deferred compensation plan or charitable giving to which you have made a commitment. Totaled, you typically need to deduct at least 20 percent and as much as 60 percent from any bonus or windfall to figure out what you have available for spending.

# Allowing for Unplanned and Emergency Expenses

Unfortunately, people lose their jobs, cars break down, and children get sick. Over the time period your budget covers, all sorts of unforeseen and unplanned events occur and cost you money. If you can afford to, the best approach is to budget and set aside a little each month to cover these unexpected expenses.

Budget planners use several rules of thumb regarding how much emergency savings is enough. If your primary reason for emergency savings is in case you lose your job—because you are well-insured for medical, disability, and life claims—the following is an approach you should use:

1. Consider the length of time you need to find a new job. (A traditional rule of thumb says that you need a month for every $10,000 of annual salary. For example, if you make $10,000 a year, figure on one month. If you make $50,000 a year, figure on five months.)

2. Take the salary you would have earned over the period of unemployment and subtract any employment benefits or severance pay you receive.

3. Reduce that remainder by the income taxes you do not pay and any amounts you do not save because you have no income.

To illustrate, suppose that it will take as long as six months to find a job; you currently earn $2,500 a month; you get half a month's severance pay if you lose your job; unemployment amounts to $100 a week; and you pay 7.65 percent social security tax and a 15 percent income tax. You then can calculate your emergency savings as:

$$((6*\$2500) - (26*\$100) - \$1250)*(1 - 7.65\% - 15\%) = \$8,625$$

## Using Zero-Based Budgeting

Large businesses use zero-based budgeting with success, and individuals and smaller businesses also can use it successfully. Basically, zero-based budgeting says that although you spent money on some category last year, you should not necessarily spend money on the same category this year.

Looking at what you spent last year can provide a valuable perspective, but this year's spending should be determined by this year's goals. Saying, "Well, last year I spent $500 on furniture, and therefore I will spend $500 this year," is dangerous. Your house or apartment may not have room for any more furniture. What about the dues for the athletic club you haven't used for months or years? Or the extra term life insurance you bought when your kids were living at home? Or the advertising money you spent to attract your first customers? Budgeting and spending amounts as you have in the past is easy to do even though your goals, your lifestyle, or your business have meanwhile made the expense unnecessary.

# Chapter Summary

This chapter outlined the budgeting process and why budgeting is important in managing your personal and business finances, described how Quicken helps with the process, and provided some tips on how to budget and manage your finances more successfully. With this information as a background, you should be able to decide whether you want to use the budgeting tools that Quicken provides.

# 17

# Using Quicken for Home Accounting

I f you read the first three parts of this book—"Getting Started with Quicken," "Learning the Basics," and "Supercharging Quicken"—you already know about the mechanics of using Quicken. Using any software, and particularly an accounting program, however, is more than just mechanics. If you are like most people, you have questions about where Quicken fits in, how Quicken changes the way you keep your financial records, and when the Quicken options should be used. This chapter answers these types of questions.

## Where Quicken Fits In

Where Quicken fits into your personal financial management or home accounting depends on what you want to get from Quicken. You can use Quicken for home accounting in three ways:

❏ To track income tax deductions

❏ To automate record keeping

❏ To monitor how closely you are following a budget

## Tracking Income Tax Deductions

When tracking income tax deductions, you need to make sure that transactions that produce an income tax deduction are entered into one of the

**387**

Quicken registers. You also need to be sure that you use a category marked as tax-related.

This process is not as difficult as it sounds. First, although you currently may make payments that represent income tax deductions from a variety of accounts, often you can change the way you make payments so that every transaction that produces an income tax deduction is recorded in one or two accounts. For example, if you currently make charitable contributions in cash and with your credit card, rather than set up a cash account and a credit card account, you can change the way you do things and start writing checks on an account you are tracking with Quicken. This way, if your only purpose in using Quicken is to track income tax deductions, you need to set up only one account—a bank account is probably easiest—and then use only that bank account for charity contributions.

Second, in many cases you probably don't need the power of Quicken to track and tally income tax deductions. The organization to which you make a tax-deductible payment may track and tally your tax deduction for you. Consider, for example, the case of a home mortgage. At the end of the year, the bank sends you a statement that identifies how much you have paid over the year in interest, principal, and, if applicable, for things like property taxes and insurance. Similarly, a charity may send a statement showing your contributions for the year. And a bank or brokerage firm may indicate your total individual retirement account contributions. Although you may need to track and tally certain income tax deductions, you may not want to go to all that work if some other organization already is tracking your deductions for you.

# Automating Record Keeping

As a general rule, any financial record keeping you now perform manually is probably a candidate for Quicken. People go to different lengths in their efforts to keep clean, precise accounting records. The obvious candidate is bank accounts—particularly checking accounts. You may be someone, however, who also tracks investments carefully, tracks personal spending in a precise manner, or keeps records of your personal assets or liabilities. In any of these cases, Quicken probably can make your job easier.

You should consider three cautions when automating your financial record keeping. First, and as with income-tax deductions, don't go to a lot of effort to account for things that someone else already tracks for you. For example, you probably don't need to go to the effort of using Quicken if all your investments appear on the same monthly statements from your broker or from the mutual fund manager. And you probably don't need to track things such as your monthly pension fund or 401(k) contributions when your employer has paid professional accountants to do just that.

A second perspective to consider is that keeping financial records isn't all that fun. Keeping records is tedious, requires attention to detail, and can take a lot of time. For these reasons, carefully consider whether you really need to keep financial records for a specific asset or liability. You can track the value of things like your home or car, but is it really worth it? In many cases, it isn't. Anytime you go to the work of keeping a detailed, transaction-by-transaction record of some asset or liability, the information should enable you to better manage your personal finances. If the information doesn't do that, it isn't worth collecting and storing.

Remember that in a Quicken register you record transactions that change the balance of an asset or liability. But the values of things like a home, stocks, or a bond change without a transaction occurring. As a result, you cannot point to an event and say, "Well, yes, that needs to be recorded." Not surprisingly, you usually have difficulty tracking changes in the value of something when you don't have actual transactions you can point to and then record.

# Monitoring a Budget

As suggested in Chapter 16, one of the most powerful home accounting uses for Quicken is monitoring how closely you are following a budget. Although the budgeting tools that Quicken provides are superb, actually using Quicken to monitor your monthly spending can be a challenge. Because you probably spend money in several ways—using checks, using your credit cards, and using cash—the only way to really track your monthly spending is to record all three spending groups in registers. Otherwise, you get only a piece of the picture. Recording all three groups can involve quite a bit of work. To simplify monitoring a budget, consider several budgeting ideas: focusing on discretionary items, aggregating spending categories, and thinking about the spending method.

## Focusing on Discretionary Items

In Chapter 16, budgeting is described as a three-step process:

1. Setting your financial goals

2. Using your financial goals as a guide to developing a financial game plan, or budget, that covers how you want to spend your money

3. Using the financial game plan, or budget, to monitor your spending to track how closely you are progressing toward your business goals

Quicken helps with the third step—using the budget to monitor your spending. You then only need to monitor your discretionary spending—and not spending that's fixed, for example, by contract or by law. Keep this in mind when you define categories and describe accounts. Some of your spending may not need to be monitored at all. Consider, for example, a mortgage payment or a rent payment: although you certainly want to include these major expenditures in a budget, you probably don't need to monitor whether you are spending money on these payments. The spending is fixed by a mortgage contract or a rental agreement. You cannot, therefore, spend less than the budgeted amount unless you want to be evicted from your home. And you won't spend more than the budgeted amount because you have no reason to do so. Even if you do, the mortgage company or landlord probably would just return your overpayment. (**Note:** The Quicken monthly budget report is the principal tool you will use to monitor a budget. Refer to Chapter 14 for more information.)

Other examples of fixed spending are loan or lease payments for a car, income and social security taxes, and child care. Which spending categories are fixed in your case depends on the specifics of your situation. But in general, anything that is already fixed, or locked in, by a contract, by law, or by the terms of employment probably doesn't need to be monitored as closely. Fixed spending does need to be included in your budget because you want to make sure that you have enough money for the item, but it doesn't need to be monitored. The general rule is that for purposes of monitoring a budget, focus on monitoring discretionary spending.

## Aggregating Spending Categories

When you monitor your discretionary spending, you find a handful of general categories, rather than a big clump of specific categories, easiest to work with. For the sake of illustration, take the case of your spending on entertainment. You can choose to track spending on entertainment by using just one category called "Entertain." Alternatively, you can break the spending down into all the various ways you actually spend your entertainment dollars:

❏ Eating at restaurants

❏ Going to the movies

❏ Seeing plays at the theater

❏ Playing golf

❏ Attending sports events

Tracking exactly how you spend your entertainment dollars takes a certain precision and usually takes effort. There are two reasons for this. The first reason is that you end up recording more transactions. For example, a credit card bill that contains charges for only the five spending groups listed needs to have one transaction recorded if only one general category is used, but five split transactions recorded if all five specific categories are used.

The second reason is that you budget by category, so the more categories you use, the more budgeted amounts you need to enter. If you feel you must have the detail that comes with using many, very specific categories, consider using subcategories that at least minimize the work of entering budgeted amounts. You don't budget by subcategory—only by category.

Consider these general rules for aggregating spending categories:

1. Lump together items that are substitutes for each other.

2. Lump together items that are of similar importance, or priority, to you and the other members of your family.

Both rules stem from the idea that if you are overspending in some category, you should consider reducing further spending in that category. A couple of examples may help you use these rules in your own budgeting. For the sake of illustration, suppose that you lump together the five spending groups listed previously into one general category. Also suppose that you go out and golf with friends three straight weekends so that you don't have any money left over for restaurants and the theater, which are favorite activities of your spouse, nor money for movies and sporting events, which are the favorite activities of your two children. In this case, you probably should not lump all five categories together because not spending money in one category may not be a practical remedy for overspending in another category. As a sensible solution, you can budget for golf as one category, for the theater and restaurants as a second category, and for the movies and sports events as a third category. You then should be able to make sure that overspending on golf doesn't occur. If your spouse overspends on the theater, a reasonable response is to minimize or curtail spending on restaurants. And if the kids insist on seeing two movies, they probably should understand that they forego a trip to the ballpark.

## Thinking about the Spending Method

Researchers have proven with empirical studies that the method people use to spend money—credit cards, checks, or cash—affects how they spend. In general, people spend more when they use a credit card than they do when they are spending cash or writing a check. And people often spend less when they use cash than when they write a check. This phenomenon doesn't directly affect how you work with Quicken, but in terms of monitoring a budget, consider this information when deciding which accounts you set up to monitor your spending.

Most people can stay within a budget more easily if they choose a spending method that is easier to control. The accounts you set up to monitor your spending probably should recognize this reality. Remember that Quicken enables you to set up special accounts for bank accounts, credit cards, and cash. For monitoring those spending categories you want to watch, choose a spending method that makes staying within your budget easier.

# How To Use Quicken

With the information covered thus far, you are in a good position to know when and where Quicken should be used for home accounting. This section covers some tips that elaborate on the previous discussion.

## Using Quicken for Bank Accounts

You generally can use Quicken for any bank accounts you want to reconcile on a monthly basis. You also can use Quicken for checking accounts for which you want to print checks. Finally, you may want to track certain bank accounts used for income tax deductions or budget monitoring reasons.

You probably don't need to use Quicken—unless you want to—for bank accounts that don't need to be reconciled. You probably don't need to use Quicken for certificates of deposit or for savings accounts with no activity other than monthly interest or fees.

# Using Quicken for Credit Cards

You don't need to use Quicken to track credit card spending for credit cards in which you pay off the balance at the end of the month. When you write the monthly check to pay off the credit card company, you can record the spending categories.

For credit cards in which you don't pay off the balance on a monthly basis, but still need to track income tax deductions or monitor spending, you should set up and use Quicken accounts. For credit cards where you want to use the reconcile feature, you also need to set up and use Quicken accounts.

If you set up accounts for credit cards, you need to enter each credit card transaction into the register. Therefore, you need to collect the credit card slips and then periodically enter them into the register.

# Using Quicken for Cash

If you spend cash making income tax deductions, you can use Quicken to track these deductions. And if you are using Quicken to monitor cash spending so that you can compare actual spending with budgeted spending, you also can use Quicken to track this information. Essentially, every time you withdraw cash from the bank, you increase your cash. Every time you spend money, you need to collect a receipt for the expense. You then periodically enter these cash transactions into the register.

One practical problem with tracking cash spending is that for some purchases, you cannot get a receipt—small things such as candy, a newspaper, or tips to a bellhop. So you either need to keep a record of these small transactions yourself, or you need to adjust your register's cash balance periodically to what you actually have in cash. The category for such an adjustment may be named something like "Sundries" or "Misc."

*CPA Tip*

For credit card and cash transactions, collect in an envelope the credit card and cash receipts you need to enter. On a periodic basis, say once a week or month, enter the receipt amounts into the appropriate register, mark the receipts as entered, and label the outside of the envelope, for example, "credit card and cash receipts from week beginning 6/1/91." If you have a large number of receipts, number the receipts and then use these numbers as the transaction numbers in the register so that you can specifically tie a transaction in the register to a receipt.

# Tracking the Adjusted Basis of Your Home

By law, the gain on the sale of your home is taxable unless you purchase another home of equal or greater value within a certain time frame, or unless you can use the one-time $125,000 exclusion to eliminate the gain. The gain on the sale of a home is calculated roughly as:

(sales price) − (original cost + cost of improvements)

The sales price and the original cost are set and are connected to your purchase and to your sale. One way to reduce the calculated gain and, therefore, minimize the income tax on the gain is to track the cost of improvements.

Improvements don't include repairs or maintenance such as fixing a roof, painting the walls, or sealing an asphalt driveway. Over the years, however, you probably will make a series of improvements that, if tracked, may reduce your gain. These improvements may include things like the landscaping you put in after you bought the house, bookshelves you added to the family room, and the extra bathroom a remodeler put in upstairs. Figure 17.1 shows an example of a register used to collect this sort of information. (Remember that the account transfer feature means

```
┌──────────────────────────────────────────────────────────────────────┐
│ F1-Help   F2-Acct/Print   F3-Edit   F4-Quick Entry  F5-Reports  F6-Activities │
│ ┌──────┬─────┬───────────────────────────┬──────────┬─┬──────────┬──────────┐ │
│ │ DATE │ REF │ PAYEE  ·  MEMO  ·  CATEGORY│ DECREASE │C│ INCREASE │ BALANCE  │ │
│ │      │     │                           │          │ │          │          │ │
│ │      │     │      ═══ BEGINNING ═══     │          │ │          │          │ │
│ │10/12 │     │ Opening Balance           │          │ │100,000 00│100,000 00│ │
│ │1987  │     │              [House]      │          │ │          │          │ │
│ │ 3/ 1 │234  │ Puget Landscaping         │          │ │  3,000 00│103,000 00│ │
│ │1988  │     │ back yard    [Big National]│         │ │          │          │ │
│ │ 6/ 3 │370  │ Tom's Remodeling          │          │ │  1,200 00│104,200 00│ │
│ │1988  │Memo:│ shelves for family room   │          │ │          │          │ │
│ │      │Cat: │ [Big National]            │          │ │          │          │ │
│ │ 6/ 3 │     │                           │          │ │          │          │ │
│ │1988  │     │          ═══ END ═══      │          │ │          │          │ │
│ │      │     │                           │          │ │          │          │ │
│ └──────┴─────┴───────────────────────────┴──────────┴─┴──────────┴──────────┘ │
│ House                                                                  │
│ Esc-Main Menu      Ctrl↵ Record              Ending Balance:  $104,200.00 │
└──────────────────────────────────────────────────────────────────────┘
```

***Fig. 17.1.*** *A Quicken register provides a convenient format to collect the costs of improvements to your home.*

you probably never will need to go into the register for the asset, House, because you can record the cost of the improvement when you write the check to pay for the improvement.)

# Tracking the Non-Deductible Portions of an IRA

One of the record-keeping nightmares from the last decade's ever-changing tax laws is the non-deductible individual retirement account (IRA) contribution. Essentially, although you may not qualify for an IRA deduction, you still may be able to contribute to an IRA. An IRA contribution can be beneficial financially, because without the income taxes on the investment earnings, your account will grow faster.

Over long periods of time, for example, you can accumulate a great deal more money—even though the original contribution didn't generate a tax deduction. Figure 16.3 in Chapter 16 shows that by contributing $25 a month over 35 years, you may accumulate $94,916 if you pay no taxes, but $47,231 if you pay the 28% federal income tax. In other words, you may accumulate almost twice as much by not paying income taxes on your earnings. Non-deductible IRA contributions enable you to defer income taxes on the money you earn until you withdraw the money.

The problem with non-deductible IRA contributions is that what you contribute is not taxed when you withdraw the money; you need a way to keep track of your non-deductible contributions. And for most people, Quicken is an excellent solution. The basic process is that you should set up an investment account for non-deductible IRA contributions. Whenever you make a non-deductible contribution, record the payment as a transfer to the account you use to track non-deductible IRA contributions. Over the years, you build a detailed record of the non-deductible contributions you have made. Figure 17.2 shows an example of an investment register that tracks the asset "Nondeduct IRA."

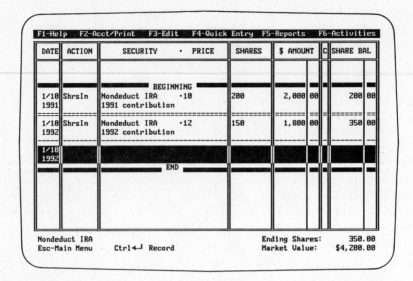

*Fig. 17.2. Use Quicken to track non-deductible IRA contributions.*

# When To Perform Quicken Tasks

One final question that people often have with regard to using Quicken is when they should perform the various Quicken tasks. Table 17.1 groups the various Quicken tasks into three groups: tasks you should perform on a daily and weekly basis, tasks you should perform on a monthly basis, and tasks you should perform on an annual basis. Consider the information in table 17.1 as a rough guideline—as you use Quicken, you will learn what works best for you.

### Table 17.1
### When To Perform Quicken Tasks

---

*Daily and Weekly Tasks*

> Record transactions in the registers.
> Print checks.
> Print a temporary copy of the month's register.
> Back up the account group.

*Monthly Tasks*

Print monthly reports.

Reconcile accounts.

Print a final copy of the month's register.

Throw away the daily or weekly copies of the register
because all that information is contained on the final copy
of the month's register.

Back up the account group.

File or store the month's bank statement, register, reports,
and backup account group files.

*Annual Tasks*

Print annual reports.

Print a permanent copy of the transaction report that
subtotals by tax deduction category. (This is your
permanent record for income tax purposes.)

Back up account group files for the year.

Create new year's budget and enter the budget.

Shrink the account group.*

* Note: When you shrink the account group, you don't want to lose the transaction
detail in accounts you are maintaining on a long-term basis for income tax purposes, such as for ultimately calculating the gain on the sale of a home or for determining the total non-deductible IRA contributions. So that this detail isn't lost in the
shrink account group operation, do not mark transactions in these registers as
cleared, and set the Include only cleared transactions switch to yes. Chapter 9
describes the **Copy/Shrink/Year-End** option.

# Chapter Summary

This chapter covered information you ultimately learn on your own
through trial and error. This chapter discussed where Quicken fits in
home accounting, how Quicken can be used for home accounting, and
when the various Quicken options and features should be used. You now
should be able to incorporate Quicken into your personal financial management activities more easily.

# 18

# Using Quicken in
# Your Business

**Y**ou may be surprised to learn that more people use Quicken as a business accounting package than as a home accounting package. The reasons for this usage are logical: you do not need to know double-entry bookkeeping, as you do for many other small-business accounting packages, and you use a simple and familiar tool, the check register. Because Quicken really isn't a full-fledged business accounting package, however, this chapter covers some of the special techniques and procedures for using Quicken in business.

The procedures for using Quicken are well-documented within the pages of this book. Accordingly, for this chapter you should know how to enter transactions into a register, set up accounts, define categories, and print reports. If you are not familiar with these features of Quicken, review the material covered in the first three sections of the book: "Getting Started with Quicken," "Learning the Basics," and "Supercharging Quicken."

This chapter begins by discussing the overall approach for using Quicken in a business. That discussion is followed by short sections that detail the seven basic accounting tasks:

- ❏ invoicing customers
- ❏ tracking receivables
- ❏ accounting for fixed assets
- ❏ preparing payroll
- ❏ tracking inventory

❏ job costing

❏ tracking loans and notes

When you combine basic bill paying and check writing, described throughout this book's chapters, with the details of the seven basic accounting tasks described in this chapter, you should have the information you need to perform your business accounting with Quicken Version 3.0 and 4.0.

# Understanding the Basics

Using Quicken for business accounting is easier if you understand the following three basic concepts: what Quicken accounts track, what should be recorded in a register, and what categories calculate.

## Knowing What Quicken Accounts Track

You use Quicken accounts to track the values of business assets or liabilities. You need to set up one account for each business asset or liability you want to track.

A business asset is anything you own. Common examples of business assets include the cash in a checking account, the receivable that some customer or client owes you, an investment in stock, inventory you resell, a piece of furniture, a piece of equipment, and real estate.

A business liability is anything you owe. Common examples of business liabilities include the loan on a car or delivery truck, payroll taxes you owe the government, the mortgage on your building, and the balance on a bank credit line.

Assets and liabilities have something in common: at any time, you can calculate the value of the asset or liability. Usually, you are not interested in the day-to-day or week-to-week change in a particular asset but rather the value at a specific time.

All the accounts you set up for a business must be included in the same account group. If you perform accounting for several businesses, each business needs its own account group. If you use Quicken at your business and at home, you need one account group for each (see Chapter 2).

*Note:* By default, Quicken enables you to define up to 64 accounts within an account group. You can increase this figure to 255 accounts.

# Defining a Transaction

Transactions are what you record in a register to show the change in the value of an asset or liability. No change ever affects only one asset or liability, though, so whenever you record the change in the value of some asset or liability, you also need to record how the change affects other accounts, or income or expenses categories. You actually perform double-entry bookkeeping without having to think or worry about debits and credits.

For example, when you transfer money from your checking account to your savings account, you record the decrease in the checking account balance with one transaction and the increase in the savings account balance with another transaction. Similarly, when you write a check to pay for your utilities, you record the decrease in your bank account due to the check and you indicate which expense category the transaction affects —probably Utilities. You always need to categorize a transaction or show the transaction as a transfer.

This discussion of transactions may seem redundant to you. But you need to verify that your assets and liabilities really are assets and liabilities. You also need to verify that the things you want to record as transactions in a register really are transactions and not assets or liabilities.

To illustrate, suppose that you want to track your receivables and record customer payments on those receivables. You need to set up an account each time you create an individual receivable. If you bill Johnson Manufacturing $1,000 for a service, you need to set up an account for this asset. The temptation with a group of similar assets, such as receivables, is to group them as one asset using one account group. Using the grouping approach, however, obscures information on specific accounts. You cannot tell whether Johnson Manufacturing still owes the $1,000 or how the $1,000 original asset value has changed. Changes in the value of that asset—such as when you receive the customer's payment—need to be recorded as transactions in the register.

The key to using Quicken as a small-business accounting system is knowing what your assets, liabilities, and transactions are. Throughout the rest of this chapter, you will find many tips and suggestions to assist you in this analysis.

# Knowing What Categories Calculate

The term *bottom line* refers to the figure at the bottom of a profit and loss statement that shows whether you made or lost money in your business. The reason you use categories within Quicken is to calculate your bottom line—to determine whether you are making or losing money. You use two kinds of categories to do this: Income and Expense. Income categories count your business revenues, or *inflows*. Common income categories include sales of products or services, interest and dividends from investments, and even the proceeds from the sale of some asset. Expense categories count your business costs, or *outflows*. Examples of expense categories include the cost of advertising, insurance, utilities, and employee wages.

Income and expense categories have something in common: they enable you to count business inflows and outflows over a period of time—such as for the week, month, or year. You can use the income and expense category information to tell whether you made or lost money during the last week, month, or year.

When you use Quicken categories to track only cash inflows and outflows—your bank and cash accounts—you are using cash-basis accounting. Cash-basis accounting means that you record income only when you deposit money, and you record expenses only when you pay money. This system makes sense. When you make the bank deposit or the check payment, you are categorizing the transaction as income or expense.

When you use Quicken categories to keep track of other assets and liabilities, however, you move toward *accrual-* or *modified accrual-basis* accounting. Accrual-basis accounting means that you record income when you earn it, and you record expenses when you use the goods or services from which the expenses stem. For example, if you use Quicken to account for customer receivables, you recognize the transaction as income when you record the receivable. If you use Quicken to account for fixed assets and depreciation, you categorize the expense of using the asset when you record depreciation.

*CPA Tip*

> Accrual-basis accounting gives you much better estimates of your income and expenses so that it better measures your profits. Accrual-basis accounting also results in better record keeping, because you keep registers for all your assets and liabilities—not just cash. If it's important in your business to measure profits accurately, try to use accrual-basis accounting. If you do, you will have a better idea of whether you're making money.

# Invoicing Customers

Quicken does not provide an invoicing feature, but you can create a report that works as an invoice. Set up an account to record the new asset you have because a customer or client now owes you money. You probably want to name the account by combining "invoice" with the actual invoice number. The account type should be 4, indicating the account type is Other Asset. Set the balance to zero and leave the description blank. Figure 18.1 shows an example of the Set Up New Account screen filled in to define such an account.

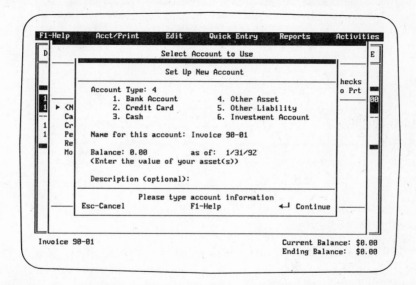

**Fig. 18.1.** *The Set Up New Account screen filled in to define the receivable that results from creating an invoice.*

Select the account so that you can access the register for the account. To record the invoice, edit the opening balance entry that Quicken makes when you set up an account. You enter the customer name in the Payee field, the total invoice amount in the Increase field, and any customer reference number in the Memo field. Select **Split Transaction** from the Edit menu or press its speed key equivalent, Ctrl-S, to provide details on the total invoice amount. Anything that has an amount associated with it must be categorized and described—even if every item has the same category.

Suppose that you are an attorney and want to create a $1,000 invoice to send to a client, Johnson Manufacturing, for $300 of work on a real estate lease, $600 of work on a bank loan agreement, and $100 for out-of-pocket expenses. Figure 18.2 shows an example of the completed Register screen and the Split Transaction window to record just such an invoice. (Remember that you can split a transaction into as many as 30 lines, so you can create an invoice that lists up to 30 charges.)

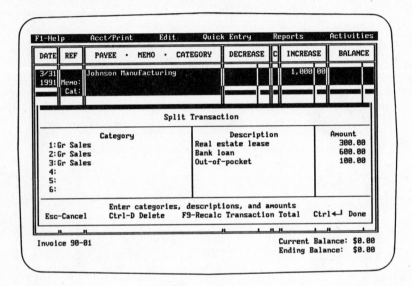

*Fig. 18.2. The Register and Split Transaction screens completed for creating an invoice.*

Now you are ready to record and print the invoice. Record the invoice by pressing Ctrl-Enter. To print the invoice, press F5 to access the Reports menu and then select the fifth option, **Transaction**. Quicken displays the Create Transaction Report screen. Enter your company name as the Report Title, enter the billing period or the billing date in the Restrict to transactions from field, and set the Subtotal by field to 12 for subtotaling by account (see fig. 18.3). Press F8 to access the Report Options screen, set Show split transaction detail to Y for yes and the Show memo/category/both field to M for memo only (see fig. 18.4). Leave the other fields set to their default values, as shown in figure 18.4. After you complete the Report Options screen, press Ctrl-Enter to return to the Create Transaction Report screen. To generate an on-screen version of the invoice, press Ctrl-Enter again. If you want to print the invoice, press F8, complete the Print Report screen, and press Ctrl-Enter.

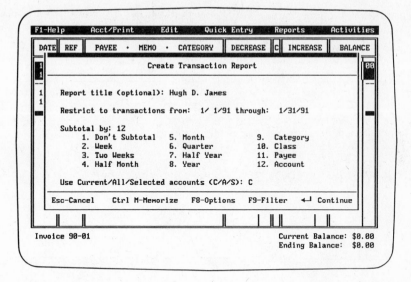

**Fig. 18.3.** *The Create Transaction Report screen for an invoice.*

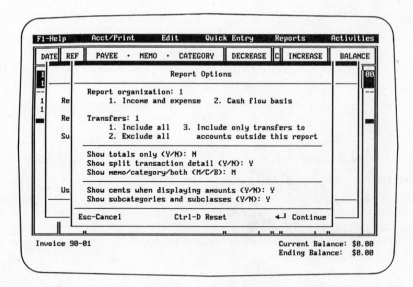

**Fig. 18.4.** *The Report Options screen for an invoice.*

Figure 18.5 shows the resulting invoice. Your business name shows at the top of the invoice, as does the billing period or billing date. Business is the name of the account group for the business. The Payee field shows the customer or client name. The Memo field shows the descriptions and amounts of the various charges that make up the invoice. Finally, the total shows the invoice amount.

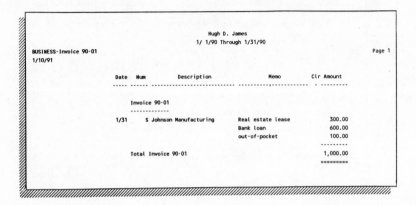

```
                                        Hugh D. James
                                    1/ 1/90 Through 1/31/90

BUSINESS-Invoice 90-01                                                          Page 1
1/10/91

          Date   Num        Description              Memo         Clr Amount
          -----  ------  --------------------------  -----------,------------  - ---------

                  Invoice 90-01
                  --------------

          1/31    S Johnson Manufacturing      Real estate lease       300.00
                                               Bank loan               600.00
                                               out-of-pocket           100.00
                                                                    ----------
                  Total Invoice 90-01                                 1,000.00
                                                                    =========
```

***Fig. 18.5.*** *An invoice generated with Quicken.*

The invoice in figure 18.5 is not as sophisticated or custom-tailored as those produced by accounting packages designed to generate invoices. Depending on the requirements of your business, however, this invoice can be satisfactory. Remember that you can export the report to an ASCII file that can be edited with almost any word processing program.

*CPA Tip*

Customers need the due date, your address, and your federal tax identification number so that they can report payments to you to the Internal Revenue Service. If you generate your invoices solely with Quicken, make sure that your customers already have this information from some other source. If you export the invoice as an ASCII text file so that you can edit the invoice, you can add the due date, your federal tax identification number, and your address.

# Tracking Customer Payments and Receivables

To track customer payments and receivables, you also need to follow the steps described in the preceding section to record the receivable as an asset. After you record the receivable as an asset, you can record customer payments on the receivable and monitor your receivables—topics covered in the following sections.

## Recording Customer Payments

To record customer payments, select the bank account you use to deposit the check and record the deposit in the usual way. To categorize the transaction, record the deposit as a transfer from the actual receivable account. For example, if you received a $500 check from Johnson Manufacturing for partial payment of the $1,000 receivable created by Invoice 90-01, you complete the register for the bank account you are depositing the money into as shown in figure 18.6. (Remember that Quicken lists the categories and the accounts when you press Ctrl-C and when you select **Categorize/Transfer** from the Quick Entry menu.)

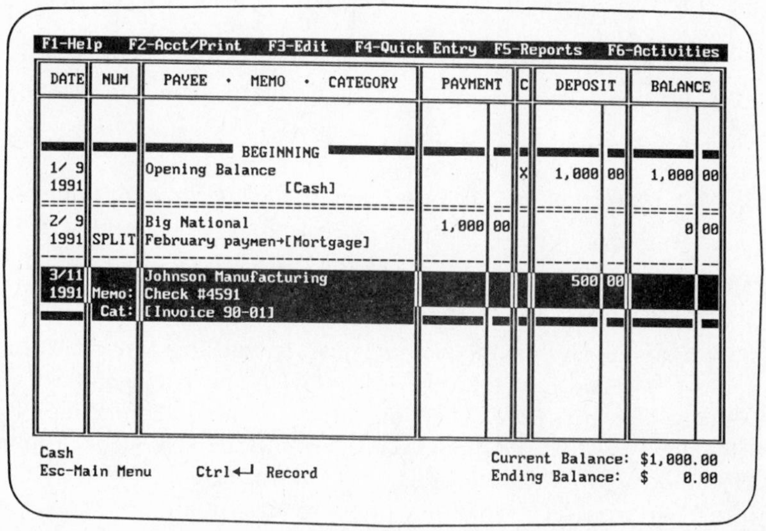

```
 F1-Help   F2-Acct/Print   F3-Edit   F4-Quick Entry   F5-Reports   F6-Activities

 DATE  NUM   PAYEE  ·  MEMO  ·  CATEGORY      PAYMENT  C   DEPOSIT    BALANCE

                      ═══ BEGINNING ═══
 1/ 9       Opening Balance                          X  1,000 00   1,000 00
 1991                    [Cash]

 2/ 9       Big National                     1,000 00                   0 00
 1991 SPLIT February paymen+[Mortgage]

 3/11       Johnson Manufacturing                        500 00
 1991 Memo: Check #4591
       Cat: [Invoice 90-01]



 Cash
 Esc-Main Menu    Ctrl←┘ Record          Current Balance: $1,000.00
                                         Ending Balance:  $    0.00
```

**Fig. 18.6.** *Recording a $500 partial payment on the $1,000 receivable created by the invoice.*

Quicken records a $500 reduction in the account you use to track the $1,000 receivable. Figure 18.7 shows the register for the Invoice 90-01 account after you record the $500 partial payment from Johnson Manufacturing as a deposit to the bank account.

Quicken records the decrease in the Invoice 90-01 receivable. After a receivable is reduced to zero, you should print a copy of the register as a record of the receivable and the customer's payments, and then delete the account to make room for more accounts.

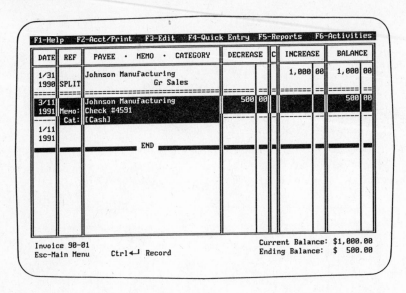

*Fig. 18.7. Quicken records the second half of the transfer transaction.*

# Tracking Customer Receivables

Another basic receivables accounting task is tracking how much customers owe you and how long they have owed you. The age of a receivable usually determines the collection efforts you make. For example, you probably don't even worry about receivables that aren't yet due. You may call customers with receivables that are more than 30 days past due. You may even turn over receivables that are more than 60 or 90 days past due to a collection agency or an attorney. To create a summary report that shows receivables account balances grouped by their age, follow these steps:

1. Select the **Summary** option from the Reports menu by pressing F5. Quicken displays the Create Summary Report screen (see fig. 18.8).

2. To complete the screen to show only receivables balances, enter a report title and a range of dates in the Restrict to transactions from and through fields that begins with the date of your oldest receivable and ends with the current date.

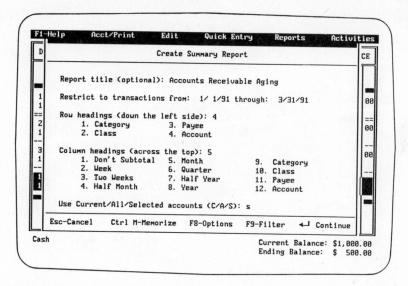

```
F1-Help      Acct/Print      Edit      Quick Entry      Reports      Activities
 D                          Create Summary Report                        CE

       Report title (optional): Accounts Receivable Aging

 1     Restrict to transactions from:  1/ 1/91 through:  3/31/91        00
 1
 ==    Row headings (down the left side): 4                             ==
 2         1. Category        3. Payee                                  00
 1         2. Class           4. Account
 --                                                                     --
 3     Column headings (across the top): 5                              00
 1         1. Don't Subtotal  5. Month         9. Category
 --        2. Week            6. Quarter       10. Class               --
 1         3. Two Weeks       7. Half Year      11. Payee
 1         4. Half Month      8. Year          12. Account
 ■                                                                      ■
       Use Current/All/Selected accounts (C/A/S): s

       Esc-Cancel    Ctrl M-Memorize    F8-Options    F9-Filter    ↵ Continue

 Cash                                          Current Balance: $1,000.00
                                               Ending Balance: $  500.00
```

**Fig. 18.8.** *The Create Summary Report screen completed for a receivables aging.*

3. Set the Row headings field to 4 for Account. Next, set the Column headings field to whatever time intervals you want to use to age receivables. (Usually, businesses age their receivables on a monthly basis.)

   *Note:* An *aging* refers to segregating receivables into different age groups. Ages are calculated as the difference between the invoice date and the current date.

4. Set the Current/All/Selected accounts field to S for selected, and press Enter.

   Quicken next displays the Select Accounts to Include screen (see fig. 18.9). You want to exclude accounts that are not receivables.

5. To exclude these accounts, move the cursor to the account you want to exclude and press the space bar. The space bar acts as a toggle between include and exclude.

6. After you complete the Select Accounts to Include screen, press Enter, and Quicken displays the Accounts Receivable Aging report summary (see fig. 18.10).

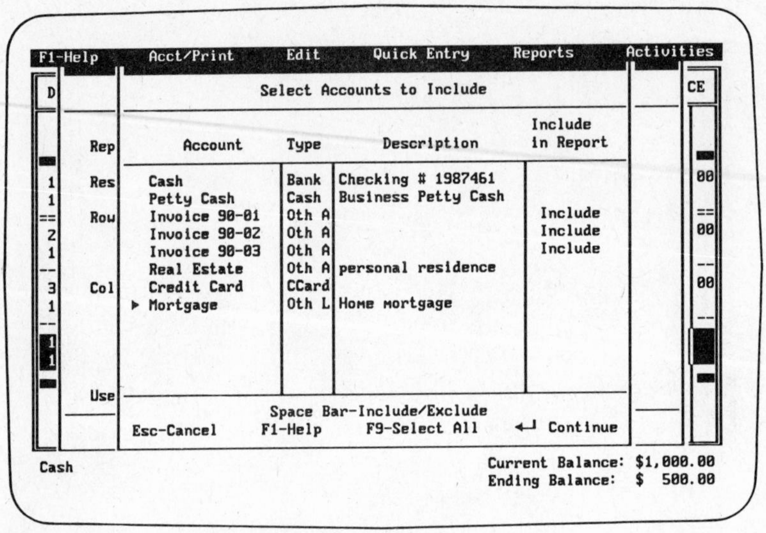

```
F1-Help      Acct/Print      Edit      Quick Entry      Reports      Activities
 D                        Select Accounts to Include                          CE

     Rep                                              Include
            Account     Type      Description       in Report
  1  Res    Cash        Bank    Checking # 1987461                             00
  1          Petty Cash  Cash    Business Petty Cash
  ==  Row    Invoice 90-01 Oth A                     Include                    ==
  2          Invoice 90-02 Oth A                     Include                    00
  1          Invoice 90-03 Oth A                     Include
  --          Real Estate  Oth A  personal residence                           --
  3  Col     Credit Card  CCard                                                 00
  1        ▶ Mortgage     Oth L  Home mortgage
  1
  1
     Use                Space Bar-Include/Exclude
            Esc-Cancel   F1-Help     F9-Select All    ↵ Continue

 Cash                                        Current Balance: $1,000.00
                                             Ending Balance:  $  500.00
```

*Fig. 18.9. The Select Accounts to Include screen.*

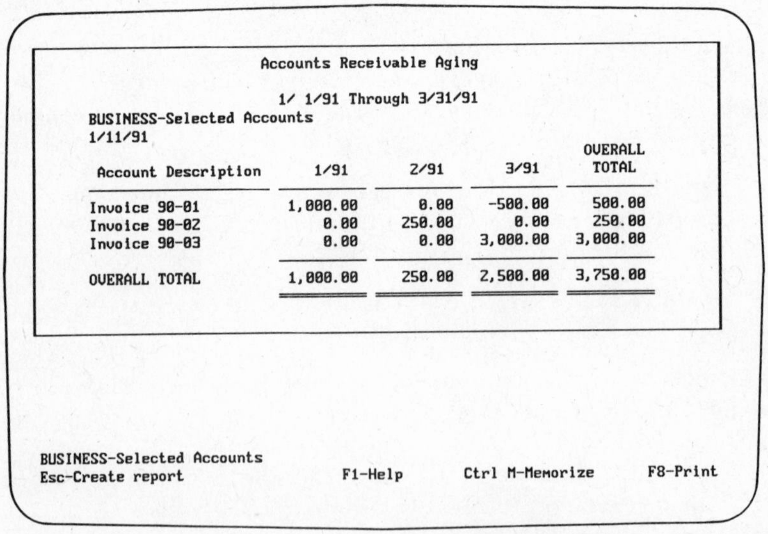

```
                    Accounts Receivable Aging

                   1/ 1/91 Through 3/31/91
        BUSINESS-Selected Accounts
        1/11/91
                                                      OVERALL
        Account Description   1/91     2/91     3/91    TOTAL

        Invoice 90-01      1,000.00     0.00  -500.00   500.00
        Invoice 90-02          0.00   250.00     0.00   250.00
        Invoice 90-03          0.00     0.00  3,000.00 3,000.00

        OVERALL TOTAL      1,000.00   250.00  2,500.00 3,750.00


        BUSINESS-Selected Accounts
        Esc-Create report          F1-Help      Ctrl M-Memorize    F8-Print
```

*Fig. 18.10. The Accounts Receivable Aging report shown on-screen.*

The summary report shows you how much money each of the receivables customers owe you and the ages of the receivables. Invoice 90-01, for example, shows up as $1,000 in January because the date of that account's first transaction is in January, and as $500 in March because that's when you received a partial payment on the receivable.

*Note:* One problem with this approach is that the account names do not indicate the customers. If you do not use Quicken to generate invoices, you can lessen this problem by naming accounts with the invoice number and the customer name. For example, you can name the account that tracks invoice 90-01 from Johnson Manufacturing as I-9001 Johnson.

*CPA Tip*

The Quicken user's manual offers another approach for recording receivables, and two other approaches for recording payments on the receivables. The manual suggests that you record all your receivables, or at least all of a specific customer's receivables, in one account. With regard to recording payments, the manual suggests that you enter the payment as a decrease transaction in a large Receivables register or as a negative transfer amount for a specific receivable transaction by using the Split Transaction window. (If you have more questions about these approaches, refer to the user's manual.) The benefit of the manual's two approaches is that you do not use up as many accounts—the limit is 255. These suggestions, however, have the following problems:

❏ If you record invoices and payment transactions in a large register, you have difficulty seeing how much money a customer owes you or has previously paid you on a specific invoice.

❏ If you use the Split Transaction window to record payments on an invoice, a second problem crops up. To apply a payment to five invoices, you must go into the Receivables register and edit five transactions to show the payment. Your bank reconciliation also is more difficult because you recorded the payment as five deposits rather than one.

❏ You cannot generate invoices if you do not set up receivables in separate accounts.

# Accounting for Fixed Assets

Accounting for fixed assets represents another activity that most businesses need to address. You may own furniture, equipment, and even real estate that needs to be depreciated. Although the assets you depreciate can be different, the mechanics of recording depreciation are consistent.

*Note:* If you need to record depletion for natural resources like timber, or if you need to record amortization expenses for intangible assets like copyrights or patents, the procedures are the same as those described here for depreciation.

# Understanding Depreciation

Suppose that you purchase a delivery truck for $12,000. You plan to use the truck for five years and then sell the truck for $2,000. The rationale for depreciating the truck is that over the five years, you need to include the expense of the truck when measuring your profits. Depreciation is a way of allocating the cost of an asset over two or more years. Several methods to make this allocation exist, but a common one is straight-line depreciation that works as follows: If you buy the truck for $12,000, intending to sell it five years later for $2,000, the overall cost of using the truck over the five years is $10,000. To calculate the yearly cost, divide the $10,000 by five years, and $2,000 is your annual depreciation expense to be included in your calculations of profits.

On balance sheets, assets are listed at an amount equal to the original cost minus the depreciation already taken. Continuing with the delivery truck example, at the end of the first year the balance sheet lists the truck at $10,000—calculated as $12,000 original cost minus $2,000 of depreciation. Similarly, at the end of the second, third, fourth, and fifth years, the balance sheet lists the truck at the original cost minus the depreciation taken to date. After the end of the fifth year, when the truck is listed at $2,000—calculated as $12,000 minus $10,000 of depreciation—you stop depreciating the asset because you do not depreciate the asset below its salvage value.

*CPA Tip*

Other depreciation methods exist, and those that the federal tax laws prescribe can be confusing. In essence, however, how you use Quicken to record depreciation works the same no matter which depreciation method you use. This chapter cannot give you complete information about how to calculate the depreciation on your assets, but if you want more information on the tax laws, call the Internal Revenue Service and ask for Internal Revenue Service Publication 534. If you want more information on how to calculate depreciation according to Generally Accepted Accounting Principles, which is different from depreciation calculated for the tax laws, consult your certified public accountant.

# Recording Fixed Assets and Depreciation

To record fixed assets and the depreciation expense related to fixed assets, set up an account for each asset that needs to be depreciated. Enter something descriptive as the account name, set the account type to 4 for Other assets, and enter the purchase price as the initial balance. Figure 18.11 shows the Set Up New Account screen filled to define a new account for a $12,000 delivery truck.

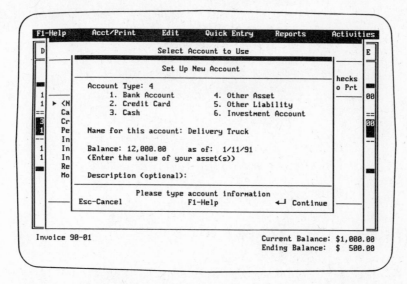

**Fig. 18.11.** *The Set Up New Account screen filled in to define a new account for a $12,000 delivery truck.*

If you have groups of similar assets with similar life spans, you usually can depreciate them as a group. For example, you probably would not depreciate individually each piece of furniture you buy during the year. Rather, you would aggregate and depreciate them together as one asset.

To record depreciation, you can enter a decrease transaction that categorizes $2,000 a year to the Depreciation Expense category. If you have not set up a category for depreciation, Quicken will prompt you to add the category. Remember that Quicken does not use a transaction in its calculations of profit unless the date is within the range you specify on the Create Report screens. Accordingly, you can enter all five years of depreciation at once by using transaction dates in each of the five years. Figure

18.12 shows the Register screen for the delivery truck filled in with the depreciation expense record for 1991, 1992, and 1993.

```
 F1-Help   F2-Acct/Print   F3-Edit   F4-Quick Entry   F5-Reports   F6-Activities
┌─────┬─────┬──────────────────────────────┬──────────┬─┬──────────┬──────────┐
│DATE │ REF │ PAYEE · MEMO · CATEGORY      │ DECREASE │C│ INCREASE │ BALANCE  │
├─────┼─────┼──────────────────────────────┼──────────┼─┼──────────┼──────────┤
│     │     │        ══ BEGINNING ══       │          │ │          │          │
│ 1/ 1│     │Opening Balance               │          │ │12,000 00 │12,000 00 │
│ 1991│     │            [Delivery Truc→    │          │ │          │          │
│     │     │                              │          │ │          │          │
│12/31│     │1991 Depreciation             │ 2,000 00 │ │          │10,000 00 │
│ 1991│     │            depreciation      │          │ │          │          │
│     │     │                              │          │ │          │          │
│12/31│     │1992 Depreciation             │ 2,000 00 │ │          │ 8,000 00 │
│ 1992│     │            depreciation      │          │ │          │          │
│     │     │                              │          │ │          │          │
│12/31│     │1993 Depreciation             │ 2,000 00 │ │          │ 6,000 00 │
│ 1993│     │            depreciation      │          │ │          │          │
│12/31│Memo:│                              │          │ │          │          │
│ 1993│Cat: │                              │          │ │          │          │
└─────┴─────┴──────────────────────────────┴──────────┴─┴──────────┴──────────┘
 Delivery Truck                               Current Balance: $12,000.00
 Esc-Main Menu      Ctrl←┘ Record             Ending Balance:  $ 6,000.00
```

*Fig. 18.12.* *The delivery truck register showing the asset depreciation schedules.*

# Preparing Payroll

One of the more common business applications of Quicken is to prepare employee payroll checks and reports. As a simple example, assume the following: You want to prepare a payroll check for an employee who earns $1,000 a month; the employee's social security tax is $76.50; and the employee's federal income tax withholding amount is $100. Also assume that the employer's matching share of social security is $76.50, and you must pay $10 for federal unemployment tax.

## Getting Ready for Payroll

To record this payroll transaction, set up a liability account for each of the payroll taxes payable accounts. Enter the account type as 5, for Other Liability, and enter the initial amount (the amount you already owe). In this example, this amount includes the federal income tax withholding, the employee's social security amount, your matching social security taxes, and the federal unemployment tax. To define each of the payroll tax accounts, use the Set Up New Account screen. Figure 18.13 shows how to set up the account for the federal income tax withholding amount. Use the screen, filled out in similar fashion, to define each of the payroll tax liability accounts.

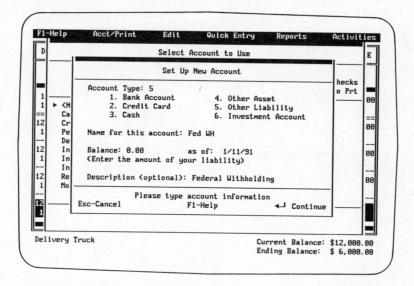

*Fig. 18.13. The Set Up New Account screen filled in to define the federal income tax withholding liability.*

You also need to define a category for each of the employer's payroll expenses: the employee's wages, the employer's matching share of the social security tax, and the federal unemployment tax. You do not define categories for the employee's social security tax or the employee's federal income tax withholding amounts, however, because these amounts are expenses of the employee, not the employer.

## Paying Employees

To record the payroll check, enter a transaction as shown in figure 18.14. If you write payroll checks using the same bank account you use to write other checks, enter the Memo description as payroll, or payroll and the pay date, so that you can use the Memo field as the basis for including transactions on reports. Select the **Split Screen** option when you are at the Category field. It is not necessary to fill in the net paycheck amount because Quicken will subtract the taxes withheld and enter the net portion in the register. If you use checks with vouchers—as you should for payroll—the employee's gross wages and the employee's deductions should appear on the first 16 lines of the Split Transaction screen, so that the split transaction shows on the voucher. (*Note:* On the Other Settings screen, make sure that the Print categories on voucher checks switch is set to yes so that the gross wages and deductions information prints on the voucher. Chapter 11 describes the Other Settings screen.)

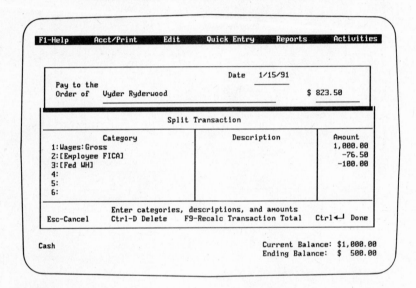

*Fig. 18.14. The gross wages and employee deductions should be entered on the first 16 lines of the Split Transaction screen.*

The other wages expenses—such as the employer's matching share of FICA and the federal unemployment tax—should be entered starting on line 17 of the Split Transaction screen, so that the expense does not appear on the payroll check's voucher (see fig. 18.15).

After you complete the Split Transaction screen, press Ctrl-Enter. Figure 18.16 shows the completed check. The net wages amount is $823.50, which is $1,000 in gross wages minus $100 in federal withholding and minus $76.50 in social security.

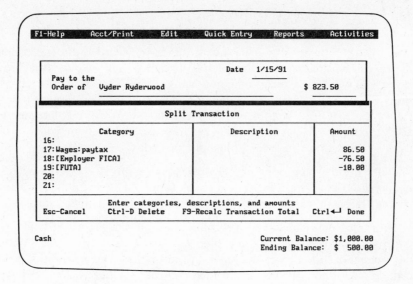

**Fig. 18.15.** *The other wages expenses start on line 17.*

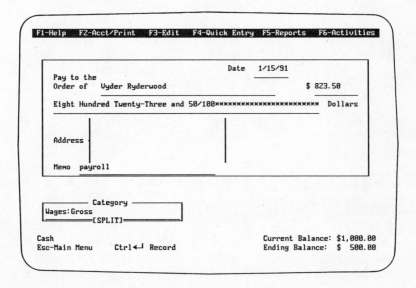

**Fig. 18.16.** *The completed payroll check.*

# Paying Payroll Taxes

When you pay the government, you already have recorded the expense of the taxes and are carrying the payroll taxes you still owe as a liability. When you write the check to the government, the Category field needs to show the payroll tax liability account. For example, if you write a check to pay the $10 in federal unemployment taxes, you enter the category as *[FUTA]*, because FUTA is the name of the liability account you use to track what you owe in federal unemployment tax.

You also use the same approach to record paying any of the other payroll tax liabilities you owe. You write a check to the government and categorize the transaction as a transfer from the payroll taxes liability account.

In real life, of course, you probably have several more payroll tax expenses and liabilities for items like state and local income taxes, state unemployment insurance, and disability insurance. The accounting procedures you follow to record and then pay each of these liabilities, however, are the same as those described in the previous paragraphs.

*CPA Tip*

You need to segregate the payroll tax liability money. The best approach is to set up a separate bank account that you use to collect and disburse payroll taxes. Do not, for any reason, "borrow" money from your payroll taxes bank account. Although the act may seem innocuous, the money is not yours to spend. The money belongs to an employee or the federal government; you only hold the money in trust.

# Completing Quarterly and Annual Tax Reports

The final aspect of preparing payroll relates to the filing of the quarterly and annual payroll forms and reports to the state and local government. You actually have a series of federal reporting requirements for W-2s, W-3s, 940s, and 941s. Depending on where you live, you also may have several state and local payroll forms and reports to complete. You should be able to retrieve the numbers for these forms by printing a summary report based on the bank account you use to write payroll checks (see fig. 18.17).

```
                                    Payroll Summary Report
                                     1/ 1/91 Through 3/31/91
  BUSINESS-Cash                                                                                    Page 1
  1/11/91
                  INC/EXP        INC/EXP        INC/EXP        INC/EXP        INC/EXP     TRANSFERS      TRANSFERS
                  EXPENSES       EXPENSES       EXPENSES       EXPENSES        TOTAL        FROM           FROM
               Wages & Job Cr Wages & Job Cr Wages & Job Cr
        Payee   Gross Wages    Payroll taxes     TOTAL                               Employee FICA  Employer FICA
  ------------- -------------- -------------- -------------- -------------- -------------- -------------- --------------
  Batum Schrag      2,500.00        216.25      2,716.25      2,716.25     -2,716.25        191.25         191.25
  Vyder Ryderwood   1,000.00         86.50      1,086.50      1,086.50     -1,086.50         76.50          76.50
                  ------------- -------------- -------------- -------------- -------------- -------------- --------------
  OVERALL TOTAL     3,500.00        302.75      3,802.75      3,802.75     -3,802.75        267.75         267.75
                  ============= ============== ============== ============== ============== ============== ==============
```

```
                                    Payroll Summary Report
                                     1/ 1/91 Through 3/31/91
  BUSINESS-Cash                                                                                    Page 2
  1/11/91
                  TRANSFERS      TRANSFERS      TRANSFERS       OVERALL
                    FROM           FROM          TOTAL          TOTAL
                    FUTA          Fed WH
        Payee
  ------------- -------------- -------------- -------------- --------------
  Batum Schrag        25.00         300.00        707.50      -2,008.75
  Vyder Ryderwood     10.00         100.00        263.00       -823.50
                  ------------- -------------- -------------- --------------
  OVERALL TOTAL       35.00         400.00        970.50      -2,832.25
                  ============= ============== ============== ==============
```

*Fig. 18.17. A transaction report that subtotals by category.*

To print the summary report, select the **Summary** option from the Reports menu. You should subtotal the report by category. If you write the payroll checks on the same account you use to write other checks and include payroll in the Memo field, you can use the F9-Filter option to specify that only transactions with *payroll* appear on the summary report.

# Completing the W-2 and W-3

You use the gross wages figures ($2,500 for Batum Schrag and $1,000 for Vyder Ryderwood) as the total wages amounts on the employees' W-2s. You use the transfers from withholding figures ($300 for Schrag and $100 for Ryderwood) as the federal income tax withholding amounts. You use the transfers from employee's FICA ($191.25 for Schrag and $76.50 for Ryderwood) as the social security taxes withheld amounts.

The W-3 summarizes the W-2 forms you complete. You enter the employer totals for each of the individual amounts on each employee's

W-2. You can use the totals from the summary report for these employer totals.

*Note:* One difference between the transaction report shown in figure 18.17 and the one you use to prepare the W-2 and W-3 forms is that your range of transaction dates encompasses the entire *calendar* year.

## Completing Other Forms and Reports

The federal and the state governments have other tax forms and reports that you must complete. You use the 940 form, for example, to calculate and report annual federal unemployment tax liability. You also use the 941 form each quarter to calculate and report federal income and social security taxes withheld and the employer's share of the social security taxes. Again, you should be able to use the summary report like the one shown in figure 18.17 to complete the quarterly return.

*Note:* For the Employer's Annual Unemployment Tax (form 940), the range of transaction dates must encompass the entire year. For the Employer's Quarterly Federal Tax (form 941), the range of transaction dates must cover the quarter.

*CPA Tip*

Typically, the Internal Revenue Service provides you with a great deal of help and information about federal payroll taxes. You should take advantage of their help. Specifically, you need the Employer's Tax Guide (often called Circular E). If you do not already have one, call the nearest Internal Revenue Service office and request a guide. If you are a sole proprietor, you also may want to request the information packet "Your Business Tax Kit for Sole Proprietor," which provides information about the taxes you pay as a sole proprietor. Some IRS locations provide free small-business tax education seminars. You also should call your state revenue office and request any information they have on the state income and payroll taxes.

## Preparing Inventory Accounting

An inventory accounting system should answer two questions: How much inventory do you currently hold? How much inventory did you sell over the year? A perpetual inventory system can answer both questions. Unfortunately, Quicken does not provide you with the tools to maintain a perpetual system. A perpetual inventory system tracks every change in inventory as the changes occur, in dollars and in units. As a result, you always know exactly how much inventory you hold, in dollars and in units. Because Quicken tracks only dollars, not units, you can answer only the second question: How much inventory did you sell over the year? You can answer this question with a simple periodic inventory system.

# Understanding Periodic Inventory Systems

A periodic system works as follows. At the end of every year, you count the inventory you are holding and add up its cost. Calculate the cost of the goods, or inventory, you sold by taking the inventory purchases you made over the year and subtracting the change in inventory.

Suppose that you sell cars and that each car costs $10,000. You held three cars in inventory at the beginning of the year, purchased ten cars over the year, and have four cars in inventory at the end of the year. Using the equation described previously, you can calculate the value of the inventory you sold over the year as follows:

Car purchases: ($10,000 * 10) = $100,000

Change over year:

Ending: ($10,000 * 4 cars) = $40,000

Beginning: ($10,000 * 3 cars) = $30,000

Minus change over year: − $10,000

Cost of inventory sold over year: $90,000

You know that over the year you bought $100,000 of cars and that you are holding $10,000 more inventory than you were last year, which means that you did not sell all the cars you bought.

# Implementing a Periodic Inventory System

If you want to enjoy the benefits of a periodic inventory system, you can use Quicken to construct a simple, but crude, inventory system.

The following steps describe how you implement a periodic inventory system using Quicken:

1. Set up an Other asset account for the inventory you buy and sell. The name can be Inventory. The account type should be 4. The starting balance should be the starting inventory balance. (If you are just starting your business, the starting inventory balance can be zero if you have not yet begun to purchase inventory.)

2. When you purchase inventory, do not categorize the purchase as an expense—transfer the total purchase amount to the inventory account.

3. When you want to calculate your net income, select the inventory account and use the **Update Account Balance** option from the Activities menu to reset the inventory account balance to whatever your physical count shows. The adjustment transaction should be categorized as cost of goods sold. You may have to add a category called "cost of goods sold" as an expense type category.

Figure 18.18 shows an inventory account register after a month of purchases and the adjustment transaction that calculates the actual cost of goods sold amount.

| F1-Help | F2-Acct/Print | F3-Edit | F4-Quick Entry | F5-Reports | F6-Activities |
| --- | --- | --- | --- | --- | --- |

| DATE | REF | PAYEE · MEMO · CATEGORY | DECREASE | C | INCREASE | BALANCE |
| --- | --- | --- | --- | --- | --- | --- |
| 1/11 1991 | | Opening Balance<br>[Inventory] | | | 30,000 00 | 30,000 00 |
| 1/23 1991 | | Inventory purchase<br>3 ragtops    [First Nationa→ | | | 30,000 00 | 60,000 00 |
| 2/10 1991 | | Inventory purchase<br>4 roadsters    [First Nationa→ | | | 40,000 00 | 100,000 00 |
| 3/ 3 1991 | | Inventory purchase<br>3 coupes    [First Nationa→ | | | 30,000 00 | 130,000 00 |
| 3/31 1991 | | Balance Adjustment<br>Cost Goods | 90,000 00 | | | 40,000 00 |
| 3/31 1991 | Memo:<br>Cat: | | | | | |

Inventory
Esc-Main Menu      Ctrl↵ Record                    Ending Balance:  $40,000.00

*Fig. 18.18. An inventory account register with sample transactions.*

# Reviewing the Problems of a Periodic System

As you know, a periodic inventory system is not without problems. You should make sure that you can live with the problems of a periodic inventory system before you spend a large amount of time and energy on implementing such a system.

Although you have accurate measures of your cash flow, you have an accurate measure of profits only through the last adjustment transaction. If you need to measure profits frequently, you must take frequent physical counts of your inventory and make the physical adjustment transaction.

You don't know the details or components of the cost of goods sold because you get the cost of goods sold from an adjustment transaction. As a result, you do not know the portion of cost of goods sold that stems from sales to specific customers or the portion that stems from breakage, shoplifting, or spoilage. This really could be true if your business has more than one type of item sold, such as books and tapes and CDs. You would have to set up separate accounts for each type of inventory and be sure to segregate all your purchases (by using the **Split Screen** option).

You also never know how much inventory you actually have on hand, except when you make physical counts of your inventory. You never can use your inventory system, therefore, to see which items need to be reordered or how many units of a specific item are in stock.

# Job Costing

*Job costing* refers to tracking the costs of a specific project, or job, and comparing these costs to what you planned to spend. Home builders, advertising agencies, and specialty manufacturers are examples of businesses with projects that must be monitored for actual and planned costs.

The Quicken user's manual suggests one approach for job costing: categorize each expense into a category and a class. When you print a transaction or summary report, you can choose to subtotal by the classes. Because you used classes to represent jobs, the total for a class is the total for a job. This approach, however, is not very strong. The following paragraphs describe alternative approaches that help you avoid two problems you encounter when categorizing expenses into categories and classes. (See Chapter 10 for a detailed discussion of categories and classes.)

The first problem with using classes as the basis for your job costing system is that within Quicken you do not budget by classes, but by categories. If you use the class approach, you omit one of the basic job costing tasks: comparing what you planned to spend with what you actually spent. Fortunately, you can solve this problem by setting up a group of categories that you use only for a specific job. You may even include some code or abbreviation in the category name to indicate the job.

For example, suppose that you are a home builder constructing a house on lot 23 in Deerfield and that you use three rough categories of expenses on all the homes you build: land, material, and labor. In this case, you can create three special categories: D23 Land, D23 material, and D23 labor, which you can use exclusively to budget and track the costs of the house you are constructing. Remember, you cannot budget for subcategories; you can budget only for categories.

A second problem with using classes as the basis for your job-costing system is that the costs you incur on a job should not always be categorized as expenses but often should be treated as assets. The costs of building the home on lot 23 in the Deerfield subdivision should be carried as inventory until the home is sold. When the home is sold, the total costs of the home should be categorized as the cost of goods sold. During the job, if you categorize the costs of building the home as expenses when you pay the costs, you overstate your expenses (which understates your profits), and you understate your assets (which understates your net worth). These understatements of profits and net worth can be a real problem if you have investors or lenders looking carefully at your financial performance and condition.

To solve this problem, create a transaction in which you move cost dollars out of the job cost categories into an asset account. The basic steps for moving these dollars from the expense categories to an asset account are as follows:

1. Set up an asset account for each job. Specify the account type as number 4, Other asset.

2. Print the budget report to see your actual costs and to show, if you want, your planned costs. From the Reports menu, select **Budget Reports**, and then enter the budgeted amounts for the job by pressing F7.

3. Create an entry *with the appropriate expense category* in the new asset account register that increases the balance of the asset and categorizes the increase so that the budget report shows the actual spending.

Figure 18.19 shows the on-screen version of the budgeting report that you can generate to monitor job costs, if you follow the approaches described in the preceding paragraphs. Figure 18.20 shows a copy of the new asset account register with the transaction that shows the reasons for the increase in the asset. Figure 18.21 shows the business balance sheet with the asset being created by the job correctly displayed on the balance sheet.

```
                              BUDGET REPORT

                         3/ 1/92 Through 3/31/92
         BUSINESS-All Accounts
         3/31/91
                               3/ 1/92    -       3/31/92
             Category Description    Actual    Budget     Diff

         INCOME/EXPENSE
           EXPENSES
             Building Lot          30,400.00  30,000.00     400.00
             Building Materials    23,456.00  25,000.00  -1,544.00
             Subcontractor labor   16,753.00  20,000.00  -3,247.00

           TOTAL EXPENSES          70,609.00  75,000.00  -4,391.00


         TOTAL INCOME/EXPENSE     -70,609.00 -75,000.00   4,391.00


         BUSINESS-All Accounts
         Esc-Create report           F1-Help    Ctrl M-Memorize   F8-Print
```

**Fig. 18.19.** *A budget report for a job.*

```
 F1-Help   F2-Acct/Print   F3-Edit   F4-Quick Entry   F5-Reports   F6-Activities
 DATE  REF   PAYEE  ·  MEMO  ·  CATEGORY   DECREASE  C  INCREASE   BALANCE

 ═══════════════ BEGINNING ═══════════════
 3/ 1       Opening Balance                                      0 00
 1991                  [Deerfield lot→

 3/31       Purchase of material                      23,456 00  23,456 00
 1991                  d23 materials

 3/31       Purchase of land                          30,400 00  53,856 00
 1991                  D23 land

 3/31       Purchase of labor                         16,753 00  70,609 00
 1991  Memo:
       Cat: d23 labor
 ─────
 3/31
 1991
 ═══════════════ END ═══════════════

 Deerfield lot 2
 Esc-Main Menu    Ctrl←┘ Record            Ending Balance:  $70,609.00
```

**Fig. 18.20.** *A transaction register showing how to record an asset.*

```
                        ACCOUNT BALANCES REPORT
                           As of 3/31/92
BUSINESS-All Accounts                                              Page 1
3/31/91
                                              3/31/92
                              Acct           Balance
                        ---------------------------  ------------
ASSETS
  Cash and Bank Accounts
    First National                            79,391.00
                                            ------------
    Total Cash and Bank Accounts              79,391.00

  Other Assets
    Deerfield lot 2                            70,609.00
    Delivery Truck                            10,000.00
    Inventory                                 40,000.00
    Invoice 90-03                              3,000.00
                                            ------------
    Total Other Assets                       123,609.00

                                            ------------
  TOTAL ASSETS                               203,000.00

LIABILITIES
  Other Liabilities
    Fed WH-Federal Withholding                   400.00
                                            ------------
    Total Other Liabilities                      400.00

                                            ------------
  TOTAL LIABILITIES                              400.00

                                            ------------
  OVERALL TOTAL                              202,600.00
                                            ============
```

*Fig. 18.21. A balance sheet showing the asset.*

# Tracking Loans and Notes

Keeping accurate records of what you pay and owe on a loan is not always easy—but is important. Interest expense is a valid business income tax deduction. What is more, you need to report how much you owe on various loans for financial statements and credit applications.

Consider using Quicken for loan record keeping. To begin, set up another liability account for the loan. The starting account balance equals what you currently owe. Define categories for the loan interest expense and any of the other expenses you pay when you make a loan payment. For a mortgage, other expense categories may include the property taxes and private mortgage insurance. For an equipment loan or lease, other expense categories may include sales tax and property insurance. Begin recording transactions. For example, you want to record a $796 loan payment—$740 of interest and $56 of principal. Suppose that you pay an additional $30 of property taxes, so that the check amount equals $826. You split portions of the payment by using the **Split** option in the Category field: $740 to interest expense and $30 to property taxes. You also record the $56 of principal reduction by transferring the $56 to the liability account you set up to track the loan balances. Figure 18.22 shows the Split Transaction screen filled to record a loan payment.

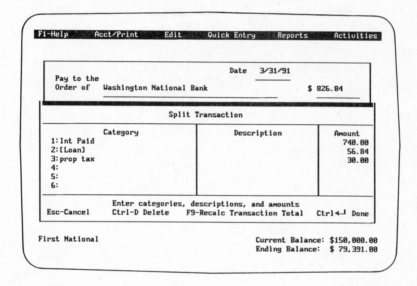

```
 F1-Help      Acct/Print      Edit      Quick Entry      Reports      Activities


    Pay to the                          Date   3/31/91
    Order of   Washington National Bank              $ 826.84

                            Split Transaction
            Category                Description          Amount
    1:Int Paid                                           740.00
    2:[Loan]                                              56.84
    3:prop tax                                            30.00
    4:
    5:
    6:
               Enter categories, descriptions, and amounts
    Esc-Cancel    Ctrl-D Delete    F9-Recalc Transaction Total   Ctrl↵ Done


    First National                           Current Balance: $150,000.00
                                             Ending Balance:  $ 79,391.00
```

*Fig. 18.22.* *Recording a loan payment.*

For amortization loans, you should get an amortization schedule. The schedule shows the principal and interest portions of the payments you make and the loan balances after each payment. The easiest place to get an amortization schedule is from the lender. Or, if you are proficient with a spreadsheet like Lotus 1-2-3 or Microsoft Excel, you can construct your own amortization schedule.

*CPA Tip*

At the end of the year, you want to adjust for interest-principal breakdown errors. Such errors can occur for several reasons. For example, the amortization schedule shows the interest and principal components of payments assuming that you pay the same day every month, but some months you may pay earlier and incur less interest, and other months you may pay later and incur more interest.

To identify a breakdown error, compare the ending balance the lender shows on the year-end statement with what your loan register shows. After you identify the dollar size of the error, making the correction is easy. If your loan register balance is $3 too high, for example, you edit the last loan payment split transaction amounts in the checking account register so that the interest is $3 less and the loan account transfer is $3 more. To double-check, compare the ending balance in the loan account register with what the lender's annual statement shows. The two amounts should be equal.

# Chapter Summary

This chapter provided you with a basic approach to accounting for any business asset or liability, and gave specific suggestions and tips for performing seven basic accounting tasks. You now should have the information necessary to use Quicken as the basis of a business accounting system.

# 19

# Preparing for Income Taxes with Quicken

A basic accounting requirement for businesses and individuals is to complete some type of federal income tax form at the end of the year in order to report income and expenses. When using Quicken, you need to use categories that enable you to complete the appropriate income tax forms. The beginning of this chapter explains using categories for income tax forms. Some Quicken users also want to know how to export the income tax deduction data inside Quicken to external income tax preparation packages such as TurboTax. The mechanics of exporting income tax data are covered near the end of the chapter.

## Using Categories

The basic rule for performing end-of-the-year income tax forms with Quicken is that you need to use Quicken categories that are easily reconcilable with the income and expense categories shown on the actual tax forms. The most straightforward approach is to create categories for each of the income and expense lines on the income tax form you file and to use these categories to account for income and expense transactions. If you want more detail than the tax form income and expense lines provide, you can use subcategories that fall under the income and expense categories. Chapter 10 describes how to create and use categories and subcategories.

For example, real estate investors complete the Schedule E tax form (see fig. 19.1); farmers complete the Schedule F tax form (see fig. 19.2); sole proprietors complete the Schedule C tax form (see fig. 19.3); partnerships complete the Schedule 1065 tax form (see fig. 19.4); and corporations complete one of the three corporate income tax forms: 1120-A for small

| SCHEDULE E | Supplemental Income and Loss | OMB No. 1545-0074 |
|---|---|---|
| (Form 1040) | (From rents, royalties, partnerships, estates, trusts, REMICs, etc.) | **1989** |
| Department of the Treasury<br>Internal Revenue Service | ▶ Attach to Form 1040 or Form 1041.<br>▶ See Instructions for Schedule E (Form 1040). | Attachment<br>Sequence No. **13** |

Name(s) shown on return | Your social security number

**Part I** Income or Loss From Rentals and Royalties  **Caution:** *Your rental loss may be limited. See Instructions.*

1 Show the kind and location of **rental property:**

A .......................................................................

B .......................................................................

C .......................................................................

2 For each rental property listed on line 1, did you or your family use it for personal purposes for more than the greater of 14 days or 10% of the total days rented at fair rental value during the tax year?

|   | Yes | No |
|---|---|---|
| A |   |   |
| B |   |   |
| C |   |   |

3 For each **rental real estate property** listed on line 1, did you actively participate in its operation during the tax year? (See Instructions.)

|   |   |   |
|---|---|---|
| A |   |   |
| B |   |   |
| C |   |   |

| Rental and Royalty Income: | | Properties | | | D Totals |
|---|---|---|---|---|---|
| | | A | B | C | (Add columns A, B, and C) |
| 4 Rents received | 4 | | | | 4 |
| 5 Royalties received | 5 | | | | 5 |
| **Rental and Royalty Expenses:** | | | | | |
| 6 Advertising | 6 | | | | |
| 7 Auto and travel | 7 | | | | |
| 8 Cleaning and maintenance | 8 | | | | |
| 9 Commissions | 9 | | | | |
| 10 Insurance | 10 | | | | |
| 11 Legal and other professional fees | 11 | | | | |
| 12 Mortgage interest paid to banks, etc. (see Instructions) | 12 | | | | 12 |
| 13 Other interest | 13 | | | | |
| 14 Repairs | 14 | | | | |
| 15 Supplies | 15 | | | | |
| 16 Taxes | 16 | | | | |
| 17 Utilities (see Instructions) | 17 | | | | |
| 18 Wages and salaries | 18 | | | | |
| 19 Other (list) ▶ ................................ | 19 | | | | |
| 20 Add lines 6 through 19 | 20 | | | | 20 |
| 21 Depreciation expense or depletion (see Instructions) | 21 | | | | 21 |
| 22 Total expenses. Add lines 20 and 21 | 22 | | | | |
| 23 Income or (loss) from rental or royalty properties. Subtract line 22 from line 4 (rents) or line 5 (royalties). If the result is a (loss), see Instructions to find out if you must file **Form 6198** | 23 | | | | |
| 24 Deductible rental loss. **Caution:** *Your rental loss on line 23 may be limited. See Instructions to find out if you must file **Form 8582*** | 24 | ( ) ( | ) ( | ) ( | ) |

25 **Income.** Add rental and royalty income from line 23. Enter the total income here . . . . . . . . | 25 |
26 **Losses.** Add royalty losses from line 23 and rental losses from line 24. Enter the total losses here . . . | 26 | ( ) |

27 Combine amounts on lines 25 and 26. Enter the net income or (loss) here . . . . . . . . . . . . | 27 |
28 Net farm rental income or (loss) from Form 4835. (Also complete line 43 on page 2.) . . . . . . | 28 |
29 Total rental and royalty income or (loss). Combine amounts on lines 27 and 28. Enter the result here. If Parts II, III, and IV on page 2 do not apply to you, enter the amount from line 29 on Form 1040, line 18. Otherwise, include the amount from line 29 in the total on line 42 on page 2 . . . . . . . . . . | 29 |

For Paperwork Reduction Act Notice, see Form 1040 Instructions. | Schedule E (Form 1040) 1989

*Fig. 19.1. The Schedule E form indicates the general income and expense categories real estate investors use to report profits and losses.*

corporations (see fig. 19.5), 1120S for S corporations (see fig. 19.6), and 1120 for all other corporations (see fig. 19.7).

Schedule E (Form 1040) 1989     Attachment Sequence No. **13**     Page **2**

Name(s) shown on return. (Do not enter name and social security number if shown on other side.)     **Your social security number**

**Note:** *If you report amounts from farming or fishing on Schedule E, you must include your gross income from those activities on line 43 below.*

**Part II**   **Income or Loss From Partnerships and S Corporations**

If you report a loss from an at-risk activity, you MUST check either column **(e)** or **(f)** to describe your investment in the activity. See Instructions. If you check column **(f)**, you must attach **Form 6198.**

| 30     **(a)** Name | **(b)** Enter P for partnership; S for S corporation | **(c)** Check if foreign partnership | **(d)** Employer identification number | **Investment At Risk?** **(e)** All is at risk | **(f)** Some is not at risk |
|---|---|---|---|---|---|
| A | | | | | |
| B | | | | | |
| C | | | | | |
| D | | | | | |
| E | | | | | |

| | **Passive Income and Loss** | | **Nonpassive Income and Loss** | | |
|---|---|---|---|---|---|
| | **(g)** Passive loss allowed from Form 8582 | **(h)** Passive income from Schedule K–1 | **(i)** Nonpassive loss from Schedule K–1 | **(j)** Section 179 deduction (see Instructions for limits) | **(k)** Nonpassive income from Schedule K–1 |
| A | | | | | |
| B | | | | | |
| C | | | | | |
| D | | | | | |
| E | | | | | |
| **31a** Totals | | | | | |
| **b** Totals | | | | | |

| | | |
|---|---|---|
| **32** Add amounts in columns (h) and (k) of line 31a. Enter the total income here . . . . . . . . . | **32** | |
| **33** Add amounts in columns (g), (i), and (j) of line 31b. Enter the total here . . . . . . . . . | **33** (     ) |
| **34** Total partnership and S corporation income or (loss). Combine amounts on lines 32 and 33. Enter the result here and include in the total on line 42 below . . . . . . . . . . . . . . . . . . | **34** | |

**Part III**   **Income or Loss From Estates and Trusts**

| 35     **(a)** Name | **(b)** Employer identification number |
|---|---|
| A | |
| B | |
| C | |

| | **Passive Income and Loss** | | **Nonpassive Income and Loss** | |
|---|---|---|---|---|
| | **(c)** Passive deduction or loss allowed from Form 8582 | **(d)** Passive income from Schedule K–1 | **(e)** Deduction or loss from Schedule K–1 | **(f)** Other income from Schedule K–1 |
| A | | | | |
| B | | | | |
| C | | | | |
| **36a** Totals | | | | |
| **b** Totals | | | | |

| | | |
|---|---|---|
| **37** Add amounts in columns (d) and (f) of line 36a. Enter the total income here . . . . . . . . | **37** | |
| **38** Add amounts in columns (c) and (e) of line 36b. Enter the total here . . . . . . . . . | **38** (     ) |
| **39** Total estate and trust income or (loss). Combine amounts on lines 37 and 38. Enter the result here and include in the total on line 42 below . . . . . . . . . . . . . . . . . . | **39** | |

**Part IV**   **Income or Loss From Real Estate Mortgage Investment Conduits (REMICs)—Residual Holder**

| 40     **(a)** Name | **(b)** Employer identification number | **(c)** Excess inclusion from Schedules Q, line 2c (see Instructions) | **(d)** Taxable income (net loss) from Schedules Q, line 1b | **(e)** Income from Schedules Q, line 3b |
|---|---|---|---|---|
| | | | | |

| | |
|---|---|
| **41** Combine amounts in columns (d) and (e) only. Enter the result here and include in the total on line 42 below. . . . . . . . . . . . . . . . . . . | **41** |

**Part V**   **Summary of Parts I Through IV**

| | |
|---|---|
| **42** TOTAL income or (loss). Combine amounts on lines 29, 34, 39, and 41. Enter the result here and on Form 1040, line 18 . . . . . . . . . . . . . . . . . . ▶ | **42** |

**Part VI**   **Reconciliation of Farming and Fishing Income**

| | | |
|---|---|---|
| **43** Farmers and fishermen: Enter your **gross** farming and fishing income reported in Parts I, II, and III (see Instructions) . . . . . . . . . | **43** | |

***Fig. 19.1.*** *Continued Schedule E, Form 1040.*

If you live in a state with income taxes, you also may have an equivalent state income tax form. Make sure that you or your accountant can prepare

| SCHEDULE F (Form 1040) | **Farm Income and Expenses** | OMB No. 1545-0074 |
| --- | --- | --- |
| Department of the Treasury Internal Revenue Service | ► Attach to Form 1040, Form 1041, or Form 1065.<br>► See Instructions for Schedule F (Form 1040). | **1989** Attachment Sequence No. **14** |

| Name of proprietor | | Social security number (SSN) |
| --- | --- | --- |

| **A** Principal product. (Describe in one or two words your principal crop or activity for the current tax year.) | **B** Agricultural activity code (from Part IV) ► |
| --- | --- |

| **C** Accounting method: ☐ Cash ☐ Accrual | **D** Employer ID number (Not SSN) |
| --- | --- |

**E** Did you make an election in a prior year to include Commodity Credit Corporation loan proceeds as income in that year? . ☐ Yes ☐ No

**F** Did you "materially participate" in the operation of this business during 1989? (If "No," see Instructions for limitations on losses.) ☐ Yes ☐ No

**G** Do you elect, or did you previously elect, to currently deduct certain preproductive period expenses? (See Instructions.) ☐ Does not apply ☐ Yes ☐ No
If you choose to revoke a prior election for animals, see the Instructions.

**Part I** Farm Income—Cash Method—Complete Parts I and II (Accrual method taxpayers complete Parts II and III, and line 11 of Part I.)
Do not include sales of livestock held for draft, breeding, sport, or dairy purposes; report these sales on Form 4797.

| | | | |
| --- | --- | --- | --- |
| 1 | Sales of livestock and other items you bought for resale . . . . | **1** | |
| 2 | Cost or other basis of livestock and other items you bought for resale . | **2** | |
| 3 | Subtract line 2 from line 1 . . . . . . . . . . . . . . . | **3** | |
| 4 | Sales of livestock, produce, grains, and other products you raised . . . | **4** | |
| 5a | Total cooperative distributions (Form(s) 1099-PATR) **5a** | 5b Taxable amount | **5b** |
| 6a | Agricultural program payments (see Instructions) **6a** | 6b Taxable amount | **6b** |
| 7 | Commodity Credit Corporation (CCC) loans: | | |
| a | CCC loans reported under election (see Instructions) . . . . . | | **7a** |
| b | CCC loans forfeited or repaid with certificates . **7b** | 7c Taxable amount | **7c** |
| 8 | Crop insurance proceeds and certain disaster payments (see Instructions): | | |
| a | Amount received in 1989 . . . . . **8a** | 8b Taxable amount | **8b** |
| c | If election to defer to 1990 is attached, check here ► ☐ | 8d Amount deferred from 1988 . | **8d** |
| 9 | Custom hire (machine work) income . . . . . . . . . . . . | **9** | |
| 10 | Other income, including Federal and state gasoline or fuel tax credit or refund (see Instructions) . . | **10** | |
| 11 | Add amounts in the right column for lines 3 through 10. If accrual method taxpayer, enter the amount from page 2, line 51. This is your **gross income** . . . . . . . . . ► | **11** | |

**Part II** Farm Expenses—Cash and Accrual Method (Do not include personal or living expenses such as taxes, insurance, repairs, etc., on your home.)

| | | | | | |
| --- | --- | --- | --- | --- | --- |
| 12 | Breeding fees . . . . . | **12** | 24 | Labor hired (less jobs credit) . | **24** |
| 13 | Chemicals . . . . . . | **13** | 25 | Pension and profit-sharing plans | **25** |
| 14 | Conservation expenses (you must attach **Form 8645**) | **14** | 26 | Rent or lease: | |
| | | | a | Machinery and equipment . | **26a** |
| 15 | Custom hire (machine work) | **15** | b | Other (land, animals, etc.) . | **26b** |
| 16 | Depreciation and section 179 deduction not claimed elsewhere (from **Form 4562**) | **16** | 27 | Repairs and maintenance . . | **27** |
| | | | 28 | Seeds and plants purchased . | **28** |
| | | | 29 | Storage and warehousing . . | **29** |
| 17 | Employee benefit programs other than on line 25 . . | **17** | 30 | Supplies purchased . . . . | **30** |
| | | | 31 | Taxes . . . . . . . | **31** |
| 18 | Feed purchased . . . . | **18** | 32 | Utilities (see Instructions) . . | **32** |
| 19 | Fertilizers and lime . . . | **19** | 33 | Veterinary fees and medicine . | **33** |
| 20 | Freight and trucking . . . | **20** | 34 | Other expenses (specify): | |
| 21 | Gasoline, fuel, and oil . . . | **21** | a | _____ | **34a** |
| 22 | Insurance (other than health) . | **22** | b | _____ | **34b** |
| 23 | Interest: | | c | _____ | **34c** |
| a | Mortgage (paid to banks, etc.) . | **23a** | d | _____ | **34d** |
| b | Other . . . . . . . | **23b** | e | _____ | **34e** |

| | | |
| --- | --- | --- |
| 35 | Add amounts on lines 12 through 34e. These are your **total expenses** . . . . . . . . . ► | **35** |
| 36 | **Net farm profit or (loss).** Subtract line 35 from line 11. If a profit, enter on Form 1040, line 19, and on Schedule SE, line 1. If a loss, you MUST go on to line 37. (Fiduciaries and partnerships, see Instructions.) | **36** |
| 37 | If you have a loss, you MUST check the box that describes your investment in this activity (see Instructions). } **37a** ☐ All investment is at risk. If you checked 37a, enter the loss on Form 1040, line 19, and Schedule SE, line 1. **37b** ☐ Some investment is not at risk. If you checked 37b, you MUST attach **Form 6198**. | |

For Paperwork Reduction Act Notice, see Form 1040 Instructions.                    Schedule F (Form 1040) 1989

*Fig. 19.2. The Schedule F form indicates the general income and expense categories farmers use to report profits and losses.*

your tax return easily with the information Quicken produces. (The more time your accountant takes, the more money you pay to have your return prepared.)

You also can work with categories that you need to combine with other categories to calculate a tax form entry. Suppose that you are a sole pro-

---

Schedule F (Form 1040) 1989                                                                                            Page **2**

**Part III   Farm Income—Accrual Method**
Do not include sales of livestock held for draft, breeding, sport, or dairy purposes; report these sales on Form 4797 and do not include this livestock on line 46 below.

| | | | |
|---|---|---|---|
| 38 | Sales of livestock, produce, grains, and other products during year . . . . . . . . | 38 | |
| 39a | Total cooperative distributions (Form(s) 1099-PATR) `39a` _____ 39b Taxable amount | 39b | |
| 40a | Agricultural program payments (see Instructions) `40a` _____ 40b Taxable amount | 40b | |
| 41 | Commodity Credit Corporation (CCC) loans: | | |
| a | CCC loans reported under election (see Instructions) . . . . . . . . . . . | 41a | |
| b | CCC loans forfeited or repaid with certificates `41b` _____ 41c Taxable amount | 41c | |
| 42 | Crop insurance proceeds . . . . . . . . . . . . . . . | 42 | |
| 43 | Custom hire (machine work) income . . . . . . . . . . . | 43 | |
| 44 | Other income, including Federal and state gasoline or fuel tax credit or refund (see Instructions) . . . | 44 | |
| 45 | Add amounts in the right column for lines 38 through 44 . . . . . . . . | 45 | |

| | | | |
|---|---|---|---|
| 46 | Inventory of livestock, produce, grains, and other products at beginning of year . . . . . . . | 46 | |
| 47 | Cost of livestock, produce, grains, and other products purchased during year . . . . . . . | 47 | |
| 48 | Add lines 46 and 47 | 48 | |
| 49 | Inventory of livestock, produce, grains, and other products at end of year | 49 | |
| 50 | Cost of livestock, produce, grains, and other products sold. Subtract line 49 from line 48* . . . . . | 50 | |
| 51 | Subtract line 50 from line 45. Enter the result here and on page 1, line 11. This is your **gross income** ▶ | 51 | |

*If you use the unit-livestock-price method or the farm-price method of valuing inventory and the amount on line 49 is larger than the amount on line 48, subtract line 48 from line 49. Enter the result on line 50. Add lines 45 and 50. Enter the total on line 51.

**Part IV   Principal Agricultural Activity Codes**

Select one of the following codes and write the 3-digit number on page 1, line B. (**Note:** *If your principal source of income is from providing agricultural services such as soil preparation, veterinary, farm labor, horticultural, or management for a fee or on a contract basis, you should file* **Schedule C** *(Form 1040), Profit or Loss From Business.*)

| | |
|---|---|
| 120 | **Field crop,** including grains and nongrains such as cotton, peanuts, feed corn, wheat, tobacco, Irish potatoes, etc. |
| 160 | **Vegetables and melons,** garden-type vegetables and melons, such as sweet corn, tomatoes, squash, etc. |
| 170 | **Fruit and tree nuts,** including grapes, berries, olives, etc. |
| 180 | **Ornamental floriculture and nursery products** |
| 185 | **Food crops grown under cover,** including hydroponic crops |

| | |
|---|---|
| 211 | **Beefcattle feedlots** |
| 212 | **Beefcattle,** except feedlots |
| 215 | **Hogs, sheep, and goats** |
| 240 | **Dairy** |
| 250 | **Poultry and eggs,** including chickens, ducks, pigeons, quail, etc. |
| 260 | **General livestock,** not specializing in any one livestock category |
| 270 | **Animal specialty,** including fur-bearing animals, pets, horses, etc. |
| 280 | **Animal aquaculture,** including fish, shellfish, mollusks, frogs, etc., produced within confined space |
| 290 | **Forest products,** including forest nurseries and seed gathering, extraction of pine gum, and gathering of forest products |
| 300 | **Agricultural production,** not specified |

---

*Fig. 19.2. Continued Schedule F, Form 1040.*

prietor and own a restaurant. Although total wages goes on one line of the Schedule C tax form, you may want to track several categories of wages, including waitresses, dishwashers, cooks, bartenders, and so on. In this

| SCHEDULE C<br>(Form 1040)<br><br>Department of the Treasury<br>Internal Revenue Service | **Profit or Loss From Business**<br>(Sole Proprietorship)<br>Partnerships, Joint Ventures, Etc., Must File Form 1065.<br>▶ Attach to Form 1040 or Form 1041.　▶ See Instructions for Schedule C (Form 1040). | OMB No 1545-0074<br>**1989**<br>Attachment<br>Sequence No. 09 |
|---|---|---|

Name of proprietor | Social security number (SSN)

**A** Principal business or profession, including product or service (see Instructions) | **B** Principal business code<br>(from page 2) ▶

**C** Business name and address ▶ ................................................................... | **D** Employer ID number (Not SSN)

**E** Method(s) used to value closing inventory.　(1) ☐ Cost　(2) ☐ Lower of cost or market　(3) ☐ Other (attach explanation).　(4) ☐ Does not apply (if checked, skip line G)

**F** Accounting method:　(1) ☐ Cash　(2) ☐ Accrual　(3) ☐ Other (specify) ▶ ........................................ | Yes | No

**G** Was there any change in determining quantities, costs, or valuations between opening and closing inventory? (If "Yes," attach explanation.)

**H** Are you deducting expenses for business use of your home? (If "Yes," see Instructions for limitations.)

**I** Did you "materially participate" in the operation of this business during 1989? (If "No," see Instructions for limitations on losses.)

**J** If this schedule includes a loss, credit, deduction, income, or other tax benefit relating to a tax shelter required to be registered, check here. ▶ ☐<br>If you checked this box, you MUST attach **Form 8271.**

**Part I　Income**

| 1 | Gross receipts or sales . . . . . . . . . | 1 | |
| 2 | Returns and allowances . . . . . . . . . | 2 | |
| 3 | Subtract line 2 from line 1. Enter the result here | | 3 |
| 4 | Cost of goods sold and/or operations (from line 39 on page 2) | | 4 |
| 5 | Subtract line 4 from line 3 and enter the **gross profit** here | | 5 |
| 6 | Other income, including Federal and state gasoline or fuel tax credit or refund (see Instructions) | | 6 |
| 7 | Add lines 5 and 6. This is your **gross income** . . . . . . . . . . ▶ | | 7 |

**Part II　Expenses**

| 8 | Advertising . . . . . . . | 8 | | 22 | Repairs . . . . . . . . | 22 | |
| 9 | Bad debts from sales or services (see Instructions) . . . . | 9 | | 23 | Supplies (not included in Part III) | 23 | |
| 10 | Car and truck expenses . . . . | 10 | | 24 | Taxes . . . . . . . . | 24 | |
| 11 | Commissions . . . . . . | 11 | | 25 | Travel, meals, and entertainment: | | |
| 12 | Depletion . . . . . . . | 12 | | **a** | Travel . . . . . . . | 25a | |
| 13 | Depreciation and section 179 deduction from **Form 4562** (not included in Part III) . . . . | 13 | | **b** | Meals and entertainment . . . | | |
| 14 | Employee benefit programs (other than on line 20) . . . . . | 14 | | **c** | Enter 20% of line 25b subject to limitations (see Instructions) . | | |
| 15 | Freight (not included in Part III) . | 15 | | **d** | Subtract line 25c from line 25b | 25d | |
| 16 | Insurance (other than health) . . | 16 | | 26 | Utilities (see Instructions) . . . | 26 | |
| 17 | Interest: | | | 27 | Wages (less jobs credit) . . . | 27 | |
| **a** | Mortgage (paid to banks, etc.) . | 17a | | 28 | Other expenses (list type and amount): | | |
| **b** | Other . . . . . . . . | 17b | | | .................................. | | |
| 18 | Legal and professional services . | 18 | | | .................................. | | |
| 19 | Office expense. . . . . . | 19 | | | .................................. | | |
| 20 | Pension and profit-sharing plans . | 20 | | | .................................. | | |
| 21 | Rent or lease: | | | | .................................. | | |
| **a** | Machinery and equipment . . . | 21a | | | .................................. | | |
| **b** | Other business property . . . | 21b | | | | 28 | |

| 29 | Add amounts in columns for lines 8 through 28. These are your **total expenses** . . . . . . . . . . ▶ | | 29 |
| 30 | **Net profit or (loss).** Subtract line 29 from line 7. If a profit, enter here and on Form 1040, line 12, and on Schedule SE, line 2. If a loss, you MUST go on to line 31. (Fiduciaries, see Instructions.) . . . . | | 30 |
| 31 | If you have a loss, you MUST check the box that describes your investment in this activity (see Instructions) . . . . | 31a ☐ All investment is at risk.<br>31b ☐ Some investment is not at risk. |

If you checked 31a, enter the loss on Form 1040, line 12, and Schedule SE, line 2.<br>If you checked 31b, you MUST attach **Form 6198.**

For Paperwork Reduction Act Notice, see Form 1040 Instructions. | Schedule C (Form 1040) 1989

***Fig. 19.3.*** *The Schedule C form indicates which income and expense categories sole proprietors use to report profits and losses.*

case, you actually have several wage categories that must be added to calculate the wages amount that goes on the tax form.

Schedule C (Form 1040) 1989        Page **2**

**Part III**   **Cost of Goods Sold and/or Operations** (See Instructions.)

| | |
|---|---|
| 32   Inventory at beginning of year. (If different from last year's closing inventory, attach explanation.) . . . . . | **32** |
| 33   Purchases less cost of items withdrawn for personal use . . . . . . . . . . . | **33** |
| 34   Cost of labor. (Do not include salary paid to yourself.) . . . . . . . . . . | **34** |
| 35   Materials and supplies . . . . . . . . . . . . . . . . | **35** |
| 36   Other costs . . . . . . . . . . . . . . . . . . | **36** |
| 37   Add lines 32 through 36 . . . . . . . . . . . . . . | **37** |
| 38   Inventory at end of year . . . . . . . . . . . . . . | **38** |
| 39   **Cost of goods sold and/or operations.** Subtract line 38 from line 37. Enter the result here and on page 1, line 4 | **39** |

**Part IV**   **Principal Business or Professional Activity Codes**   (**Caution:** Codes have been revised. Check your code carefully.)

Locate the major business category that best describes your activity (for example, Retail Trade, Services, etc.). Within the major category, select the activity code that most closely identifies the business or profession that is the principal source of your sales or receipts. **Enter this 4-digit code on page 1, line B.** (**Note:** If your principal source of income is from farming activities, you should file **Schedule F** (Form 1040), Farm Income and Expenses.)

### Construction

Code
0018   Operative builders (for own account)

**General contractors**
0034   Residential building
0059   Nonresidential building
0075   Highway and street construction
3889   Other heavy construction (pipe laying, bridge construction, etc.)

**Building trade contractors, including repairs**
0232   Plumbing, heating, air conditioning
0257   Painting and paper hanging
0273   Electrical work
0299   Masonry, dry wall, stone, tile
0414   Carpentering and flooring
0430   Roofing, siding, and sheet metal
0455   Concrete work
0885   Other building trade contractors (excavation, glazing, etc.)

### Manufacturing, Including Printing and Publishing
0638   Food products and beverages
0653   Textile mill products
0679   Apparel and other textile products
0695   Leather, footware, handbags, etc.
0810   Furniture and fixtures
0836   Lumber and other wood products
0851   Printing and publishing
0877   Paper and allied products
1032   Stone, clay, and glass products
1057   Primary metal industries
1073   Fabricated metal products
1099   Machinery and machine shops
1115   Electric and electronic equipment
1883   Other manufacturing industries

### Mining and Mineral Extraction
1511   Metal mining
1537   Coal mining
1552   Oil and gas
1719   Quarrying and nonmetallic mining

### Agricultural Services, Forestry, Fishing
1933   Crop services
1958   Veterinary services, including pets
1974   Livestock breeding
1990   Other animal services
2113   Farm labor and management services
2212   Horticulture and landscaping
2238   Forestry, except logging
0836   Logging
2246   Commercial fishing
2469   Hunting and trapping

### Wholesale Trade—Selling Goods to Other Businesses, Etc.
**Durable goods, including machinery, equipment, wood, metals, etc.**
2618   Selling for your own account
2634   Agent or broker for other firms—more than 50% of gross sales on commission

**Nondurable goods, including food, fiber, chemicals, etc.**
2659   Selling for your own account

2675   Agent or broker for other firms—more than 50% of gross sales on commission

### Retail Trade—Selling Goods to Individuals and Households
3012   Selling door-to-door, by telephone or party plan, or from mobile unit
3038   Catalog or mail order
3053   Vending machine selling

**Selling From Showroom, Store, or Other Fixed Location**
**Food, beverages, and drugs**
3079   Eating places (meals or snacks)
3086   Catering services
3095   Drinking places (alcoholic beverages)
3210   Grocery stores (general line)
0612   Bakeries selling at retail
3236   Other food stores (meat, produce, candy, etc.)
3251   Liquor stores
3277   Drug stores

**Automotive and service stations**
3319   New car dealers (franchised)
3335   Used car dealers
3517   Other automotive dealers (motorcycles, recreational vehicles, etc.)
3533   Tires, accessories, and parts
3558   Gasoline service stations

**General merchandise, apparel, and furniture**
3715   Variety stores
3731   Other general merchandise stores
3756   Shoe stores
3772   Men's and boys' clothing stores
3913   Women's ready-to-wear stores
3939   Women's accessory and specialty stores and furriers
3939   Family clothing stores
3954   Other apparel and accessory stores
3970   Furniture stores
3996   TV, audio, and electronics
3988   Computer and software stores
4119   Household appliance stores
4317   Other home furnishing stores (china, floor coverings, etc.)
4333   Music and record stores

**Building, hardware, and garden supply**
4416   Building materials dealers
4432   Paint, glass, and wallpaper stores
4457   Hardware stores
4473   Nurseries and garden supply stores

**Other retail stores**
4614   Used merchandise and antique stores (except motor vehicle parts)
4630   Gift, novelty, and souvenir shops
4655   Florists
4671   Jewelry stores
4697   Sporting goods and bicycle shops
4812   Boat dealers
4838   Hobby, toy, and game shops
4853   Camera and photo supply stores
4879   Optical goods stores
4895   Luggage and leather goods stores
5017   Book stores, excluding newsstands
5033   Stationery stores
5058   Fabric and needlework stores
5074   Mobile home dealers
5090   Fuel dealers (except gasoline)
5884   Other retail stores

### Finance, Insurance, Real Estate, and Related Services
5520   Real estate agents or brokers
5579   Real estate property managers
5710   Subdividers and developers, except cemeteries
5538   Operators and lessors of buildings, including residential
5553   Operators and lessors of other real property
5702   Insurance agents or brokers
5744   Other insurance services
6064   Security brokers and dealers
6080   Commodity contracts brokers and dealers, and security and commodity exchanges
6130   Investment advisors and services
6148   Credit institutions and mortgage bankers
6155   Title abstract offices
5777   Other finance and real estate

### Transportation, Communications, Public Utilities, and Related Services
6114   Taxicabs
6312   Bus and limousine transportation
6361   Other highway passenger transportation
6338   Trucking (except trash collection)
6395   Courier or package delivery services
6510   Trash collection without own dump
6536   Public warehousing
6551   Water transportation
6619   Air transportation
6635   Travel agents and tour operators
6650   Other transportation services
6676   Communication services
6692   Utilities, including dumps, snowplowing, road cleaning, etc.

### Services (Personal, Professional, and Business Services)
**Hotels and other lodging places**
7096   Hotels, motels, and tourist homes
7211   Rooming and boarding houses
7237   Camps and camping parks

**Laundry and cleaning services**
7419   Coin-operated laundries and dry cleaning
7435   Other laundry, dry cleaning, and garment services
7450   Carpet and upholstery cleaning
7476   Janitorial and related services (building, house, and window cleaning)

**Business and/or personal services**
7617   Legal services (or lawyer)
7633   Income tax preparation
7658   Accounting and bookkeeping
7518   Engineering services
7682   Architectural services
7708   Surveying services
7245   Management services
7260   Public relations
7286   Consulting services
7716   Advertising, except direct mail
7732   Employment agencies and personnel supply
7799   Consumer credit reporting and collection services

7856   Mailing, reproduction, commercial art and photography, and stenographic services
7872   Computer programming, processing, data preparation, and related services
7922   Computer repair, maintenance, and leasing
7773   Equipment rental and leasing (except computer or automotive)
7914   Investigative and protective services
7880   Other business services

**Personal services**
8110   Beauty shops (or beautician)
8318   Barber shop (or barber)
8334   Photographic portrait studios
8532   Funeral services and crematories
8714   Child day care
8730   Teaching or tutoring
8755   Counseling (except health practitioners)
8771   Ministers and chaplains
6882   Other personal services

**Automotive services**
8813   Automotive rental or leasing, without driver
8839   Parking, except valet
8953   Automotive repairs, general and specialized
8896   Other automotive services (wash, towing, etc.)

**Miscellaneous repair, except computers**
9019   TV and audio equipment repair
9035   Other electrical equipment repair
9050   Reupholstery and furniture repair
2881   Other equipment repair

**Medical and health services**
9217   Offices and clinics of medical doctors (MDs)
9233   Offices and clinics of dentists
9258   Osteopathic physicians and surgeons
9241   Podiatrists
9274   Chiropractors
9290   Optometrists
9415   Registered and practical nurses
9431   Other health practitioners
9456   Medical and dental laboratories
9472   Nursing and personal care facilities
9886   Other health services

**Amusement and recreational services**
8557   Physical fitness facilities
9597   Motion picture and video production
9688   Motion picture and tape distribution and allied services
9613   Videotape rental
9639   Motion picture theaters
9670   Bowling centers
9696   Professional sports and racing, including promoters and managers
9811   Theatrical performers, musicians, agents, producers, and related services
9837   Other amusement and recreational services

8888   Unable to classify

*Fig. 19.3. Continued Schedule C, Form 1040.*

If you are using Quicken for a sole proprietorship and you hold and resell inventory, you need Part III of the Schedule C form to calculate your cost of goods sold and your inventory balances (see fig. 19.3). You can use the

| Form **1065** | **U.S. Partnership Return of Income** | | OMB No. 1545 0099 |
|---|---|---|---|
| Department of the Treasury Internal Revenue Service | ► See separate Instructions. For calendar year 1989, or fiscal year beginning _____, 1989, and ending _____ , 19 ___ | | **1989** |

| A Principal business activity | Name | | D Employer identification number |
|---|---|---|---|
| Retail | 10-9876543          DEC89          D71 | | 10 - 9876543 |
| B Principal product or service | AbleBee Book Store | I | E Date business started |
| Books | 334 WEST MAIN STREET | R | 10/1/78 |
| C Business code number | ANYTOWN     MD          20904 | S | F Total assets (see Specific Instructions) |
| 5942 | | | $     45,691 |

G Check applicable boxes: (1) ☐ Initial return     (2) ☐ Final return     (3) ☐ Change in address     (4) ☐ Amended return

H Enter number of partners in this partnership . . . . . . . . . . . . . . . . . . ► _____ 2 _____

I Check this box if this is a limited partnership . . . . . . . . . . . . . . . . . . . . . . . ► ☐

J Check this box if any partners in the partnership are also partnerships . . . . . . . . . . . . . . ► ☐

K Check this box if this partnership is a partner in another partnership . . . . . . . . . . . . . . ► ☐

See page 4, items L through T, for Additional Information Required.

**Designation of Tax Matters Partner** (See instructions.)

Enter below the general partner designated as the tax matters partner (TMP) for the tax year of this return:

Name of designated TMP ► _____

Identifying number of TMP ► _____

Address of designated TMP ► _____

**Caution:** *Include only trade or business income and expenses on lines 1a–21 below. See the instructions for more information.*

| | | | | |
|---|---|---|---|---|
| **Income** | 1a Gross receipts or sales . . . . . . . . . | 1a | 409,465 | |
| | b Less returns and allowances . . . . . . . . . | 1b | 3,365 | 1c    406,100 |
| | 2 Cost of goods sold and/or operations (Schedule A, line 7) . . . . . | | | 2    267,641 |
| | 3 Gross profit (subtract line 2 from line 1c) . . . . . . . . | | | 3    138,459 |
| | 4 Ordinary income (loss) from other partnerships and fiduciaries (attach schedule) . . | | | 4 |
| | 5 Net farm profit (loss) (attach Schedule F (Form 1040)) . . . . . | | | 5 |
| | 6 Net gain (loss) (Form 4797, Part II, line 18) . . . . . . . | | | 6 |
| | 7 Other income (loss) . . . . . . . . . . . | | | 7    559 |
| | 8 Total income (loss) (combine lines 3 through 7) . . . . . . | | | 8    139,018 |
| **Deductions (see instructions for limitations)** | 9a Salaries and wages (other than to partners) . . . . . . | 9a | 29,350 | |
| | b Less jobs credit . . . . . . . . . . . | 9b | | 9c    29,350 |
| | 10 Guaranteed payments to partners . . . . . . . . | | | 10    25,000 |
| | 11 Rent . . . . . . . . . . . . . . . | | | 11    18,000 |
| | 12 Interest (see instructions) . . . . . . . . . . | | | 12    451 |
| | 13 Taxes . . . . . . . . . . . . . . | | | 13    350 |
| | 14 Bad debts . . . . . . . . . . . . . | | | 14    250 |
| | 15 Repairs . . . . . . . . . . . . . . | | | 15    1,125 |
| | 16a Depreciation (attach Form 4562) (see instructions) . . . | 16a | 1,174 | |
| | b Less depreciation reported on Schedule A and elsewhere on return | 16b | | 16c    1,174 |
| | 17 Depletion (**Do not deduct oil and gas depletion.**) . . . . | | | 17 |
| | 18a Retirement plans, etc. . . . . . . . . . . | | | 18a |
| | b Employee benefit programs . . . . . . . . . | | | 18b |
| | 19 Other deductions (attach schedule) . . . . . . . . | | | 19    13,948 |
| | 20 Total deductions (add lines 9c through 19) . . . . . . | | | 20    89,648 |
| | 21 Ordinary income (loss) from trade or business activities (subtract line 20 from line 8) . . . | | | 21    49,370 |

**Please Sign Here** ► Under penalties of perjury, I declare that I have examined this return, including accompanying schedules and statements, and to the best of my knowledge and belief, it is true, correct, and complete. Declaration of preparer (other than general partner) is based on all information of which preparer has any knowledge.

► *Frank W. Able*
Signature of general partner

► 4/3/90
Date

| **Paid Preparer's Use Only** | Preparer's signature ► | Date | Check if self-employed ► ☐ | Preparer's social security no. |
|---|---|---|---|---|
| | Firm's name (or yours if self employed) and address ► | | E.I. No. ► | |
| | | | ZIP code ► | |

For Paperwork Reduction Act Notice, see page 1 of separate instructions.          Form **1065** (1989)

***Fig. 19.4.*** *The 1065 form indicates which income and expense categories partnerships use to report profits and losses.*

periodic inventory approach described in Chapter 18 to produce the information for Part III of the Schedule C form.

If you are using Quicken for a partnership or a corporation, you must report asset and liability amounts on the tax return (see figs. 19.4 through 19.7). You also want to verify that Quicken provides the raw data neces-

---

Form 1065 (1989)                                                                                              Page 2

**Schedule A   Cost of Goods Sold and/or Operations**

| | | |
|---|---|---|
| 1  Inventory at beginning of year . . . . . . . . . . . . . . . . . . . . . . . . | 1 | 18,125 |
| 2  Purchases less cost of items withdrawn for personal use . . . . . . . . . . . . . . . . . | 2 | 268,741 |
| 3  Cost of labor . . . . . . . . . . . . . . . . . . . . . . . . . . . . | 3 | |
| 4a Additional section 263A costs (see instructions—attach schedule) . . . . . . . . . | 4a | |
| b  Other costs (attach schedule) . . . . . . . . . . . . . . . . . . . . . . . | 4b | |
| 5  Total (add lines 1 through 4b) . . . . . . . . . . . . . . . . . . . . . | 5 | 286,866 |
| 6  Inventory at end of year . . . . . . . . . . . . . . . . . . . . . . . . | 6 | 19,225 |
| 7  Cost of goods sold (subtract line 6 from line 5). Enter here and on page 1, line 2 . . . . . . . . | 7 | 267,641 |

8a Check all methods used for valuing closing inventory:
   (i)  ☐ Cost
   (ii)  ☑ Lower of cost or market as described in Regulations section 1.471-4
   (iii)  ☐ Writedown of "subnormal" goods as described in Regulations section 1.471-2(c)
   (iv)  ☐ Other (specify method used and attach explanation) ▶ ............................................. ▶ ☐
   b  Check if the LIFO inventory method was adopted this tax year for any goods (if checked, attach Form 970) . . . . . . . ▶ ☐
   c  Do the rules of section 263A (with respect to property produced or acquired for resale) apply to the partnership? . . ☐ Yes  ☑ No
   d  Was there any change in determining quantities, cost, or valuations between opening and closing inventory? . . . . ☐ Yes  ☑ No
     If "Yes," attach explanation.

**Schedule H   Income (Loss) From Rental Real Estate Activities**

1  In the space provided below, show the kind and location of each rental property. Attach a schedule if more space is needed.
   Property A ...............................................................................................................
   Property B ...............................................................................................................
   Property C ...............................................................................................................

| Rental Real Estate Income | | Properties | | | Totals (add columns A, B, C, and amounts from any attached schedules) |
|---|---|---|---|---|---|
| | | A | B | C | |
| 2  Gross income . . . . . . . | 2 | | | | 2 |
| **Rental Real Estate Expenses** | | | | | |
| 3  Advertising . . . . . . . | 3 | | | | |
| 4  Auto and travel . . . . . . | 4 | | | | |
| 5  Cleaning and maintenance . . | 5 | | | | |
| 6  Commissions . . . . . . . | 6 | | | | |
| 7  Insurance . . . . . . . . | 7 | | | | |
| 8  Legal and other professional fees . . . . . . . . . . | 8 | | | | |
| 9  Interest . . . . . . . . . | 9 | | | | |
| 10  Repairs . . . . . . . . . | 10 | | | | |
| 11  Taxes . . . . . . . . . . | 11 | | | | |
| 12  Utilities . . . . . . . . . | 12 | | | | |
| 13  Wages and salaries . . . . | 13 | | | | |
| 14  Depreciation from Form 4562 | 14 | | | | |
| 15  Other (list) ▶ ............... ........................ ........................ | 15 | | | | |
| 16  Total expenses. Add lines 3 through 15 . . . . . . . . | 16 | | | | 16 |
| 17  Net income (loss) from rental real estate activities. Subtract line 16 from line 2. Enter net income (loss) from the total column on Schedule K, line 2 . | 17 | | | | 17 |

*Fig. 19.4. Continued Form 1065.*

sary to complete these lines of the tax return. The easiest approach probably is to set up accounts to track each asset and liability that appears on
the tax return. Another approach is to use accounts that can be combined
to calculate the total asset or liability figure that needs to be entered on
the tax return.

| Form 1065 (1989) | | Page 3 |
|---|---|---|
| **Schedule K** Partners' Shares of Income, Credits, Deductions, Etc. | | |
| (a) Distributive share items | | (b) Total amount |

| | | (b) Total amount |
|---|---|---|
| **Income (Loss)** | 1 Ordinary income (loss) from trade or business activities (page 1, line 21) | **1** 49,370 |
| | 2 Net income (loss) from rental real estate activities (Schedule H, line 17) | **2** |
| | 3a Gross income from other rental activities ... **3a** | |
| | b Less expenses (attach schedule) **3b** | |
| | c Net income (loss) from other rental activities | **3c** |
| | 4 Portfolio income (loss) (see instructions): | |
| | a Interest income | **4a** |
| | b Dividend income | **4b** 150 |
| | c Royalty income | **4c** |
| | d Net short-term capital gain (loss) (Schedule D, line 4) | **4d** 100 |
| | e Net long-term capital gain (loss) (Schedule D, line 9) | **4e** 200 |
| | f Other portfolio income (loss) (attach schedule) | **4f** |
| | 5 Guaranteed payments to partners | **5** 25,000 |
| | 6 Net gain (loss) under section 1231 (other than due to casualty or theft) (see instructions) | **6** |
| | 7 Other income (loss) (attach schedule) | **7** |
| **Deduc-tions** | 8 Charitable contributions (attach list) | **8** 650 |
| | 9 Section 179 expense deduction (attach Form 4562) | **9** |
| | 10 Deductions related to portfolio income (do not include investment interest expense) | **10** |
| | 11 Other deductions (attach schedule) | **11** |
| **Credits** | 12a Credit for income tax withheld | **12a** |
| | b Low-income housing credit: (1) Partnerships to which section 42(j)(5) applies | **12b(1)** |
| | (2) Other than on line 12b(1) | **12b(2)** |
| | c Qualified rehabilitation expenditures related to rental real estate activities (attach schedule) | **12c** |
| | d Credits (other than credits shown on lines 12b and 12c) related to rental real estate activities (attach schedule) | **12d** |
| | e Credits related to other rental activities (see instructions) (attach schedule) | **12e** |
| | 13 Other credits and expenditures (attach schedule) | **13** |
| **Self-Employ-ment** | 14a Net earnings (loss) from self-employment | **14a** 74,370 |
| | b Gross farming or fishing income | **14b** |
| | c Gross nonfarm income | **14c** |
| **Adjustments and Tax Preference Items** | 15a Accelerated depreciation of real property placed in service before 1987 | **15a** |
| | b Accelerated depreciation of leased personal property placed in service before 1987 | **15b** |
| | c Depreciation adjustment on property placed in service after 1986 | **15c** |
| | d Depletion (other than oil and gas) | **15d** |
| | e (1) Gross income from oil, gas, and geothermal properties | **15e(1)** |
| | (2) Deductions allocable to oil, gas, and geothermal properties | **15e(2)** |
| | f Other adjustments and tax preference items (attach schedule) | **15f** |
| **Invest-ment Interest** | 16a Interest expense on investment debts | **16a** |
| | b (1) Investment income included on lines 4a through 4f above | **16b(1)** 450 |
| | (2) Investment expenses included on line 10 above | **16b(2)** |
| **Foreign Taxes** | 17a Type of income | |
| | b Foreign country or U.S. possession | |
| | c Total gross income from sources outside the U.S. (attach schedule) | **17c** |
| | d Total applicable deductions and losses (attach schedule) | **17d** |
| | e Total foreign taxes (check one): ▶ ☐ Paid ☐ Accrued | **17e** |
| | f Reduction in taxes available for credit (attach schedule) | **17f** |
| | g Other foreign tax information (attach schedule) | **17g** |
| **Other** | 18a Total expenditures to which a section 59(e) election may apply (attach schedule) | **18a** |
| | b Attach schedule for other items and amounts not reported above (see instructions) | |
| **Analysis** | 19a Total distributive income/payment items (combine lines 1 through 7 above) | **19a** |
| | b Analysis by type of partner: | |

| | (a) Corporate | (b) Individual | | (c) Partnership | (d) Exempt organization | (e) Nominee/Other |
|---|---|---|---|---|---|---|
| | | i. Active | ii. Passive | | | |
| 1. General partners | | 74,820 | | | | |
| 2. Limited partners | | | | | | |

**Fig. 19.4.** *Continued Form 1065.*

This chapter contains copies of the 1989 federal income tax forms for businesses (see figs. 19.1 through 19.7). (The 1990 forms were unavailable when this book was written.) You can use these forms to build your

Form 1065 (1989)  Page **4**

**Schedule L**  **Balance Sheets**
(See the instructions for Question N on page 8 of the Instructions before completing Schedules L and M.)

| | | Beginning of tax year | | End of tax year | |
|---|---|---|---|---|---|
| Assets | | (a) | (b) | (c) | (d) |
| 1 | Cash | | 3,455 | | 4,650 |
| 2 | Trade notes and accounts receivable | 7,150 | | 10,990 | |
| a | Less allowance for bad debts | | 7,150 | | 10,990 |
| 3 | Inventories | | 18,125 | | 19,225 |
| 4a | U.S. government obligations | | | | |
| b | Tax-exempt securities | | 1,000 | | 1,000 |
| 5 | Other current assets (attach schedule) | | | | |
| 6 | Mortgage and real estate loans | | | | |
| 7 | Other investments (attach schedule) | | 1,000 | | — |
| 8a | Buildings and other depreciable assets | 15,000 | | 15,000 | |
| b | Less accumulated depreciation | 4,000 | 11,000 | 5,174 | 9,826 |
| 9a | Depletable assets | | | | |
| b | Less accumulated depletion | | | | |
| 10 | Land (net of any amortization) | | | | |
| 11a | Intangible assets (amortizable only) | | | | |
| b | Less accumulated amortization | | | | |
| 12 | Other assets (attach schedule) | | | | |
| 13 | Total assets | | 41,730 | | 45,691 |
| | **Liabilities and Capital** | | | | |
| 14 | Accounts payable | | 10,180 | | 10,462 |
| 15 | Mortgages, notes, bonds payable in less than 1 year | | 4,000 | | 3,600 |
| 16 | Other current liabilities (attach schedule) | | | | |
| 17 | All nonrecourse loans | | | | |
| 18 | Mortgages, notes, bonds payable in 1 year or more | | — | | 7,739 |
| 19 | Other liabilities (attach schedule) | | | | |
| 20 | Partners' capital accounts | | 27,550 | | 23,890 |
| 21 | Total liabilities and capital | | 41,730 | | 45,691 |

**Schedule M**  **Reconciliation of Partners' Capital Accounts**
(Show reconciliation of each partner's capital account on Schedule K-1 (Form 1065), Item K.)

| (a) Partners' capital accounts at beginning of year | (b) Capital contributed during year | (c) Income (loss) from lines 1, 2, 3c, and 4 of Sch. K | (d) Income not included in column (c), plus nontaxable income | (e) Losses not included in column (c), plus unallowable deductions | (f) Withdrawals and distributions | (g) Partners' capital accounts at end of year (combine columns (a) through (f)) |
|---|---|---|---|---|---|---|
| 27,550 | | 49,820 | 50 | ( 650 ) | ( 52,880 ) | 23,890 |

**Additional Information Required** (continued from page 1)

| | | Yes | No |
|---|---|---|---|
| L | Check accounting method: (1) ☐ Cash  (2) ☑ Accrual  (3) ☐ Other | | |
| M | Check this box if this is a partnership subject to the consolidated partnership audit procedures of sections 6221 through 6233 (see instructions) ▶ ☐ | | |
| N | Does the partnership meet all the requirements shown in the Instructions for **Question N**? | | ✔ |
| O | Was there a distribution of property or a transfer (for example, by sale or death) of a partnership interest during the tax year? | | ✔ |
| | If "Yes," see the instructions concerning an election to adjust the basis of the partnership's assets under section 754. | | |
| P | Does the partnership have any foreign partners? | | ✔ |
| Q | At any time during the tax year, did the partnership have an interest in or a signature or other authority over a financial account in a foreign country (such as a bank account, securities account, or other financial account)? (See the instructions for exceptions and filing requirements for form TD F 90-22.1.) | | ✔ |
| | If "Yes," write the name of the foreign country. ▶ | | |
| R | Was the partnership the grantor of, or transferor to, a foreign trust which existed during the current tax year, whether or not the partnership or any partner has any beneficial interest in it? If "Yes," you may have to file Forms 3520, 3520-A, or 926 | | ✔ |
| S | Check this box if the partnership has filed or is required to file **Form 8264**, Application for Registration of a Tax Shelter ▶ ☐ | | |
| T | Check this box if the partnership is a publicly traded partnership as defined in section 469(k)(2) ▶ ☐ | | |

*Fig. 19.4. Continued Form 1065.*

lists of required categories and accounts. The forms, however, change almost every year. Unfortunately—and thank your congressman for this—the forms are not finalized until late in the year. You cannot know

| SCHEDULE D (Form 1065) | Capital Gains and Losses | | | | OMB No. 1545-0099 |
|---|---|---|---|---|---|
| Department of the Treasury Internal Revenue Service | ▶ Attach to Form 1065. | | | | **1989** |

Name of partnership: **AbleBee Book Store**  Employer Identification number: **10-9876543**

**Part I** Short-Term Capital Gains and Losses—Assets held one year or less

| (a) Description of property (Example, 100 shares 7% preferred of ''Z'' Co.) | (b) Date acquired (mo., day, yr.) | (c) Date sold (mo., day, yr.) | (d) Sales price (see instructions) | (e) Cost or other basis (see instructions) | (f) Gain (loss) ((d) minus (e)) |
|---|---|---|---|---|---|
| 1 XYZ Chemical Co. 20 shares common | 12/5/88 | 5/1/89 | 600 | 500 | 100 |
| | | | | | |
| | | | | | |
| | | | | | |

2 Short-term capital gain from installment sales from Form 6252, line 22 or 30 . . . . . . . . .

3 Partnership's share of net short-term capital gain (loss), including specially allocated short-term capital gains (losses), from other partnerships and from fiduciaries

4 Net short-term capital gain (loss)—Combine lines 1 through 3. Enter each partner's share on Schedule K-1 (Form 1065), line 4d . . . . . . . . .  **100**

**Part II** Long-Term Capital Gains and Losses—Assets held more than one year

| 5 ABC Motors Inc. 10 shares common | 12/7/87 | 6/5/89 | 700 | 500 | 200 |
|---|---|---|---|---|---|
| | | | | | |
| | | | | | |
| | | | | | |

6 Long-term capital gain from installment sales from Form 6252, line 22 or 30 . . . . . . . . .

7 Partnership's share of net long-term capital gain (loss), including specially allocated long-term capital gains (losses), from other partnerships and from fiduciaries . . . . . . . . .

8 Capital gain distributions . . . . . . . . .

9 Net long-term capital gain (loss)—Combine lines 5 through 8. Enter each partner's share on Schedule K-1 (Form 1065), line 4e . . . . . . . . .  **200**

## General Instructions

*(Section references are to the Internal Revenue Code.)*

**Caution:** At the time these instructions were printed, Congress was considering tax legislation that would change the treatment of certain dispositions of property that qualify as long-term capital gains. If this legislation is passed, we will take the steps necessary to publicize the final rules.

**Purpose of Schedule.**—Use Schedule D (Form 1065) to report sales or exchanges of capital assets, except capital gains (losses) that are specially allocated to any partners.

Specially allocated capital gains (losses) received by the partnership as a partner in other partnerships and from fiduciaries are to be entered on Schedule D, line 3 or 7, whichever applies. Capital gains (losses) of the partnership that are specially allocated to partners should be entered directly on line 4d of Schedules K and K-1 or line 4e of Schedules K and K-1, whichever applies. Do not include these amounts on Schedule D. See **How Income Is Shared Among Partners** in the General Instructions for Schedules K and K-1 of the Instructions for Form 1065 for more information.

**General Information.**—To report sales or exchanges of property other than capital assets, including the sale or exchange of property used in a trade or business and involuntary conversions (other than casualties and thefts), see **Form 4797,** Sales of Business Property, and related instructions.

For amounts received from an installment sale, the holding period rule in effect in the year of sale will determine the treatment of the amounts received as long-term or short-term capital gain.

Report every sale or exchange of property in detail, even though there is no gain or loss.

For more information, see **Publication 544,** Sales and Other Dispositions of Assets.

**Note:** *For information on liquidations of corporations, see* **Publication 542,** *Tax Information on Corporations, and Publication 544.*

**What Are Capital Assets?**—Each item of property the partnership held (whether or not connected with its trade or business) is a capital asset **except:**

1. Assets that can be inventoried or property held mainly for sale to customers.

2. Depreciable or real property used in the trade or business.

3. Certain copyrights; literary, musical, or artistic compositions; letters or memorandums; or similar property.

4. Accounts or notes receivable acquired in the ordinary course of trade or business for services rendered or from the sale of property described in 1 above.

5. A U.S. Government publication (including the Congressional Record) received from the Government or any of its agencies in a manner other than by buying it at the price offered for public sale, which is held by a taxpayer who received the publication or by a second taxpayer in whose hands the basis of the publication is determined, for purposes of determining gain from a sale or exchange, by referring to its basis in the hands of the first taxpayer.

**Items for Special Treatment and Special Cases.**—The following items may require special treatment:

• Transactions by a securities dealer.

• Bonds and other debt instruments.

• Certain real estate subdivided for sale that may be considered a capital asset.

• Gain on the sale of depreciable property to a more than 50% owned entity, or to a trust in which the partnership is a beneficiary, is treated as ordinary gain.

• Gain on disposition of stock in an Interest-Charge Domestic International Sales Corporation or a Foreign Sales Corporation.

For Paperwork Reduction Act Notice, see the instructions for Form 1065.  Schedule D (Form 1065) 1989

***Fig. 19.4.*** *Continued Form 1065.*

with certainty which income and expense categories or which asset and liability accounts you should be using until the year is almost over. The

| Form **1120-A** | **U.S. Corporation Short-Form Income Tax Return** | OMB No. 1545-0890 |
|---|---|---|

Department of the Treasury Internal Revenue Service
Instructions are separate. See them to make sure you qualify to file Form 1120-A.
For calendar year 1989 or tax year beginning ................., 1989, ending ................., 19 ......  **1989**

A Check this box if corp. is a personal service corp. (as defined in Temp. Regs. sec. 1.441-4T— see instructions) ▶ ☐

Use IRS label. Other-wise, please print or type.

Name
10-2134657   DEC 89   D89   5995
ROSE FLOWER SHOP, INC.
38 SUPERIOR LANE
FAIR CITY, MD   20715

B Employer identification number
10-2134657

C Date incorporated
7-1-82

D Total assets (see Specific Instructions)
$ 65,987

E Check applicable boxes: (1) ☐ Initial return   (2) ☐ Change in address
F Check method of accounting: (1) ☐ Cash   (2) ☑ Accrual   (3) ☐ Other (specify) ..... ▶

| | | | | | | |
|---|---|---|---|---|---|---|
| **Income** | 1a | Gross receipts or sales | 248,000 | b Less returns and allowances | 7,500 | c Balance ▶ | 1c | 240,500 |
| | 2 | Cost of goods sold and/or operations (see instructions) | | | | 2 | 144,000 |
| | 3 | Gross profit (line 1c less line 2) | | | | 3 | 96,500 |
| | 4 | Domestic corporation dividends subject to the 70% deduction | | | | 4 | |
| | 5 | Interest | | | | 5 | 942 |
| | 6 | Gross rents | | | | 6 | |
| | 7 | Gross royalties | | | | 7 | |
| | 8 | Capital gain net income (attach Schedule D (Form 1120)) | | | | 8 | |
| | 9 | Net gain or (loss) from Form 4797, Part II, line 18 (attach Form 4797) | | | | 9 | |
| | 10 | Other income (see instructions) | | | | 10 | |
| | 11 | **Total income**—Add lines 3 through 10 ▶ | | | | 11 | 97,442 |

| | | | | | | |
|---|---|---|---|---|---|---|
| **Deductions** (See instructions for limitations on deductions.) | 12 | Compensation of officers (see instructions) | | | | 12 | 23,000 |
| | 13a | Salaries and wages | 24,320 | b Less jobs credit | | c Balance ▶ | 13c | 24,320 |
| | 14 | Repairs | | | | 14 | |
| | 15 | Bad debts | | | | 15 | |
| | 16 | Rents | | | | 16 | 6,000 |
| | 17 | Taxes | | | | 17 | 3,320 |
| | 18 | Interest | | | | 18 | 1,340 |
| | 19 | Contributions **(see instructions for 10% limitation)** | | | | 19 | 1,820 |
| | 20 | Depreciation (attach Form 4562) | | 20 | | 21b | |
| | 21 | Less depreciation claimed elsewhere on return | | 21a | | | |
| | 22 | Other deductions (attach schedule) *(Advertising)* | | | | 22 | 3,000 |
| | 23 | **Total** deductions—Add lines 12 through 22 ▶ | | | | 23 | 62,800 |
| | 24 | Taxable income before net operating loss deduction and special deductions (line 11 less line 23) | | | | 24 | 34,642 |
| | 25 | **Less: a** Net operating loss deduction (see instructions) | | 25a | | | |
| | | **b** Special deductions (see instructions) | | 25b | | 25c | |
| | 26 | Taxable income—Line 24 less line 25c | | | | 26 | 34,642 |
| | 27 | **Total tax** (Part I, line 7) | | | | 27 | 5,196 |

| | | | | | | |
|---|---|---|---|---|---|---|
| **Tax and Payments** | 28 | **Payments:** | | | | | |
| | a | 1988 overpayment credited to 1989 | 28a | | | | |
| | b | 1989 estimated tax payments | 28b | 6,000 | | | |
| | c | Less 1989 refund applied for on Form 4466 | 28c ( | ) Bal ▶ | 28d | 6,000 | |
| | e | Tax deposited with Form 7004 | | | 28e | | |
| | f | Credit from regulated investment companies (attach Form 2439) | | | 28f | | |
| | g | Credit for Federal tax on fuels (attach Form 4136) | | | 28g | | |
| | h | **Total payments**—Add lines 28d through 28g | | | | 28h | 6,000 |
| | 29 | Enter any **penalty** for underpayment of estimated tax—Check ▶ ☐ if Form 2220 is attached | | | | 29 | |
| | 30 | **Tax due**—If the total of lines 27 and 29 are larger than line 28h, enter amount owed | | | | 30 | |
| | 31 | **Overpayment**—If line 28h is larger than the total of lines 27 and 29, enter amount overpaid | | | | 31 | 804 |
| | 32 | Enter amount of line 31 you want: **Credited to 1990 estimated tax** ▶ | 804 | Refunded ▶ | | 32 | |

**Please Sign Here**
Under penalties of perjury, I declare that I have examined this return, including accompanying schedules and statements, and to the best of my knowledge and belief, it is true, correct, and complete. Declaration of preparer (other than taxpayer) is based on all information of which preparer has any knowledge.

▶ *George Rose*   2/14/90   ▶ President
Signature of officer   Date   Title

**Paid Preparer's Use Only**
Preparer's signature ▶   Date   Check if self-employed ☐   Preparer's social security number
Firm's name (or yours if self-employed) and address ▶   E.I. No. ▶   ZIP code ▶

For Paperwork Reduction Act Notice, see page 1 of the instructions.   Form **1120-A** (1989)

**Fig. 19.5.** *The 1120-A form indicates which income and expense categories small corporations should use to report profits and losses.*

practical approach is to use the categories and accounts indicated by the preceding year and make adjustments when the new forms come out.

Form 1120 A (1989)      Page **2**

### Part I   Tax Computation

| | | | |
|---|---|---|---|
| **1** Income tax (see instructions to figure the tax) Check this box if the corp. is a qualified personal service corp. (see instructions). ▶ ☐ | **1** | 5,196 |
| **2a** General business credit. Check if from: ☐ Form 3800 ☐ Form 3468 ☐ Form 5884 ☐ Form 6478 ☐ Form 6765 ☐ Form 8586 | **2a** | | |
| **b** Credit for prior year minimum tax (attach Form 8801) | **2b** | | |
| **3** Total credits—Add lines 2a and 2b | **3** | | |
| **4** Line 1 less line 3 | **4** | 5,196 |
| **5** Recapture taxes. Check if from ☐ Form 4255 ☐ Form 8611 | **5** | | |
| **6** Alternative minimum tax (attach Form 4626) | **6** | | |
| **7** Total tax—Add lines 4 through 6. Enter here and on line 27, page 1 | **7** | 5,196 |

**Additional Information** (See instruction F.)

**G** Refer to the list in the instructions and state the principal:

(1) Business activity code no. ▶   5995

(2) Business activity ▶   Flower Shop

(3) Product or service ▶   Flowers

**H** Did any individual, partnership, estate, or trust at the end of the tax year own, directly or indirectly, 50% or more of the corporation's voting stock? (For rules of attribution, see section 267(c).)   Yes ☐ No ☑
If "Yes," attach schedule showing name, address, and identifying number.

**I** Enter the amount of tax-exempt interest received or accrued during the tax year   ▶ |$   -0-

**J** (1) If an amount for cost of goods sold and/or operations is entered on line 2, page 1, complete (a) through (c):

| | | |
|---|---|---|
| (a) Purchases (see instructions) | 134,014 |
| (b) Additional sec. 263A costs (see instructions—attach schedule) | |
| (c) Other costs (attach schedule) | 9,466 |

(2) Do the rules of section 263A (with respect to property produced or acquired for resale) apply to the corporation?   Yes ☐ No ☑

**K** At any time during the tax year, did you have an interest in or a signature or other authority over a financial account in a foreign country (such as a bank account, securities account, or other financial account)? (See instruction F for filing requirements for form TD F 90-22.1.)   Yes ☐ No ☑
If "Yes," enter the name of the foreign country ▶

**L** Enter amount of cash distributions and the book value of property (other than cash) distributions made in this tax year ▶ |$   -0-

### Part II   Balance Sheets

| | (a) Beginning of tax year | (b) End of tax year |
|---|---|---|
| **Assets** | | |
| **1** Cash | 20,540 | 18,498 |
| **2a** Trade notes and accounts receivable | | |
| **b** Less allowance for bad debts | ( ) | ( ) |
| **3** Inventories | 2,530 | 2,010 |
| **4** U.S. government obligations | 13,807 | 45,479 |
| **5** Tax-exempt securities (see instructions) | | |
| **6** Other current assets (attach schedule) | | |
| **7** Loans to stockholders | | |
| **8** Mortgage and real estate loans | | |
| **9a** Depreciable, depletable, and intangible assets | | |
| **b** Less accumulated depreciation, depletion, and amortization | ( ) | ( ) |
| **10** Land (net of any amortization) | | |
| **11** Other assets (attach schedule) | | |
| **12** Total assets | 36,877 | 65,987 |
| **Liabilities and Stockholders' Equity** | | |
| **13** Accounts payable | 6,415 | 6,079 |
| **14** Other current liabilities (attach schedule) | | |
| **15** Loans from stockholders | | |
| **16** Mortgages, notes, bonds payable | | |
| **17** Other liabilities (attach schedule) | | |
| **18** Capital stock (preferred and common stock) | 20,000 | 20,000 |
| **19** Paid-in or capital surplus | | |
| **20** Retained earnings | 10,462 | 39,908 |
| **21** Less cost of treasury stock | ( ) | ( ) |
| **22** Total liabilities and stockholders' equity | 36,877 | 65,987 |

### Part III   Reconciliation of Income per Books With Income per Return (Must be completed by all filers)

| | | | |
|---|---|---|---|
| **1** Net income per books | 29,446 | **5** Income recorded on books this year not included on this return (itemize) | |
| **2** Federal income tax | 5,196 | | |
| **3** Income subject to tax not recorded on books this year (itemize) | | **6** Deductions on this return not charged against book income this year (itemize) | |
| **4** Expenses recorded on books this year not deducted on this return (itemize) | | **7** Income (line 24, page 1). Enter the sum of lines 1 through 4 less the sum of lines 5 and 6 | 34,642 |

**Fig. 19.5.** *Continued Form 1120–A.*

Sole proprietors must consider one other thing: you actually may need to complete more than one Schedule C form. You cannot aggregate a series of dissimilar businesses and report the consolidated results on one Schedule C. For example, if you own a tavern, practice law, and run a small

| Form **1120S** Department of the Treasury Internal Revenue Service | **U.S. Income Tax Return for an S Corporation** For the calendar year 1989, or tax year beginning _____ 1989, ending _____ , 19 ___ ▶ For Paperwork Reduction Act Notice, see page 1 of separate instructions. | OMB No. 1545-0130 **1989** |
|---|---|---|

**A** Date of election as an S corporation  *12-1-88*

**B** Business code no (see Specific Instructions)  *5008*

Use IRS label. Otherwise, please print or type.

10-4487965    DEC89    D74    3070
ESTEX, INC.
482 WINSTON ST.
METRO CITY    OH    43705

I R S

**C** Employer identification number

**D** Date incorporated  *3-1-72*

**E** Total assets (see Specific Instructions)  $ *825,714*

**F** Check applicable boxes   (1) ☑ Initial return   (2) ☐ Final return   (3) ☐ Change in address   (4) ☐ Amended return

**G** Check this box if this is an S corporation subject to the consolidated audit procedures of sections 6241 through 6245 (see instructions before checking this box) . . . ▶ ☑

**H** Enter number of shareholders in the corporation at end of the tax year . . . . . . . . . . . . . . . . . . . . ▶ **6**

Caution: Include **only** trade or business income and expenses on lines 1a through 21. See the instructions for more information.

| | | | |
|---|---|---|---|
| **Income** | **1a** Gross receipts or sales *1,545,700*   **b** Less returns and allowances *21,000*   **c** Bal ▶ | **1c** | *1,524,700* |
| | **2** Cost of goods sold and/or operations (Schedule A, line 7) . . . . . . . . . | **2** | *954,700* |
| | **3** Gross profit (subtract line 2 from line 1c) . . . . . . . . . | **3** | *570,000* |
| | **4** Net gain (or loss) from Form 4797, line 18 (see instructions) . . . . . . | **4** | *-0-* |
| | **5** Other income (see instructions—attach schedule) . . . . . . . . . | **5** | *-0-* |
| | **6** Total income (loss)—Combine lines 3, 4, and 5 and enter here . . . . . . ▶ | **6** | *570,000* |
| **Deductions (See instructions for limitations.)** | **7** Compensation of officers . . . . . . . . . | **7** | *170,000* |
| | **8a** Salaries and wages *144,000*   **b** Less jobs credit *6,000*   **c** Bal ▶ | **8c** | *138,000* |
| | **9** Repairs . . . . . . . . . | **9** | *800* |
| | **10** Bad debts (see instructions) . . . . . . . . . | **10** | *1,600* |
| | **11** Rents . . . . . . . . . | **11** | *9,200* |
| | **12** Taxes . . . . . . . . . | **12** | *15,000* |
| | **13** Interest (see instructions) . . . . . . . . . | **13** | *24,200* |
| | **14a** Depreciation (attach Form 4562) (see instructions) . . . **14a** *5,200* | | |
| | **b** Depreciation reported on Schedule A and elsewhere on return . . **14b** *-0-* | | |
| | **c** Subtract line 14b from line 14a . . . . . . . . . | **14c** | *5,200* |
| | **15** Depletion (**Do not deduct oil and gas depletion. See instructions.**) . . . | **15** | *-0-* |
| | **16** Advertising . . . . . . . . . | **16** | *8,700* |
| | **17** Pension, profit-sharing, etc. plans . . . . . . . . . | **17** | *-0-* |
| | **18** Employee benefit programs . . . . . . . . . | **18** | *-0-* |
| | **19** Other deductions (attach schedule) . . . . . . . . . | **19** | *78,300* |
| | **20** Total deductions—Add lines 7 through 19 and enter here . . . . . ▶ | **20** | *451,000* |
| | **21** Ordinary income (loss) from trade or business activities—Subtract line 20 from line 6 . . . | **21** | *119,000* |
| **Tax and Payments** | **22** Tax: | | |
| | **a** Excess net passive income tax (attach schedule) . . . . . **22a** | | |
| | **b** Tax from Schedule D (Form 1120S) . . . . . **22b** | | |
| | **c** Add lines 22a and 22b (see instructions for additional taxes) . . . . . | **22c** | *-0-* |
| | **23** Payments: | | |
| | **a** Tax deposited with Form 7004 . . . . . **23a** | | |
| | **b** Credit for Federal tax on fuels (attach Form 4136) . . . **23b** | | |
| | **c** Add lines 23a and 23b . . . . . | **23c** | *-0-* |
| | **24** Tax due—If line 22c is larger than line 23c, enter amount owed. See instructions for Paying the Tax . . . . . . . . . ▶ | **24** | *-0-* |
| | **25** Overpayment—If line 23c is larger than line 22c, enter amount overpaid . . . . . . ▶ | **25** | *-0-* |

**Please Sign Here**

Under penalties of perjury, I declare that I have examined this return, including accompanying schedules and statements, and to the best of my knowledge and belief, it is true, correct, and complete. Declaration of preparer (other than taxpayer) is based on all information of which preparer has any knowledge.

▶ *John H. Anders*    Signature of officer    *3-10-90*    Date    ▶ *President*    Title

**Paid Preparer's Use Only**

| Preparer's signature | | Date | Check if self-employed ▶ ☐ | Preparer's social security number |
|---|---|---|---|---|
| Firm's name (or yours if self employed) and address ▶ | | | E.I. No. ▶ | |
| | | | ZIP code ▶ | |

Form **1120S** (1989)

**Fig. 19.6.** *The 1120S form indicates which income and expense categories S corporations should use to report profits and losses.*

manufacturing business, you must complete three Schedule C forms: one for the tavern, one for the law practice, and still another for the manufacturing firm. Quicken can handle this situation, but you need to account for each business that needs a separate Schedule C in its own account group. (Chapter 3 describes how to set up and select different account groups.)

Form 1120S (1989)                                                                    Page **2**

**Schedule A** **Cost of Goods Sold and/or Operations** (See instructions for Schedule A.)

| | | |
|---|---|---|
| 1 Inventory at beginning of year | 1 | 126,000 |
| 2 Purchases | 2 | 1,127,100 |
| 3 Cost of labor | 3 | -0- |
| 4a Additional section 263A costs (attach schedule) (see instructions) | 4a | -0- |
| b Other costs (attach schedule) | 4b | -0- |
| 5 Total—Add lines 1 through 4b | 5 | 1,253,100 |
| 6 Inventory at end of year | 6 | 298,400 |
| 7 Cost of goods sold and/or operations—Subtract line 6 from line 5. Enter here and on line 2, page 1 | 7 | 954,700 |

**8a** Check all methods used for valuing closing inventory:

(i) ☐ Cost

(ii) ☑ Lower of cost or market as described in Regulations section 1.471-4

(iii) ☐ Writedown of "subnormal" goods as described in Regulations section 1.471-2(c)

(iv) ☐ Other (specify method used and attach explanation) ▶

**b** Check this box if the LIFO inventory method was adopted this tax year for any goods (if checked, attach Form 970) . . . . ▶☐

**c** If the LIFO inventory method was used for this tax year, enter percentage (or amounts) of closing inventory computed under LIFO . . . . . . . . . . . . . . . . . . . . . . . | 8c |

**d** Do the rules of section 263A (with respect to property produced or acquired for resale) apply to the corporation? . . . ☐ Yes ☑ No

**e** Was there any change in determining quantities, cost, or valuations between opening and closing inventory? . . . . ☐ Yes ☑ No
If "Yes," attach explanation.

**Additional Information Required** (continued from page 1)

| | Yes | No |
|---|---|---|
| **I** Did you at the end of the tax year own, directly or indirectly, 50% or more of the voting stock of a domestic corporation? For rules of attribution, see section 267(c). If "Yes," attach a schedule showing: (1) name, address, and employer identification number; and (2) percentage owned. | | ✓ |
| **J** Refer to the listing of business activity codes at the end of the Instructions for Form 1120S and state your principal: | | |
| (1) Business activity ▶ 5008 - Distributor (2) Product or service ▶ Heavy equipment | | |
| **K** Were you a member of a controlled group subject to the provisions of section 1561? | | ✓ |
| **L** At any time during the tax year, did you have an interest in or a signature or other authority over a financial account in a foreign country (such as a bank account, securities account, or other financial account)? (See instructions for exceptions and filing requirements for form TD F 90-22.1.) | | ✓ |
| If "Yes," enter the name of the foreign country ▶ | | |
| **M** Were you the grantor of, or transferor to, a foreign trust which existed during the current tax year, whether or not you have any beneficial interest in it? If "Yes," you may have to file Form 3520, 3520-A, or 926 | | ✓ |
| **N** During this tax year did you maintain any part of your accounting/tax records on a computerized system? | | ✓ |
| **O** Check method of accounting: (1) ☐ Cash (2) ☑ Accrual (3) ☐ Other (specify) ▶ | | |
| **P** Check this box if the S corporation has filed or is required to file **Form 8264**, Application for Registration of a Tax Shelter . . . . . . . . . . . . . . . . . . . . . ▶☐ | | |
| **Q** Check this box if the corporation issued publicly offered debt instruments with original issue discount . . . . ▶☐ | | |
| If so, the corporation may have to file **Form 8281**, Information Return for Publicly Offered Original Issue Discount Instruments. | | |
| **R** If the corporation: (1) filed its election to be an S corporation after December 31, 1986, (2) was a C corporation prior to making the election, and (3) at the beginning of the tax year had net unrealized built-in gain as defined in section 1374(d)(1), enter the net unrealized built-in gain (see instructions) ▶ 37,200 | | |

**Designation of Tax Matters Person** (See instructions.)

Enter below the shareholder designated as the tax matters person (TMP) for the tax year of this return:

Name of designated TMP ▶ John H. Anders

Identifying number of TMP ▶ 458 - 00 - 0327

Address of designated TMP ▶ 4340 Holmes Parkway
Metro City, OH 43704

*Fig. 19.6. Continued Form 1120S.*

As long as you use Quicken's categories, extracting the information you need to complete a form is simple. You simply print the report that summarizes the categories that track income tax deductions. For individuals,

Form 1120S (1989)     Page **3**

### Schedule K   Shareholders' Shares of Income, Credits, Deductions, Etc. (See Instructions.)

| (a) Pro rata share items | | (b) Total amount |
|---|---|---|
| **Income (Loss) and Deductions** | | |
| **1** Ordinary income (loss) from trade or business activities (page 1, line 21) . . . . . . . | 1 | 119,000 |
| **2a** Gross income from rental real estate activities . . . . . .   2a | | |
|   **b** Less expenses (attach schedule). . . . . . . . .   2b | | |
|   **c** Net income (loss) from rental real estate activities . . . . . . . . . . . | 2c | |
| **3a** Gross income from other rental activities . . . . .   3a | | |
|   **b** Less expenses (attach schedule) . . . . . . .   3b | | |
|   **c** Net income (loss) from other rental activities . . . . . . . . . . . . | 3c | |
| **4** Portfolio income (loss): | | |
|   **a** Interest income . . . . . . . . . . . . . . . . . . | 4a | 4,000 |
|   **b** Dividend income . . . . . . . . . . . . . . . . | 4b | 16,000 |
|   **c** Royalty income . . . . . . . . . . . . . . . . . | 4c | |
|   **d** Net short-term capital gain (loss) (Schedule D (Form 1120S)) . . . . . . . | 4d | |
|   **e** Net long-term capital gain (loss) (Schedule D (Form 1120S)) . . . . . . . | 4e | |
|   **f** Other portfolio income (loss) (attach schedule) . . . . . . . . . . | 4f | |
| **5** Net gain (loss) under section 1231 (other than due to casualty or theft) (see instructions) . . . | 5 | |
| **6** Other income (loss) (attach schedule) . . . . . . . . . . . . . . | 6 | |
| **7** Charitable contributions (attach list) . . . . . . . . . . . . . . | 7 | 24,000 |
| **8** Section 179 expense deduction (attach Form 4562) . . . . . . . . . | 8 | |
| **9** Expenses related to portfolio income (loss) (attach schedule) (see instructions) . . . | 9 | |
| **10** Other deductions (attach schedule) . . . . . . . . . . . . . . | 10 | |
| **Credits** | | |
| **11a** Credit for alcohol used as a fuel (attach Form 6478) . . . . . . . . . | 11a | |
|   **b** Low-income housing credit: **(1)** From partnerships to which section 42(j)(5) applies . . . . . . | 11b(1) | |
|      **(2)** Other than on line 11b(1) . . . . . . . . . . . . . . | 11b(2) | |
|   **c** Qualified rehabilitation expenditures related to rental real estate activities (attach schedule) . . . | 11c | |
|   **d** Credits (other than credits shown on lines 11b and 11c) related to rental real estate activities (attach schedule) | 11d | |
|   **e** Credits related to other rental activities (see instructions) (attach schedule) . . . . . | 11e | |
| **12** Other credits and expenditures (attach schedule)   *Jobs Credit* . . . . . . . . . | 12 | 6,000 |
| **Investment Interest** | | |
| **13a** Interest expense on investment debts . . . . . . . . . . . . . | 13a | 3,000 |
|   **b (1)** Investment income included on lines 4a through 4f above . . . . . . . | 13b(1) | 20,000 |
|      **(2)** Investment expenses included on line 9 above . . . . . . . . | 13b(2) | |
| **Adjustments and Tax Preference Items** | | |
| **14a** Accelerated depreciation of real property placed in service before 1987. . . . . . . | 14a | |
|   **b** Accelerated depreciation of leased personal property placed in service before 1987 . . . . . | 14b | |
|   **c** Depreciation adjustment on property placed in service after 1986 . . . . . . | 14c | |
|   **d** Depletion (other than oil and gas) . . . . . . . . . . . . . | 14d | |
|   **e (1)** Gross income from oil, gas, or geothermal properties . . . . . . . | 14e(1) | |
|      **(2)** Deductions allocable to oil, gas, or geothermal properties . . . . . . | 14e(2) | |
|   **f** Other adjustments and tax preference items (attach schedule) . . . . . . | 14f | |
| **Foreign Taxes** | | |
| **15a** Type of income ................................................. | | |
|   **b** Name of foreign country or U.S. possession ................................ | | |
|   **c** Total gross income from sources outside the U.S. (attach schedule) . . . . . . | 15c | |
|   **d** Total applicable deductions and losses (attach schedule) . . . . . . . | 15d | |
|   **e** Total foreign taxes (check one): ▶ ☐ Paid   ☐ Accrued . . . . . . | 15e | |
|   **f** Reduction in taxes available for credit (attach schedule) . . . . . . . | 15f | |
|   **g** Other foreign tax information (attach schedule) . . . . . . . . . | 15g | |
| **Other Items** | | |
| **16** Total property distributions (including cash) other than dividends reported on line 18 below . . . | 16 | 65,000 |
| **17** Other items and amounts not included on lines 1 through 16 above, that are required to be reported separately to shareholders (attach schedule). | | |
| **18** Total dividend distributions paid from accumulated earnings and profits contained in other retained earnings (line 27, Schedule L) . . . . . . . . . . . . | 18 | |

*Fig. 19.6. Continued Form 1120S.*

the Tax Summary Report is valuable; for businesses, the Profit and Loss statement is valuable.

| Form **1120** | **U.S. Corporation Income Tax Return** | OMB No. 1545 0123 |
|---|---|---|
| Department of the Treasury Internal Revenue Service | For calendar year 1989 or tax year beginning _____ 1989, ending _____ 19 ____ ▶ Instructions are separate. See page 1 for Paperwork Reduction Act Notice. | **1989** |

| | | |
|---|---|---|
| Check if a— | Use IRS label. Other- wise, please print or type. | **D** Employer identification number 10-0395674 |
| **A** Consolidated return ☐ | Name  10-0395674  DEC89  071  3998 | **E** Date incorporated 3-1-72 |
| **B** Personal holding co. ☐ | TENTEX TOYS, INC. | |
| **C** Personal service corp (as defined in Temp. Regs. sec. 1 441 4T—see instructions) ☐ | 36 DIVISION STREET ANYTOWN, IL 60930 | **F** Total assets (see Specific Instructions) $ 879,417 |

**G** Check applicable boxes: (1) ☐ Initial return (2) ☐ Final return (3) ☐ Change in address

|  | Income | | | |
|---|---|---|---|---|
| 1a | Gross receipts or sales $2,010,000  **b** Less returns and allowances $20,000  **c** Bal ▶ | | 1c | 1,990,000 |
| 2 | Cost of goods sold and/or operations (Schedule A, line 7) | | 2 | 1,520,000 |
| 3 | Gross profit (line 1c less line 2) | | 3 | 470,000 |
| 4 | Dividends (Schedule C, line 19) | | 4 | 10,000 |
| 5 | Interest | | 5 | 4,500 |
| 6 | Gross rents | | 6 | |
| 7 | Gross royalties | | 7 | |
| 8 | Capital gain net income (attach Schedule D (Form 1120)) | | 8 | |
| 9 | Net gain or (loss) from Form 4797, Part II, line 18 (attach Form 4797) | | 9 | |
| 10 | Other income (see instructions—attach schedule) | | 10 | 1,000 |
| 11 | **Total** income—Add lines 3 through 10 ▶ | | 11 | 485,500 |

|  | Deductions (See instructions for limitations on deductions.) | | | |
|---|---|---|---|---|
| 12 | Compensation of officers (Schedule E, line 4) | | 12 | 70,000 |
| 13a | Salaries and wages 44,000  **b** Less jobs credit 6,000  **c** Balance ▶ | | 13c | 38,000 |
| 14 | Repairs | | 14 | 800 |
| 15 | Bad debts | | 15 | 1,600 |
| 16 | Rents | | 16 | 9,200 |
| 17 | Taxes | | 17 | 15,000 |
| 18 | Interest | | 18 | 27,200 |
| 19 | Contributions (**see instructions for 10% limitation**) | | 19 | 23,150 |
| 20 | Depreciation (attach Form 4562) | 20 17,600 | | |
| 21 | Less depreciation claimed on Schedule A and elsewhere on return | 21a 12,400 | 21b | 5,200 |
| 22 | Depletion | | 22 | |
| 23 | Advertising | | 23 | 8,700 |
| 24 | Pension, profit-sharing, etc., plans | | 24 | |
| 25 | Employee benefit programs | | 25 | |
| 26 | Other deductions (attach schedule) | | 26 | 78,300 |
| 27 | **Total** deductions—Add lines 12 through 26 ▶ | | 27 | 277,150 |
| 28 | Taxable income before net operating loss deduction and special deductions (line 11 less line 27) | | 28 | 208,350 |
| 29 | **Less: a** Net operating loss deduction (see instructions) | 29a | | |
| | **b** Special deductions (Schedule C, line 20) | 29b 8,000 | 29c | 8,000 |

|  | Tax and Payments | | | |
|---|---|---|---|---|
| 30 | Taxable income—Line 28 less line 29c | | 30 | 200,350 |
| 31 | **Total tax** (Schedule J, line 10) | | 31 | 55,387 |
| 32 | **Payments: a** 1988 overpayment credited to 1989 | 32a | | |
| | **b** 1989 estimated tax payments | 32b 69,117 | | |
| | **c** Less 1989 refund applied for on Form 4466 | 32c (          ) **d** Bal ▶ 32d 69,117 | | |
| | **e** Tax deposited with Form 7004 | 32e | | |
| | **f** Credit from regulated investment companies (attach Form 2439) | 32f | | |
| | **g** Credit for Federal tax on fuels (attach Form 4136) | 32g | 32h | 69,117 |
| 33 | Enter any **penalty** for underpayment of estimated tax—Check ▶ ☐ if Form 2220 is attached | | 33 | |
| 34 | **Tax due**—If the total of lines 31 and 33 is larger than line 32h, enter amount owed | | 34 | |
| 35 | **Overpayment**—If line 32h is larger than the total of lines 31 and 33, enter amount overpaid | | 35 | 13,730 |
| 36 | Enter amount of line 35 you want: **Credited to 1990 estimated tax** ▶ 13,730  **Refunded** ▶ | | 36 | |

| **Please Sign Here** | Under penalties of perjury, I declare that I have examined this return, including accompanying schedules and statements, and to the best of my knowledge and belief, it is true, correct, and complete. Declaration of preparer (other than taxpayer) is based on all information of which preparer has any knowledge. |
|---|---|
| | ▶ James Q. Barclay  Signature of officer  9/7/90 Date  ▶ President Title |

| **Paid Preparer's Use Only** | Preparer's signature ▶ | Date | Check if self-employed ☐ | Preparer's social security number |
|---|---|---|---|---|
| | Firm's name (or yours if self-employed) and address ▶ | | E.I. No. ▶ ZIP code ▶ | |

*Fig. 19.7. The 1120 form indicates which income and expense categories some corporations should use to report profits and losses.*

Form 1120 (1989)                                                                                                          Page **2**

## Schedule A  Cost of Goods Sold and/or Operations (See instructions for line 2, page 1.)

| | | | |
|---|---|---|---|
| 1 | Inventory at beginning of year | 1 | 126,000 |
| 2 | Purchases | 2 | 1,127,100 |
| 3 | Cost of labor | 3 | 402,000 |
| 4a | Additional section 263A costs (see instructions—attach schedule) | 4a | |
| b | Other costs (attach schedule) | 4b | 163,300 |
| 5 | Total—Add lines 1 through 4b | 5 | 1,818,400 |
| 6 | Inventory at end of year | 6 | 298,400 |
| 7 | Cost of goods sold and/or operations—Line 5 less line 6. Enter here and on line 2, page 1 | 7 | 1,520,000 |

**8a** Check all methods used for valuing closing inventory:

(i) ☐ Cost  (ii) ☑ Lower of cost or market as described in Regulations section 1.471-4 (see instructions)

(iii) ☐ Writedown of "subnormal" goods as described in Regulations section 1.471-2(c) (see instructions)

(iv) ☐ Other (Specify method used and attach explanation.) ▶ - - - - - - - - - - - - - - - - - - - - - - - - - - - - - - - - - - - -

**b** Check if the LIFO inventory method was adopted this tax year for any goods (if checked, attach Form 970) . . . . . ☐

**c** If the LIFO inventory method was used for this tax year, enter percentage (or amounts) of closing inventory computed under LIFO . . . . . . . . . . . . . . . . . . | 8c |

**d** Do the rules of section 263A (with respect to property produced or acquired for resale) apply to the corporation? . . ☑ Yes ☐ No

**e** Was there any change in determining quantities, cost, or valuations between opening and closing inventory? If "Yes," attach explanation . . . . . . . . . . . . . . . . . . . . . . . . . . . . ☐ Yes ☑ No

## Schedule C  Dividends and Special Deductions (See instructions.)

| | | (a) Dividends received | (b) % | (c) Special deductions: (a) × (b) |
|---|---|---|---|---|
| 1 | Dividends from less-than-20%-owned domestic corporations that are subject to the 70% deduction (other than debt-financed stock) | | 70 | |
| 2 | Dividends from 20%-or-more-owned domestic corporations that are subject to the 80% deduction (other than debt-financed stock) | 10,000 | 80 | 8,000 |
| 3 | Dividends on debt-financed stock of domestic and foreign corporations (section 246A) | | see instructions | |
| 4 | Dividends on certain preferred stock of less-than-20%-owned public utilities | | 41.176 | |
| 5 | Dividends on certain preferred stock of 20%-or-more-owned public utilities | | 47.059 | |
| 6 | Dividends from less-than-20%-owned foreign corporations and certain FSCs that are subject to the 70% deduction | | 70 | |
| 7 | Dividends from 20%-or-more-owned foreign corporations and certain FSCs that are subject to the 80% deduction | | 80 | |
| 8 | Dividends from wholly owned foreign subsidiaries subject to the 100% deduction (section 245(b)) | | 100 | |
| 9 | **Total**—Add lines 1 through 8. See instructions for limitation | | | 8,000 |
| 10 | Dividends from domestic corporations received by a small business investment company operating under the Small Business Investment Act of 1958 | | 100 | |
| 11 | Dividends from certain FSCs that are subject to the 100% deduction (section 245(c)(1)) | | 100 | |
| 12 | Dividends from affiliated group members subject to the 100% deduction (section 243(a)(3)) | | 100 | |
| 13 | Other dividends from foreign corporations not included on lines 3, 6, 7, 8, or 11 | | | |
| 14 | Income from controlled foreign corporations under subpart F (attach Forms 5471) | | | |
| 15 | Foreign dividend gross-up (section 78) | | | |
| 16 | IC-DISC and former DISC dividends not included on lines 1, 2, or 3 (section 246(d)) | | | |
| 17 | Other dividends | | | |
| 18 | Deduction for dividends paid on certain preferred stock of public utilities (see instructions) | | | |
| 19 | Total dividends—Add lines 1 through 17. Enter here and on line 4, page 1. ▶ | 10,000 | | |

**20** Total deductions—Add lines 9, 10, 11, 12, and 18. Enter here and on line 29b, page 1 . . . . . . . . ▶ | 8,000 |

## Schedule E  Compensation of Officers (See instructions for line 12, page 1.)

Complete Schedule E only if total receipts (line 1a, plus lines 4 through 10, of page 1, Form 1120) are $500,000 or more.

| (a) Name of officer | (b) Social security number | (c) Percent of time devoted to business | Percent of corporation stock owned (d) Common | (e) Preferred | (f) Amount of compensation |
|---|---|---|---|---|---|
| 1  James Q. Barclay | 581-00-0936 | 100 % | 45 % | % | 40,000 |
| | | % | % | % | |
| George M. Collins | 447-00-2604 | 100 % | 15 % | % | 21,000 |
| | | % | % | % | |
| Samuel Adams | 401-00-2611 | 50 % | 2 % | % | 9,000 |

**2** Total compensation of officers . . . . . . . . . . . . . . . . . . . . . . | 70,000 |

**3** Less: Compensation of officers claimed on Schedule A and elsewhere on return . . . . . . . ( )

**4** Compensation of officers deducted on line 12, page 1 . . . . . . . . . . . . . . . . | 70,000 |

***Fig. 19.7. Continued Form 1120.***

Form 1120 (1989)      Page **3**

**Schedule J**    **Tax Computation**

1   Check if you are a member of a controlled group (see sections 1561 and 1563) . . . . . . ▶ ☐

2   If the box on line 1 is checked:

    a   Enter your share of the $50,000 and $25,000 taxable income bracket amounts (in that order):

      (i) ⌊$      ⌋    (ii) ⌊$      ⌋

    b   Enter your share of the additional 5% tax (not to exceed $11,750) ▶ ⌊$      ⌋

3   Income tax (see instructions to figure the tax). Check this box if the corporation is a qualified personal service corporation (see instructions). ▶ ☐ . . . . . . . . . . | 3 | **61,387**

4a   Foreign tax credit (attach Form 1118) . . . . . . . | 4a |

   b   Possessions tax credit (attach Form 5735) . . . . . | 4b |

   c   Orphan drug credit (attach Form 6765) . . . . . . | 4c |

   d   Credit for fuel produced from a nonconventional source (see instructions) . . . . . . . | 4d |

   e   General business credit. Enter here and check which forms are attached:

      ☐ Form 3800   ☐ Form 3468   ☑ Form 5884

      ☐ Form 6478   ☐ Form 6765   ☐ Form 8586    | 4e | **6,000**

   f   Credit for prior year minimum tax (attach Form 8801) | 4f |

5   Total—Add lines 4a through 4f . . . . . . . . . . | 5 | **6,000**

6   Line 3 less line 5 . . . . . . . . . . . . . . | 6 | **55,387**

7   Personal holding company tax (attach Schedule PH (Form 1120)) . . . | 7 |

8   Recapture taxes. Check if from:   ☐ Form 4255   ☐ Form 8611 . . | 8 |

9a   Alternative minimum tax (attach Form 4626) . . . . . . . | 9a |

   b   Environmental tax (attach Form 4626) . . . . . . . . | 9b |

10   Total tax—Add lines 6 through 9b. Enter here and on line 31, page 1 . . . . | 10 | **55,387**

---

**Additional Information** (See instruction F.)    | Yes | No |

H   Refer to the list in the instructions and state the principal:

   (1) Business activity code no. ▶   *3998*

   (2) Business activity ▶   *Manufacturing*

   (3) Product or service ▶   *Toys*

I   (1) Did the corporation at the end of the tax year own, directly or indirectly, 50% or more of the voting stock of a domestic corporation? (For rules of attribution, see section 267(c).) .   | | ✓ |

     If "Yes," attach a schedule showing: (a) name, address, and identifying number; (b) percentage owned; and (c) taxable income or (loss) before NOL and special deductions of such corporation for the tax year ending with or within your tax year.

   (2) Did any individual, partnership, corporation, estate, or trust at the end of the tax year own, directly or indirectly, 50% or more of the corporation's voting stock? (For rules of attribution, see section 267(c).) If "Yes," complete (a) through (c) . .   | | ✓ |

     (a) Attach a schedule showing name, address, and identifying number.

     (b) Enter percentage owned ▶ _____

     (c) Was the owner of such voting stock a person other than a U.S. person? (See instructions.) **Note:** *If "Yes," the corporation may have to file Form 5472.* . . . . .

       If "Yes," enter owner's country ▶ _____

J   Was the corporation a U.S. shareholder of any controlled foreign corporation? (See sections 951 and 957.) . . . . . . .   | | ✓ |

   If "Yes," attach Form 5471 for each such corporation.

K   At any time during the tax year, did the corporation have an interest in or a signature or other authority over a financial account in a foreign country (such as a bank account, securities account, or other financial account)? . . . . . . . . . .   | | ✓ |

   (See instruction F and filing requirements for form TD F 90-22.1.)

   If "Yes," enter name of foreign country ▶ _____

L   Was the corporation the grantor of, or transferor to, a foreign trust that existed during the current tax year, whether or not the corporation has any beneficial interest in it? . . . . .   | | ✓ |

   If "Yes," the corporation may have to file Forms 3520, 3520-A, or 926.

M   During this tax year, did the corporation pay dividends (other than stock dividends and distributions in exchange for stock) in excess of the corporation's current and accumulated earnings and profits? (See sections 301 and 316.) . . . . . . . .   | | ✓ |

   If "Yes," file Form 5452. If this is a consolidated return, answer here for parent corporation and on **Form 851, Affiliations Schedule,** for each subsidiary.

N   During this tax year, did the corporation maintain any part of its accounting/tax records on a computerized system? . . . . .   | | ✓ |

O   Check method of accounting:

   (1) ☐ Cash

   (2) ☑ Accrual

   (3) ☐ Other (specify) ▶ _____

P   Check this box if the corporation issued publicly offered debt instruments with original issue discount . . . . . . . . ☐

   If so, the corporation may have to file Form 8281.

Q   Enter the amount of tax-exempt interest received or accrued during the tax year ▶ ⌊$   **5,000**   ⌋

R   Enter the number of shareholders at the end of the tax year if there were 35 or fewer shareholders ▶

**Fig. 19.7.** *Continued Form 1120.*

Form 1120 (1989)                                                                                     Page **4**

**Schedule L** | **Balance Sheets**

| Assets | Beginning of tax year (a) | (b) | End of tax year (c) | (d) |
|---|---|---|---|---|
| 1 Cash | | 14,700 | | 28,331 |
| 2a Trade notes and accounts receivable | 98,400 | | 103,700 | |
| b Less allowance for bad debts | | 98,400 | | 103,700 |
| 3 Inventories | | 126,000 | | 298,400 |
| 4 U.S. government obligations | | | | |
| 5 Tax-exempt securities (see instructions) | | 100,000 | | 120,000 |
| 6 Other current assets (attach schedule) | | 26,300 | | 17,266 |
| 7 Loans to stockholders | | | | |
| 8 Mortgage and real estate loans | | | | |
| 9 Other investments (attach schedule) | | 100,000 | | 80,000 |
| 10a Buildings and other depreciable assets | 272,400 | | 296,700 | |
| b Less accumulated depreciation | 88,300 | 184,100 | 104,280 | 192,420 |
| 11a Depletable assets | | | | |
| b Less accumulated depletion | | | | |
| 12 Land (net of any amortization) | | 20,000 | | 20,000 |
| 13a Intangible assets (amortizable only) | | | | |
| b Less accumulated amortization | | | | |
| 14 Other assets (attach schedule) | | 14,800 | | 19,300 |
| 15 Total assets | | 684,300 | | 879,417 |
| **Liabilities and Stockholders' Equity** | | | | |
| 16 Accounts payable | | 28,500 | | 34,834 |
| 17 Mortgages, notes, bonds payable in less than 1 year | | 4,300 | | 4,300 |
| 18 Other current liabilities (attach schedule) | | 6,800 | | 7,400 |
| 19 Loans from stockholders | | | | |
| 20 Mortgages, notes, bonds payable in 1 year or more | | 176,700 | | 264,100 |
| 21 Other liabilities (attach schedule) | | | | |
| 22 Capital stock: a Preferred stock | | | | |
| b Common stock | 200,000 | 200,000 | 200,000 | 200,000 |
| 23 Paid-in or capital surplus | | | | |
| 24 Retained earnings—Appropriated (attach schedule) | | 30,000 | | 40,000 |
| 25 Retained earnings—Unappropriated | | 238,000 | | 328,783 |
| 26 Less cost of treasury stock | | ( ) | | ( ) |
| 27 Total liabilities and stockholders' equity | | 684,300 | | 879,417 |

**Schedule M-1** | **Reconciliation of Income per Books With Income per Return** (You are not required to complete this schedule if the total assets on line 15, column (d), of Schedule L are less than $25,000.)

| | | | |
|---|---|---|---|
| 1 Net income per books | 147,783 | 7 Income recorded on books this year not included on this return (itemize): | |
| 2 Federal income tax | 55,387 | | |
| 3 Excess of capital losses over capital gains | 3,600 | a Tax-exempt interest $ 5,000 | |
| 4 Income subject to tax not recorded on books this year (itemize): _____ | | b Insurance Proceeds 9,500 | 14,500 |
| 5 Expenses recorded on books this year not deducted on this return (itemize): | | 8 Deductions on this return not charged against book income this year (itemize): | |
| a Depreciation . . . $ | | a Depreciation . . . $ 1,620 | |
| b Contributions carryover $ 850 | | b Contributions carryover $ | |
| c Travel and entertainment . $ | | _____ | |
| See Itemized | | | 1,620 |
| Statement Attached $ 16,850 | 17,700 | 9 Total of lines 7 and 8 | 16,120 |
| 6 Total of lines 1 through 5 | 224,470 | 10 Income (line 28, page 1)—line 6 less line 9 | 208,350 |

**Schedule M-2** | **Analysis of Unappropriated Retained Earnings per Books (line 25, Schedule L)** (You are not required to complete this schedule if the total assets on line 15, column (d), of Schedule L are less than $25,000.)

| | | | |
|---|---|---|---|
| 1 Balance at beginning of year | 238,000 | 5 Distributions: a Cash | 65,000 |
| 2 Net income per books | 147,783 | b Stock | |
| 3 Other increases (itemize): | | c Property | |
| Refund of 1987 Income Tax | | 6 Other decreases (itemize): | |
| Due to IRS Examination | | Reserve for Contingencies | 10,000 |
| | 18,000 | 7 Total of lines 5 and 6 | 75,000 |
| 4 Total of lines 1, 2, and 3 | 403,783 | 8 Balance at end of year (line 4 less line 7) | 328,783 |

*Fig. 19.7. Continued Form 1120.*

*CPA Tip*

> Although tax forms give most of the general information about the types of expenses, the instructions and regulations by the IRS may require additional information to be gathered. One example is that the business usage of a vehicle owned by a business is subject to different limitations, which are not necessarily found in Quicken. Your tax advisor should be consulted when you have areas that are questionable.

# Importing Quicken Data into TurboTax

The financial data you collect and store in Quicken can be imported directly into several popular income tax preparation packages. TurboTax, for example, imports Quicken data as long as you follow general steps. (*Note:* Even if you don't have TurboTax, you still may be able to apply the same general steps).

First, you need to track income and expense categories for each line of the income tax forms you need to fill out. At the end of the tax year, you edit the category descriptions for those categories that track income and expense for income tax accounting purposes. You should use as category descriptions the TurboTax code for the category. You need to refer to the TurboTax documentation for the list of codes, which has been expanded greatly since last year's version of the product.

Next, you need to create an ASCII disk file version of the report that summarizes the category totals you want to import. Then follow the instructions described in the TurboTax user's manual for importing the data contained in the ASCII disk file you create. (For this information and other help with TurboTax, you may want to read *Using TurboTax*, published by Que Corporation, which will be available at the end of 1990 or early in 1991.)

# Chapter Summary

This chapter described the basic steps you should take to make sure that Quicken produces the raw data necessary to complete federal and state income tax returns. The steps are neither complex nor difficult. You are required from the very beginning, however, to use categories that enable you to summarize income and expense data correctly.

# V

## Protecting Yourself from Forgery, Embezzlement, and Other Disasters

### Includes

Protecting Against Forgery and
Embezzlement

Protecting Against System Disasters

# Protecting Against
## Forgery and
## Embezzlement

**B** y this point, you have installed the Quicken software on your computer, set up your accounts, fine-tuned the system settings, and defined any of the categories you want to use. Now you need to protect your system and your money.

First, you should know how Quicken can help you protect yourself from forgery and embezzlement. This issue is very important, particularly for small businesses. The U.S. Department of Commerce estimates that employee theft costs American business about $40 billion annually.

Second, you should know about internal controls—ways in which you can minimize intentional and unintentional human errors within the Quicken system. Internal controls protect the accuracy and the reliability of your data files and the cash you have in your bank accounts.

## Defining Forgery and Embezzlement

Forgery is fraudulently marking or altering any writing that changes the legal liability of another person. When someone signs your name to one of your checks or endorses a check made payable to you, that person has committed forgery. Forgery also occurs when somebody alters a check that you wrote.

Embezzlement is fraudulently appropriating property or money owned by someone else. In a home or small business accounting system, an embezzler usually is an insider—employee, partner, friend, or family member —who intercepts incoming deposits or makes unauthorized withdrawals from a bank account. The steps you can take to prevent either crime are not difficult. Providing your system with protection is not an accusation of guilt. Making embezzlement and forgery more difficult or almost impossible is a wise investment of money and time.

# Preventing Forgery

Typically, a professional forger finds out when the bank mails your monthly statements. The forger intercepts one of your monthly bank statements, which provides him or her with samples of your signature and information about your average balances and when you make deposits and withdrawals. The forger is ready to go into action; he can order pre-printed checks from a printer just as you would or he or she can steal blank check forms from you. If the forger follows the latter course of action, the forms usually are taken from the back of your checkbook or from an unused set of blank checks so that you do not notice their disappearance as quickly. Unfortunately, you may not discover the forged checks until they clear your account or until you reconcile your bank account.

You should know a few things about forgery. First, your bank is responsible for paying only on checks with genuine signatures. The bank should use the signature card that you signed when you opened your account to judge the authenticity of the signature on your checks. The bank, therefore, cannot deduct from your account amounts stemming from forged checks. If the bank initially deducts money based on forged checks, the amounts must be added back to your account later. In certain cases, however, you are responsible for the money involved with forged checks.

You can make mistakes that cause you to bear the cost of a forgery. One mistake is to be careless and sloppy, or negligent, in managing your checking account. For example, your business may use a check-signing machine easily available to anyone within the company, including a check forger. Another example of negligence is to routinely leave your checkbook on the dashboard of your red convertible. The courts are responsible for determining whether such behavior represents negligence; if the court determines that your conduct falls short of the care a reasonable person would exercise, the bank may not have to pay for the forger's unauthorized transactions.

Another mistake that may leave you liable for forgery losses is failure to review monthly statements and canceled checks. You should examine these items closely for any forged signature, and you must report the forgeries promptly. If you do not—generally, you have one year—your bank is not obligated to add back to your account the amount stolen by the check forger.

If you do not examine your monthly statements and canceled checks within 14 days of receiving them, you lose your right to force the bank to add back to your account additional amounts stolen by the same check forger. If a forger writes ten checks for $50 on your account, for example, and you look at the bank statement a month later, the bank must add back the first forged $50 check, but is not liable for the nine other checks that followed.

> Never allow someone to occasionally sign checks for you. If you are out of town, for example, do not allow an employee or neighbor to use your checkbook to pay urgent bills for you. If that person signs a check for you and you do not report the signature as a forgery to the bank within 14 days, and if that person forges checks at a later date without your knowledge, the bank probably will not be responsible for payment on those forgeries.

*CPA Tip*

At the very least, check forgery wastes your time and the bank's time. If you are not careful, forgery can cost you all the money you have. Following are some useful precautions that you may take to avoid this catastrophe:

1. Treat your blank checks as you would treat cash. Do not leave check forms in places easily accessible to others. Better yet, lock your checks up or at least put them away in a desk drawer or cabinet so that they are not easy to find. (This rule also goes for the box of Quicken computer checks.)

2. Use Quicken to keep your check register up-to-date. This precaution enables you to notify the bank immediately to stop payment on checks that have not been recorded in your check register, but are missing from your pad or box of blank checks.

3. Watch for your monthly bank statement and canceled checks. If they do not arrive at the usual time of the month, call the bank to

find out whether the statements are late that month. You want to make sure that your statement has not been intercepted by a forger who will use your canceled checks to practice your signature.

4. Review the canceled checks you receive with your bank statement and verify that you or one of the other signers on the checking account wrote the checks. Also verify that none of the checks were altered.

5. Reconcile the balance shown in your check register with the balance shown on the monthly bank statement as soon as possible. The reconciling process does not take very long. For more information on reconciling your account, see Chapter 8.

6. Be sure to write *VOID* in large letters across the face of checks you do not use. If you have old blank check forms you no longer need—your name or address changed or you have closed the account, for example—destroy the check forms.

7. Fill in all the blanks, particularly the payee and amount fields on a check form, to prevent a forger from altering a check you actually wrote and signed. If you have set the alignment correctly on your printer, Quicken completely fills out each of the required check form fields. For those checks that you write manually, however, do not leave space on the payee line for a forger to include a second payee, and do not leave space on one of the amount fields so that $5.00 can be changed to $500.00 (see figs. 20.1 and 20.2.) The first figure is a perfect example of a check so poorly filled out that it almost invites forgery. The second figure shows how a check written like the one shown in figure 20.1 can be modified by a forger.

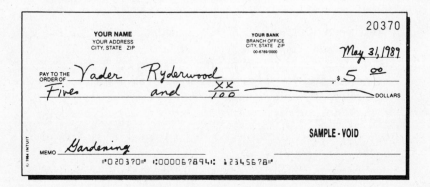

**Fig. 20.1.** *A good example of a bad way to write a check.*

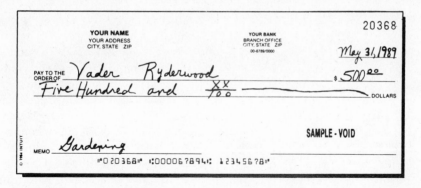

**Fig. 20.2.** How your check can be altered by a forger.

# Preventing Embezzlement

Embezzlement is more of an issue for business users of Quicken than for home users. Accordingly, the next few paragraphs focus on the business aspects of the problem.

Generally, embezzlement is a risk anytime you have others working with business assets (cash, inventory, or equipment, for example), or with a business's financial records. Because embezzlement takes so many different forms, the process cannot be generalized. You should take precautions against embezzlement, even if you have no suspicions that this crime may be a risk to you. When you fail to erect barriers to embezzlement, you become an appealing target. Often the embezzler is the least likely person to be expected of such a crime.

# Keeping Complete Financial Records

In many small-business embezzlement cases, messy or incomplete financial records are involved. If the accounting records are a mess, locating certain transactions usually is difficult or impossible—especially fraudulent transactions.

By using Quicken, you keep complete financial records for most parts of your business. If other areas exist in which you are not using Quicken, however, such as in billing and collecting from customers, be especially diligent and careful.

## Segregating Duties

Try to separate physical custody of an asset, such as cash or accounts receivable, from the records for the asset. If one employee keeps the company checking account records using Quicken, for example, another employee should sign all the checks and collect all the cash. If another employee keeps track of the amounts customers owe and how much they pay on their bills, someone else should count and deposit the incoming cash. In these examples, the person who keeps the records indirectly double-checks the work of the person with physical custody of the asset, and the person with physical custody of the asset indirectly checks the work of the person keeping the records.

## Checking Employee Backgrounds

Before hiring anyone, check his or her background and references carefully. Be sure to check carefully the background of persons you rely on for important parts of your business, such as counting cash and accounting. Embezzlement tends to be a habit with some people. In many cases, you find that an embezzler has stolen from his or her previous employer.

## Requiring Vacations

Even if you follow the three precautions described previously, a clever embezzler still can steal from you, but embezzling becomes difficult. Usually such schemes require a lot of on-going effort and maintenance on the part of the embezzler. You should require people to take vacations. By following this precaution, you can take over or reassign a person's duties, and the embezzlement scheme crumbles or becomes obvious to others if an embezzler skims a portion of the incoming cash deposits. If an embezzler writes checks for more than the actual amount and pockets the difference, you may notice that cash expenses decrease during his or her vacation.

# Using Internal Controls

Internal controls are rules and procedures that protect your business assets—including cash—and the accuracy and reliability of your financial records. You can use internal controls to protect yourself from forgery and embezzlement and to make recovering from forgery and embezzlement easier, if you are unlucky enough to become a victim. Within Quicken, you can use three internal controls to further protect your system:

❏ Leave a paper audit trail

❏ Retain your documents

❏ Use the Quicken password feature

# Creating Paper Trails

One of the most important internal control procedures you can use is to create paper evidence that accurately describes and documents each transaction. The capability to produce this paper evidence is one of Quicken's greatest strengths—a strength that you should take advantage of as much as possible.

Obviously, you record every check you write and every deposit you make in the check register. But you also should record individual cash with-drawals from automated tellers machines, bank service fees, and monthly interest expenses. Entering these transactions provides you with solid descriptions of each transaction that affects your cash flow.

The extensive reports that Quicken offers provide you with another important piece of the paper trail for transactions. As an audit trail, the check register links the individual checking account transactions to the summary reports. For example, suppose that you notice a balance in some expense category that is much larger than you expected. Using the Reports feature, you can look through the check register for the specific transactions that affected the expense category.

Computer-based accounting systems, including Quicken, probably use and generate more paper than any manual system. From an internal control perspective, this fact is comforting. The clean, easy-to-read, and well-organized information produced by Quicken makes reviewing transactions, checking account balances, and researching suspicious income or expense conditions much easier. As a result, you are more likely to find any errors of omission—and even fraudulent transactions—in your checking account records.

# Retaining Documents

After looking at all the paper a computer-based accounting system can generate (check forms, registers, and other special reports), you may wonder how long you need to keep this paperwork.

Table 20.1 provides guidelines on the length of time you should keep canceled checks, check registers, and any of the other special reports generated by Quicken. These guidelines are based on statutory and regulatory requirements and statutes of limitations. If you have more questions about other personal or business financial records and documents, talk to your tax advisor.

**Table 20.1**
**Document Storage Guidelines**

| Reports and Forms | 1 year | 3 years | 7 years | Permanent |
|---|---|---|---|---|
| Check register | | | | X |
| Backup files | X | | | |
| Canceled checks | | | | X |
| Category lists | | | | X |
| Monthly personal income/expense statements | | X | | |
| Yearly personal income/expense statements | | | X | |
| Other personal reports | X | | | |
| Monthly business income/expense statements | | X | | |
| Yearly business income/expense statements | | | X | |
| Other business reports | X | | | |

# Using Passwords

Passwords represent a third internal control mechanism. With Quicken, you can use passwords to limit access to the account groups you use to store your financial records. To set a password, select the **Password** option from the Change Settings menu (see fig. 20.3). Quicken then displays the Password menu shown in figure 20.4.

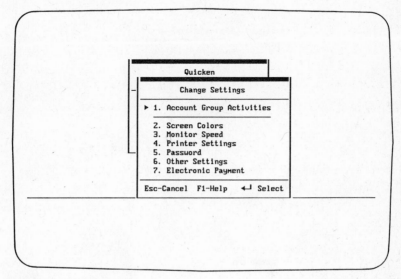

*Fig. 20.3.* *The Change Settings menu.*

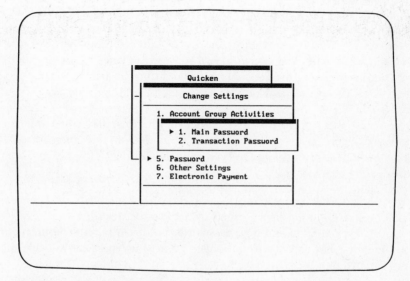

*Fig. 20.4.* *The Password menu.*

You can use two types of passwords in Quicken: main and transaction date passwords. The main password provides access to an account group. If you want each account group to have a password, you need to set up a password for each group. If you select the **Main Password** option, Quicken displays the Set Up Password screen shown in figure 20.5.

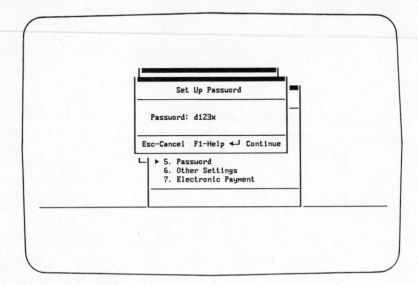

*Fig. 20.5. The Set Up Password screen.*

To define a main password, type the combination of letters and numbers you want to use as a password. You can use up to 16 characters. (*Note:* Quicken does not distinguish between the use of upper- and lowercase letters in establishing or using passwords.) After setting the password, Quicken asks you for the password before allowing you to view or modify transactions in any of the accounts with the group. Figure 20.5, for example, shows the main password set to d123x. The next time you try to access the Write Checks, Register, or Reports screen for the account group with the password d123x, Quicken requires that you enter the password. Figure 20.6 shows the screen on which you type the password. As an additional precaution, Quicken does not display the password you type.

If you want to change or remove the password, reselect the **Main Password** option. Quicken displays the Change Password screen shown in figure 20.7. Type the old and new passwords and press Enter. You now can use the new password. If you no longer want to use passwords, leave the New Password field blank.

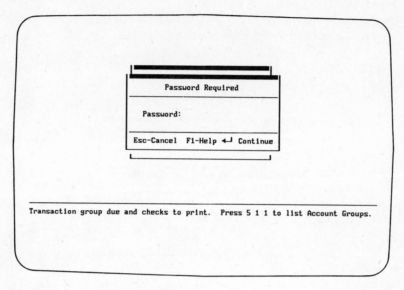

*Fig. 20.6. Entering the main password.*

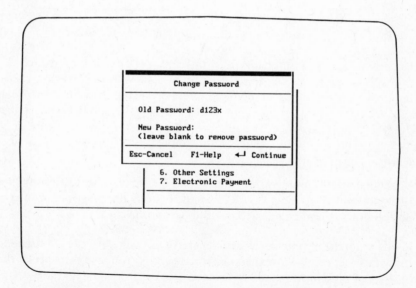

*Fig. 20.7. The Change Password screen.*

You can require transaction date passwords to make changes to the account before a certain date. These passwords are useful if you want to restrict or limit transactions recorded or modified for prior months. To define a transaction password, select the **Transaction Password** option. The screen shown in figure 20.8 appears.

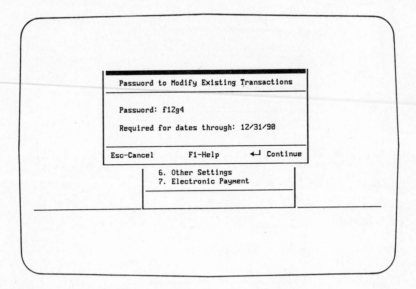

**Fig. 20.8.** *The Password to Modify Existing Transactions screen.*

On this screen, you enter the password and the date through which the transaction password is required. Figure 20.8 shows the password, f12g4, required for entering or modifying transactions dated through 12/31/90. If you want to record a transaction dated 12/31/90, Quicken requires that the transaction password be entered on the screen shown in figure 20.9. As with main passwords, Quicken does not display the transaction password as you type it.

*Note:* Quicken enables you to enter all the information, and when you are ready to record the transaction, Quicken requests the password. You cannot record the transaction without the password.

If you want to change a transaction password, reselect the Transaction Password menu and the old and new passwords. You also can specify the old and new passwords (see fig. 20.10).

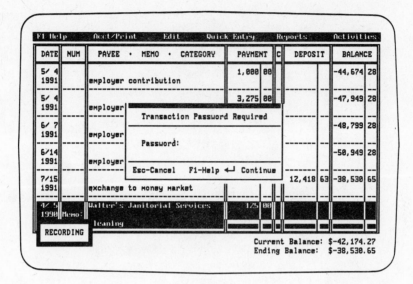

**Fig. 20.9.** *Entering the transaction password.*

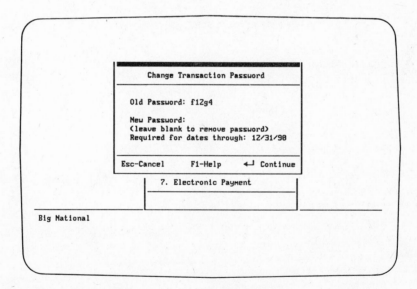

**Fig. 20.10.** *The Change Transaction Password screen.*

*CPA Tip*

You should consider the following three conventions when using passwords:

1. Make sure that you do not lose your password. If you lose your password, you lose your data. Record your password in a safe place in case you forget it.

2. If you are worried about someone accessing Quicken and then writing computer checks, initiating electronic payments, or modifying your account group information, use nonsensical passwords of at least six characters. The passwords you create then are much more difficult to guess.

3. Be sure that you don't use some seemingly clever password scheme, such as month names or colors, as passwords. If you set the transaction password to *blue*, the curious user will not take long to figure out the main password—even if the password is *chartreuse to mauve*.

# Chapter Summary

This chapter described actions you can take to protect yourself from forgery and embezzlement. Admittedly, these topics are unpleasant. By thinking about this subject and taking some precautions, however, you can minimize the chances of something that is even more unpleasant—being a victim.

# 21

# Protecting Against
# System Disasters

System disasters don't affect only the Quicken program and data files. System disasters may, in fact, affect every program and all the data on your computer. For many users, however, the creation of financial records with Quicken is the most important function the computer performs. The data that Quicken collects and stores are, for many businesses, essential to stay in business. For many individuals, the data Quicken collects and stores are critical to tax preparation and investment management. It is important, therefore, for Quicken users to understand the reasons for and some of the precautions against some of the more common and the more dangerous system errors.

The information in this chapter doesn't apply just to Quicken program and data files. Although the information covered here is in the interest of protecting your financial records, the information also applies to your other software and data.

## Defining a Few Basic Terms

One of the most appealing features of Quicken is that you don't have to be a computer wizard to make good use of the program. In fact, you really don't need to know much at all about computers, how they work, and how they are put together. You may want to keep it that way—you may have no desire or inclination to increase your computer knowledge. If you want to look into the ways you can prevent system disasters, however, you should learn a few computer terms before getting into specifics.

# Files

Files are the basic storage tools of computers. For example, if you upgraded from Quicken 3.0 and look in the QUICKEN3 directory, you see a list of files. (***Note:*** If you are a new user of Quicken, your files probably are stored in QUICKEN4 instead of QUICKEN3.) You can try this yourself by typing *dir c:\quicken3* at the C› prompt (see fig. 21.1). Generally, two types of files exist: program files and data files.

```
                                                  1
     Volume in drive C has no label
     Directory of  C:\QUICKEN3

     .            <DIR>      5-19-90    7:25a
     ..           <DIR>      5-19-90    7:25a
     Q      EXE   200160     6-29-90    2:53p
     Q      HLP   100873     6-29-90   12:00p
     QCHECKS DOC    6097     6-29-90   12:00p
     PRINTERS DAT   4991     6-29-90   12:00p
     BILLMIND EXE  10497     6-29-90   12:00p
     Q      OVL   362384     6-29-90   12:00p
     Q      CFG     1009     3-31-91   10:03a
     QDATA  QDT     4352     1-10-91    1:43p
     QDATA  QNX     1270     1-10-91    1:43p
     QDATA  QMT     3405     1-10-91    1:43p
     QDATA  QDI      728     1-06-91    4:07p
     Q3     DIR       51     3-31-91   10:03a
     BUSINESS QDT    9856    3-31-91   10:03a
     BUSINESS QNX    3190    3-31-91   10:03a
     BUSINESS QMT    1926    3-31-91   10:03a
     BUSINESS QDI     544    3-31-91   10:03a
            18 File(s)    8341504 bytes free

     C:\QUICKEN3>
```

***Fig. 21.1.*** *A list of the files in the QUICKEN3 directory.*

Program files store the instructions, or software, that tell your computer what to do. You usually can tell program files by their extensions because program files are named with EXE, COM, or BAT file extensions.

Data files store information. For example, the checking account information you enter into the Quicken register actually is stored in data files. (***Note:*** If you are interested in which Quicken files are program files and which are data files, refer to Chapter 9.)

# Software

The software represents actual instructions that tell your computer what to do. People often segregate software into system software, which generally controls the physical components of your computer system, and application software, which uses the operating software to create and process data. DOS, which is an acronym for *disk operating system*, is an example of system software. Quicken is an example of application software.

## Hardware

Hardware refers to the actual, physical components of your computer, such as the monitor, keyboard, printer, disk drives, memory, microprocessor chips, and so on.

# Preventing Hardware Disasters

Computers, like people, don't always operate perfectly. Although you probably shouldn't worry about your personal computer breaking down, you need to be prepared for a breakdown. Better yet, you can work to prevent a breakdown.

## Dealing with Dirty Power

The electric power you use to run your computer and everything else in your home or office may pose a danger to your computer and the data you store on and with it. The danger comes from dirty electrical power —power that surges and sags in strength. Most of the time, these fluctuations don't cause a problem. But if the surge is severe enough, the surge may cause your computer to reset itself. In effect, the power surge causes your computer to temporarily turn itself off, which means, at the very least, that you lose the transactions you have entered as part of the current session of Quicken. Unfortunately, the situation can get worse: if a power surge causes your computer to reset at the same time the computer is writing or reading data from your hard disk or a floppy disk, the data on the disk may be damaged.

To prevent this particular disaster, you can use a simple device called a "surge protector" or "surge suppressor." You plug the surge protector into the wall socket and then plug your computer into the surge protector. The surge protector removes power surges, which means that your computer, because it gets its power from the surge protector, will never get power surges. Talk to your local computer supplier to see which type of surge protector is best for your system. You shouldn't have to pay much more than about $50.

# Handling Hard Disk Failures

Hard disks are remarkably reliable when you consider that while your computer runs, the hard disk is spinning constantly. Sooner or later, however, the hard disk probably will fail, so remember to back up regularly—that way you minimize the work you lose by re-entering transactions. (Chapter 9 describes the process for backing up your files.)

Consider two preventive measures against hard disk failure. First, don't turn on and off your machine several times a day. Instead, just leave the machine running. Your computer doesn't use much electrical power—probably about the same as your desk lamp. By leaving the computer running all day—even while you are out running errands, going to lunch, or working with customers—you minimize the most wearing and stressful operation your computer goes through: being turned on.

A second preventive measure relates to the fact that heat really isn't very good for your computer. Keep the room your computer is in at a comfortable temperature. For the same reason, don't stack books, a computer manual, or check forms on top of the computer so that they block the ventilation holes. Some of the circuitry, like the microprocessor, needs to stay below a certain temperature to work correctly. You may have heard horror stories about the personal computer circuit boards—the laminated cardboard boards that the electronic circuitry plugs into—delaminating when temperatures become extreme.

# Handling Floppy Disk Problems

You undoubtedly will use floppy disks to store Quicken data files—even if you have a hard disk on your computer. You should know a little about preventing floppy disk failures.

Floppy disks are amazingly durable. Floppy disks store data on a thin plastic disk coated with a material that can store magnetic charges. Magnetic charges on the disk's surface represent the binary digits, or bits, that are the basic building blocks of program and data files. As long as you treat floppy disks with a reasonable degree of care, you really shouldn't have problems. You should consider a few things, however, when handling floppy disks.

First, because the actual disk is plastic, you don't want the disk to become very cold or very hot. A very cold floppy disk—one whose temperature drops below freezing—becomes brittle and may change shape. A very hot disk—one whose temperature rises above 140 degrees—may warp or even melt. In either case, because the actual plastic disk becomes damaged, you can lose the data on the disk. You shouldn't, therefore, leave floppy disks in your car if you car is parked outside and the temperature is below freezing. You also shouldn't leave disks on the dashboard of your car on a hot, sunny day. And you shouldn't set a steaming mug of hot coffee on top of the disk.

A second set of problems relates to the fact that the information on the disk is stored as a series of magnetic charges on the disk's surface. Because of this, you don't want to do things that change or foul the charges. Don't, for example, store disks next to a magnet, even if the magnet is only a small one for holding paper clips. And don't store disks next to appliances that generate magnetic fields, such as refrigerators, televisions, and telephones. You also don't want to touch the actual disk surface (which you can see through the opening on the plastic sleeve of the disk), spill things on the disk, or write on the disk with a sharp object.

# Reviewing and Preventing Software Disasters

Software poses as many potential dangers to your computer and to your use of Quicken, and the Quicken files, as does the hardware. Potential problems include the possibility of accidentally deleting files, of somehow "catching" a computer virus, and the myriad difficulties that can come from working with "beta" (pre-release) software, freeware, and shareware. All these things can damage your computer, the Quicken data files, and your ability to use Quicken.

## Recovering Deleted Files

You can use a variety of ways to delete files: with DOS commands such as DEL or ERASE, with Quicken, and with other application programs, such as Lotus 1-2-3 and Microsoft Word. You can accidentally delete files in many different ways—much as you can accidentally throw out an important financial document. You should know, however, that if you do accidentally delete a file, you can recover the file as long as you understand what happens when you delete a file. You also need to know which tools you can use to recover, or "undelete," previously deleted files.

*Caution:* Do not change or add to the files on the hard disk or floppy disk that contains the deleted files. When DOS marks a file as erased in its list of files and file locations, DOS assumes that the portion of the disk that contains the deleted file can be used to store other program and data files. If you create any new data files, increase the size of existing data files, or install new program files—such as the software to recover the deleted files—you may overwrite the files you want to recover. For this reason, if you accidentally delete your files and want to recover the deleted files, do so immediately.

When DOS deletes a file, DOS doesn't actually remove the file from the hard disk or floppy disk. Instead, DOS erases the first letter of the file's name on its list of files and file locations. At this point in time, the file and the file name—minus its first letter—are still there. But DOS considers the deleted file gone. You can still recover the file—although you cannot use DOS to do so. Several relatively inexpensive programs that provide an undelete file feature are available. These programs include PC Tools Deluxe, Norton Utilities, Lotus Magellan, and Mace Utilities.

If you need to recover a deleted file, you can go down to the local software store, purchase one of the these utilities—PC Tools Deluxe, for example—and use the program to undelete the deleted files. Whichever program you choose, the process works the same way. PC Tools Deluxe looks at the DOS list of files and file locations and gives you a list of the files on the list that have their first letters erased. Quicken data files that usually appear as

    QDATA.QDT
    QDATA.QNX
    QDATA.QMT
    QDATA.QDI

instead appear on a list as

    ?DATA.QDT
    ?DATA.QNX
    ?DATA.QMT
    ?DATA.QDI

You follow the program's directions for undeleting the files, which means you tell the software that is replacing the files the first letter of the file names that were deleted—in this example, the letter "Q."

# Protecting Against Viruses

Viruses have been around for some time—probably for almost 20 years. Some say their existence and, therefore, their danger have been exaggerated. Others counter by pointing to the widely reported examples of viruses that you may have read about in your local newspaper. Whatever the truth, you should understand a thing or two about viruses and how to protect yourself from them.

## Defining Viruses

Viruses actually are small programs. Sometimes viruses do rather innocuous things like displaying political or supposedly humorous messages randomly or on specific dates—such as April 1—as you work on your computer. Oftentimes, they operate more nefariously. A virus, for example, may secretly and slowly destroy program and data files bit by bit. Because the corruption of your data files is so slow, you don't notice the virus's effect until it is too late and the virus has infected even your backup copies of data files. Another virus may incrementally use more of your computer's power so that the computer operates more and more slowly. In each of these cases, however, you don't want your machine infected. And in most cases, the steps for making sure that your machine isn't infected or for "disinfecting" your computer aren't all that difficult—as long as you understand where viruses come from and how you can detect and get rid of them.

## Determining Where Viruses Originate

Because a virus is actually a program, for your machine to be infected, the virus program file somehow needs to be copied to your computer. Usually, that means the virus program file is copied to your computer from an infected floppy disk. You also can infect you computer by copying an infected file from a computer bulletin board by modem. For this reason, the basic rule is that you should not copy program files blindly.

You probably don't need to worry about copying program files as part of installing a program from a major software company. Software companies, for most the part, thoroughly test all the parts of a program long before you ever install the program. But—and this is highly recommended—you should be leery about copying program files on a floppy disk that came from a friend, or a friend of a friend. Aside from the legal and moral issues (you shouldn't copy pirated software), and even though the original software is fine, the floppy disk that you are copying the program files from may be infected.

Although not everyone agrees, you probably should not use the free software that people pass around, for basically for the same reason. Ensuring that the program files aren't infected is just too difficult. If you insist on using these programs, take the effort to contact the original writer to confirm that the program files you are copying are, in fact, the ones he or she wrote. You also should confirm that the file date and file size, which appear when you list the program files using the DOS DIR command shown in figure 21.1, are the same as the original program files he or she created.

## Detecting Viruses

If you have, in the past, indiscriminately copied program files to your hard disk, your machine already may be infected. Predictably, the steps for curing your machine really depend on the virus. Different viruses behave differently, but you should be on the watch for several things.

First, keep a sharp eye out for program files that you don't understand or that don't seem related to the programs you use. If you find a suspicious-looking file, refer to the appropriate software user's manual to confirm that the file is indeed a valid program file. (As noted earlier, program files use the file extensions COM, EXE, or BAT.) If you find a program file you know you don't use, remove the file from the disk.

Second, watch for increases in the file size of program files. Some viruses don't actually appear as a separate program file, but rather append themselves to existing program files. If you see program files increasing in size for no apparent reason, consider the possibility that the existing program file is being contaminated by a virus. You should be able to check quite easily with the software manufacturer if you have questions about this possibility. For obvious reasons, any software manufacturer will be extremely interested if a virus is specifically infecting one of their programs.

A third thing to watch for are hidden files. You may have two or three hidden files on a disk. PC DOS uses the two hidden files IBMIO.COM and IBMDOS.COM. MS-DOS uses the two hidden files IO.SYS and MSDOS.SYS. If you use volume labels on your hard disk or floppy disks, a third hidden file for the label may exist. Your disks should not have any other hidden files. If other hidden files are present, either you or someone else hid the files. That someone else may be the creator of the virus.

To check for the presence of hidden files, you can use the DOS CHKDSK command. To use the CHKDSK command, type *chkdsk*, followed by a space, the drive letter, and a colon. To look for hidden files on your C hard disk, type *chkdsk c:*. DOS then displays information about the disk, including the number of hidden files (see fig. 21.2). (For an example of the other information that the CHKDSK command displays, refer to the DOS user's manual that came with your computer.)

```
C:\>chkdsk c:

  31344640 bytes total disk space
     55296 bytes in 3 hidden files
    133120 bytes in 59 directories
  22822912 bytes in 1317 user files
   8333312 bytes available on disk

    655360 bytes total memory
    519376 bytes free

C:\>
```

**Fig. 21.2.** *Use the DOS CHKDSK command to look for hidden files.*

*Note:* Some software packages search disks specifically for viruses. If you are someone who is rather careless about what you copy to your disks, you may want to consider purchasing one of these programs. Ask your local software dealer for help.

# Working with Beta Software

Beta software is the pre-release software that software manufacturers distribute to small groups of users—usually very experienced and sophisticated users—to test before the program actually is released to the software-buying public. In some people's minds, working with beta copies of software has a certain prestige—particularly beta copies of popular programs. You probably should not work with the beta on any machine that stores something as important as your personal or business financial records. Beta copies may have programming bugs, or errors, that cause the program to abort unexpectedly or that may damage or destroy data files.

A related point is that you shouldn't, for the same reason, use a beta copy of the software in place of an actual released-to-the-public version.

# Chapter Summary

This chapter covered a topic that most people don't regularly think about: preventing system disasters. If you use a computer as a tool for managing something as important as your money, you should understand how to prevent hardware and software disasters.

# A

# Tips for Specific Business Situations

This appendix gives you some tips for using Quicken in specific business situations. You should read the previous sections of the book before starting this appendix, because this appendix does not focus on the mechanics of menu options or the way in which you complete screens.

## Tips for Lawyers, Consultants, and Other Professionals

Probably the simplest kind of business to perform accounting for is a professional service business. You should be able to run your accounting records out of a checkbook. As long you record an income category when you make deposits, and record an expense category when you write checks or withdraw money, you can produce helpful financial reports that enable you to gauge your performance.

If you sell services, think about your billing. Billing produces what is probably your other major asset besides cash—receivables—in addition to determining your cash inflow.

If your volumes of invoices and clients are low, you probably can perform billing and collecting by using a combination of manual techniques and Quicken. You may be able to track the hours you spend with various clients in an appointment calendar.

If your volumes of invoices and clients are high, you need a fast way to accumulate the amounts your clients owe you, to aggregate these amounts, and to produce an invoice. You also need an easy way to track outstanding invoices. If you are not happy with the way your current billing and receivables tracking works, consider acquiring a stand-alone billing package. One popular package is Timeslips III, which provides a convenient way to record the hours you spend on a client's behalf, account for the out-of-pocket expenses you incur, and generate invoices at the end of the month.

# Tips for Restaurants

You can use Quicken for restaurant accounting. As part of closing out the cash register, you can record the daily cash and credit-card sales as a deposit transaction into your register. You also can record expenses directly into Quicken as they occur by categorizing any checks you write.

Although you may be tempted to carry your inventory in an account because inventory is an asset, this method is probably not worth the effort. Food inventories are too short-lived. What you record on Monday as food inventory, you probably use up or throw out by the following Monday. Categorize food purchases in an expense category instead of setting up a food inventory account that you must adjust every time you calculate your profits. You need to calculate an inventory balance for your income tax return, but only once per year.

# Tips for Retailers

Retail businesses, especially those that do not have to prepare invoices or statements, also can use Quicken with good results. You need a point-of-sale system like a cash register to ring up sales, make change, and so forth. At the end of the day, you can enter the total sales for the day as a deposit transaction into your check register.

For a retail business that holds extensive inventory, Quicken has one weakness—you do not have a good way to track the units and dollars of inventory you hold. You may want to implement a manual inventory-tracking system and use a common tool for setting priorities: ABC analysis and classification.

*ABC analysis and classification* is a common-sense approach to breaking down your inventory into classes—A, B, or C—to show their relative value to you. Items in the A class are the most valuable, and items in the C class are the least valuable. After categorizing items in the three classes, you decide which control and management procedures are appropriate and cost-effective for each class.

Typically, class A items constitute 20 percent of the total number of items in your inventory and make up 80 percent of your inventory's dollar value. You may want (or be required by law) to count class A items on a weekly or daily basis and maintain precise manual records of balances and changes in the balances.

Class B items are at the next level of importance and value. These items usually constitute 40 to 50 percent of the total number of items in inventory, but they may account for less than 15 percent of the dollar value of your inventory. Accordingly, you may want to use a periodic inventory approach for class B items and take a physical count of your inventory once per quarter or month.

For some retailers and manufacturers, class C items may be as much as 40 percent of the total number of items in inventory, although they account for less than 5 percent of the inventory's value. Naturally, the effort expended on controlling this inventory is considerably less than the effort connected with classes A and B. For example, you may decide to count class C items annually.

ABC analysis and classification is a straightforward approach to setting priorities in your inventory control and management efforts. Although every item in your inventory may be important, do not succumb to the temptation to classify all your items as class A. Categorize your inventory holdings into meaningful and manageable groups.

# Tips for Churches, Synagogues, and Nonprofit Organizations

Most churches, synagogues and nonprofit organizations have simple accounting, and tracking of donations and disbursements fits easily into the checkbook register structure. A couple of common accounting requirements exist, however, for nonprofit businesses.

# Tracking Pledges

Some nonprofit organizations, as part of the budgeting process, solicit pledges from the donors who support the organization. Often, the organization tracks actual donations and compares these donations to the pledged amounts—just as a for-profit business tracks actual income and compares that amount to budgeted income.

If you want to make these sorts of comparisons, set up income categories for each person who pledges donations and enter a budgeted amount as the pledged amount. When you record donations, categorize donations as coming from a specific donor. If you have pledges from Vyder Ryderwood and Batum Schrag, for example, you have income categories for both donors. That way, at any time, you can generate a budget report that compares the budgeted, or pledged, donation income category amounts with the actual donation income category amounts.

# Tracking Fund Designations

Some nonprofit businesses accept designated donations. A contributor may, for example, designate that he wants his donation to go into the new building fund or for the children's breakfast program. The easiest way to track such designations is to set up separate bank accounts for each designation. When someone designates a donation for a specific purpose, you can deposit the money into the separate fund.

# Outgrowing Quicken

Quicken's simplicity and friendliness make the program a popular package. However, you may outgrow the product. You may become more sophisticated in your financial management, or your business may grow too large or complex for Quicken. This book concludes with some pointers on where you go when you need to move to something new.

## Becoming More Sophisticated

Even if you are not an accountant, you may want to become more sophisticated in your financial management. The more sophisticated you become, the harder it is to get what you want from Quicken. You may, for example, want to create elaborate invoices or monthly customer statements, generate recurring invoices or purchase orders, use a perpetual inventory system, use double-entry bookkeeping, and account for multiple companies that you later want to consolidate. You sometimes can accomplish these tasks with Quicken, but your solution probably will be awkward and incomplete compared to what is available from a more advanced accounting package.

You may consider taking two or three community college or university accounting classes. Often, colleges offer two introductory accounting courses and a managerial accounting course. An introductory course on business financial management also may be helpful. If you want to become more sophisticated in your financial management, the place to start is often your own knowledge base.

## Becoming Too Large for Quicken

Increased business volumes can make you outgrow Quicken. You can find yourself, for example, spending most of your time printing checks, entering transactions into Quicken registers, and generating reports. You may not have time to be a full-time accountant or bookkeeper. To be quite candid, if you have applied all the tricks and techniques described in Chapter 18, you are probably expecting too much from Quicken.

If this situation sounds familiar, look at similar batches of transactions that seem to be taking an inordinate amount of time and consider moving them to an outside service bureau or processing them with a more convenient tool. If you are spending too much time preparing payroll, for example, outside service bureaus such as ADP and PayChex can prepare your payroll checks and payroll tax forms. If you are spending a great deal of time recording invoices and customer payments, consider using one of the stand-alone billing packages, such as Timeslips III, which enables you to generate invoices and record payments much faster than Quicken.

You can still use Quicken as your master accounting system, but groups of similar transactions can be processed elsewhere. All you need to do is enter at the end of the month single transactions that summarize the individual transactions recorded elsewhere. If Quicken seems to be coming up short in several areas, you may need a full-fledged accounting system, such as DacEasy or Peachtree.

# Appendix Summary

This appendix gave you some tips and ideas for using Quicken in specific accounting situations. Not all the material covered will apply to your business, but some of the information presented should make using Quicken easier.

The information also should help you decide whether you have outgrown Quicken—and what to do if you have.

# B

# Using This Book with Version 3.0

If you are working with Version 3.0 of Quicken, you should find *Using Quicken: IBM Version*, 2nd Edition, helpful, even though the book is written for Version 4.0. To use this book for Version 3.0, you need to be aware of the features that exist only in Version 4.0. You may simply ignore those portions of the book that deal exclusively with Version 4.0.

*Note:* Some slight menu differences exist between Version 3.0 and Version 4.0. If you have trouble finding a specific option or the screen required for a certain report, the menu maps in the back of this book provide a quick reference source.

## Version 4.0's Two Major New Features

One major new feature of Version 4.0 is the investment account type that enables you to easily monitor your investments. This feature may seem like a small enhancement, but this feature is very powerful. Quicken 4.0 provides special tools for tracking and measuring the performance of mutual funds, stocks, bonds, and other investments. Chapter 13 describes the new investment tracking features that Quicken 4.0 provides. If you're working with Version 3.0, skip Chapter 13.

A second major new feature is Version 4.0's electronic payment capability. Quicken 4.0 now enables users to pay bills electronically using the Check-

Free electronic payment service. The electronic payment feature, which didn't exist in Quicken 3.0, is described in Chapter 15. Version 3.0 users can skip this chapter, too.

*Note:* Some Version 3.0EP (not the same as Version 3.0) users may have the electronic payment capability. If you're in that boat, you may find Chapter 15 helpful.

# Reviewing Other Miscellaneous Changes

Version 4.0 also contains some smaller changes. If you are using this book for Version 3, you can just ignore the sentences and paragraphs, interspersed throughout the book, that reference these minor differences.

Quicken Version 4.0 enables you to memorize report settings so that you can use and re-use the report description you create with the report request screens. Ignore the sections of Chapter 14 that describe how to create and use memorized reports.

Quicken Version 4.0 includes an auto-completion feature. This addition is handy. When you enter a piece of information that Quicken validates against a list Quicken keeps in memory, Quicken enables you to type just enough of the piece of information to uniquely identify it. You then can press Enter and Quicken enters the rest of the piece of information for you. This sounds complicated, but it's not. Take the case of categories. Say you have a category named Entertainment. If only this one category starts with the characters "Ent," you can just type *ent* and press Enter. Quicken completes the rest of the category name for you. The auto-completion feature works several places in the system, including for categories, accounts, investment securities, and investment goals. If you're a Version 3.0 user, ignore the sections of Chapters 4, 6, and 13 that allude to auto-completion.

Quicken Version 4.0 enables you to reprint a reconciliation report. This feature is discussed in Chapter 8.

Quicken Version 4.0 warns you if you re-use a check number. Keep that in mind as you enter transactions into the check register.

Quicken Version 4.0 enables you to start the program with parameters that allow you to control which account and account groups are selected. Version 4.0 also enables you to start the program so that it uses less memory. Chapter 11 describes starting Version 4.0 with parameters.

# C

# Planning for Your Retirement

**M**ost people aspire to quit working someday, and most people support themselves with a paycheck. How do you pay for your living expenses when the paycheck stops? You may think this topic should interest only those readers who are retiring soon, but that is not the case. The irony is that the easiest time to prepare for retirement is when it's still a long way off, and the hardest time to prepare for retirement is when it's right around the bend.

The problem resembles that of the swimmer who chooses a river that goes over a waterfall some distance downstream. Because the waterfall is still a long way off—perhaps the swimmer can hear only faintly the roar of the falls—swimming to shore is still easy. But as the sound of the waterfall becomes louder, the current also becomes stronger. And the swimmer must work harder and harder to reach the shore safely. If the swimmer doesn't try to escape from the river until the very end, the current is too strong. At that point, the sound of the waterfall is deafening and the danger obvious, but the swimmer is at the mercy of the river's increasing strength.

The opening paragraphs of this book suggested that your reasons for using Quicken probably stem from a desire to make better financial decisions, to increase your well-being, and to enjoy life more. The chapter on budgeting, Chapter 16, talked about the benefits of creating and using a financial game plan. This appendix walks you through the steps you can take to increase the chance that your retirement years also will be your golden years. You learn how to estimate your living expenses, how to figure what you may receive in pension and social security benefits, and how to make

**485**

up any shortfall between your income and your expenses. Although this whole topic may seem like something only 50 year olds should read, younger readers who peruse the paragraphs that follow may find the information beneficial. Contrary to what you may think, preparing for retirement at age 30 is much easier than at age 50 or 60.

# Preparing a Living Expenses Budget

The first step in planning for your retirement is to estimate what your living expenses should be. Obviously, the further away your retirement, the less precise your estimates will be. But even if retirement is twenty years away, your current spending should provide a useful benchmark for estimating future expenses. The general rule of thumb is that your retirement expenses will be roughly 80 percent of your current living expenses. Generally, three reasons account for this calculation:

❏ Your housing expenses may go down, either because you own a home and will have paid off the mortgage by then or you move to a smaller house or apartment.

❏ Children grow up and, probably, cease to be financial responsibilities.

❏ Work expenses, such as special clothing, transportation, tools, dues, and so on, stop because you stop working.

Be careful, however, about drastically reducing your planned living expenses. Remember that certain expenses also may increase because you age or retire. Medical expenses—such as the insurance your employer paid previously—may increase. Entertainment and vacation expenses may increase because you have more free time on your hands. Consider also that retirement may mean new hobbies or activities with attendant costs.

In any event, the reports that Quicken provides should prove immensely helpful. In particular, Quicken's Itemized Category Report should be useful because the report shows the ways you currently are spending money. (Refer to Chapter 14 if you have questions about how to print a particular report.) Figure C.1 provides a worksheet you can use to estimate the living expenses you may have during retirement. You can fill in the first column, the one that records your current expenses, using the Itemized Category Report. (Refer to Chapter 14 for information on using the Itemized Category Report.) Using that information and the ideas already touched on, you should be able to fill in the second column to come up with an estimate of your retirement expenses. Remember that Quicken's calculator provides a convenient way to compute the total expenses for retirement. Figure C.2 provides a sample completed worksheet.

| Estimated Living Expenses Worksheet | | |
|---|---|---|
| Expense | Current | Retirement |
| Housing | | |
|   Mortgage or rent | | |
|   Property taxes | | |
|   Property insurance | | |
|   Maintenance | | |
| Food | | |
| Transportation | | |
| Work | | |
| Hobby | | |
| Vacation | | |
| Recreation | | |
| Healthcare/Insurance | | |
| Clothing | | |
| Other | | |
| Total Expenses | | |

**Fig. C.1.** *A worksheet you can use to estimate your living expenses.*

You should keep in mind two more things about estimating your retirement living expenses. First, don't adjust your expense estimates for the inflation that probably will occur between now and the time you retire, because you address the ravages of inflation elsewhere. Second, although the worksheet in figure C.1 doesn't provide space to budget taxes, you will cover this important topic later.

# Estimating Tentative Retirement Income

Estimating your tentative retirement income is the second step in planning your retirement income. In general, a person's retirement income

| Estimated Living Expenses Worksheet | | |
|---|---|---|
| Expense | Current | Retirement |
| Housing | | |
|   Mortgage or rent | 8,000 | 0 |
|   Property taxes | 1,000 | 1,000 |
|   Property insurance | 500 | 500 |
|   Maintenance | 500 | 500 |
| Food | 3,000 | 500 |
| Transportation | 3,000 | 3,000 |
| Work | 1,500 | 0 |
| Hobby | 0 | 1,500 |
| Vacation | 1500 | 1,500 |
| Recreation | 500 | 500 |
| Healthcare/Insurance | 0 | 3,000 |
| Clothing | 1,000 | 1,000 |
| Other | 1,000 | 1,000 |
| Total Expenses | 21,500 | 14,000 |

*Fig. C.2. A sample completed worksheet.*

essentially consists of three components: social security, investment income, and pension income. To tally these three sources, you need to do the following:

1. Contact your local Social Security office and ask for the form called "Request for Earnings and Benefit Estimate Statement." Figure C.3 shows a sample of the form.

2. Complete the "Request for Earnings and Benefit Estimate Statement" by following the directions on the form. You need to enter your social security number, information about your earnings, and indicate when you plan to retire. After you complete the form, send the form to the address given. In a few weeks, you will receive an estimate of what you should receive in social security benefits when you retire. Enter the social security benefits estimate on Line 1 of the Estimated Retirement Income Worksheet shown in figure C.4.

Form Approved
OMB No. 0960-0466 ☐ SP

## SOCIAL SECURITY ADMINISTRATION

### Request for Earnings and Benefit Estimate Statement

To receive a free statement of your earnings covered by Social Security and your estimated future benefits, all you need to do is fill out this form. Please print or type your answers. When you have completed the form, fold it and mail it to us.

1. Name shown on your Social Security card:

   First      Middle Initial      Last

2. Your Social Security number as shown on your card:

   ☐☐☐-☐☐-☐☐☐☐

3. Your date of birth: ___ Month ___ Day ___ Year

4. Other Social Security numbers you have used:

   ☐☐☐-☐☐-☐☐☐☐
   ☐☐☐-☐☐-☐☐☐☐

5. Your Sex: ☐ Male ☐ Female

6. Other names you have used (including a maiden name):

7. Show your actual earnings for last year and your estimated earnings for this year. Include only wages and/or net self-employment income covered by Social Security.

   A. Last year's actual earnings:

   $ ☐☐☐,☐☐☐.☐0☐0
   Dollars only

   B. This year's estimated earnings:

   $ ☐☐☐,☐☐☐.☐0☐0
   Dollars only

8. Show the age at which you plan to retire: ☐☐
   (Show only one age)

9. Below, show the average yearly amount that you think you will earn between now and when you plan to retire. Your estimate of future earnings will be added to those earnings already on our records to give you the best possible estimate.

   Enter a yearly average, not your total future lifetime earnings. Only show earnings covered by Social Security. Do not add cost-of-living, performance or scheduled pay increases or bonuses. The reason for this is that we estimate retirement benefits in today's dollars, but adjust them to account for average wage growth in the national economy.

   However, if you expect to earn significantly more or less in the future due to promotions, job changes, part-time work, or an absence from the work force, enter the amount in today's dollars that most closely reflects your future average yearly earnings.

   **Most people should enter the same amount that they are earning now (the amount shown in 7B).**

   Your future average yearly earnings:

   $ ☐☐☐☐,☐☐☐.☐0☐0
   Dollars only

10. Address where you want us to send the statement:

    Name

    Street Address (Include Apt. No., P.O. Box, or Rural Route)

    City      State      Zip Code

    I am asking for information about my own Social Security record or the record of a person I am authorized to represent. I understand that if I deliberately request information under false pretenses I may be guilty of a federal crime and could be fined and/or imprisoned. I authorize you to send the statement of earnings and benefit estimates to the person named in item 10 through a contractor.

    ▶

    Please sign your name (Do not print)

    Date      (Area Code) Daytime Telephone No.
    ABOUT THE PRIVACY ACT
    Social Security is allowed to collect the facts on this form under Section 205 of the Social Security Act. We need them to quickly identify your record and prepare the earnings statement you asked us for. Giving us these facts is voluntary. However, without them we may not be able to give you an earnings and benefit estimate statement. Neither the Social Security Administration nor its contractor will use the information for any other purpose.

Form SSA-7004-PC-OP1 (9-89) Destroy Prior Edition

**Fig. C.3.** *The Social Security Administration's "Request for Earnings and Benefit Estimate Statement."*

3. If you qualify for an employer's pension, contact the pension fund administrator or trustee and ask for whatever information you need to estimate what your future retirement benefits will be. They should be more than happy to give this information to you. In fact, the pension fund trustee is required to give the information to you. (***Note:*** If you feel uncomfortable asking, tell the trustee or administrator that you need the information for a personal financial plan that's being prepared.) Enter any pension fund benefits estimate on Line 2 of the Estimated Retirement Income Worksheet shown in figure C.4.

4. Enter your current retirement savings on Line 3 of the Estimated Retirement Income Worksheet. (***Note:*** If you use Quicken to keep track of the investments and savings you have made for retirement, you should be able to obtain this information from the Portfolio Value Report. Refer to Chapter 14 if you have questions about how to print a report.)

**Estimated Retirement Income Worksheet**

Line 1 - Social security benefits

Line 2 - Pension benefits

Line 3 - Current savings

Line 4 - Future value factor

Line 5 - Future value of savings
(Note: multiply line 4 by line 3.)

Line 6 - Annual interest rate

Line 7 - Interest Income Savings
(Note: multiply line 7 by line 6)

Line 8 - Total Retirement Income
(Note: Add lines 1, 2 and 7)

Line 9 - Estimated Income Taxes

Line 10 - Spendable Income
(Note: Subtract line 9 from line 8.)

*Fig. C.4. The Estimated Retirement Income Worksheet.*

5. Enter the appropriate future value factor as shown in the Future Value Factors table in figure C.5. Find the number in the Years of Interest column that matches the number of years until you begin drawing on your money. For example, if you won't retire for another 20 years, locate the number 20. Next, choose the factor that corresponds to the interest rate. If you will retire in 20 years and expect an annual return of 5 percent, for example, you use the factor 2.6533.

| Future Value Factors | | | | |
|---|---|---|---|---|
| Years of | Annual Interest Rates | | | |
| Interest | 3% | 4% | 5% | 6% |
| 1 | 1.0300 | 1.0400 | 1.0500 | 1.0600 |
| 2 | 1.0609 | 1.0816 | 1.1025 | 1.1236 |
| 3 | 1.0927 | 1.1249 | 1.1576 | 1.1910 |
| 4 | 1.1255 | 1.1699 | 1.2155 | 1.2625 |
| 5 | 1.1593 | 1.2167 | 1.2763 | 1.3382 |
| 6 | 1.1941 | 1.2653 | 1.3401 | 1.4185 |
| 7 | 1.2299 | 1.3159 | 1.4071 | 1.5036 |
| 8 | 1.2668 | 1.3686 | 1.4775 | 1.5938 |
| 9 | 1.3048 | 1.4233 | 1.5513 | 1.6895 |
| 10 | 1.3439 | 1.4802 | 1.6289 | 1.7908 |
| 11 | 1.3842 | 1.5395 | 1.7103 | 1.8983 |
| 12 | 1.4258 | 1.6010 | 1.7959 | 2.0122 |
| 13 | 1.4685 | 1.6651 | 1.8856 | 2.1329 |
| 14 | 1.5126 | 1.7317 | 1.9799 | 2.2609 |
| 15 | 1.5580 | 1.8009 | 2.0789 | 2.3966 |
| 16 | 1.6047 | 1.8730 | 2.1829 | 2.5404 |
| 17 | 1.6528 | 1.9479 | 2.2920 | 2.6928 |
| 18 | 1.7024 | 2.0258 | 2.4066 | 2.8543 |
| 19 | 1.7535 | 2.1068 | 2.5270 | 3.0256 |
| 20 | 1.8061 | 2.1911 | 2.6533 | 3.2071 |
| 21 | 1.8603 | 2.2788 | 2.7860 | 3.3996 |
| 22 | 1.9161 | 2.3699 | 2.9253 | 3.6035 |
| 23 | 1.9736 | 2.4647 | 3.0715 | 3.8197 |
| 24 | 2.0328 | 2.5633 | 3.2251 | 4.0489 |
| 25 | 2.0938 | 2.6658 | 3.3864 | 4.2919 |
| 26 | 2.1566 | 2.7725 | 3.5557 | 4.5494 |
| 27 | 2.2213 | 2.8834 | 3.7335 | 4.8223 |
| 28 | 2.2879 | 2.9987 | 3.9201 | 5.1117 |
| 29 | 2.3566 | 3.1187 | 4.1161 | 5.4184 |
| 30 | 2.4273 | 3.2434 | 4.3219 | 5.7435 |
| 31 | 2.5001 | 3.3731 | 4.5380 | 6.0881 |
| 32 | 2.5751 | 3.5081 | 4.7649 | 6.4534 |
| 33 | 2.6523 | 3.6484 | 5.0032 | 6.8406 |
| 34 | 2.7319 | 3.7943 | 5.2533 | 7.2510 |
| 35 | 2.8139 | 3.9461 | 5.5160 | 7.6861 |

**Fig. C.5.** *The Future Value Factors table.*

*CPA Tip*

To adjust for inflation interest rates, deduct inflation from the stated interest rate or rate of return. For example, if you invest in certificates of deposit that pay 8 percent interest and inflation runs at 5 percent, your real rate of return is 3 percent. Similarly, if you invest in common stocks that pay an average 10 percent return, and inflation runs at 4 percent, your real rate of return is 6 percent. By removing inflation from the calculations, your calculations can be made in current-day dollars, which makes things simpler and yet recognizes the effect of inflation.

As a frame of reference in picking appropriate real rates of return, you may find several pieces of data helpful. Over the last 60 years or so, inflation has averaged a little more than 3 percent, common stocks have averaged 10 percent, long-term bonds have averaged around 5 percent, and short-term treasury bills have averaged roughly 3.5 percent. Therefore, when you subtract inflation, stocks produced real returns of 7 percent, long-term bonds produced real returns of about 2 percent, and treasury bills essentially broke even. Accordingly, if half of your retirement savings is invested in long-term bonds yielding 2 percent and the other half invested in common stocks yielding 7 percent, you may want to guess your return as somewhere between 4 and 5 percent.

6. On Line 5, calculate the future value of your current retirement savings by multiplying the savings amount on Line 3 by the future value factor on Line 4. If the appropriate factor is 2.6533 and your current savings amounts to $10,000, the future value of your savings amounts to $26,533.

7. On Line 6, enter the annual real interest rate you expect to earn on your retirement savings. (Refer to the preceding CPA Tip for help with this figure.)

8. On Line 7, calculate the annual investment or interest income you will earn on your retirement savings by multiplying on Line 5 by the figure on Line 6.

9. On Line 8, calculate your total retirement income by adding the figures on Lines 1, 2, and 7.

10. On Line 9, estimate the income taxes you will owe on your total retirement income figure shown on Line 8.

Of course, you don't know what the tax law and tax rates will be next year, let alone by the time you retire. The best approach, however, is to apply the current income tax laws. You calculate what your income taxes would be based on the current laws—and assume this figure will be close to what you actually pay when you retire. (**Note:** For help on how to calculate your income taxes, refer to Chapter 16, "Budgeting with Quicken," which describes the steps for estimating the income and social security taxes you will owe based on the 1990 income tax laws and rates.)

11. On Line 10, calculate the actual money you will have to spend on living expenses by subtracting your estimated income taxes expense on Line 9 from the total retirement income figure on Line 8. Figure C.6 shows a sample completed Estimated Retirement Income Worksheet.

---

**Estimated Retirement Income Worksheet**

| | |
|---|---|
| Line 1 - Social security benefits | 3,500 |
| Line 2 - Pension benefits | 5,174 |
| Line 3 - Current savings | 10,000 |
| Line 4 - Future value factor | 2.6533 |
| Line 5 - Future value of savings (Note: multiply line 4 by line 3.) | 26,533 |
| Line 6 - Annual interest rate | 5% |
| Line 7 - Interest Income Savings (Note: multiply line 7 by line 6) | 1,326 |
| Line 8 - Total Retirement Income (Note: Add lines 1, 2 and 7) | 10,000 |
| Line 9 - Estimated Income Taxes | 1,000 |
| Line 10 - Spendable Income (Note: Subtract line 9 from line 8.) | 9,000 |

---

**Fig. C.6.** *A sample completed Estimated Retirement Income Worksheet.*

If the total spendable income shown on Line 10 of the Retirement Income Worksheet equals or exceeds the total living expenses figure you developed on the Living Expenses Worksheet, congratulations! Assuming everything goes well, you are in good shape financially for your retirement. If, however, your estimate of your total spendable income in retirement is less than your estimate of your retirement living expenses, you need to save additional money for retirement—something that is described next.

# Estimating Needed Retirement Savings

Don't be discouraged if you worked through the steps described in the preceding two sections only to conclude that you cannot retire the way you might want. Recognizing the problem means you are in a lot better shape than most people who don't even realize they have a problem just over the horizon. You have the option of doing something about the potential shortfall—you can save additional money.

To figure out what you need to save over the years, follow these steps using the Retirement Savings Worksheet (see fig. C.7):

**Retirement Savings Worksheet**

Line 1 - Extra Income Needed

Line 2 - Annual real interest rate

Line 3 - Extra Savings Needed
(note: divide line 1 by line 2.)

Line 4 - Monthly Savings Factor

Line 5 - Monthly Savings Required
(note: multiply line 3 by line 4.)

*Fig. C.7. The Retirement Savings Worksheet.*

1. On Line 1, enter the extra retirement income you will need. This figure should be the difference between what the Estimated Living Expenses Worksheet shows and what the Estimated Retirement Income Worksheet shows.

2. On Line 2, enter the annual real interest rate you think you will earn based on the investments you will make with the money you save.

---

*CPA Tip*

The Retirement Savings Worksheet doesn't recognize the income taxes you will have to pay on the interest you earn on the additional retirement savings you accumulate. The assumption simplifies your calculations, but may cause imprecision in your estimates. If you feel that you cannot live with such imprecision, you need to calculate an "adjusted for income taxes" annual real interest rate. To do so, use the following formula:

(annual interest rate * ( 1 − income tax rate)) − inflation rate

---

3. On Line 3, calculate the extra savings you need to accumulate by dividing the extra retirement income figure (Line 1) by the annual real interest rate (Line 2). For example, if the extra retirement income needed is $5,000 and the annual real interest rate is 5 percent, you need an extra $100,000 of savings, calculated as ($5,000 / 5 percent).

4. On Line 4, enter the appropriate monthly savings factor from the Monthly Savings Factors table (see fig. C.8). To locate the appropriate monthly savings factor, look down the Years of Savings column until you come to the number that equals the same number of years you will be saving. Pick the factor in the same column as the annual real rate of return you assume you will earn on your investments. For example, if you want to save some amount on a monthly basis over the next twenty years and you think you can earn a 4 percent real rate of return, enter *.002726*.

*Note:* The Monthly Savings Factor table assumes that you save for retirement using investment options in which you don't have to pay taxes on the interest you earn, such as individual retirement accounts, employer-provided 401(k) plans, tax-deferred annuities, and so forth.

| Monthly Savings Factors | | | |
|---|---|---|---|
| Years of Savings | Annual interest rates | | |
| | 3% | 4% | 5% | 6% |
| 1 | 0.082194 | 0.081817 | 0.081441 | 0.081066 |
| 2 | 0.040481 | 0.040092 | 0.039705 | 0.039321 |
| 3 | 0.026581 | 0.026191 | 0.025804 | 0.025422 |
| 4 | 0.019634 | 0.019246 | 0.018863 | 0.018485 |
| 5 | 0.015469 | 0.015083 | 0.014705 | 0.014333 |
| 6 | 0.012694 | 0.012312 | 0.011938 | 0.011573 |
| 7 | 0.010713 | 0.010335 | 0.009967 | 0.009609 |
| 8 | 0.009230 | 0.008856 | 0.008493 | 0.008141 |
| 9 | 0.008077 | 0.007708 | 0.007351 | 0.007006 |
| 10 | 0.007156 | 0.006791 | 0.006440 | 0.006102 |
| 11 | 0.006404 | 0.006043 | 0.005698 | 0.005367 |
| 12 | 0.005778 | 0.005422 | 0.005082 | 0.004759 |
| 13 | 0.005249 | 0.004898 | 0.004564 | 0.004247 |
| 14 | 0.004797 | 0.004450 | 0.004122 | 0.003812 |
| 15 | 0.004406 | 0.004064 | 0.003741 | 0.003439 |
| 16 | 0.004064 | 0.003727 | 0.003410 | 0.003114 |
| 17 | 0.003764 | 0.003431 | 0.003120 | 0.002831 |
| 18 | 0.003497 | 0.003169 | 0.002864 | 0.002582 |
| 19 | 0.003259 | 0.002935 | 0.002636 | 0.002361 |
| 20 | 0.003046 | 0.002726 | 0.002433 | 0.002164 |
| 21 | 0.002853 | 0.002538 | 0.002251 | 0.001989 |
| 22 | 0.002679 | 0.002368 | 0.002086 | 0.001831 |
| 23 | 0.002520 | 0.002214 | 0.001937 | 0.001688 |
| 24 | 0.002375 | 0.002074 | 0.001802 | 0.001560 |
| 25 | 0.002242 | 0.001945 | 0.001679 | 0.001443 |
| 26 | 0.002120 | 0.001827 | 0.001567 | 0.001337 |
| 27 | 0.002007 | 0.001719 | 0.001464 | 0.001240 |
| 28 | 0.001903 | 0.001619 | 0.001369 | 0.001151 |
| 29 | 0.001806 | 0.001526 | 0.001282 | 0.001070 |
| 30 | 0.001716 | 0.001441 | 0.001202 | 0.000996 |
| 31 | 0.001632 | 0.001361 | 0.001127 | 0.000927 |
| 32 | 0.001554 | 0.001288 | 0.001058 | 0.000864 |
| 33 | 0.001481 | 0.001219 | 0.000995 | 0.000806 |
| 34 | 0.001413 | 0.001154 | 0.000935 | 0.000752 |
| 35 | 0.001349 | 0.001094 | 0.000880 | 0.000702 |

**Fig. C.8.** *The Monthly Savings Factors table.*

5. On Line 5, calculate your approximate required monthly savings by multiplying Line 4 by Line 3. If Line 3 shows $100,000 as the extra savings you need to accumulate and Line 4 shows a factor of .002726, you need to save $272.60 each month to accumulate $100,000 in today's dollars—not inflated dollars—by the end of the twenty-year period. Figure C.9 shows an example of a completed Retirement Savings Worksheet.

| Retirement Savings Worksheet | |
|---|---|
| Line 1 - Extra Income Needed | *5,000* |
| Line 2 - Annual real interest rate | *5%* |
| Line 3 - Extra Savings Needed (note: divide line 1 by line 2.) | *100,000* |
| Line 4 - Monthly Savings Factor | *.002726* |
| Line 5 - Monthly Savings Required (note: multiply line 3 by line 4.) | *272.60* |

**Fig. C.9.** *A sample completed Retirement Savings Worksheet.*

# Some More Tips on Retirement Planning

Planning for retirement can be frustrating and actually is never that easy. Before you decide you never will be able to quit working, however, here are a few suggestions and observations.

First, invest your retirement money in tax-deferred investments, such as individual retirement accounts, 401(k)s, annuities, and so forth. You should consider these types of investments even if you don't get an immediate tax deduction. The reason is that paying income taxes on the interest or investment income you earn greatly reduces the real interest rate you enjoy. Suppose, for the sake of illustration, that you choose to invest in a mutual fund that you expect will return around 7.5 percent annually. If you don't have to pay income taxes on the interest, you may be left with a real interest rate of around 4.5 percent (calculated as the 7.5 percent minus the 3 percent historical inflation rate). If you do have to pay income taxes, however, it's a different story. Suppose that your highest dollars of income are taxed at the 33 percent tax rate. To subtract the income taxes you will pay, multiply the 7.5 percent by $(1 - 33$ percent$)$. That means the "adjusted-for-income-taxes" interest rate is actually 5 percent. When you calculate the real interest rate by taking this 5 percent interest rate and subtracting the 3 percent inflation rate, your annual real interest rate amounts to a measly 2 percent—less than half of what you receive if you use an investment option that allows you to defer income taxes. In this case, using investment options in which you can defer the taxes more than doubles your return—which will make a huge difference in the amounts you accumulate over the years you save.

A second consideration is that the longer you postpone retirement, the more retirement income you typically will enjoy when you do retire. This tactic isn't much of a revelation, of course, because it makes intuitive sense. However, the difference postponed retirement makes may surprise you. If you postpone retirement, you have several things working in your favor. Social security benefits may increase because you begin drawing benefits later or because your average earnings are higher. Any retirement savings you accumulate have a few more years to earn interest, and you probably will be able to save more money. Finally, pension plans usually pay benefits based on years of service, so working a little longer can increase that source of retirement income. You can rework the numbers using the planning worksheets given in this appendix to see the specific numbers in your case.

A third and final point to consider relates to a fundamental assumption of the worksheets. The worksheets assume that you live off only your annual investment income, social security, and your pensions. This means that you never will actually spend the money you save—only the interest those savings earn. For example, if you have $100,000 in savings that earns $5,000 in annual interest, you spend only the $5,000, and you leave the $100,000 intact. As a practical matter, however, you probably can spend some of the $100,000. The trick is to make sure that the $100,000 doesn't run out before you do.

# Index

1065 tax form, 436-440
1120-A tax form, 441-442
1120 tax form, 446-449
1120S tax form, 443-445

## A

ABC analysis and classification, 478-479
Above field, 341
Account Balances option, 350
Account Group Activities menu, 184
Account Group Copied Successfully screen, 194
Account Group menu, 54
account groups
    defining new, 53-57
    deleting, 58-59
    editing names, 57-58
    selecting, 59
Account is a single mutual fund field, 262
accounting
    accrual-basis, 402
    nonprofit organization, 479-480
    restaurant, 478
    retail, 478-479
accounts
    adding, 47-51
    asset/liability, 240-242
    bank, checking cleared transactions, 162-163
    business accounting, tracking, 400-401
    cash, 247-248
    checking
        balance adjustment transactions, 173-176
        reconciliation reports, 167-169
        reconciling, 161-176
        transactions, troubleshooting, 176-179
        transposition errors, 177
        verifying balances, 167-168
    credit card, 251-256
    deleting existing, 51-52
    describing, 47-60
    determining suitability of use with Quicken, 50-51
    editing existing, 51
    entering all transactions at one time, 53
    investment, reconciling, 292-297
    naming conventions, 49
    report, selecting, 338
    selecting, 52-53
    starting Quicken with, 235
    transfers, recording, 73-74
    updating balances, 248-251
accounts payable (A/P) by vendor, business report, 320-321
Accounts Payable (Unprinted Checks) by Vendor screen, 321
Accounts Receivable by Customer screen, 322
accounts receivable (A/R) by customer, business report, 321-324
accrual-basis accounting, 402
Acct/Print menu, 76-77, 124, 196
Activities menu, 111-113
Adding Balance Adjustment Entry screen, 174
Adjust Balance menu, 294-295
Adjust Balance option, 294
Adjust Cash Balance screen, 295-296
Adjust Share Balance screen, 295-296
Alternate Printer Settings option, 27
amortization schedule, 427

annual tax report, business accounting, 418-419
ASCII file, 450
    exporting to, 196-198
    importing price history data, 290
    printing, 78-79
    printing reports to, 169, 306
asset accounts, 240-242
assets, market value, 257
Assign Transactions to Group screen, 107, 154
asterisks (*****) in check number field, 131
audit trails, Register, 85
auto-completion, 68, 120
AUTOEXEC.BAT file, 20
AUTOEXEC.BOO file, 20
automated record keeping, 388-389

## B

backing up files, 182-186
Balance Sheet screen, 327
balance sheets, 256-257
    business report, 326-328
balances, updating account, 248-251
bank accounts
    abbreviating bank name, 23
    CheckFree, identifying, 359-361
    home accounting, 392
bank service fees, 72
bank statement, 162
BCAT.QMT file, 182
Below field, 341
beta software, 475-476
BILLMIND.EXE file, 182
Billminder
    message box, 123
    option, 18-20
    program, 122-124
bills
    CheckFree, transmitting, 364-367
    early payment, 66, 118
    paying electronically, 353-372
budget report, creating, 348-349
Budget option, 348
budgets
    after-tax bonus shares, 384
    aggregating spending categories, 390-391
    categories, 380-381
    defining, 373
    designing, 375-380
    discretionary items, 389-390
    effects of raises on, 384
    emergency expenses, 384-385
    goals, 374-375
    individual retirement accounts (IRA), 383
    monitoring, 380, 389-392
    reports, 381-382
    saving money, 382-383
    spending methods, 392
    tips for success, 382-385
    zero-based, 385
BUFFERS, DOS statement, 17
business accounting
    accounts, tracking, 400-401
    categories, calculating, 402
    customer
        invoicing, 403-406

recording payments, 407-408
tracking receivables, 408-411
depreciation
calculating, 412
recording, 413-414
federal tax forms, 420
fixed assets, 411-412
recording, 413-414
payroll
preparing, 414-415
recording checks, 415-417
taxes, 418
reports, tax, 418-419
state tax forms, 420
transactions, defining, 401
W-2 form, 429-420
W-3 form, 429-430
business reports
accounts payable (A/P) by vendor, 320-321
accounts receivable (A/R) by customer, 321-324
balance sheet, 326-328
cash flow, 319-320
customer aging, 324
job/project, 324
payroll, 324-326
profit and loss statement, 317-319
Business Reports menu, 303

## C

calculator screen, 43
Calculator option, 112, 158
calculators
tape, 43
using, 42-44
capital gain distribution, mutual fund accounts, 270
capital gains (Schedule D), investment report, 331-332
Capital Gains (Schedule D) Report screen, 332
cash accounts, 247-248
cash expenditures, home accounting, tracking, 393
cash flow
business report, 319-320
personal report, 308-309
cash receipts, 393
Cash Account Register screen, 247
Cash Flow Report screen, 304, 308, 319
function keys, 309, 319
categories
adding, 213-215
budget, 380-381
business accounting, calculating, 402
deleting, 216-217
editing, 217-218
income tax, 429-450
listing, 205-210
printing, 218-219
report
matching, 339
selecting, 340
tax-related, 341
setting up, 212-213
subcategories, 210-212
working with, 203-205
Categorize/Transfer option, 104-105, 151-152, 213
Category and Transfer List screen, 105, 151, 213
Category field, 73, 415, 418, 427
Category matches field, 339
Category Not Found box, 215
Change Color Scheme screen, 229
Change Password screen, 461
Change Settings menu, 27, 54, 184, 227-234, 356, 459
Change Settings option, 27, 354

Change Transaction Password screen, 463
characters
special, 93-94
wildcard searches, 92-94
check forms
multipart, 14
numbering, 12
one-part, 14
options, 12-13
ordering, 11-14
two-part, 14
voucher stub, 14
vouchers, 138
check number field, asterisks (*****) in, 131
Check Printer Settings option, 27
Check Printer Settings screen, 29
Check Register Does Not Balance with Bank Statement
screen, 174
CheckFree
bank accounts, identifying, 359-361
bills
identifying payees, 362-364
transmitting, 364-367
functions, 367-370
modem, configuring, 357-358
payment inquiry, 369
service form, 354-355
setting up electronic bill paying, 354-358
stop payments, issuing, 369
CheckFree Corporation, 354
checking accounts
describing, 22-26
distinguishing between bank accounts, 23
first time setup, 23-26
reconciliation reports, 167-169
reconciling, 161-176
transaction adjustment feature, 176
transactions
balance adjustment, 173-176
troubleshooting, 176-179
transposition errors, 177
verifying balances, 163
checks
aligning, 127
canceled, checking for authenticity, 162
combining exact matches and key word matches,
142-143
deleting, 134
editing, 122
exact match search, 139-141
finding, 139-144
incorrect printing, 130
key word match search, 142
manual, 12
numbering, 129
outstanding, 163
payroll, 415-417
pointer line, 126
postdating, 122-124
preventing forgery, 454-457
printing, 124-131
recording, 134
recording in Register, 65-70
reprinting, 131-132
reviewing, 122
sample, 126, 130
searches, repeating, 143
split transactions, 134-138
stop payments, 131
transaction group
creating, 152-155
deleting, 156-157
executing, 155-156
modifying, 156-157

transactions
　　deleting memorized, 149
　　listing memorized, 150-151
　　memorizing, 145-147
　　recalling, 147-148
　　voided, 86
　　voiding, 131, 138-139
　　writing, 117-121
　　writing/printing, 115-124
CHKDSK, DOS command, 473
Class List screen, 221
Class matches field, 340
classes
　　defining, 219-221
　　deleting, 222-223
　　editing, 222-223
　　problems with, 225
　　recording, 224-225
　　report
　　　matching, 340
　　　selecting, 341
　　subclasses, 224-225
Cleared status is blank field, 342
Cleared Transaction Detail report, 171
colors
　　default, 229
　　screen, 228-229
Column headings field, 337
commands, DOS
　　CHKDSK, 475
　　executing, 113, 159
CONFIG.SYS file, 17
context-sensitive help, 35-36
conversion date, 14-15
CONVERT.COM file, 182
Copy Account Group screen, 191
Copy/Shrink/Year-End option, 191
Create Account Balances Report screen, 350
Create Budget Report screen, 349
Create Opening Share Balance screen, 265
Create Summary Report screen, 335-336, 349, 409
Create Transaction Report screen, 346, 405
credit card
　　accounts, 251-256
　　home accounting, 393
　　paying bills, 252-256
　　receipts, 393
Credit Card Transactions List screen, 254
Credit Card Register screen, 252
Credit Card Statement Information screen, 253
cursor-movement keys
　　fields, 41
　　help screens, 35-36
　　Register, 74-75
　　selecting options, 37
　　Write Checks screen, 122
Custom Modem Initialization screen, 358
customer aging, business report, 324
customers
　　business accounting
　　　invoicing, 403-406
　　　recording payments, 406-407
　　　tracking receivables, 408-411

**D**

data
　　collecting, 40-42
　　entering/editing, 40-42
　　saving, 42
deduction categories, 206-207
Delete Transaction option, 84, 134
Deleting Account Group message box, 59

Deleting Account message box, 52
deposits in transit, 163
deposits, recording in Register, 70-72
depreciation, business accounting
　　calculating, 412
　　recording, 413-414
Describe Group screen, 106, 153
Description field, 73
directories, QUICKEN4, 16
disk, printing to, 78-79, 169
documents, as internal control, 460
DOS
　　commands
　　　CHKDSK, 475
　　　executing, 113, 159
　　BUFFERS statement, 17
　　FILES statement, 17
　　prompt, 113

**E**

Edit Category screen, 218
Edit Class screen, 223
Edit menu, 83-98, 133-145
electronic bill paying, 353-372
Electronic Payee List screen, 363
Electronic Payment Account Settings screen, 360
Electronic Payment Inquiry option, 367
Electronic Payment menu, 356
Electronic Payment option, 356
Electronic Payment Settings screen, 357
embezzlement
　　defining, 453-454
　　preventing, 457-458
Employer's Tax Guide, 420
Equal field, 341
exact match search, 92
　　checks, 139-141
　　combining with key word match, 94-95, 142-143
Export option, 196
Export Transactions to QIF File screen, 197
exporting files, 195-198

**F**

federal tax identification number, 406
fields
　　Above, 341
　　Account is a single mutual fund, 262
　　Below, 341
　　Category, 73, 415, 418, 427
　　Category matches, 339
　　check number, asterisks (*****) in, 131
　　Class matches, 340
　　Cleared status is blank, 342
　　Column headings, 337
　　cursor-movement keys, 41
　　Description, 73
　　Equal, 341
　　Goal, 283-284
　　Increase, 403
　　Maximum short-term gain holding period, 331-332
　　Memo, 271, 406, 415
　　Memo matches, 339
　　moving between, 40
　　Payee, 403, 405
　　Payee matches, 339
　　Payments/Deposits/Unprinted checks/All, 342
　　report title, 350
　　Report at intervals of, 351
　　Report balances on dates from, 351
　　Report balances on dates through, 351
　　Report organization, 343

Report performance from, 331
Report performance to, 331
Report title, 336
Report value as of, 329
Restrict to transactions from, 337, 404
Restrict to transactions through, 337
Row heading, 337
Security, 271
Select categories to include, 340
Select classes to include, 341
Show cents when displaying amounts, 343
Show memo/category/both, 343, 404
Show subcategories and subclasses, 343
Sub-total by Short- vs Long-Term, 331
Subtotal by, 404
Tax-related categories only, 341
Turn On Electric Payment, 359
Type, 282
Use Current/All/Selected accounts, 338, 351
files, 468
    ASCII, 78-79, 169, 196-198, 290, 306, 450
    AUTOEXEC.BAT, 20
    AUTOEXEC.BOO, 20
    backing up, 182-186
    BCAT.QMT, 182
    BILLMIND.EXE, 182
    CONFIG.SYS, 16
    CONVERT.COM, 182
    converting Version 2.0, 25
    exporting, 195-198
    HCAT.QMT, 182
    hidden, 473
    IBMDOS.COM, 472
    IBMIO.COM, 472
    importing, 198-199
    INSTALL, 16-21
    IO.SYS, 475
    locating, 194-195
    MSDOS.SYS, 473
    PRINTERS.DAT, 182
    program, 181-182
    Q-EXE, 181
    Q.BAT, 16, 182
    Q.CFG, 182
    Q.HLP, 182
    Q.OVL, 181
    Q2.BAT, 16
    Q3.DIR, 182
    QCHECKS.DOC, 182
    QDATA.QDI, 182
    QDATA.QDT, 182
    QDATA.QMT, 182
    QDATA.QNX, 182
    recovering deleted, 471-472
    restoring backed-up, 186-190
    shrinking, 190-194
    TCAT.QMT, 182
FILES statement, DOS, 17
financial records, 243-246
Find option, 90-92, 139-144
First Time Setup screen, 23-24, 273
fixed assets, business accounting, 411-412
    recording, 413-414
floppy disks
    days in advance setting, 232
    installing Quicken, 22
    protecting against failure, 470-471
forgery
    defining, 453-454
    preventing, 454-457
forms
    check, ordering, 11-14
    CheckFree Service, 354-355
    income tax, 429-431

fractions, with stocks/bonds, 265
function-key options, 38-39
function keys, 116-117, 309, 312, 314, 319, 334-335
    Write Checks screen, 116-117
    Register screen, 65
functions, CheckFree, 367-370
fund designations, nonprofit organization, 480

**G**

Go to Date option, 95-96, 143-144
Go to Date screen, 96
Go to Transfer option, 96-98, 144, 245
Goal field, 283-284

**H**

hard disks
    days in advance setting, 232
    installing Quicken, 16-21
    protecting against failure, 470
hardware, 469
    preventing disaster, 469-471
    requirements, 16
HCAT.QMT file, 182
help, context-sensitive, 35-36
Help (F1) key, 35-36
Help option, 35
help screens, cursor-movement keys, 35-36
hidden files, 475
home accounting
    automating record keeping, 388-389
    bank accounts, 392
    budget
        aggregating spending categories, 390-391
        discretionary items, 389-390
        monitoring, 389-392
        spending methods, 392
    cash expenditures, tracking, 393
    credit cards, 393
    home equity, 394-395
    income tax deductions, 387-388
    IRA, non-deductible portions, 395-396
    scheduling tasks, 396-397
home equity, home accounting, tracking, 394-395

**I**

IBMDOS.COM file, 474
IBMIO.COM file, 474
Import from QIF File or CheckFree screen, 199
Import option, 198-199
Import Price Data screen, 291
importing files, 198-199
income categories, 206
income tax
    categories, 429-450
    deductions, 387-388
    forms, 429-450
Increase field, 403
individual retirement accounts (IRA), 383, 395-396
information bar
    Register screen, 65
    Write Checks screen, 116
inquiry, CheckFree, payment, 369
Install screen, 17
INSTALL program, 16-21
installation
    to floppy disk system, 22
    to hard disk system, 16-21
Installation of Quicken is Complete screen, 21
Installing Quicken Billminder screen, 19

internal controls
  documents, storage guidelines, 460
  paper trails, 459
  passwords, 461-466
inventory accounting
  job costing, 423-426
  periodic systems, 421-423
investment accounts,
  first-in, first-out (fifo) recording keeping, 298
  reconciling, 292-297
  updating cash balance, 295
  updating share balance, 295-297
investment actions
  investment and cash accounts, 274-275
  mutual fund accounts, 267-268
investment and cash account, 259-260
  investment actions, 274-275
  reconciling, 293-295
  register, 272-280
investment goal
  defining, 283-284
  deleting, 284
  editing, 284
Investment Goals List screen, 263
investment income, investment reports, 332-333
Investment Income Report screen, 333
investment, market value, recording, 286-288
investment performance, investment report, 330-331
Investment Performance Report screen, 330
investment records
  market values, updating, 285-291
  price history, 288
  price history, importing, 290-291
investment register, 280-297
investment reports
  capital gains (Schedule D), 331-332
  investment income, 332-333
  investment performance, 330-331
  investment transactions, 334
  portfolio value, 329-330
Investment Reports menu, 303
investment transactions, investment report, 334
Investment Transactions Report screen, 334
Investment Types List screen, 263
investments, monitoring, 259-264
IO.SYS file, 473
IRA, home accounting, tracking non-deductible portions, 395
itemized category, personal report, 312-313
Itemized Category Report screen, 312
  function keys, 312

**J**

job costing, inventory accounting, 423-426
job/project, business report, 324
Job/Project Report screen, 325

**K**

key definitions
  Version 3.0, 237
  Version 4.0, 237
key word match search, 92-94
  check, 142
  combining with exact match, 94-95, , 142-143
keyboard shortcuts
  Ctrl-B (Repeat Find backwards), 95
  Ctrl-C (Categorize/Transfer), 104-105
  Ctrl-C (List Categories), 73
  Ctrl-D (Delete Transaction), 84, 134
  Ctrl-Enter (Record Transaction), 84, 134
  Ctrl-F (Find), 90

  Ctrl-G (Go to Date), 95, 143
  Ctrl-M (Memorize Transaction), 99, 344
  Ctrl-N (Repeat Find next), 95
  Ctrl-O (Calculator), 112
  Ctrl-S (Split Transaction), 86
  Ctrl-T (Recall Transaction), 101, 147
  Ctrl-V (Void Transaction), 85, 138
  Ctrl-W (Write Checks), 111
  Ctrl-X (Go to Transfer), 96, 144
  Ctrl-X (Toggle Between Registers), 74
  Ctrl-Y (Security List), 281
keys
  cursor-movement
    fields, 41
    help screens, 35-36
    Register, 74-75
    selecting options, 37
    Write Checks screen, 122
  F1 (Help), 35-36
  function, 65
  Num Lock, 42

**L**

liability accounts, 240-242
load funds, mutual fund shares, 272
loan balance register, 244
loans
  amortization schedule, 427
  tracking, 426-428
Lotus 1-2-3, printing reports to, 307

**M**

Main menu, 23, 48, 236
Main Password option, 460
Make Credit Card Payment screen, 255
Mark Range of Check Numbers as Cleared screen, 166
market value
  determining, 257
  investment, recording, 286-288
  updating investment records, 285-291
Maximum short-term gain holding period field, 331-332
Memo field, 271, 406, 415
Memo matches field, 339
Memorize Transaction option, 99-100, 146
Memorized Reports option, 344-345
Memorized Transaction option, 151
Memorizing Report screen, 344
memory, conserving, 236-237
memos, report, matching, 339
menu bars
  Register screen, 65
  Write Checks screen, 116
menu options, selecting, 37-39
menus
  Account Group, 54
  Account Group Activities, 184
  Acct/Print, 76-77, 124, 196
  Activities, 111-113
  Adjust Balance, 294-295
  Business Reports, 303
  Change Settings, 27, 54, 184, 227-234, 356, 461
  Edit, 83-98, 133-145
  Electronic Payment, 356
  Investment Reports, 303
  Main, 23, 48, 236
  Password, 459
  Personal Reports, 302
  Quick Entry, 39, 98-111, 145-157, 288
  Reports, 301-302
  Write/Checks Activities, 157-159

message box
Billminder, 123
Category Not Found, 215
Deleting Account, 52
Deleting Account Group, 59
OK to Record Transaction?, 69
Print to Disk, 79
messages
Account Group backed up successfully, 186
Account Group restored successfully, 188
Cannot Restore the Current Account Group, 189
Duplicate check number. Are you sure?, 234
No matching transactions were found, 92, 141
OK to Delete Transaction?, 85, 135
OK to Record Transaction?, 121
Overwrite Existing Account Group, 188
Please insert your Backup Disk in Drive A, 185
RECORDING, 68, 120
Transaction Group Entered, 110
You are about to delete a memorized transaction, 149
modem, configuring, 357-358
Monitor Speed option, 229-230
monthly budget, personal report, 309-312
Monthly Budget for Category screen, 311
Monthly Budget Report screen, 309
function keys, 309
MSDOS.SYS file, 475
multipart check forms, 14
mutual fund account, 259-260
action descriptions, 270
capital gain distribution, 270
investment actions, 267-268
reconciling, 292-295
register, recording transactions, 265-272
stock split transaction, 271
mutual funds, recording initial purchase, 264-265

**N**

net worth
measuring, 256-257
personal report, 315-317
Net Worth Report screen, 316
New Price screen, 289
no load funds, mutual fund shares, 272
nonprofit organization accounting, 479-480
notes, tracking, 426-428
Num Lock key, 42

**O**

OK to Record Transaction? message box, 69
on-line calculator, 42-44
one-part check forms, 14
options
*see also* screens
Account Balances, 350
Adjust Balance, 294
Alternate Printer Settings, 27
Billminder, 18-20
Budget, 348
Calculator, 112, 158
Categorize/Transfer, 104-105, 151-152, 213
Change Settings, 27, 354
check forms, 12-13
Check Printer Settings, 27
Copy/Shrink/Year-End, 191
Delete Transaction, 84, 134
Electronic Payment, 356
Electronic Payment Inquiry, 367
Export, 196

Find, 90-92, 139-144
function-key, 38-39
Go to Date, 95-96, 143-144
Go to Transfer, 96-98, 144, 245
Help, 35
Import, 198-199
Main Password, 460
Memorize Transaction, 99-100, 146
Memorized Reports, 344
Memorized Transaction, 151
menu, 37-39
Monitor Speed, 229-230
Order Supplies, 111, 158
Password, 459
Pay Credit Card Bill, 248, 252
Price History, 288
Print Checks, 124
Print Register, 76
Print to Disk, 198
Printer Settings, 27
Recall Transaction, 101-103, 147, 149
Reconcile, 158, 292-293
Record Transaction, 84, 134
Register, 23, 74, 158, 243
Reminder, 271
Repeat Find (backwards), 95, 143
Repeat Find (next), 95, 143
report, 342-343
Report Printer Settings, 27
Security List, 280-286
segregating transactions, 337
Select Account, 48, 243
Select/Set Up Account Group, 191
Send Electronic Mail, 367, 369-370
Set Account Group Location, 194-195
Set Up New Goal, 283
Split, 427
Split Screen, 415
Split Transaction, 86-89, 134-138, 403
starting Quicken with, 235-236
Stop Payment Request, 367
Summary, 348
Transaction, 404
Transaction Groups, 115-111, 152-157
Transaction Password, 462
Update Account Balances, 244-245, 248-250
Use DOS, 113, 158-159
Void Transaction, 85, 138-139
Write Checks, 111
Write/Print Checks, 40, 65, 115
Order Supplies option, 111, 158
Other Settings screen, 230-234
outstanding checks, 163

**P**

paper trails, internal controls, 457
parallel printer port, 30
parameters, starting Quicken with, 234-238
Password menu, 461
Password option, 461
Password to Modify Existing Transactions screen, 464
passwords
changing/removing, 462-463
defining, 462
internal controls, 461-466
naming conventions, 462, 466
transaction date, 463-464
Pay Credit Card Bill option, 248, 252
Payee field, 403, 405
Payee matches field, 339
payees
CheckFree, identifying, 362-364

report, matching, 339
payment inquiry, CheckFree, 369
Payments/Deposits/Unprinted checks/All field, 342
payroll
    business accounting
        preparing, 414-415
        segregating tax liability, 418
        taxes, 418
    business report, 324-326
    checks, recording, 415-417
Payroll Report screen, 326
periodic inventory systems, 421-423
personal reports
    cash flow, 308-309
    itemized category, 312-313
    monthly budget, 309-312
    net worth, 315-317
    tax summary, 314-315
Personal Reports menu, 302
personal tax deduction categories, 205-206
petty-cash expenditures, 247
pledges, nonprofit organization, 478
pointer line, check, 126
portfolio value, investment report, 329-330
Portfolio Value Report screen, 329
power surges, 467-468
Preview Transmission to CheckFree screen, 367
price history, importing to investment record, 290-291
Price History option, 288-289
Print Checks option, 124
Print Checks screen, 125
Print Reconciliation Report screen, 168
Print Register option, 76
Print Register screen, 78
Print Report screen, 305
Print Report to Lotus 1-2-3 File screen, 307
Print Supply Order Form screen, 111-112, 159
Print to Disk box, 79
Print to Disk option, 198
Print to Disk screen, 169, 306
Printer Control Codes screen, 32
Printer List screen, 27-29
Printer Settings option, 27
Printer Settings submenu, 27-28
PRINTERS.DAT file, 182
printers
    describing, 27-32
    impact, 126
    parallel port, 30
    serial port, 30
printing
    categories, 218-219
    checks, 124-131
    reconciliation reports, 167-169
    Register, 75-80
        to disk, 78-79
    reports, 304-307
        to ASCII file, 307
        to Lotus 1-2-3 file, 307
    securities list, 285
    transfer list, 218-219
professional accounting, 477
profit and loss statement, 317-319
Profit & Loss Statement screen, 318
programs
    Billminder, 122-124
    files, 181-182
    hardware requirements, 16
    INSTALL, 16-21
    installing
        to floppy disk system, 22
        to hard disk system, 16-21
    starting parameters, 234-238

**Q**

Q-EXE file, 181
Q.BAT file, 16, 182
Q.CFG file, 182
Q.HLP file, 182
Q.OVL file, 181
Q2.BAT file, 16
Q3.DIR file, 182
QCHECKS.DOC file, 182
QDATA account group, 53
QDATA.QDI file, 182
QDATA.QDT file, 182
QDATA.QMT file, 182
QDATA.QNX file, 182
quarterly tax report, business accounting, 418-419
Quick Entry menu, 39, 98-111, 145-157, 288
Quicken
    data, importing into TurboTax, 450
    hardware requirements, 16
    moving around in, 35-46
    outgrowing, 480-481
    overview, 2-3
    preparing to use, 9-34
    program files, 181-182
    starting parameters, 234-238
    Version 3.0, using book with, 483
    Version 4.0, new features, 483-484
QUICKEN4 directory, 16

**R**

real estate asset register, 243
Recall Transaction option, 101-103, 147, 149
receipts
    cash, 393
    credit card, 393
Reconcile Investment Account screen, 293-294
Reconcile Mutual Fund Account screen, 292
Reconcile option, 158, 292-293
Reconcile Register with Bank Statement screen, 164
reconciliation reports
    printing, 167-169
    reviewing, 169-172
Reconciliation Is Not Complete screen, 173
Record Transaction option, 84, 134
records, financial, 243-246
Register
    accounts, recording transfers, 73-74
    audit trails, 85
    auto-completion, 68
    bank service fees, 72
    checks
        dating, 66
        recording, 65-70
    cursor-movement keys, 74-75
    deposit, recording, 70-72
    entering transactions in, 245
    investment, 280-297
    investment and cash account, 272-280
    loan balance, 244
    printing, 75-80
    printing monthly copies, 80
    real estate asset, 243
    transactions
        deleting, 84-86
        deleting memorized, 102-103
        listing memorized, 103-104
        locating, 89-95
        memorizing, 99-100
        postdated, 75
        recalling, 101-102
        recording, 84-86

repeating find request, 95
reviewing/editing, 74-75
splitting, 86-89
voiding, 84-86
using, 63-82
withdrawals, recording, 72
Register Adjusted to Agree with Statement screen, 175
Register option, 23, 64-65, 74, 158, 243
Register screen, 26, 64-65, 404
  function keys, 65
  information bar, 65
  menu bar, 65
Reminder option, 271
Rename an Account Group screen, 58
Repeat Find (backwards) option, 95, 143
Repeat Find (next) option, 95, 143
report title field, 350
Report at intervals of field, 351
Report balances on dates from field, 351
Report balances on dates through field, 351
Report Options screen, 342-343, 405
Report organization field, 343
Report performance from field, 331
Report performance to field, 331
Report Printer Settings option, 27
Report title field, 336
Report value as of field, 329
reports
  accounts balances, 350-351
  accounts, selecting, 338
  budget, 348-349, 381-382
  business accounting, tax, 418-419
  business
    accounts payable (A/P) by vendor 320-321
    accounts receivable (A/R) by customer, 321-324
    balance sheet, 326-328
    cash flow, 319-320
    customer aging, 324
    job/project, 324
    payroll, 324-326
    profit and loss statement, 317-319
  categories
    matching, 339
    selecting, 340
    tax-related, 341
  classes
    matching, 340
    selecting, 341
  Cleared Transaction Detail, 171
  customizing, 334-338
  entering title, 336-337
  filtering, 338-342
  function keys, 334-335
  investment
    capital gains (Schedule D), 331-332
    investment income, 332-333
    investment performance, 330-331
    investment transactions, 334
    portfolio value, 329-330
  memorizing, 344-345
  memos, matching, 339
  options, setting, 342-343
  payees, matching, 339
  personal
    cash flow, 308-309
    itemized category, 312-313
    monthly budget, 309-312
    net worth, 315-317
    tax summary, 314-315
  printing, 304-307
    to ASCII file, 307
    to Lotus 1-2-3 file, 307

reconciliation, 167-172
  summary, 348
  transaction, 346-348
    matching amounts, 341-342
    restricting, 337
    segregating, 337-338
    sorting, 337
    specifying
      cleared/uncleared, 342
      types, 342
  Uncleared Transaction Detail, 171
Reports menu, 301-302
restaurant accounting, 476
Restrict to transactions from field, 337, 404
Restrict to transactions through field, 337
retail accounting, 478-479
retirement planning, 487-500
Row heading field, 337

## S

Schedule C tax form, 434-435
Schedule E tax form, 430-431
Schedule F tax form, 432-433
screen colors, changing, 228-229
screens
  see also options
  Account Group Copied Successfully, 194
  Accounts Payable (Unprinted Checks) by Vendor, 321
  Accounts Receivable by Customer, 322
  Adding Balance Adjustment Entry, 174
  Adjust Cash Balance, 295-296
  Adjust Share Balance, 295-296
  Assign Transactions to Group, 107, 154
  Balance Sheet, 327
  calculator, 43
  Capital Gains (Schedule D) Report, 332
  Cash Account Register, 247
  Cash Flow Report, 304, 308, 319
  Category and Transfer List, 105, 151, 213
  Change Color Scheme, 229
  Change Password, 461
  Change Transaction Password, 463
  changing update speed, 229-230
  Check Printer Settings, 29
  Check Register Does Not Balance with Bank
    Statement, 174
  Class List, 221
  Copy Account Group, 191
  Create Account Balances Report, 350
  Create Budget Report, 349
  Create Opening Share Balance, 265
  Create Summary Report, 335-336, 349, 409
  Create Transaction Report, 346, 405
  Credit Card Transactions List, 254
  Credit Card Register, 252
  Credit Card Statement Information, 253
  Custom Modem Initialization, 358
  Describe Group, 106, 153
  Edit Category, 218
  Edit Class, 223
  Electronic Payee List, 363
  Electronic Payment Account Settings, 360
  Electronic Payment Settings, 357
  Export Transactions to QIF File, 197
  First Time Setup, 23-24, 273
  Go to Date, 96
  Import from QIF File or CheckFree, 199
  Import Price Data, 291
  Install, 17
  Installation of Quicken is Complete, 21
  Installing Quicken Billminder, 19

Investment Goals List, 263
Investment Income Report, 333
Investment Performance Report, 330
Investment Transactions Report, 334
Investment Types List, 263
Itemized Category Report, 312
Job/Project Report, 325
Make Credit Card Payment, 255
Mark Range of Check Numbers as Cleared, 166
Memorized Report, 345
Memorizing Report, 344
Monthly Budget for Category, 311
Monthly Budget Report, 309
Net Worth Report, 316
New Price, 289
Other Settings, 230-234
Password to Modify Existing Transactions, 462
Payroll Report, 326
Portfolio Value Report, 329
Preview Transmission to CheckFree, 367
Price History, 289
Print Checks, 125
Print Reconciliation Report, 168
Print Register, 78
Print Report, 305
Print Report to Lotus 1-2-3 File, 307
Print Supply Order Form, 111-112, 159
Print to Disk, 169, 306
Printer Control Codes, 32
Printer List, 27-29
Profit & Loss Statement, 318
Reconcile Investment Account, 293-294
Reconcile Mutual Fund Account, 292
Reconcile Register with Bank Statement, 164
Reconciliation Is Not Complete, 173
Register, 26, 404
Register Adjusted to Agree with Statement, 175
Rename an Account Group, 58
Report options, 342-343, 405
Search Direction, 91
Securities List, 277, 281
Security Not Found, 276
Select Account Group to Back Up, 185
Select Account Group to Restore, 187
Select Account to Use, 48, 51-52, 241, 260
Select Accounts to Include, 323, 410
Select Categories to Include, 340
Select Checks to Print, 128
Select Classes to Include, 341
Select Help Topic, 35-36
Select/Set Up Account Group, 55, 57-58
Select Transaction Group to Execute, 106, 153
Set Account Group Location, 56, 195
Set Check Type, 127
Set Maximum Accounts in Group, 193
Set Up Account for Electronic Payment, 359
Set Up Account Group, 56
Set Up Category, 214
Set Up Class, 221
Set Up Electronic Payee, 363
Set Up Investment Goal, 283-284
Set Up Mutual Fund Security, 262
Set Up New Account, 25, 50, 241, 261, 403, 413
Set Up Password, 460
Set Up Security, 277
Set Up Security Type, 283
Specify Budget Amounts, 309-310
Specify Directory, 19
Split Transaction, 87, 136-138, 404, 416
Tax Summary Report, 314
Transaction Group Date, 109, 156
Transaction Group Entered, 157
Transaction to Find, 142, 90, 94

Transmit Inquiry to CheckFree, 370
Type Check Number, 129
Type of Checks, 128
Type Position Number, 126
Update Account Balance, 249
Update Prices and Market Value, 287-288, 291
Write Checks, 37, 116-117
Write/Print Checks, 63, 115, 362
search argument, 139
    special characters, 93-94
Search Direction screen, 91
searches
    combining exact and key word matches, 94-95
    exact match, 92
    key word, 92-94
securities, adding to securities list, 282-285
securities list
    investment goal
        defining, 283-284
        deleting, 284
        editing, 284
    printing, 285
    securities
        adding, 282-285
        deleting, 282, 285
        editing, 283, 285
        hiding, 285-286
Securities List screen, 281
Security field, 271
Security List option, 280-286
Security Not Found screen, 276
segregating transactions, options, 337
Select Account Group to Back Up Screen, 185
Select Account Group to Restore screen, 187
Select Account option, 48, 243
Select Account to Use screen, 48, 51-52, 241, 260
Select Accounts to Include screen, 323, 410
Select categories to include field, 340
Select Categories to Include screen, 340
Select Checks to Print screen, 128
Select classes to include field, 341
Select Classes to Include screen, 341
Select Help Topic screen, 35-36
Select/Set Up Account Group option, 191
Select/Set Up Account Group screen, 55, 57-58
Select Transaction Group to Execute screen, 106, 153
Send Electronic Mail option, 367, 369-370
serial printer port, 30
service fees, 72
Service Form, CheckFree, 354-355
Set Account Group Location option, 194-195
Set Account Group Location screen, 56, 195
Set Check Type screen, 127
Set Maximum Accounts in Group screen, 193
Set Up Account for Electronic Payment screen, 359
Set Up Account Group screen, 56
Set Up Category screen, 214
Set Up Class screen, 221
Set Up Electronic Payee screen, 363
Set Up Investment Goal screen, 283-284
Set Up Mutual Fund Security screen, 262
Set Up New Account screen, 25, 50, 241, 261, 403, 413
Set Up New Goal option, 283
Set Up Password screen, 460
Set Up Security screen, 277
Set Up Security Type screen, 283
shortcut keys, 38
Show cents when displaying amounts field, 343
Show memo/category/both field, 343, 404
Show subcategories and subclasses field, 343
software, 468
    beta, 475-476
    preventing disaster, 469-474

special characters, search arguments, 93-94
Specify Budget Amounts screen, 309-310
Specify Directory screen, 19
Split option, 427
Split Screen option, 415
Split Transaction option, 86-89, 134-138, 403
Split Transaction screen, 87, 136-137, 404, 416
    check forms, 138
statements, DOS
    BUFFERS, 17
    FILES, 17
stock split transactions, 271
stocks, working with fractions, 265
stop payments, 131
    issuing, 369
Stop Payment Request option, 367
Sub-total by Short- vs Long-Term field, 331
subcategories, 210-212
subclasses, recording, 224-225
submenus, Printer Settings, 27-28
Subtotal by field, 404
summary report, 348
Summary option, 348
surge protector, 467-468

**T**

tasks, home accounting, scheduling, 396-397
tax summary report, 314-315
Tax-related categories only field, 341
Tax Summary Report screen, 314
    function keys, 314
taxes
    budgeting, 377
    payroll, 418
TCAT.QMT file, 182
Securities List screen, 277
titles, report, 336-337
transaction date password, 463-464
transaction group
    checks
        creating, 152-155
        deleting, 156-157
        executing, 155-156
        modifying, 156-157
    deleting, 110-111
    executing, 108-110
    modifying, 110-111
    setting up, 105-108
transaction report, 346-348
Transaction Group Date screen, 109, 156
Transaction Group Entered screen, 157
Transaction Groups option, 115-111, 152-157
Transaction option, 404
Transaction Password option, 462
Transaction to Find screen, 90, 94, 142
transactions
    business accounting, defining, 401
    check
        deleting memorized, 149
        listing memorized, 150-151
        memorizing, 145-147
        recalling, 147-148
        splitting, 134-138
    electronic payments, 365
    mutual fund accounts, stock split, 271
    mutual fund register, 265-272
    Register
        deleting, 84-86
        deleting memorized, 102-103
        listing memorized, 103-104
        locating, 89-95

    memorizing, 99-100
    postdated, 75
    recalling, 101-102
    recording, 84-86
    reviewing/editing, 74-75
    splitting, 86-89
    voiding, 84-86
repeating find request, 95
report
    matching amounts, 341-342
    restricting, 337
    segregating, 337-338
    sorting, 337
    specifying cleared/uncleared, 342
    specifying types, 342
segregating, options, 337
transfer list, printing, 218-219
Transmit Inquiry to CheckFree screen, 370
transposition errors, checking account, 177
TurboTax, importing Quicken data, 450
Turn on electric payment field, 359
two-part check forms, 14
Type Check Number screen, 129
Type field, 282
Type of Checks screen, 128
Type Position Number screen, 126

**U**

Uncleared Transaction Detail report, 171
Update Account Balance screen, 249
Update Account Balances option, 244-245, 248-250
Update Prices and Market Value screen, 287-288, 291
Use Current/All/Selected accounts field, 338, 351
Use DOS option, 113, 158-159

**V**

Version 3.0
    key definitions, 237
    using book with, 481
Version 4.0
    key definitions, 237
    new features, 481-482
viruses
    defining, 473
    detecting, 474-475
    determining origination, 473-474
    disinfecting disks, 474-475
Void Transaction option, 85, 138-139
voucher stub, 14
vouchers, check forms, 138

**W**

W-2 form, business accounting, 419-420
W-3 form, business accounting, 429-430
wildcard characters, key word match searches, 92-94
withdrawals, recording in Register, 72
Write/Checks Activities menu, 157-159
Write Checks option, 37, 111, 116-117
Write Checks screen
    cursor-movement keys, 122
    function keys, 116-117
    menu bar, 116
Write/Print Checks option, 40, 65, 115
Write/Print Checks screen, 63, 115, 362

**Z**

zero-based budgeting, 385

# Free Catalog!

Mail us this registration form today, and we'll send you a free catalog featuring Que's complete line of best-selling books.

Name of Book _____

Name _____

Title _____

Phone ( ____ ) _____

Company _____

Address _____

City _____

State _____ ZIP _____

*Please check the appropriate answers:*

1. Where did you buy your Que book?
   - ☐ Bookstore (name: _____)
   - ☐ Computer store (name: _____)
   - ☐ Catalog (name: _____)
   - ☐ Direct from Que
   - ☐ Other: _____

2. How many computer books do you buy a year?
   - ☐ 1 or less
   - ☐ 2-5
   - ☐ 6-10
   - ☐ More than 10

3. How many Que books do you own?
   - ☐ 1
   - ☐ 2-5
   - ☐ 6-10
   - ☐ More than 10

4. How long have you been using this software?
   - ☐ Less than 6 months
   - ☐ 6 months to 1 year
   - ☐ 1-3 years
   - ☐ More than 3 years

5. What influenced your purchase of this Que book?
   - ☐ Personal recommendation
   - ☐ Advertisement
   - ☐ In-store display
   - ☐ Price
   - ☐ Que catalog
   - ☐ Que mailing
   - ☐ Que's reputation
   - ☐ Other: _____

6. How would you rate the overall content of the book?
   - ☐ Very good
   - ☐ Good
   - ☐ Satisfactory
   - ☐ Poor

7. What do you like *best* about this Que book?
   _____
   _____

8. What do you like *least* about this Que book?
   _____
   _____

9. Did you buy this book with your personal funds?
   ☐ Yes          ☐ No

10. Please feel free to list any other comments you may have about this Que book.
    _____
    _____
    _____

**que**

# Order Your Que Books Today!

Name _____

Title _____

Company _____

City _____

State _____ ZIP _____

Phone No. ( ____ ) _____

Method of Payment:

Check ☐  (Please enclose in envelope.)

Charge My: VISA ☐    MasterCard ☐

American Express ☐

Charge # _____

Expiration Date _____

| Order No. | Title | Qty. | Price | Total |
|-----------|-------|------|-------|-------|
|  |  |  |  |  |
|  |  |  |  |  |
|  |  |  |  |  |
|  |  |  |  |  |
|  |  |  |  |  |
|  |  |  |  |  |
|  |  |  |  |  |
|  |  |  |  |  |
|  |  |  |  |  |

You can **FAX** your order to **1-317-573-2583**. Or call **1-800-428-5331, ext. ORDR** to order direct.

Please add $2.50 per title for shipping and handling.

Subtotal _____

Shipping & Handling _____

**Total** _____

**que**

## BUSINESS REPLY MAIL
First Class Permit No. 9918      Indianapolis, IN

*Postage will be paid by addressee*

11711 N. College
Carmel, IN 46032

## BUSINESS REPLY MAIL
First Class Permit No. 9918      Indianapolis, IN

*Postage will be paid by addressee*

11711 N. College
Carmel, IN 46032